GW00391103

RE-ORIENTING CUISINE

Food, Nutrition, and Culture

Series Editors: Rachel Black, Boston University
Leslie Carlin, University of Toronto

Published by Berghahn Books in Association with the Society for the Anthropology of Food and Nutrition (SAFN).

While eating is a biological necessity, the production, distribution, preparation, and consumption of food are all deeply culturally inscribed activities. Taking an anthropological perspective, this book series provides a forum for thought-provoking work on the bio-cultural, cultural, and social aspects of human nutrition and food habits. The books in this series bring timely food-related scholarship to the graduate and upper-division undergraduate classroom, to a research-focused academic audience, and to those involved in food policy.

Re-Orienting Cuisine

East Asian Foodways in the Twenty-First Century

Edited by
Kwang Ok Kim

berghahn
NEW YORK · OXFORD
www.berghahnbooks.com

Published by

Berghahn Books

www.berghahnbooks.com

© 2015 Kwang Ok Kim

All rights reserved.

Except for the quotation of short passages for the purposes
of criticism and review, no part of this book may be reproduced
in any form or by any means, electronic or mechanical,
including photocopying, recording, or any information
storage and retrieval system now known or to be invented,
without written permission of the publisher.

Library of Congress Cataloging-in-Publication Data

Re-orienting cuisine : East Asian foodways in the twenty-first century / edited by
Kwang Ok Kim.
    pages cm. — (Food, nutrition, and culture ; volume 3)
    Includes bibliographical references and index.
    ISBN 978-1-78238-562-2 (hardback) — ISBN 978-1-78238-563-9 (ebook)
    1. Food habits—East Asia. 2. Diet—East Asia. I. Kim, Kwang-ok, editor of
compilation.
    GT2853.E18R46 2015
    394.1'2095—dc23

                                                                    2014033554

British Library Cataloguing in Publication Data

A catalogue record for this book is available from the British Library.

Printed on acid-free paper.

ISBN: 978-1-78238-562-2 hardback
ISBN: 978-1-78238-563-9 ebook

Contents

Part III. Health, Safety, and Food Consumption

Figures and Tables

Figures

Tables

Acknowledgments

This book has been a long time in the making, requiring much patience through several stages of rewriting and editing toward its present fruition. Special thanks are due to the Institute of Cross-Cultural Studies of the Seoul National University, Korea, the Foundation of Chinese Dietary Culture, Taiwan, and the Center for Asia-Pacific Area Studies of Academia Sinica, Taiwan, that provided various forms of help and support to the authors. In addition, the Chiang Ching Kuo Foundation is deeply appreciated for its generous financial support for a scientific workshop at its incubating stage of the long process of development. Also, I would like to extend my warm thanks to the editorial staff at Berghahn Books, especially Molly Mosher and Elizabeth Berg, for constant support and thoughtful suggestions to improve this volume.

Introduction

Kwang Ok Kim

Positing food and food practice in the context of time and space, this book aims to further expand a genre of anthropological study of human agency in and through material culture. Previously, most studies of food, like other subfields of material culture, have been focused on the so-called authentic culinary methods, forms, and meanings of a particular "national" or "ethnic" cuisine or dish, produced and consumed in its supposedly "original" social place. However, as the movement of foods and the emergence of foodways across national and geographical boundaries produce a world in motion (Inda and Rosaldo, eds. 2002), the boundaries of authenticity and originality are blurred and multiplied. In this global fashion, the image, meaning, value, or identity of a nation or an ethnic group is competed over, negotiated, and compromised through the rediscovery, regeneration, remaking, and even invention of cuisine and dishes. Faced with this newly emerging cultural landscape of food, the authors here offer ethnographic observations of various forms of the transnational and cross-boundary movement of culinary cultures. In so doing, they address related topics, such as the dynamic process of cultural encounters, cultural brokerage, the relations between producers and consumers, markets of imagination, and the politics of culture that emerge in relation to the social biography of a food practice. Food itself becomes a world in motion.

In the field of food studies, the most popular current is perhaps what may be categorized as "nutritional and medicinal studies." In this vein, cultural materialists have provided us with many ethnographic studies that attempt to explain and rationalize a given people's food substance as something "good to eat," in the sense that the food can be understood ultimately as a reflection of an adaptation to the ecological condition in which people are placed (see Harris 1985), or in the sense that food practice is an alternative form of folk knowledge of medical sciences. We can observe this in postmodern cultural fashions such as alternative medicine movements or well-being lifestyle movements. In the field of Chinese food studies, for example, scholars usually focus on a particular item within a cuisine to explore its cultural meanings, as well as regional variation in terms of ingredients and tastes in the context of ecological and environmental conditions (see Chang, ed. 1977).

Food, however, is laden with much deeper meanings than simply providing necessary nutritional and medicinal results. It is a space for social and cultural practice. Anthropologists have also observed that various kinds and forms of food are something "good to think." Numerous studies have approached food as a mechanism to materialize modes of thought and to express a group's identity, cultural system, or social classificatory system. Many new attempts began to appear to illuminate the symbolic meanings (see Douglas 1966) as well as political and social functions (see Goody 1982) embedded in particular food practices. These studies have shown how particular social and historical conditions determine the forms of certain foods, the specific ways foods are prepared and consumed, and by extension, how food practices have evolved in adapting to the changes of those conditions.

On the other hand, there is also a danger of essentializing certain foods and foodways as unchanging and linked to a specific region or an ethnic group. Countering the tendency toward this kind of crystallization, anthropological study reveals that the food and foodways of a particular region or a group are continuously constructed for various purposes. It is important, therefore, not to lose sight of the selectively constructed nature of an ethnic or national cuisine which, like tradition, is a process of selection, remaking, and even invention (Hobsbawm and Ranger, eds. 1983).

More recently, as food industries and agribusiness have increasingly commoditized food, various efforts have been made to promote the national and local cuisine competitively, and also to expand the cross-boundary marketization of these cuisines at the global level, a project that sometimes involves state-driven initiatives. It is in these contexts that competitive discourses appear and claim the uniqueness and superiority of a specific national/local cuisine. These claims are not confined to straightforward production and consumption patterns or nutritional and scientific values, but also draw on the aesthetic and philosophical meanings attached to certain foods. Accumulation of such studies has helped us understand how specific forms of cuisine have emerged under specific kinds of historical or ecological conditions and how they have acquired particular cultural meanings. It is in this context that food can be understood as genre of the politics of culture.

The characteristic features of a local cuisine thus formed are gradually treated as a brand of the region concerned. By examining culinary biographies, therefore, we can understand the historical processes by which ethnic and local cuisines are continuously invented, reproduced, and standardized for various political and social purposes. In specific contexts, we can approach a dynamic process of transformation and recuperation of a local cuisine by focusing on culinary practices of cultural resistance, negotiation, and accommodation between the traditional and the modern. The expansion of colonial encounters and the increasing transnational flow of migration and lifestyles in modern history have stimulated a radical and rapid process that constitutes multiple kinds of alternative or new dietary trends. It is often in postcolonial contexts that we find native intellectuals seeking to rediscover and to elaborate the purportedly unique local cuisines as a venue for reclaiming the national cultural identity.

When discussing foodways, therefore, the concept of authenticity does not seem particularly useful. Searching for authenticity can be a futile endeavor. The same Chinese cuisine, for instance, can change in its taste, ingredients, forms, and cooking process with time and place as all of these dimensions are constantly being reinvented and redefined. What is needed, in this regard, is to find a way to approach and understand food as a genre of cultural history by trying to illuminate the process by which a certain food acquires a particular position and definition over history, rather than approaching it as a stationary cultural item that is unchanging over time and space.

Another notable aspect of food and foodways in modern times is its potential for "culture splash" (Bestor 2000). The industrialization of food and the development of information, knowledge, and technology have accelerated the movement of food and foodways across boundaries. The development of media technology in particular has brought about new fashions and styles in food and culinary practices, even without the actual movement of the people with whom the food is traditionally associated. It is necessary in this global age, therefore, to approach the changing cultural meanings that a particular food has come to acquire when it crosses national boundaries by treating it as a venue for the practice of, competition over, and negotiation of cultural meanings. James Watson's study (1997) of McDonald's hamburgers is considered as a pioneering work in this area. It is an ethnographic study of how the icon of American fast food is differently localized and consumed in East Asia including Korea, Japan, China, Taiwan, and Hong Kong.

Within these transnational movements, food is not simply relocated but also is re-created through mutual borrowing and copying. While this phenomenon has often been referred to by such terms as *fusion* or *hybridization*—thereby suggesting its temporary nature—it often takes root as an independent culture in and of itself. We may find good examples of such a phenomenon in the foods of Mexican Americans or Koreans living in Japan. When food crosses boundaries, it is important to identify the main initiators of such changes. For instance, we find in most societies that those of an older generation are so accustomed to their own cultural practices that they are often much slower and more reluctant to accept a different culture, while the younger, by comparison, tend to be more adventurous and responsive to new cultural experiences. Food is no exception to this general tendency, as can be seen in the fact that the recent popularity of Asian cuisines in Western societies is driven mostly by such young adventurers.

Here it is noted that fashion is shaped by the combined efforts of producers, mediators, and consumers. Well-known chefs, locally recognized cooks, experienced women with the image of a mother or a grandmother, or faceless industrial companies and chain restaurants produce their own brand dishes with "secretly endowed" or "newly invented" recipes and ingredients. Through expanded networks with multiple channels, mass-media organizations broadcast cooking programs and documentaries on the varieties of human food throughout the world. Gastronomic business companies, consumer journals, and culinary magazines propagate new lifestyle trends through the discourse of fancy food adventures. Tourism plays a significant role in developing people's world of taste. Young people in particular use the internet and other forms of digital mediation to exchange their individual experiences of "new," "foreign," and "exotic" as well as "fancy" and "high-class" foods. The market is expanding to introduce new opportunities to experience "authentic" as well as "extraordinary" dishes, local as well as foreign cuisines, and traditional as well as modern foods. So, the transnational expansion and penetration of networks of transportation, information technology, cultural industries, migration, and so on have promoted the transnational marketing structure of agribusiness and the food industry. Experiences of new foodways are evaluated through the discourses of modernity, refined taste, and contemporary lifestyles. Eating a foreign dish means opening and practicing a new world in everyday life. Various human agents such as tourists and travelers, business people, short- and long-term migrant workers, returnees from study abroad, and so on, return with new tastes and styles of life that are foreign to their neighbors at home. Local people are stimulated to consume newly fashionable foods and their related knowledge and information as a space in which people can "taste" a different imagination of modernity or globality. By confronting "parallel modernities" through food, they participate in the imagined realities of other cultures as part of their daily lives (Larkin 1997).

It is in this context that we note the rapid increase of transnational migration in the transformation of food and foodways, where migrants and travelers often assume the role of cultural innovators. In search for a taste of different culture, people in this global age enjoy leaving their familiar surroundings to set out for various foreign corners of the world. It is these innovators who introduce, commoditize, and industrialize new and exotic ways of life by bringing the food they have experienced in far-off regions back to their own society. Similarly, the migrant-settlers may start an ethnic restaurant in their new society as a means of preserving their livelihood and also as a way of maintaining their identity. They do not simply reproduce the ethnic food of the hinterland but also invent and re-create the food in negotiation with the taste and preferences of the local consumers. It is by this means that localized ethnic food is often very different from the food eaten in the migrants' homeland. The food consumed in the name of Chinese, Indian, Thai, Vietnamese, Japanese, and Korean cuisine in different parts of the world is often very different from what is eaten in their places of origin. Nevertheless, these cuisines are promoted and accepted as "authentic." Authenticity here is something that is invented and imagined through mutual recognition and collaboration between the producers and consumers (see Caldwell 2009).

In this regard, what is essential in the study of food seems to be an inquiry into its life trajectory that shows how the form, cooking method, ingredients, tastes, aroma, etc., of a specific food have come to be formulated over the course of time and as a consequence of its traveling over space. It will then be followed by an analysis of its social and cultural aspects, as the same food may also be differently classified or be given different meanings in different contexts of time and space. Food is a part of material culture because the way it is produced, transacted, and consumed constitutes a part of culture. In this sense, food can be seen as "en-culturated material" and "en-culturated nature," and it thus needs to be studied with an insight that goes beyond the usual dichotomy of culture and nature.

The fourteen chapters included in this volume have approached food through the framework of cultural dynamics discussed above. They explicitly and implicitly raise questions about "authentic ethnic cuisine," as well as about ethnic or national boundaries with regard to food. The authors present interesting ethnographic observations on why people come to claim the place of an ethnic group or a nationality through food while they also pursue a so-called global standard for modernity. Caught in between the two grand forces of globalization and localization, food provides a venue for a close examination of the political, economic, social, and cultural dynamics practiced through various forms of competition, negotiation, and complementarity among capital, technology, power, and ideology.

The four chapters included in part I are concerned with the question of how local/national identity is constructed through food practice. Okpyo Moon (chapter 1) addresses the phenomenon of the rapid popularization of a specific genre of food known as royal court cuisine in South Korea. Various intellectual projects to rediscover and reestablish this cultural tradition were attempted as a postcolonial response to the violence impinged upon the Korean nation by Japanese colonial power. The reproduction of and even invention of tradition have been attempted at various historical junctures and, here, it is royal court tradition that was abruptly discontinued by colonial aggression. Court culture had epitomized the most sophisticated of Korean tradition, and the recent revival and popularization of courtly culture is seen as an expression of the desire and ideology to restore the essence of the lost and subsequently distorted national culture. In the name of cultural heritage, a cultural entrepreneur offers royal court cuisine reconstructed for foreign visitors as a specific brand of haute cuisine through a form of commoditization that leads foreign consumers to imagine the host country, nation, and culture in a more desirable fashion.

It is according to the same logic that state banquets are often designed to provide a special cultural space to taste food as an emblem of national cultural tradition. For example, the different foods offered at a People's Republic of China (PRC) state banquet are believed to be drawn from the recipes and dishes of the emperor's meal in the prerevolutionary historical past. They are considered to be a selective representation of prerevolutionary culture. In the same vein, Hsin-Huang Michael Hsiao and Khay-Thiong Lim (chapter 2) discuss how certain food is selected for state banquets in Taiwan and Malaysia and treated as representative of, and having the status of, national cuisine. Both being multiethnic societies with a rich variety of different ethnic cuisines, the state uses banquets to provide a political space to define and delineate both the content and boundaries of newly created national cuisines.

Jean DeBernardi's study of the Daoist tea culture of Wudang mountain in China (chapter 3) shows a strategic compromise between the state and a global trend toward commoditization to create a local brand for a tourist market. The representation of Daoism constitutes an important part of cultural politics that emphasize the unique features of Chinese culture. It seems that the state is deeply involved in this process by combining tea and Daoist culture in its attempt to revitalize the glorious Chinese civilization of the past. The participation of the state leaders in the opening ceremony of a reconstructed Daoist temple and the performance of martial art and tea ceremonies in the name of cultural heritage transform a local culture into a space for the political production of national identity, thus contributing to the sanctification of tea, Daoism, and the state all at once.

While the above studies focus on the reproduction of specific food as haute cuisine often in the form of state banquet menus and national cultural heritage, Kwang Ok Kim (chapter 4) highlights reinvention of more common food items, such as rice, as a response to global modernity. In response to the growing multinationalization of dietary life, numerous items of rice cuisine are invented and reproduced in Korea to emphasize the positive quality of its national food. Kim maintains that the phenomenon can be understood both as an expression of cultural nationalism vis-à-vis Western modernity and as a reflection of the postmodern lifestyle of middle-class people who are deeply conscious of health, aesthetics, well-being, and environmental issues.

The six chapters in part II deal with the formation of new cultural spaces in the process of crossing boundaries. A dish that crosses national boundaries is often redefined and reinterpreted depending on the social and cultural context of the local place where it is consumed. Noting that noodles are considered nearly as important as rice in East Asian diet, Kyung-Koo Han (chapter 5) shows how a specific noodle, known as *ramyeon,* has come to occupy different positions in

Chinese, Japanese, and Korean dietary life with different functions and meanings. What is particularly emphasized in this observation is the process of its industrialization, commoditization, and market competition. David Wu (chapter 6), on the other hand, discusses the recent popularization of Japanese cuisine in Taiwan as a combined phenomenon of nostalgia for the particular Taiwanese experience under Japanese colonialism and newly rising concerns about globalization. In early 2000s, there emerged a street of Korean food in an urban district of Taipei. This emergence was due partly to the influence of overseas Chinese returnees from Korea and partly to the impact of the more recent boom of Korean popular culture known as the Korean Wave (*hallyu*). More recently, however, Japanese cuisine has come into vogue, taking over Korean cuisine as the most popular ethnic food in Taiwan. According to Wu's interpretation, the Taiwanese consider things Japanese to represent the more global and thus the more sophisticated and modern. The phenomenon is indicative of a growing materialistic concern of the young in particular, a yearning that overrides the adverse historical memories of colonial oppression of a particular sector of the population.

By comparing the very different nature of the appeal of the Chinese, Japanese, and Korean cuisines to Russian consumers, Melissa Caldwell (chapter 7) shows how food reveals larger cultural attitudes about Russia's stakes and position within the global flows of immigration and capital. This analysis is intended to challenge prevailing paradigms in globalization and consumption studies that have privileged a West-to-East geographic orientation by shifting the vantage point to a very different set of East-to-West interactions. Yuson Jung's analysis of Chinese food consumption in postsocialist Bulgaria (chapter 8) can be placed in a similar vein, as she also attempts to challenge the notion of a one-way flow of commodities and ideas from the West to the East often advocated by globalization theorists. Noting that Bulgarians use Chinese food-consumption practices to evaluate their political economic position within the global hierarchy during intensive social transformation, Jung argues that the meanings attached to the Chinese food consumption by the Bulgarians are nonetheless filtered through a Western lens that projects the hegemonic standards of modern consumption practices.

Also addressing the transformation of food and food ways in the context of globalization, Sangmee Bak (chapter 9) explores the domestication process of ethnic food restaurants in contemporary Korea. She argues that, while Koreans construct and express global identities by consuming these ethnic cuisines, each ethnic cuisine acquires its own global identity in this process of localization. Michael Herzfeld (chapter 10) observes, on the other hand, the subtle differences between the domestic and global consumption of Thai cuisine. He maintains that a tension between hierarchy and egalitarianism plays out in the consumption and presentation of Thai food (in both current and historical practices) through complex tastes created by a careful mingling of spices designed to orchestrate the intricate timing of gustatory experiences. He argues that these complexities and ambiguities are often erased in the tourist and overseas versions of the Thai cuisine.

As a source of life, food is produced and consumed not only in relation to symbols, meanings, and power but also with a concern for safety. As food production and distribution have come to be increasingly dominated by capitalism, market relations, and mass production, these processes have also become closely connected with issues of safety, health, and environmental concerns. These are the issues addressed by the four chapters included in part III, showing that they have become key areas of anthropological studies of food.

In chapter 11, Young-Kyun Yang analyzes the changing position and meaning of Chinese food in contemporary Korea. When Chinese food was introduced as one of the first foreign cuisines in the country during the last decade of the nineteenth century, it was mostly the nutritional value that was appreciated by the Korean consumers. More recently, however, with the growing concern for "well-being" along with changes in the overall criteria for what counts as health, the nutritional value of the Chinese food has come to be reinterpreted with new concerns about obesity, hygiene, and environmentalism. The growing popularity of Vietnamese noodle dishes, Indian curry, and Thai cuisine, which Koreans understand to be based on rice and vegetables and to use fewer meat ingredients or other food flavorings, may also be understood in relation to the widely held belief in Korea that Vietnamese, Indian, and Thai bodies have a slim constitution.

On the other hand, Sidney Cheung (chapter 12) shows how crayfish harvested in the United States were imported into China via Japan and have been reinvented and transformed into a new local specialty food of the Nanjing area, now serving as a critical source of income for the local residents. What is particularly emphasized in this process is the fact that the reinvention of crayfish into an economically profitable crop in the fish farms of Nanjing and its restaurants involves serious ecological destruction, but such consequences do not draw the slightest attention of the local authorities, the farmers, and the consumers.

Jakob Klein (chapter 13) discusses the meanings and practices surrounding the consumption of "organics" and other ecologically certified foods in Kunming, the capital of Yunnan province in southwest China. Noting that the depiction of the Chinese consumption of organic foods as the practices of a "health-conscious" or "quality-seeking" elite has little relevance to "ordinary" Chinese, Klein nevertheless maintains that this consumption is both shaped by and influential to wider food culture and experiences of change in urban China. Yunxiang Yan (chapter 14) reviews the development of food safety problems in China, identifying the shift from the public hazard of food poisoning to the social fear of poisonous food. Emphasizing that food safety is not a singular issue in contemporary Chinese society, Yan argues that, socially and ethically, it is the unsafe food caused by modern modes of farming and food processing that presents the severest challenge to the public trust, regulatory governance, and general well-being of Chinese individuals.

The fourteen chapters briefly reviewed above all indicate that an analysis of specific forms of food without considering its changes over time and across space is no longer meaningful. Food must be observed and analyzed in the global contexts where different tastes, lifestyles and imaginations easily cross boundaries and blend with each other to create new forms. Food is constantly changing and being adopted by new consumers, making the concept of authenticity useful only in a very limited sense for food studies. A dish that originated in Beijing and is reproduced in New York under the same name is not necessarily of the same form, ingredients, or taste, even though authenticity is often claimed and utilized for marketing its newer forms.

Foods are invented, modified, and re-created not only by those who produce and supply them but also by those who consume them. Thus, foods that were once tied with specific ethnic groups or classes are now being consumed by others beyond the traditional ethnic or class boundaries, offering opportunities for an ever-varied and dynamic cultural life, and forming the basis of new communities of heterogeneity. The contributors to this volume have attempted to expand the scope of food studies from medicinal or nutritional studies to social scientific approaches, pursuing food's social and cultural meanings, and functions and aesthetic considerations. Furthermore, these authors show that foods with the same origin, history, and narrative grow out of the meanings of a specific locality and time, being transformed and consumed by different people in different regions according to different imaginations. Food and foodways thus become a genre of explaining culture and its changes.

References

Bestor, Theodore C. 2000. "How Sushi Went Global." *Foreign Policy.* December: 54–63.

Caldwell, Melissa L., ed. 2009. *Food and Everyday Life in the Post-Socialist World.* Bloomington: Indiana University Press.

Chang, K. C. 1977. *Food in Chinese Culture.* New Haven, CT: Yale University Press.

Douglas, Mary. 1966. *Purity and Danger.* London: Barrie and Rockliff.

Goody, Jack. 1982. *Cooking, Cuisine and Class.* Cambridge: Cambridge University Press.

Harris, Marvin. 1985. *Good to Eat: Riddles of Food and Culture.* New York: Simon Schuster.

Hobsbawm, Eric, and Terrence Ranger, eds. 1983. *The Invention of Tradition.* Cambridge: Cambridge University Press.

Inda, Jonathan Xavier, and Renato Rosaldo, eds. 2002. *The Anthropology of Globalization: A Reader.* Oxford: Blackwell Publishers Ltd.

Larkin, Brian. 1997. "Indian Films and Nigerian Lovers: Media and the Creation of Parallel Modernities." *Africa* 67(3): 406–439.

Watson, James L., ed. 1997. *Golden Arches East: McDonald's in East Asia.* Stanford: Stanford University Press.

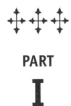

National/Local Food in the (Re)Making

CHAPTER 1

Dining Elegance and Authenticity
Archaeology of Royal Court Cuisine in Korea

Okpyo Moon

The age-old traditions of the Korean royal court were lost with the fall of the Joseon dynasty at the hands of Japanese imperial forces at the beginning of the twentieth century. Many court-life traditions faded away and disappeared as displaced royal family members and their former attendants grew older and more impoverished after the establishment of the Japanese colonial administration in 1910. It was only in the 1970s that royal court cuisine began to receive official attention as part of efforts to reconstruct and preserve national cultural heritage that had been lost or was in danger of vanishing. In 1970, a former court lady named Han Hui sun was designated by the state as the skill holder of Important Intangible Cultural Property (IICP) No. 38, the Royal Court Cuisine of the Joseon dynasty.

In the following year, the title was bestowed upon a gastronomist named Hwang Hye-seong, who had been key in having royal cuisine listed as an IICP for state protection. It was also Hwang who cited former court lady Han as the "legitimate heir" and recommended designation as the first holder. Later, in the early 1990s, a new Korean table d'hôte (*hanjeongsik*) restaurant opened in Seoul, claiming to serve "royal court cuisine." Its advertisement reads:

> In March 1991, the cuisine of the royal court was reconstructed for the first time at Jihwaja restaurant.... Using only the best seasonal ingredients, its taste is light and simple, giving a unique character to Jihwaja's dishes. Those who work at Jihwaja do so with a spirit of "enlightening the public of the royal court cuisine" rather than simply of "selling food." (from the promotional pamphlet of Jihwaja)

This chapter examines the process by which "royal court cuisine" was identified and redefined within the framework of the Intangible Cultural Property System introduced in 1962, and how the royal cuisine thus reconstructed came to be established, recognized, and successfully commoditized by the entrepreneurial efforts of the Hwang family in particular as a specific brand of haute cuisine in the dietary culture of late twentieth- and early twenty-first-century Korea.

The restaurant mentioned is one of several successful haute cuisine restaurants serving traditional Korean meals in courses that began to appear in big cities in South Korea starting in the early 1980s and becoming popular in the 1990s and 2000s. The spread of exclusive restaurants combining Western and traditional practices in serving reflects both the growing desire of the urban middle-class population to dine with enhanced elegance and to introduce more sophisticated aspects of Korean tradition to foreign guests. In the case of Jihwaja and others that followed, the fact that they specialize in royal cuisine is intended to attract particular attention.

Given the widespread acceptance of the notion of "invented tradition" (Hobsbawm and Ranger 1983), it would not suffice to merely acknowledge that certain cultural elements conceived of as age-old tradition are often not transmitted intact from the ancient past but in fact have relatively recent origins. Dietary practices are no exception. What should be understood and explained is, at any given particular historical moment, why and by whom particular elements are emphasized or claimed as valuable tradition and how they are subsequently accepted as such by the general public.[1] I will attempt first to examine how the new type of Korean table d'hôte restaurants combining traditional and newly arising needs in dietary practices has evolved over the past three decades, and analyze the historical background against which royal court cuisine has come to occupy a notable position.

Korean Meal: Its Basic Structure and Changes

The Korean dishes most well known outside the peninsula are arguably marinated beef (*bulgogi*), pickled cabbage (*gimchi*), and rice mixed with vegetables (*bibimbap*). Indeed, in Japan where some 500,000 Korean residents still live as a legacy of colonial rule, *yakiniku,* the Japanese term for Korean style grilled beef, has come to function as a synecdoche for Korean cuisine and Korean restaurants in general. In countries where large-scale Korean migration started later and more visible Korea towns have emerged, such as Los Angeles, New York, or Beijing, restaurants have more specialized menus focusing on foods like *sundubu* (soft tofu stew), *agujjim* (braised monkfish), or *seolleongtang* (bone marrow soup with noodles), reflecting trends popular in Korea at the time of their migration. Whatever their specialty is, one distinct feature of these Korean restaurants is how the food is served. The basic structure of a Korean meal is cooked rice and soup with a number of "side dishes" that almost invariably include *gimchi*. Cooked rice is so central to the Korean meal that a table set for a meal is called cooked rice table (*bapsang* or *bansang*). A basic meal is usually accompanied by soup, stew, broth, or some liquid dish. The status of a meal is often measured by the number of side dishes such as "three side dish rice table" (*samcheop bansang*), "seven side dish rice table" (*chilcheop bansang*) or "twelve side dish rice table" (*sibicheop bansang*).[2]

Another distinct structural feature of a Korean meal is simultaneous service wherein all dishes including dessert are placed on the table at the same time and eaten according to the preference of the diner. The same feature can be noted not only in everyday meals, but also at ceremonial repasts such as those for a new bride, sixtieth birthday celebrations, or ancestral rituals. In addition to the basic rice and soup, the side dishes at these ritual tables include meat, fish, cooked vegetables, pickled vegetables, rice cakes, noodles, fresh and preserved fruit, honey pastries, and various other foodstuffs depending on the region and the individual.

One of the most distinctive aspects of Korean table setting is that the foods are offered in large quantity and are not supposed to be consumed entirely by the person to whom it is offered so that the remaining food can be shared by others. It is the generosity and sincerity of the people who prepare and present the meal that is displayed to the observers. After the meal, the table is handed down to subordinates to be shared, from the king to officials and servants, from elders in the family to those of younger generations, and from ancestors to descendants. Ceremonial meals (*eosang*) for the king were distributed among officials, while ordinary meals (*surasang*) were eaten by servants, mostly the court ladies who prepared and served the food to the king, starting with elderly and high-ranking court ladies and moving down the salle to lower-level female attendants (Hwang, Han, and Jeong 2003: 31; M. Kim 1977: 71, 100–102).

The custom of handing down the table was firmly institutionalized in the concept of *toeseon*, a term that may be translated as "to move the table and to offer the food." Commensality was emphasized not by eating together at the same time but from the same surface. Eating together from a common table with family members and guests was introduced during the Japanese colonial period (1910–1945) along with the modern concept of *danran katei*, a convivial family circle (Sand 1998: 198–201).[3]

Since the early 1980s, however, some restaurants in Seoul, such as Yongsusan, began to serve Korean dishes set out in European-style courses, rather than all at once. This was a major innovation in two respects: first, it replaced the simultaneous traditional serving style and introduced a rough structure of starters, main courses, and desserts to Korean meals, an element undoubtedly adopted from the West. These new type of Korean table d'hôte restaurants became more popular and widespread in the 1990s and 2000s in the urban, middle-class areas of Seoul and nearby satellite cities such as Bundang and Ilsan, while in provincial cities, even newly emerged Korean table d'hôte restaurants continued to serve dishes simultaneously except for the dessert course.

The first use of the term *hanjeongsik* was during the colonial period. *Hanjeongsik* was offered as an equivalent to the *teishoku* service available in Japanese restaurants, which were usually located on the top floors of modern department stores and also served Korean set menus (Han 2001: 339). On other occasions, the term was used at *yojeong* type restaurants where it meant a large banquet table on which all the dishes were placed at the same time and shared by a group of people, commonly male dignitaries. According to Jeong Hye-gyeong (2007: 101), it was at these *yojeong* restaurants that the communal table was first commonly adopted over the traditional individual table. She also notes that since many of the chefs employed at colonial *yojeong* restaurants were displaced chefs who had formerly worked at court, some of the dishes derived from royal court cuisine began to be introduced to a limited public. However, due to the fact that they often included *gisaeng* (female entertainers) and were frequented by Japanese colonizers and collaborators, *yojeong* carried negative associations that prevented their evolution into modern haute cuisine restaurants (2007: 105).[4]

The new type of Korean table d'hôte restaurants that I refer to here by the term *hanjeongsik* adopted Western conceptions of course meals, emerging in the early 1980s as exclusive, high-class, metropolitan restaurants, partially in response to the growing need for entertaining foreign (Western) guests. A set meal served in these restaurants typically includes porridge or soup, "fusion"-style salad dishes with innovative dressings, cold vegetables, pan-fried meat, fish, or vegetables, barbecued beef, steamed pork, cooked vegetables, and other delicacies, with the number and intricacy of dishes adjusted to the price and status of the selected set option. They are often served on at Western-style tables set with wine glasses, napkins, and other non-traditional place settings instead of Korean-style low tables with cushions on the floor. It is possible to trace certain Western influences on the meal structure from the combination and order of the dishes included in each particular set. One of the most unique features of the newly developed Korean set meals is that they offer a course comprised of cooked rice, soup, and side dishes in a "main (*siksa*) course" distinct from all the dishes served beforehand. This demonstrates that the basic structure of Korean meals has not been abandoned altogether, even with so many innovations and compromises.

The second feature of the new Korean table d'hôte restaurants is that although the food is served in courses, each course dish is shared between two to four diners depending on the number of people, instead of individual dishes for each diner. The communal table is maintained, with each person transferring their individual portion from the communal dish to their own plate (sharing plate) rather than eating directly from the communal dish. Soup, stew, or broth is also served in a communal bowl for the table before being individually portioned and consumed. This reflects the increasing influence of the concept of hygiene, although within the family circle the communal aspect of eating is still widely emphasized.

Authenticity Claimed: Identifying and Defining Royal Court Cuisine

Even among this new type of Korean table d'hôte restaurants, the previously mentioned restaurant Jihwaja was innovative for claiming reconstructed royal court cuisine before it had emerged as a popular merchandising option. "Royal court cuisine" is a concept inherently difficult to define, with a number of different dynasties controlling the peninsula over the course of Korea's history. Even if confined to the most recent Joseon dynasty (1392–1910), court cuisine must have undergone numerous transformations during over the past five hundred years: adoption and evolution of new ingredients, spices, and cooking methods.

Jack Goody, in his discussion of the development of haute cuisine in Asia and Europe, noted that, "in terms of class and cuisine, the higher in the hierarchy, the wider the contacts, the broader the view" (1982: 105). The royal court must have been among the first to adopt and incorporate exotic elements. According to the recollections of a former court lady, Kim Myeong-gil, the favorite dish of the last two kings of the Joseon period, Gojong and Sunjong, was fried fish prepared by a chef trained in Russia.[5]

> Around the time of the Gabo Reforms in 1894, sweets called *piori* and drinks known as coffee were presented to the court and enjoyed by King Gojong, Queen Min, and the Crown Prince in the pastime chamber. An official interpreter of Russian, Kim Hong-ryuk called in Kim Jong-ho who had been wandering around Siberia to cook Western food for the king. King Gojong and Crown Prince Sunjong enjoyed fried fish the most. Fragrant coffee was an exotic taste that was compared to millet gruel or medicinal broth that the king used to have before breakfast. (M. Kim 1977: 31–32)

This shows that the royal family enjoyed exotic and foreign delicacies, indicating that royal court cuisine constantly adopted new elements and ingredients. There were hundreds of people to be fed in the court at any given time, including the king and queen, their offspring, relatives, concubines, officials, soldiers, guards, and servants. Different occasions, such as everyday meals, celebrations, foreign guests, hunting expeditions, and ancestral rituals all required different foods and protocol (Song 1998). This complicates the task of delineating the boundaries and actual contents of "royal court cuisine" and means that any attempt to reconstruct it is bound to be partial and open to contestation.

The authenticity of claim of Jihwaha was chiefly derived from being opened by Hwang Hye-seong (1920–2006), a key figure in listing Royal Court Cuisine of the Joseon dynasty as an Important Intangible Cultural Property. The pamphlet of another royal court cuisine restaurant named Gungyeon, opened in Seoul in 2006 by the Hwang family, reads:

The royal court cuisine [we offer] is the crystallization of the highest culinary culture of our country that combines the best ingredients, the excellent art of cooking, and utmost sincerity. The cuisine you are offered is handed down from Han Hui-sun, a court lady who attended the last two kings, Gojong and Sunjong of the Joseon dynasty, to Hwang Hye-seong and Han Bok-ryeo. In 1971, the Royal Court Cuisine of the Joseon dynasty was designated [by the state] as Important Intangible Cultural Heritage No. 38, and Han was named the first holder of the art. In the same year, the Research Institute of Korean Royal Cuisine was established and has provided the focal point for transmitting that knowledge until today. The cuisine of Gungyeon will be the main vehicle of conveying and familiarizing the taste of tradition perfected in these historical developments.

As a professor of gastronomy, the now-deceased Hwang Hye-seong, the first owner of the restaurant Jihwaja, began to study Korean royal court cuisine before anyone else took interest in the field.[6] Hwang began to visit Nakseonjae, where the last queen of the discontinued dynasty resided until her death in 1966 and began researching court cuisine, recipes, methods of table setting, names of utensils, protocols, and terminologies concerning the diet of the king and his family. She also learned about institutional arrangements of the courtly kitchen and so forth, mainly by taking notes from the former court ladies who attended the queen at Nakseonjae.

In order to have the former court lady Han Hui-sun designated as the first specialist in royal court cuisine, Hwang produced and submitted an extended report to the Bureau of Cultural Heritage (later expanded and renamed as the Cultural Heritage Administration) emphasizing the need for preserving royal court cuisine and strongly recommending Han for the position (Hwang 1970). The report contained more than one hundred recipes and introduced numerous court terminologies that had been previously unrecorded, reconstructed from Han's memories. Given that scholarly substantiation, including meticulous research and rigorous examination, is deemed the most critical element in the designation of a particular person as a specialist in IICP, it can be said that Hwang had almost singlehandedly established Han as an IICP specialist. Furthermore, she had also created an outline of the scope and meaning of the royal court cuisine.

IICP skill holders and the scholars who submit the initial recommendation often continue in close relationships, each lending authority to the other. As the initial skill holder is often a relatively uneducated artisan, the role of the supporting scholar(s) is critical. It is this academic authority that legitimizes official recognition of a particular art or craft.[7] What was unusual in Hwang's case was that she succeeded Lady Han as the next heritage holder. Han was already eighty-two when she was designated as the skill holder of Royal Court Cuisine in 1971 and passed away the next year. Hwang was designated the next holder in 1973. She established the private Research Institute of Korean Royal Cuisine in 1971, where she formulated "court cuisine" centered on the high cuisine offered to the king and began to teach classes based on those dishes. Since Hwang was then a fulltime professor at Hanyang University, the Institute was run with assistance from her three daughters, all of whom became specialists in royal cuisine. Hwang died in 2006 and her eldest daughter, Han Bok-nyeo, was elevated by the Korean government as the next skill holder.[8] In addition to succeeding to the office of IICP holder in Royal Court Cuisine of the Joseon Dynasty and running the Research Institute, Hwang's daughter, as well as other family members, has opened four royal court cuisine restaurants in the major neighborhoods of Seoul since Jihwaja's establishment in 1991.

Authenticity Maintained: Branding and Merchandising Royal Court Cuisine

The Important Intangible Cultural Property System of Korea was introduced in the early 1960s in order to protect disappearing traditional arts and crafts. This system aids in identifying such arts and crafts and providing practical means to transmit and preserve skills that would have otherwise vanished. The state designation ratifies the authenticity of a particular person or group among many practitioners; however, it often results in the fossilization of a particular version of the skill concerned (UNESCO 2004). By lending state authority, the system also tends to give hegemonic privileges to a particular person or group designated as the official holder of the heritage while discriminating against other practitioners. This applies not only to the area of cuisine, but also to other arts and crafts including the design and making of traditional clothes, furniture making, shamanic dance, court music, or other skills. However, the hegemonic status is not always maintained to the same extent in all areas. Especially when there are doubts and challenges, it needs to be defended via what might be termed "politics of authenticity."

In the case of royal court cuisine, Hwang's family successfully maintained hegemonic status through careful coordination of family relations, official connections, academic authority, and business acumen. Hwang Hye-seong served as a member of the governmental committee for cultural properties, and her eldest daughter is the head of the Research Institute of Korean Royal Cuisine and maintains close ties with the Cultural Properties Administration, sitting on most of the relevant committees and serving as a professional consultant for state dinners and other official government functions.[9] Hwang's second daughter runs an independent cooking school and her youngest daughter, a university professor, researches Korean cuisine. Hwang's son is CEO of the family business, including four restaurants, a cooking school connected to the research institute, catering services, and factories that manufacture foodstuffs such as rice cakes (see figure 1.1).

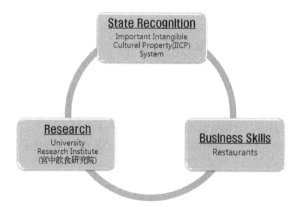

Figure 1.1. The Hwang family's politics of authenticity.

Despite efforts to protect their claim, some doubts have been raised about the authenticity of the Hwang family's version of royal court cuisine and the authority of former court lady Han Hui-sun (1889–1972). Han was admitted to the palace in 1901 at the age of thirteen and became "the court lady responsible for the king's meal" (*sura sanggung*) in 1907. According to the common practice of the time, female servants usually became an attendant court lady about fifteen years after joining the court and it took another fifteen years or so to become a full-fledged court lady (*sanggung*) (Y. Kim 1987: 40, 44). Some critics find it implausible that Han became a *sura sanggung* in 1907, seven years after her admission to the court, at the age of eighteen.

Even if Han was able to learn about royal cuisine in the king's kitchen, the meal preparation she would have observed must have been much reduced following Korea's annexation by Japan in 1910, resulting in a loss of court ritual and pomp.[10] Defining and understanding the royal court cuisine of the Joseon period solely on the basis of the memories of Lady Han and as reproduced by Hwang and her family members is problematic. The concept requires a more systematic redefinition on the basis of thorough research that traces its evolution.

The Hwang family is fully aware of such skepticism but maintains the authenticity and superiority of the knowledge and skills transmitted from court lady Han to Hwang and her daughter. This assertion is evident in the following comments by Hwang, which were included in the 1970 report submitted to the Bureau of Cultural Properties:

> In addition, there were male chefs who belonged to the court and prepared the food for the king. However, they scattered after the fall of the Yi dynasty and it is not possible to trace them to gain information now.[11] Fortunately, four court ladies who attended the last queen, Yun, at Nakseonjae are still alive, and

the oldest of them, Lady Han (aged 82) is the only surviving female attendant who served in the royal kitchen. ... I have been learning from her since 1943, studying with her in Nakseonjae, but have always regretted that her knowledge and skill is not conveyed to a wider audience. It is only meaningful, therefore, to open a way for a more correct and wider transmission of the knowledge and skill by recognizing her as an Intangible Cultural Heritage. (1970: 65–66)

What Hwang and her successors have pursued for the past few decades with considerable success may be described as a process of defining, formalizing, and standardizing royal court cuisine. Hwang Hye-seong played a critical role in the initial introduction and popularization of the concept of royal cuisine, especially by translating knowledge concerning royal court cuisine into the modern language of gastronomy nutrition (Han, Hwang, and Yi 1957; Hwang 1970; Hwang, Han, and Cheong 2003; Han 2005). It was largely thanks to the efforts of Hwang and her disciples that royal court cuisine has become firmly established as part of university curricula in culinary science.[12]

In the course of popularizing it, however, Hwang and her family members effectively monopolized its development, especially through the Intangible Cultural Property System, developing court cuisine into a merchandisable commodity. Although they could not copyright the term, they are reported to have discouraged the use of the term through various informal channels. Some of Hwang's rivals have complained of pressure from the Hwang family not to use the term "royal court cuisine" in other research and publications. Even the development of college courses on "Royal Court Cuisine" met with strong protests from the Hwang family. As a result, some authors have adopted terms like *banga eumsik,* referring to *yangban* (traditional elite class) households instead of the royal court, even though there is essentially no difference between the two (from an interview).

On the other hand, on the pamphlet of a restaurant recently opened by the family, royal court cuisine is now presented as "Dietary Culture of Hwang Hye-seong Family" along with a picture of Hwang and her four children in reconstructed court costume (see figure 1.2), conveying a message that the tradition is owned by the family. During her long years as IICP specialist (1972–2006), Hwang supervised the preparation of numerous state dinners, including the North-South Summit Meeting held in Pyeongyang in 2000. More recently, the Research Institute of Korean Royal Cuisine, established and run by the Hwang family, provided consulting services for many Korean TV dramas and films, such as *Jewel in the Palace* (Dae Jang Geum, 2003), *Beyond the Years* (Cheonnyeonhak, 2006), and *Le Grand Chef* (Sikgaek, 2007), further bolstering their status. The unprecedented success of *Jewel in the Palace* in particular, both domestically and abroad, has contributed significantly to the popularity of royal cuisine among the general public.

Figure 1.2. Royal court cuisine as dietary culture of Hwang Hye-seong's family.

Despite these achievements, at least content-wise, these restaurants as well as the Research Institute of Korean Royal Cuisine struggle to maintain a distinctively unique character of the cuisine with respect to other kinds of traditional cuisine these days. Once-scarce ingredients have become widely available. The growth of the Korean middle class has resulted in greater innovations and elaborations in both presentation and cooking methods, targeting those who seek and can afford distinction and exclusivity in their diet. It is also not possible to prevent other restaurants from emulating and reproducing specific dishes that are believed to be drawn from court cuisine.

As a result, although it used to be thought that such dishes as *neobiani* (grilled beef), *sinseollo* (a broth of vegetables, meat, and seafood cooked in a brass or silver chafing dish), and *gujeolpan* (a dish with nine divided sections containing meat, vegetables, egg, and mushrooms) were all derived from royal court cuisine, all have nonetheless become widely available at traditional Korean restaurants. It has never been clear what divides royal court cuisine from the cuisine of aristocrats, considering a "trickle-down" effect on the dietary consumption patterns of the nobility (McCracken 1988).

More serious contestation and challenges to the authenticity claim of the Hwang family version of royal court cuisine come from the academic sphere. The major basis for most contemporary scholarship on Korean traditional cuisine is a large body of classical Chinese and Hangeul literature (Y. Jeong 1975; Hwang 1970; S. Kim 2005; H. Jeong 2007). As reconstruction of food and dietary practices of the past is based on existing texts as well as orally transmitted knowledge, any attempt at reconstruction is bound to be open to contestation. For instance, food historian Kim Sang-bo has raised questions regarding Hwang's argument that the everyday repast of the Joseon kings was usually a "twelve side dish rice table" (Hwang and Ishige 1988: 69). Kim speculates that Hwang might have misread the relevant texts (S. Kim 2005: 452–455).

Royal Court Cuisine in Twenty-First-Century Korea

According to diners who have visited a prestigious royal court cuisine restaurant, the food served there is neither particularly tasty nor uniquely distinct, apart from the many unfamiliar terms used. Restaurant owners, on the other hand, claim that people are unable to judge royal court cuisine as "delectable" because people nowadays are too accustomed to the taste of modern artificial flavorings. Such court cuisine purveyors point to the lack of flavor or diminished flavor as evidence for the authenticity of their cuisine. As the continued patronage of royal court cuisine restaurants shows, the subjective judgments of previous customers do not seem to discourage others from visiting these places to taste the real hauté cuisine of Korea or from introducing it to foreign guests. Indeed, despite numerous criticisms, suspicions, and challenges, royal court cuisine restaurants thrive in today's Korean cities, especially in the capital, Seoul, the most globalized center of the country. All the restaurants run by the Hwang family, for instance, are now listed on the pages of most popular tourist guide books as places that one ought to visit in order to understand Korean traditional culture. Also, as officially recognized authorities of the Royal Court Cuisine of the Joseon dynasty, Hwang Hyeseong and her daughter Han Bok-nyeo not only operate their own restaurants but also have advised most of the institutions or events related to royal cuisine such as Daejanggeum Theme Park and Korean food festivals held overseas.

The branding and commodification of royal court cuisine in the 1990s cannot be solely attributed to the entrepreneurship and resources of a particular family. It must be understood against the general social milieu of the time: a rising interest in rediscovering forgotten national cultural traditions that reflected newly gained economic prosperity and cultural vitality. Within this context, there have been various attempts to foster appreciation of other lost or forgotten cultural heritage, especially those related to royal court culture abruptly terminated by the Japanese encroachment.[13] Although the Korean royal family nominally continued until the death of King Sunjong in 1926, much of its heritage was distorted and lost through drastic budget cuts and degradations imposed by the colonial administration. Recovering a sense of national pride and identity became intertwined with rediscovering precolonial heritage.

In addition to the Institute of Korean Royal Cuisine run by the Hwang family, there is also a Korean Royal Costume Research Institute whose activities include exhibitions of reconstructed royal costumes and fashion shows. In 2007, the National Palace Museum of Korea was finally inaugurated at Gyeongbokgung palace, expanding the former Exhibition Hall of the Remains of the Royal Court that was opened at Deoksugung palace in 1992.

On the consumers' side, such heritage provides a chance to display distinction and exclusivity. Many Koreans considers royal court culture to epitomize style, sophistication, elegance, and the utmost refinement. Before the 1980s in Korea, many of these extravagances had not been available to most Koreans due to sumptuary regulations as well as financial constraints. In the 1980s and 1990s, however, accurate knowledge and understanding of elaborate and refined "high-culture" heritage emerged as a new sign of status and identity for modern urban Korean people; in particular, an interested few began to reconstruct and consume elaborate royal costumes for special occasions such as birthdays, weddings, and other celebrations (Moon 1997). Many bridal or cooking classes also functioned as a mechanism for introducing and popularizing haute cuisine, including royal court cuisine.

Eating is not just an act of satisfying physiological needs or a matter of nutritional supply. It indicates more of cultural practices that include style and aesthetics. Anthropologist Jack Goody notes that the spread of haute cuisine in

England can be attributed in part to the changing nature of social stratification and the increasing dominance of the middle class, writing,

> The opposition between high and low took on a different shape, more closely related to expenditure than to birth. But the real revolution in the daily food of England occurred as the results of the events and inventions of the nineteenth century. The industrialization of production was accompanied by the industrialization of food, which led to the "complete revolution" associated with an industrial cuisine. Originally middle-class, it extended rapidly with the expanding economy leading to the "bourgeoisification" of the whole culture of food, accomplished through the vigorous support of the mass media. (1982: 152–153).

The successful commodification of royal court cuisine in the late twentieth and early twenty-first century in South Korea can be seen as reflecting the developments in the stage following modern industrialization, in which, once again, hand-picked specialties and uniqueness have come to be valued as markers of distinction. For some people, a visit to a royal court restaurant is a chance to experience a fantasy world of the lost Korean court life.

> We aspire to be a space where one can taste the essence of royal court cuisine, the apex of [Korean] dietary culture. It is our belief that anyone who visits this place is entitled to be treated with the utmost courtesy, as though he is a king in past times. We intend to inherit the spirit of royal cuisine of the Joseon period, created by chefs of highest skill, with the ingredients from every corner of the country, and with utmost sincerity for only one person, the king. (from the pamphlet of Gungyeon)

Conclusion

Dietary practices undergo transformations over time. Quite apart from the food consumed in everyday context by the majority population, different items of food are emphasized for different political, ideological, and cultural reasons at different periods. Court cuisine had only attracted minimal attention until the 1990s, when it became more widely spotlighted as part of a broader movement to reconstruct tradition and authenticity in Korean society. Increased globalization, along with the growth of the middle class, contributed to its development; efforts to globalize Korean food triggered the need for reconstruction of Korean royal court cuisine. In addition, the concept of royal court cuisine was appealing to those seeking distinction and exclusivity in the midst of increasingly ubiquitous modern Korean table d'hôte restaurants.

Hwang Hye-seong and her family have been at the center of the evolution of Korean royal court cuisine in recent decades. One of the first to take a serious interest in the topic, Hwang began her research by exhuming as well as inventing a "legitimate" heir of the heritage, while also collecting and documenting relevant knowledge and skills. These efforts resulted in her teacher and then herself being designated as a holder of Important Intangible Cultural Property. Once recognized, however, the hegemonic privileges accompanying IICP designation have been used by Hwang and her family to maintain authoritative status over other practitioners in the field through careful coordination of state power, scholarly substantiation, and merchandising skills.

The successful branding and commodification of royal court cuisine by the Hwang family has been accomplished not simply through entrepreneurship, but also with the support of the state and mass media. In particular, the unprecedented success of a television drama, *Jewel in the Palace,* contributed to popularizing royal cuisine among the general public. Increasing international tourism also played a significant role in reviving interest in national cultural heritage. "Royal court cuisine" seems to have had particular appeal to the general public. Food and dietary practices of the past are reconstructed through literature, drawings, and oral tradition, thus making the claim of authenticity by any single party more vulnerable to contestation. Nevertheless, royal court cuisine, reconstructed as the epitome of national high cultural heritage, continues to interest people with an urge for differentiation, exclusivity, and national identity in a globalizing, postindustrial, and postmodern Korea.

Notes

An earlier version of the present article was published in *Korea Journal* (2010) vol. 50, no. 1: 36–59.

1. It is more than a quarter of a century since the thesis of "invented tradition" was first raised. A useful critical reconsideration of the thesis can be found in Vlastos (1998).
2. It is believed that a "twelve side dish table" was an appropriate status marker for a king in the past (M. Kim 1977: 97–98; Hwang, Han, and Jeong 2003: 31). It is said, however, that, to the dismay of his mother, the Lady Hong, King Jeongjo, who had been known for his frugality, had always insisted on three side dish table for an ordinary meal (Y. Kim 1987: 404).
3. According to Sand (1998: 200), synchronizing meal times, sharing an eating place, and introducing the common table was a major device for "imposing a regime on the household's time, and bringing about, at least in appearance, a convivial domestic group governed by egalitarian rules" in late nineteenth- and early twentieth-century Japan. Sand also notes that this was a reverse of the process that occurred in Europe and the United States, where the refinement of table manners and increased variety of household goods engendered the replacement of a common pot with individual dishes.

4. Many *yojeong* restaurants of colonial origin could be found in big cities well into the 1970s and were used to entertain Japanese businessmen and burgeoning numbers of male tourists in the postcolonial era, especially after the normalization of diplomatic ties between Japan and Korea in 1965 (Moon 2009).

5. King Gojong enjoyed coffee in his later years as well. In one incident, the coffee that the king and his crown prince drank was poisoned with opium. The king noticed the taste was strange and immediately spit it out but the young crown prince who drank the whole cup was nearly paralyzed and lost some of his teeth. Kim Hong-ryuk was arrested as a suspect but as "his tongue was pulled out by somebody while in prison," the plot's orchestrator was never disclosed (M. Kim 1977: 30–32). At the very least, this episode illustrates how sensitive a palate for coffee King Gojong had.

6. Not much is known about Hwang apart from the fact that she was born in Cheonan in Chungcheongnam-do province in 1920 to a well-to-do family that ran a local rice mill, and went to Japan to study. She graduated from high school in Fukuoka, on the island of Kyushu in Japan in 1937, and then from a women's junior college in Kyoto in 1940, where she studied Japanese Cuisine and Nutrition. She started teaching at Sukmyeong Women's Junior College in 1941 (Lee 2001).

7. For further discussion of issues surrounding the protection of intangible cultural heritage in various different contexts, please see UNESCO (2004).

8. It is often the case in the Korean IICP system that a child of the previous holder succeeds to the same office. Although each IICP holder must be designated by the nomination committee appointed by the Cultural Properties Administration, the children of the existing holder usually benefit from the advantage of being qualified as an officially recognized potential candidate during the lifetime of the previous holder.

9. An incident that hints at a close connection between the Hwang family and government officials concerns the location of the first royal court cuisine restaurant they opened in 1991. It is said that the Minister of Culture and Sports at the time first suggested and subsequently arranged for the restaurant to be located within the complex of the National Theatre so that it would be convenient to bring foreign guests to experience traditional Korean cuisine (from an interview).

10. According to one record, as a result of drastic budget cuts forced by Ito Hirobumi, the number of female attendants at the court in 1926 was about one-tenth the number of pre-colonial attendants, and there were only about ten women working in the royal kitchen, with Han Hui-sun occupying one of the lowest positions in terms of salary (Y. Kim 1987: 59).

11. Despite these claims, it is said that Hwang actively discouraged male court chefs coming forward in order to protect her version (from an interview).

12. In the 1960s, Hwang arranged for Lady Han to teach courses at Sukmyeong Women's University, where Hwang worked at the time.

13. In addition to the Institute of Korean Royal Cuisine, the Korean Royal Costume Research Institute was established in 1979 and provides exhibitions of reconstructed royal costumes and fashion shows. In 2007, the National Palace Museum of Korea was inaugurated at Gyeongbokgung palace, expanding the former Exhibition Hall of the Remains of the Royal Court that was opened at Deoksugung palace in 1992.

References

Appadurai, Arjun. 1988. "How to Make a National Cuisine: Cookbooks in Contemporary India." *Comparative Studies in Society and History* 30: 3–24.

Goody, Jack. 1982. *Cooking, Cuisine, and Class: A Study in Comparative Sociology.* Cambridge: Cambridge University Press.

Han, Bok-jin. 2001. *Uri saenghwal 100 nyeon—eumsik* (Hundred Years of Our Life—Food). Seoul: Hyeonamsa.

———. 2005. *Joseon sidae gungjung-ui siksaenghwal munhwa* (Dietary Culture of the Royal Court during the Joseon Period). Seoul: Seoul National University Press.

Han, Hui-sun, Hwang Hye-seong, and Yi Hye-gyeong. 1957. *Ijo gungjung yori tonggo* (A Study of Royal Court Cuisine of the Yi Dynasty). Seoul: Hageopsa.

Hobsbawm, Eric J., and Terence O. Ranger, eds. 1983. *The Invention of Tradition.* Cambridge: Cambridge University Press.

Hwang, Hye-seong. 1970. *Muhyeong munhwajae josa bogoseo, je 75 ho—gungjung yoribeop mit sayong-haneun dogu* (Intangible Cultural Property Report 75—Cooking Methods of Royal Court Cuisine and Utensils Used). Seoul: Bureau of Cultural Properties.

Hwang, Hye-seong, and Naomichi Ishige. 1988. *Kankoku no shoku* (Korean Food). Tokyo: Heibonsha.

Hwang, Hye-seong, Han Bok-nyeo, and Jeong Gil-ja. 2003. *Joseon wangjo gungjung eumsik* (Royal Court Cuisine of the Joseon Dynasty). Seoul: Research Institute of Korean Royal Cuisine.

Jeong, Hye-gyeong. 2007. *Hanguk eumsik odisei* (An Odyssey of Korean Food). Seoul: Thinking Tree Publishing.

Jeong, Yang-wan. 1975. *Bingheogak Yi-ssi, gyuhap chongseo* (*Gyuhap chongseo* by Bingheogak Yi). Seoul: Bojinjae.

Kang, In-hui. 1987. *Hanguk-ui mat* (Taste of Korea). Seoul: Daehan Textbook Co.

Kim, Ho. 2008. "Joseon-ui sikchi jeontong-gwa wangsil-ui sikchi eumsik" (Tradition of Dietary Treatment of Joseon and Treatment Foods of the Royal Court). *Joseon sidae sahakbo* (The Journal of Joseon Dynasty History) 45: 135–177.

Kim, Kwang Ok. 2001. "Contested Terrain of Imagination: Chinese Food in Korea." In *Changing Chinese Foodways in Asia,* edited by Wu David Y. H. and Tan Chee-being, 201–218. Hong Kong: The Chinese University Press.

Kim, Myeong-gil. 1977. *Nakseonjae jubyeon: namgigo sipeun iyagideul* (Near Nakseonjae: Stories that I Want to Leave Behind). Seoul: Tongyang Broadcasting Company.

Kim, Sang-bo. 2004. *Hanguk-ui eumsik saenghwal munhwasa* (A Cultural History of Korean Dietary Life). Seoul: Suhaksa.

———. 2005. "20 segi Joseon wangjo gungjung yeonhyang eumsik munhwa" (Dietary Culture of the Royal Banquet of the Joseon Dynasty in the 20th Century). In vol. 3 of *Joseon hugi gungjung yeonhyang munhwa* (The Culture of Royal Banquet during the Late Joseon Period), edited by Academy of Korean Studies, 324–552. Seoul: Minsokwon.

Kim, Yong-suk. 1987. *Joseonjo gungjung pungsok yeongu* (A Study of Royal Court Customs of the Joseon Period). Seoul: Iljisa Publishing House.

Lee, Hyoung-kwon. 2001. "Hwang Hye-sung: Keeper of the Ancient Recipes of Changdeokgung Palace." *Koreana* 15(4): 46–49.

Lu, Shun, and Gray Alan Fine. 1995. "The Presentation of Ethnic Authenticity: Chinese Food as a Social Accomplishment." *The Sociological Quarterly* 36(3): 535–553.

McCracken, Grant. 1988. *Culture and Consumption: New Approaches to the Symbolic Character of Consumer Goods and Activities.* Bloomington and Indianapolis: Indiana University Press.

Mintz, Sidney W., and Christine M. Du Bois. 2002. "The Anthropology of Food and Eating." *Annual Review of Anthropology* 31: 99–119.

Moon, Okpyo. 1997. "Jeontong-ui saengsan-gwa sobi: hanbok-eul jungsim-euro" (Production and Consumption of Tradition: The Case of Korean Costume). In *Hangugin-eui sobi-wa yeoga saenghwal* (Consumption and Leisure Life in Contemporary Korea), edited by Moon Okpyo, 9–74. Seongnam: Academy of Korean Studies Press.

———. 2009. "Japanese Tourists in Korea: Colonial and Postcolonial Encounters." In *Japanese Tourism and Travel Culture,* edited by Anguis Sylvie-Gichard and Okpyo Moon, 147–171. London: Routledge.

Sand, Jordan. 1998. "At Home in the Meiji Period: Inventing Japanese Domesticity." In *Mirror of Modernity: Invented Traditions of Modern Japan,* edited by Stephen Vlastos, 191–207. Berkeley, Los Angeles, and London: University of California Press.

Seremetakis, C. Nadia. 1993. "Memory of the Senses: Historical Perception, Commensal Exchange and Modernity." *Visual Anthropology Review* 9(2): 2–18.

Song, Su-hwan. 1998. "Joseon jeongi-ui saongwon" (A Study on the Bureau for Overseeing Ceramic Production in the Early Joseon Dynasty). *Hanguksa hakbo* (The Journal for the Studies of Korean History) 3: 121–166.

United Nations Educational, Scientific and Cultural Organization (UNESCO). 2004. "Intangible Heritage." *International Museum*: 221–222.

Vlastos, Stephen. 1998. "Tradition: Past/Present Culture and Modern Japanese History." In *Mirror of Modernity: Invented Traditions of Modern Japan,* edited by Stephen Vlastos, 1–18. Berkeley, Los Angeles, and London: University of California Press.

Wilk, Richard R. 1999. "'Real Belizean Food': Building Local Identity in the Transnational Caribbean." *American Anthropologist, New Series* 101(2): 244–255.

Yun, Seo-seok. 2009. *Yeoksa-wa hamkkehan hanguk siksaenghwal munhwa* (Korean Dietary Cultures throughout the History) Seoul: Shinkwang Publishing Co.

Transliterations

agujjim	아구찜
banga eumsik	班家飮食
bansang	飯床
bapsang	밥상
bibimbap	비빔밥
bulgogi	불고기
Cheonnyeonhak	千年鶴
chilcheop bansang	七楪飯床
Daejanggeum	大長今
danran katei (J.)	團欒家庭
gisaeng	妓生
gujeolpan	九折坂
naengchae	冷菜
neobiani	너비아니

samcheop bansang	三楪飯床
sanggung	尙宮
seolleongtang	설렁탕
shinseollo	神仙爐
sibicheop bansang	十二楪飯床
Sikgaek	食客
siksa	食事
sundubu	순두부
sura sanggung	水喇尙宮
surasang	水喇床
teishoku (J.)	定食
toeseon	退膳
yakiniku (J.)	燒肉
yojeong	料亭

CHAPTER 2

History and Politics of National Cuisine

Malaysia and Taiwan

Hsin-Huang Michael Hsiao and Khay-Thiong Lim

Food serves to help solidify group membership and to distinguish oneself from others. It is therefore argued that there exists a relationship between food and identities such as ethnicity, race, nationality, class, and gender. But since ethnicity and nationhood are "constructed," the associated cuisines may also be "imagined." However, "once imagined, such cuisines provide added concreteness to the idea of national or ethnic identity" (Mintz and Du Bois 2002: 109). There are various ways to imagine or create an ethnic or national cuisine, such as by using cookbooks to create an Indian national cuisine (Appadurai 1988), or by inventing the "Royal Rat" as real Belizean food (Wilk 1999), or by using fish sauce in crafting Vietnamese community (McIntyre 2002). It therefore clearly suggests that the discourse about ethnic or national food can add to a "cuisine's conceptual solidity and coherence" (Mintz and Du Bois 2002: 109). In this chapter we will look into the discourses about national food in Taiwan and Malaysia, and compare their historical backgrounds and political contexts.

Taiwan and Malaysia as Multiethnic Societies

Both Malaysia and Taiwan have long been multiethnic countries with diverse composition of ethnic groups. Malaysia is currently composed of three major ethnic groups: Malays, Chinese, and Indians.[1] Among them, Malays are the majority, with dominant political power in the country, and many of them are descendants of people now also residing in Indonesia. Groups of heterogeneous origins had gradually become one common ethnicity called Malays in the early decades of the twentieth century when Malay nationalism rose up against the

British colonialism of the period. Islam, language, and the sultanate have been the three essential elements in the identification of Malayness.

All ethnic Chinese of Malaysia are descendants of migrants from southeastern China during the nineteenth and twentieth centuries. Some earlier Chinese migrants, mostly Min-nanese (or Hokkien, as they are commonly termed in Malaysia), ended up intermarrying with indigenous Malay females and eventually became a particular indigenized mixed-blood Chinese *peranakan* ethnic group. There are other Chinese migrants, mostly Hakka, inhabiting the remote or rural areas in Malaya, who have intermingled with the indigenous minority peoples. However, the Hakka did not establish and evolve into a different Chinese *peranakan* society, and still maintained their ethnic and cultural Hakkaness (Skinner 1996).

The Indians in Malaysia were migrants from the Indian subcontinent. Some of them were Indian Muslims, who also intermarried with Malays and became a unique group called "*Jawi peranakan.*" Others, most of them originating from southern India, were Tamil Hindus, who were labor migrants recruited by the British colonial authorities to build infrastructure in colonial Malaya, such as roads and railway construction, and to serve as the labor pool of colonial rubber plantation estates operated by British companies.

There are other ethnic minorities in Malaysia, apart from the three major ethnic groups mentioned above. Eurasians, such as descendants of cross-marriages between Portuguese and other Europeans and local women, are another ethnic legacy left by the colonialists. There are also various indigenous peoples in Malaysia, such as Orang Asli in the Malay Peninsular, Dayaks in Sarawak, and Kadazan-Dusun in Sabah. These non-Muslim indigenous peoples are grouped with Muslim Malays under the banner of "Bumiputra" (sons of the soil) since the 1970s.

Similarly, Taiwan is also a country with multiple ethnicities and cultures, and the descendants of southern Chinese migrants in the sixteenth and seventeenth centuries have become the majority group. Under Japanese rule, from 1895 to 1945, especially since the 1930s, Taiwanese were aggressively educated to become "Japanese" by learning the Japanese language, culture, and lifestyle. The legacy of Japanese rule is still evident in today's Taiwan, including even the relatively positive attitudes toward the Japanese shown by some among Taiwan's older generation. In 1945, Taiwan was "liberated" by the Chinese nationalist army led by the Generalissimo Chiang Kai-shek. The exiled KMT (Kuomintang or Chinese Nationalist Party) government and its army complicated and multiplied the already multiethnic nature of Taiwanese society.

At present, there are five major ethnic groups in Taiwan: Min-nanese, Hakka, Chinese mainlanders, indigenous Austronesians, and foreign spouses and laborers since the 1990s. Within a total population of around 23 million, 72 percent are of Min-nanese origin and about 12 percent are Hakka in origin. The ancestors of the Min-nanese and Hakka originated from Fujian and Guangdong provinces and were earlier migrants to Taiwan, four hundred years ago. Both the Min-nanese and Hakka are grouped together and categorized as Taiwanese or "*benshengren.*" Apart from them, there is another category of Chinese people who migrated to Taiwan in a mass exodus during the end of the civil war in the 1940s; they are normally called mainlanders or "*waishengren.*" Making up only 12 percent of the total population, the mainlanders have wielded most of the political power. The fourth group is indigenous Austronesian peoples or "*yuanzhumin,*" who make up only 2 percent of the total population. The last category of population in Taiwan, emerging since the 1990s under the globalization trend, is the "foreign spouses and workers." One subgroup of these is the marriage migrants, mainly from mainland China and Southeast Asia (Vietnam in particular), whose numbers equal those of the indigenous Austronesian peoples, about 2 percent of the population.

The multiplicity of ethnic groups of both Malaysia and Taiwan is certainly reflected in the variety of ethnic foods. In Malaysia, Malays, Chinese, and Indians have their own ethnic foods and cuisines. In Taiwan, Min-nanese, Hakka, and mainlanders have also developed their own distinctive ethnic foods. There exist similarities and differences among the ethnic foods in Malaysia and Taiwan, respectively. Sometimes different ethnic foods cut across the ethnic boundaries, but at other times it is difficult or even impossible to achieve this. For instance, the Muslim Malays are prohibited for religious reasons to consume pork, while the ethnic Chinese are the major pork consumers in Malaysia. In Taiwan, though no food taboo is found among the different ethnic groups, distinct tastes of certain foods can still be identified.

Here we try to answer the following questions: Would the similarities of food consumption within the three Han (Chinese) ethnic groups in Taiwan make it easy to facilitate the identification of a Taiwanese "national cuisine"? How is it possible with the more complicated ethnic foods in Malaysia to intentionally construct a Malaysian national cuisine? Whose cuisine after all is "represented" as part of the national cuisine in these two countries? Finally, what constitute the elements of official discourses of national cuisine in both Taiwan and Malaysia? Based on the similarities of colonial experiences as well as the nature of multiethnic society, a comparison between the two countries can provide a clearer picture about the development of the official discourses on national cuisine. We also explore the different political contexts articulated through government-initiated discourses of the two countries' national cuisine.

The Making of the Malaysian National Cuisine

More and more attention has been paid to the role of culinary traditions to support and even initiate tourism development in many industrialized modern countries. As Fabio Parasecoli (2008: 128–129) argues, "symbolically, economically, and materially, tourists consume and ingest the communities they visit." What tourists expect to consume is dishes that are defined as "typical" or "local" through "tradition" and "authenticity." However, identifying the types of cuisine that really constitute a "typical" or "local" food of a certain ethnic group or nation is always problematic, especially in a society with many different ethnic groups. In this chapter, we will pursue the question of what the relations are between tourism and culinary traditions in Malaysia, as well as what are recognized as "typical" or "local" Malaysian foods that have been considered to be attractive to foreign tourists, and why.

During the Visit Malaysia Year 2007 campaign, the Malaysia Tourism Department (MTD) produced a TV advertisement, "Malaysia Truly Asia," in which beaches, islands, and comfortable villas with Malaysian scenery are all presented to the viewers. The theme song, sung by a Malaysian idol, Jaclyn Victor, has the following lyrics:

> Everything I've wanted, all that I've asked of you
> Everything I've dreamed of, it's all coming true
> So stay with me (with me), as we walk hand in hand
> Malaysia, truly Asia
> The mountains and the sea
> Malaysia, truly Asia
> It's calling out, to you and me
> Malaysia, truly Asia.

It seems that the theme song tries to portray Malaysia as a place incorporating many Asian characteristics, such as having many ethnic groups and diverse cultures into one destination, Malaysia, in order to lure international tourists into this country. Therefore, it implies that if tourists wish to visit many different Asian countries and to experience many different cultures, they can simply come to Malaysia, for it is a truly Asian country. But, by portraying Malaysia as "true Asia," what does it say about the food and food-related culture of Malaysia?

Bringing Culture Back to Tourism

Tourism in Malaya[2] was developed out of British colonialism. The emergence of tourism in British Malaya reflects the consolidation of European political control in the region, and also indicates the rapid growth of the travel industry in the late nineteenth and twentieth century in Europe. However, during this period, most European travelers "moved through a network of personal contacts and introductions, staying … at Government House or the Residency." (Stockwell 1993:

267) This means that the earliest European travelers tended to meet and stay only with their colonial counterparts in Malaya, rather than being involved in or having interacted with the indigenous communities of the colony. Although A. J. Stockwell does not mention the meals European travelers usually took, we could reasonably suspect that these early European travelers ate only Western-style cuisine when staying at Government House or Residency where most of the colonial officials lived.

After independence in 1957, the Federation of Malaya then incorporated Sabah, Sarawak, and Singapore in 1963 and became the Federation of Malaysia.[3] During the first decade of independence, the Malaysian government had dedicated many efforts to the building of infrastructure in the country for developing tourism. It was not until 1972 that tourism in Malaysia became a special task for a newly established department, the Malaysian Tourist Development Corporation (TDC). Toward the late 1970s, major tourism promotions were finally initiated by the TDC. Nevertheless, the creation of the TDC in 1972 signified a new strategy upheld by the Malaysian government toward culture and tourism development of the country. From that point onward, the concept of culture began to gradually enter into the tourism policy of Malaysia. It was historically related to the 13 May incident of 1969 as well as the national culture policy in 1971.[4]

In order to avoid the reoccurrence of bloody racial riots after 1969, which the government believed to be caused by lack of mutual understanding and economic discrepancy among different ethnic groups, the Malaysia government began to implement policies emphasizing national unity and promoting ethnic harmony. A National Culture Congress was held in 1971, and a three-principle national culture was recommended, which was later adopted by the government. The three principles of national culture are: (1) the national culture of Malaysia must be based on the cultures of the people indigenous to the region; (2) elements from other cultures that are suitable and reasonable may be incorporated into the national culture; and (3) Islam will be an important element in the national culture.[5] From these, we can see that the specified elements of Islam and cultures of people indigenous to the region have been designated to represent the essence of Malaysian national culture. The "national culture issue" sparked a hot debate among local scholars and officials in the 1980s (for a discussion of this, see Carsten 2005).

In 1987, the TDC's tasks were taken over by the Ministry of Culture and Tourism (MCT). This is the first time culture entered into the sector of tourism in Malaysia. In the very beginning, in tourism the concept of culture was normally used to indicate only the infrastructure of cultural buildings and centers, or what we call "cultural hardware."

It was not until the 1990s that the government began to recognize the importance of culture to tourism development. And this time, the "cultural software," such as peoples' way of life and other cultural and art elements, was emphasized. In the Sixth Malaysian Plan (1991–1995), the government admitted that the tourism industry would shape "an image and identity of Malaysia by itself." The government began to encourage tourism to "reflect the values and way of life of Malaysian people." The government further acknowledged that "the variety of cultures in Malaysia should be an additional asset for the sector of tourism." This variety of cultures, according to the Plan, consisted of different and colorful local cultures, art performances, traditions, handicrafts, architecture and special cuisine, which would produce many kinds of merchandise and would eventually bring in lots of foreign money.[6]

It was clear from the above statement that the Malaysian government began to treat "culture" not only in terms of performing arts, museums, art galleries, and handicrafts, but also, for the first time after independence, to infuse the idea of "everyday life of people" into tourism. The most significant and convenient aspect of people's way of life is food or cuisine traditions. In the Seventh Malaysian Plan (1996–2000), continuously underscoring the importance of culture in promoting tourism, the government put more effort into the cultural infrastructure, including places for cultural exhibitions, state cultural centers, and cultural activities. In short, "the uniqueness of Malaysian cultural heritages will be stressed through costume, music, cuisine, handicraft and local arts."[7]

Food or cuisine has gradually turned out to be a major element in tourism promotion and development in Malaysia. In the Ninth Malaysian Plan (2006–2010), food has been put at the forefront of tourism, along with history and handicrafts. The Plan stated that "the attraction of culture will be promoted by displaying the variety of ethnic groups and cultural carnivals. Malaysia will also be promoted as a meeting point of many different dishes from various ethnic groups inhabiting here."[8]

The Malaysian government gradually brought culture back to tourism by introducing cultural elements of various ethnic groups in the country. In addition to the elements of Islam and indigenous cultures, other cultures considered as possible contributors to the progress of tourism were also pinpointed in tourism. The government came to pay more attention to food, while strategically avoided the use of Islam in its promotion of tourism (King 1993). Although ethnic foods were used in publicity efforts for Malaysia, only certain foods were officially accepted. The basis of selection has been the principle of Islam.

Is There a Malaysian National Cuisine?

The website introducing the theme of Malaysia Truly Asia opens with the following: "To know Malaysia is to love Malaysia. A bubbling and bustling melting pot of races and religions where Malays, Indians, Chinese and many other ethnic groups live together in peace and harmony."[9] The melting pot of races and religions, in the official's conception, has not only made Malaysia a "gastronomical paradise," but has also shaped "a people, Malaysians" who are "very laid back, warm and friendly." The Malaysian people, it further argues, possess a "Malaysian culture." In the official definition, a "Malaysian culture" is made up of Malays, Chinese, Indians, and many other ethnic groups [who] have lived together in Malaysia for generations. All these cultures have influenced each other, creating a truly Malaysian culture.

This is to expound upon the multiethnic and multicultural reality of Malaysian society. But what does the "Malaysian culture" mean in terms of food? How is "Malaysian culture" presented by the Malaysian government in terms of food? We look at the e-brochure of Tourism Malaysia and use some data collected from our interview to clarify these questions. The 54-page e-brochure entitled "Culinary Delights" aims to introduce Malaysian foods to foreigners. In the brochure, there are descriptions of, introductions to, and even recipes for various selected ethnic foods in Malaysia. The last seven pages are devoted to some useful tourist information, with sections such as "Eating Out," "Cooking Classes," "Malaysia at a Glance," and "Gourmet Tour Packages."

In the e-brochure, Malaysia is represented as a country with an amalgamation of Malays, Chinese, Indians, and great variety of minority groups in Sabah and Sarawak. It was further enriched with the influences from Thai, British, and Portuguese cultures. To understand Malaysian culture, one should venture into the myriads of ethnic groups of the country. In the e-brochure, each ethnic group is portrayed and their "ethnic characters" are described. For instance, in depicting Malay people, the brochure states the following: "In Malaysia, the term Malay refers to a people who practice Islam and Malay traditions, speak the Malay language and whose ancestors are Malays. ... The Malays are known for their gentle mannerism and rich arts heritage." Unlike the autochthonism of local Malays, the brochure stresses the allochthonous nature of the Chinese and Indians. The Chinese, especially, are categorized into three subgroups in terms of the dialects they use: "Hokkien who live predominantly on the northern island of Penang; the Cantonese who live predominantly in the capital city Kuala Lumpur; and the Mandarin-speaking group who live predominantly in the southern state of Johor." In fact, this does not equate to the formal classification of Chinese dialect groups, which comprise Hokkien, Hakka, Cantonese, Hainanese, and so on. And in the classification of Chinese subgroups, Mandarin speaking is seldom regarded as a distinct group of Chinese, because the Mandarin-speaking group cuts across all Chinese dialect groups. With regard to their "ethnic characters," the brochure characterizes the Chinese as a people of "diligence and keen business sense." For the Indian people, the brochure does not further classify their detailed subethnic groups, but highlights "their colorful culture such as ornate temples, spicy cuisine and exquisite sarees."

In the introduction of Malay food, the brochure summarizes Malay cuisine as inheriting "influence from the Indonesian, Indian, Thai, Arabic and Chinese cooking styles." Rice is the staple food of the Malay. There are a variety of rice dishes, such as *nasi lemak, nasi dagang, nasi goreng, nasi kerabu, nasi himpit, ketupat,* and *bubur nasi.*[10] Malay meals are characterized as using many fresh, fragrant herbs and roots, for instance lemongrass, ginger, garlic, kaffir lime leaves, fresh and dried chilies, basil, polygonum, torch ginger, turmeric roots, galangal, and pandanus leaves. Coconut milk and tamarind are also common ingredients in Malay dishes. Pungent food is a favorite of Malay people, thus, *sambal* or spicy paste became the most common condiment in Malay cuisine.

Again in the e-brochure, *ketupat, lemang, rendang, roti jala, nasi lemak, laksa, satay, ais kacang, dodol,* and *pengat pisang* are selected as representative foods of the Malay.[11] Among them, *nasi lemak* is said to be an unofficial national meal of Malaysia: "If there is anything that is quintessentially Malaysian, nasi lemak would definitely sum it up." *Laksa* is another food that different ethnic groups share; however, "there are significant differences between the Chinese, Peranakan and Malay laksa but the base and essence are the same."

For Chinese food, apart from the influence of local cooking methods, "the inherited culinary traditions of the Cantonese, Szechuan, Hokkien, Hakka, Teochew and Hainanese make Malaysian Chinese food one of the most tantalizing and diverse." The brochure argues that as adaptations occur over time, the classic Chinese cuisine, by adding new local ingredients, has led to "the birth of delicious new recipes that are uniquely Malaysian." The Chinese foods in the brochure are: *char kuay teow,* curry mee (curry noodles), Hainanese chicken rice, *yong tau foo, joo hoo eng chai* (cuttlefish salad), *popiah, yee sang,* clay pot rice, and moon cakes.[12] Two of these, curry noodles and cuttlefish salad, are said to be "uniquely Malaysian." The uniqueness of curry noodles, as the brochure states, comes from the "curry powder, coconut milk and a host of other spices and ingredients" that make it a highly localized and creative food among Malaysians. Cuttlefish salad can only be found in Malaysia, and perhaps Singapore, making it uniquely Malaysian. The list of representative Chinese foods in the brochure contains no dishes with pork or lard. This is because Islam is the national religion of Malaysia, so *halal* food (food that is permissible for Muslims) is strictly observed. It is therefore understandable that certain popular Chinese foods, usually with pork or lard, such as *bah kut teh,* or *Hokkien mee*[13] (to cite only two examples) are consciously neglected and omitted in the brochure officially produced by the government.

Unlike Chinese cuisine, which is usually "*haram,*" or impermissible for Muslims, most of the Indian cuisine is *halal.* In the e-brochure, Indian cuisine is described as "spicy, flavorful and piquant as spices are the essence of Indian fare." We can crudely classify Indian cuisine into two types: south Indian cuisine and north Indian cuisine. The former consists of rice, curry, side dishes, and yoghurt served on a banana leaf, while the latter comprises *briyani* rice, grilled meat, and a variety of breads, such as *naan, roti parata,* and *chapathi,* served with spice-laden curries and chutney.[14] In Malaysia, a unique variant of Indian cuisine has developed out of the Tamil Muslim community. The food stalls run by Tamil Muslims are known as *mamak* stalls. In Tamil, *mamak* means uncle. According to the e-brochure, the signature *mamak* dishes are curry fish head, *nasi kandar, mee goreng mamak,* and *rojak mamak.*[15] The *mamak* cuisine is *halal,* and is thus acceptable for Muslims to consume.

The e-brochure also publishes cuisine of other minorities of Malaysia, namely the Nyonya (or Chinese *peranakan*), Portuguese, and indigenous peoples of Sabah and Sarawak. Nyonya cuisine is a "marriage of Chinese cooking style with Malay ingredients and condiments." Similarly, the Malaysian Portuguese food is a highly hybridized cuisine "with traces of Dutch, British and local ingredients," and is influenced by "Malay, Chinese, Indian and Nyonya styles of cooking."

It is therefore clear that in the official discourse, there is a Malaysian culture. This Malaysian culture is actually constituted by the cultures of various ethnic groups inhabiting the country. The Malaysian culture should comply with the principles of national culture set in 1971. Thus, in tourism, especially under the theme of Malaysia Truly Asia, ethnic cultures are, in effect, appropriated with purposes. The government carefully and consciously selects cultural elements of the non-Muslim peoples so as not to violate the principle of Islam in making up the national culture. In the realm of tourism, food has become one of the major attractions, and some Chinese and Indian foods are selectively chosen as representatives of ethnic foods. Is there then a Malaysian cuisine? The answer is both yes and no. It depends on the definition of Malaysian cuisine. If by Malaysian cuisine we mean a "kind" of food that is particularly and officially chosen to be the representative of the country, then the answer is no. But if we define Malaysian cuisine as an array of food produced and consumed in Malaysia, then the answer is yes. Officially, the two most important principles for Malaysian national culture, i.e. Islam and indigenous cultures, continually play a very important role in delimiting the constitutions of Malaysian culture. For the cuisine of non-Malay, only those that use local ingredients, especially coconut milk and spices—and, of course, those that avoid pork-related ingredients—can be identified as "uniquely Malaysian."

Finally, a simple survey was carried out from January to February of 2009 among university students of different ethnic groups in Malaysia. Responses from twenty-seven students were collected, of which eleven are Malay, eleven are Chinese and five are Indians. Of course this is not a representative sample survey, but the data can give us a glimpse into some implicit meanings related to food as well as national culture in people's ordinary lives.

It is interesting to note that *nasi lemak* is the food most frequently mentioned by the respondents as representing Malaysia, irrespective of ethnic background. There are thirteen respondents choosing *nasi lemak* as a cuisine representing the nation. The reasons given by our respondents are its popularity, prevalence, status as genuine local cuisine, something consumed by all ethnic groups, the ease of getting the ingredients, and its being uniquely Malaysian. This is confirms the status of *nasi lemak* as the unofficial national dish raised in the e-brochure mentioned above. However, respondents can clearly differentiate the ethnic ways of cooking *nasi lemak*. With regard to the chili paste (*sambal*) served with *nasi lemak*, a Malay respondent said "Indians add more spices, and Malays add coconut milk and sugar," and a Chinese respondent states that "Malay food is more sweet, while Chinese food is saltier." The different ethnic ways of cooking can also be found in *laksa*, a popular food that is consumed by all ethnic groups. Therefore, when respondents give their answers, ethnic taste rather than a national cuisine is the priority. Apart from the ethnic way of cooking, some respondents, especially those of Malay ethnic background, will prefer regional food of their origins, such as certain special foods from Kelantan, Trengganu, or Perlis states.

It is therefore clear from this simple survey that, for the respondents, what really exists, in the end, is only in the ethnic or regional sense of food. There is no well-defined and fixed national cuisine at the moment. Most of the respondents also tend to argue about the multiethnic and multicultural nature of Malaysian society. In terms of food, many also maintain that every ethnic food should be treated equally in the creation of a so-called Malaysian cuisine. This coincides with and echoes the way the Malaysian government has deliberately presented the topic to the world.

The Making of Taiwan's National Cuisine

Local food in colonial Taiwan under Japan was recognized, and the term "Taiwanese cuisine" (*Taiwan liao-li*) was even coined. Two sources stated different dates when the term was first used in public occasions and official publications. One indicated that as early as 1898, only three years after the Japanese imperial force invaded, the term was used by a local newspaper reporting on the New Year's celebration banquet organized by the colonial government's Tainan office. It reported that at the banquet, in addition to Japanese officials, some local Taiwanese gentry were invited, so the food prepared had local flavor and features. It is interesting to note that even at the early phase of its colonial rule, "Taiwanese cuisine" had been offered at Japanese official occasions, and a Taiwanese cuisine stand was even set up at the 1903 Osaka National Expo (Chen 2008). The other date given for the term's origin was 1915, when the phrase was used and described in a book entitled *Taiwan,* written by Takeuchi Sadayoshi and published by *Taiwan Daily Newspaper* (*Taiwan Nichinichi Shimpo*).

Recognizing Taiwanese Cuisine under Japanese Colonialism

Under the category of Taiwanese cuisine, it was specifically reserved for the banquet dishes prepared and consumed only in high-class restaurants. The ordinary daily dishes cooked and consumed by Taiwanese locals at home could only be referred to as "Taiwanese food" (Chang 2008). The recognition of the coexistence of and the difference between "Taiwanese food" and "Taiwanese cuisine" was already made clear at the beginning of the Japanese colonialism. However, the designation of "cuisine" to the particular selection, preparation, presentation, location, and even consumers of Taiwan's food had its social and political significance and implications.

First, "Taiwanese cuisine" was local cuisine for Taiwan, not a national cuisine for Japan. It somewhat fit the classic definition of cuisine in a local scope; it was local identity rather than national identity that was implied (Cwiertka 2006). Secondly, "Taiwanese cuisine" deliberately referred to the banquet or feast served only in fancy high-class restaurants, and consumed by only well-to-do Japanese residents in Taiwan and the local Taiwan landlords, gentry, and merchants (Chen 2008). In that sense, the Japanese colonial idea of the cuisine of Taiwan was also used as a means to differentiate class distinctions In a divided and hierarchical colony, Taiwan. It was in line with conception of cuisine and class (Goody 1982). Thirdly, it goes without saying that the identification of the localized "Taiwanese cuisine" also made a clear distinction from the national "Japanese cuisine," a separation of local vs. nation, colonized vs. colonizer, a difference that definitely went beyond food, custom, culture, ethnicity, or race alone.

The British ignorance of "Malaysian cuisine" in its colonial rule had suppressed the identification and development of local Malaysian food culture, while the Japanese recognition of "Taiwanese cuisine" has helped the shaping and growth of local Taiwanese food culture during the era under colonialism. The two colonial governments' attitudes toward colonies' food and related local customs and cultures appeared to be very different, and that might also have reflected the different modes of colonial rule. The British colonialism was separatist in nature by isolation of and ignorance of the colonized society, while the Japanese colonialism was also separatist in essence by recognition and acceptance of the colonized culture.

In the case of Taiwan, in contrast to Malaysia, by the beginning of the early twentieth century, both terms—"Taiwanese food" and "Taiwanese cuisine"—had already been created and popularized, not only among the Japanese colonials, but also among the Taiwanese locals, particularly the local elites. Thus, recognition of the existence of Taiwanese food and cuisine has a longer and socially richer history.

To take the menu of the Taiwanese cuisine shop at the Osaka Expo in 1903 for example (Yueh 1903: 14, cited in Chen 2008: 147), one will notice that among the forty-three "regular" dishes and ten "special" dishes, in terms of three out of the five criteria to constitute a cuisine, as pointed out by Warren Belasco (1999), a Taiwanese cuisine could then be defined. For example, the seafood and chicken constituted the most "dominant selected edible foods," though the variety was quite large; stir fry, steam, and soup making made up the "preferred ways of cooking"; and rich flavors with spices had certainly also made it "distinctive from the Japanese cuisine." One additional unique specialty of Taiwanese cuisine for many Japanese was shark's fin soup. On the 1903 Expo menu, nine methods of preparation for shark's fin soup were listed. It was also reported that about 38,000–39,000 Japanese customers stopped by and consumed the food with delight (Chen 2008).

Furthermore, a difference could be made as well between "low cuisine" and "high cuisine," to borrow Jack Goody's (1982) concepts, by the two typical menus for either middle-income families at home or an expensive restaurant banquet. Table 2.1 lists the sample dishes taken from Takeuchi's *Taiwan* in 1915 (cited in Chang 2008). From the different sets of dishes listed for comparison, it is no surprise that even the middle-income Taiwanese families under colonial rule normally could not afford chickens or ducks for their everyday meals. On the other hand, dishes made of chicken and duck were, in fact, the second most popular dishes in restaurants, following seafood. Though seafood was consumed both at home and in restaurants, the variety and quality differed greatly. Seafood served as high cuisine was prepared in very sophisticated ways, and the variety of seafood used was diverse. Pork and vegetables were less often selected for restaurant dishes, and were usually cooked at home. Table 2.1 demonstrates the distinction of homemade Taiwanese food and the Taiwanese cuisine prepared in restaurants, and that was a direct reflection of class differences at the time.

Table 2.2 further illustrates the list of typical and popular dishes representing "Taiwanese cuisine" in 1907 and 1934–1935, respectively (cited in Chen 2008). One can see that the style of cooking and flavors of the dishes that constituted Taiwanese cuisine over nearly three decades during Japanese colonial rule had not changed much. What changed was actually the inclusion of a few more local dishes originating from various places in Taiwan. So by the 1930s, "Taiwan cuisine" as first invented and propagandized by the Japanese colonial government from outside had also undergone the experience of further "localization" so as to make it more authentically "Taiwanese."

Table 2.1. Comparison of homemade Taiwanese food and restaurant-prepared Taiwanese cuisine

Materials	Middle-income Taiwanese family food	Taiwanese cuisine prepared in a restaurant
poultry	none	duck soup (清湯鴨, *ching-tang-ya*)
		duck with eight delicacies (八寶鴨, *pa-pao-ya*)
		braised duck with spiced cabbage (冬菜鴨, *tung-tsai-ya*)
		chicken with mushroom (毛菰雞, *mao-ku-chi*)
		curry chicken (加里雞, *chia-li-chi*)
		marinated duck (鹵胖鴨, *lu-pang-ya*)
		fried sliced chicken (炒雞片, *chao-chi-pien*)
		fried chicken with scallion (炒雞蔥, *chao-chi-tsung*)
		chicken biscuit (搭雞餅, *ta-chi-ping*)
seafood	fried bamboo shoots with shrimp (竹笋炒金釣蝦, *chu-sun-chao-chin-tiao-hsia*)	abalone (鮑魚肚, *pao-yu-tu*)
	sauteed fish (煎魚仔, *chien-yu-tzu*)	shark's fin broth (清湯魚翅, *ching-tang-yu-chih*)
	sauteed yellow sea bream (煎亦螺魚, *chien-chih-tsung-yu*)	abalone broth (清湯鮑魚, *ching-tang-pao-yu*)
	pickled cucumbers with scallop (瓜仔煮干貝, *kua-tzu-chu-kan-pei*)	sea cucumber broth (清湯參, *ching-tang-sen*)
	small fish (烹勿仔魚, *peng-wu-tzu-yu*)	crab balls (蟳丸, *hsun-wan*)
	well-sauteed fish (煎熟魚, *chien-shou-yu*)	hot pot with mixed meat, seafood, and vegetables (什錦火膏, *shih-chin-huo-kao*)
	smoked tofu with fish floss (豆腐煮魚脯, *tou-fu-chu-yu-fu*)	braised fish (紅燒魚, *hung-shao-yu*)
		braised fish with trimmings, fish with five shredded ingredients (大五柳居, *ta-wu-liu-chu*)
		crab with eight delicacies (八寶蟳羹, *pa-pao-hsun-keng*)
		assorted fish stewpot (什錦魚羹鍋, *shih-chin-yu-hsun-kuo*)
		fried shrimp (炒蝦仁, *chao-hsia-jen*)
		fried frog (炒水蛙, *chao-shui-wa*)
		shrimp balls (燒蝦丸, *shao-hsia-wan*)

(continued)

meat	smoked meat with calabash (匏仔焄肉, *pao-tzu-hsun-jou*)	mushroom (合菰, *ho-ku*)
		fried tripes (炒肚尖, *chao-tu-chien*)
	smoked meat with pickled cucumbers (肉焄醬瓜, *jou-hsun-chiang-kua*)	bamboo shoots (火腿笋炒豆水, *huo-tui-sun-chao-tou-shui*)
	smoked meat with golden needle (金針焄肉, *chin-chen-hsun-jou*)	
	smoked meat with dried tofu (豆干焄肉, *tou-kan-hsun-jou*)	
	smoked meat with "tree mushroom" (木耳焄肉, *mu-erh-hsun-jou*)	
	smoked meat with big cucumber (刺瓜焄肉, *tzu-kua-hsun-jou*)	
vegetables	pickled small cucumber (瓜仔, *kua-tzu*)	yam soup (芋羹, *yu-keng*)
	dried radish (菜脯, *tsai-fu*)	lotus seed soup (蓮子湯, *lien-tzu-tang*)
	"water spinach" soup (煮應菜湯, *chu-ying-tsai-tang*)	
	braised eggplant (煮茄, *chu-chieh*)	
	pickled peach (鹹桃仔, *hsien-tao-tzu*)	
	Chinese pickled vegetables with smoked bamboo shoots (鹹菜焄竹笋, *hsien-tsai-hsun-chu-sun*)	
	fried Chinese pickled vegetables (炒鹹菜, *chao-hsien-tasi*)	
	braised cabbage (煮白菜, *chu-pai-tsai*)	
	braised bean sprouts (煮豆菜, *chu-tou-tasi*)	
	braised three-colored amaranth (煮莧菜, *chu-hsien-tsai*)	
	noodles with leek (麵線煮韭菜, *mien-hsien-chu-chiu-tsai*)	
egg, beans	sauteed tofu (煎豆腐, *chien-tou-fu*)	almond tofu (杏仁豆腐, *hsing-jen-tou-fu*)
	egg with leek (韭菜煮蛋, *chiu-tsai-chu-tan*)	
	peanut (土豆仁, *tu-tou-jen*)	
	vermicelli with duck's egg (鴨蛋麵線湯, *ya-tan-mien-hsien-tang*)	
starch (others)	deep-fried bread stick (油食粿, *yu-chia-kuo*)	

Source: Takeuchi Sadayoshi, 1915, *Taiwan, Taiwan Daily Newspaper,* cited in Chang, 2008: 41.

Table 2.2. Selected menu of Taiwanese cuisine (1907 and 1934–1935)

Taiwanese cuisine as introduced in *Taiwan Daily Newspaper*, 1907	braised fish (紅燒魚, *hung-shao-yu*), fish biscuit (塔魚餅, *ta-yu-ping*), duck biscuit (塔鴨餅, *ta-ya-ping*), braised beef (紅燒牛肉, *hung-shao-niu-jou*), spring chicken (櫻桃小雞, *ying-tao-hsiao-chi*), cold sliced chicken meat dressed with sauce (涼拌雞, *liang-pan-chi*)
Taiwanese cuisine as introduced in *Taiwan Daily Newspaper*, 1934–1935	fried meat with vegetables (炒生菜肉, *chao-sheng-tsai-jou*) hot pot with three delicacies (mixed sea food) (三鮮火鍋, *san-hsien-huo-kuo*) assorted vegetable rice (什菜飯, *shih-tsai-fan*) shrimp (吐絲蝦仁, *tu-szu-hsia-jen*) almond tofu (杏仁豆腐, *hsing-jen-tou-fu*) braised dongpo pork (東坡方肉, *tung-po-fang-jou*) fried tofu sheet with meat (炸豆腐皮包肉, *cha-tou-fu-pi-pao-jou*) traditional braised pork (古滷肉, *ku-lu-jou*) braised fish with trimmings, fish with five shredded ingredients (大五柳居, *ta-wu-liu-chu*) braised fish (紅燒魚, *hung-shao-yu*) three delicacies soup (清湯三絲, *ching-tang-san-szu*)

Source: "Taiwanese Cuisine," *Taiwan Daily Newspaper*, 5–20 February 1907; "Taiwanese Cuisine," essays appearing in *Taiwan Daily Newspaper*, June 1934–April 1935. Cited in Chen 2008, 153.

Downgrading "Taiwanese Cuisine" to "Taiwanese Dishes" Under Early KMT Rule

It is popularly believed that "Taiwanese food" gained its popularity and reputation for the first time in the 1990s, when it was promoted to the status of "Taiwanese cuisine." This assertion implies that the food culture of Taiwan had never been developed before. From what has been examined and discussed in this chapter, such a belief is absolutely wrong and historically misleading. But what happened then after the end of World War II and the termination of Japanese colonial rule? It was the exiled regime of the KMT from the Chinese mainland that both unintentionally and intentionally downgraded and suppressed the development of the local food culture of Taiwanese society. It was unintentionally suppressed by the government's financial austerity policy and social pressure for thrift due to the postwar economic difficulties. Intentionally, the food culture from China and various recognized forms of "Chinese cuisine" were promoted, while the long-established "Taiwanese cuisine" was downgraded or ignored.

The KMT government policy on food culture starting in the 1950s deliberately treated "Jiangze cuisine" (*chiang-che-liao-li*) as prestigious and high cuisine, and at official banquets and gatherings the rich and powerful were offered that selection. Even as late as 1985, in a tourism-promotion booklet entitled "Chinese Delicacies in Taiwan," put out by the Government Information Office of the Executive Yuan, "Jiangze cuisine" was still given the greatest space and was praised as the champion of Chinese food. Only a quarter of the pages were devoted to "Taiwanese cuisine," and the focus was on seafood and congee with light snacks. We can see that Taiwanese food, previously recognized as a unique cuisine of its own under Japanese colonial rule, was demoted in status under Chinese KMT control, and only recognized as home food, casual snacks, or prepared dishes served only at hostess restaurants (cf., Chen: 2008: 174–177).

Therefore, the connotation of the term "Taiwanese dish" (*tai-tsai*) has been local, low, cheap, unsophisticated, unofficial, homemade, street food, and outdoor catering food (*Bando*) for occasions of celebration or grief. In short, for over two to three decades, the food culture has been defined only as some collection of dishes originating from Taiwan and popular among Taiwanese. To Chinese KMT officials and mainlander elites, "Taiwanese dish" was inferior to "Chinese cuisine." In the 1960s, a few famous Taichai restaurants in Taipei, like Green Leaf (Ching-yeh, since 1964) and Umei (Mei-tzu, since 1965), though popular and welcomed by local Taiwanese, never enjoyed high status in Taiwan's gourmet circle, which was still dominated by Chinese mainlanders. Not until the late 1970s and early 1980s did several new restaurants begin to claim to offer Taiwanese cuisine. Typical restaurants are Hsin Ye (Hsin-yeh, since 1977), Orchid Restaurant of Brothers Hotel (Hsiung-ti-fan-tien-lan-hua-ting, since 1979), and Howard Plaza Hotel's Formosa (Fu-hua-fan-tien-Peng-lai-tun, since 1985), to name a few.

Resurrection of "Modern Taiwanese Cuisine"

The reestablishment of the reputation or status of "Taiwanese cuisine" has been a recent phenomenon. It was as late as the 1990s when the term "Taiwanese cuisine" returned to the food-culture circle in Taiwan. Since then, there have been many publications on menus, dishes, and cookbooks under the name of "Taiwanese cuisine" widely read and appreciated among a wider audience. As a part of the tradition of Taiwanese food culture, two broad groups of Taiwan dishes have been recognized and they are clearly specified in the publications: "Taiwanese snacks" and "Taiwanese cuisine." Table 2.3 compiles the most frequently listed dishes for both snacks and cuisine. From the two lists, one can easily see that the primary origins of the dishes, especially those classified as cuisine, have been local in Taiwan, not the provinces of China's Mainland, and the diverse localities where the most popular Taiwanese snacks have come from can actually be identified. Therefore, the return of Taiwanese cuisine also brought about a second level of localization, namely, the rise of recognition of regions, counties, and cities in Taiwan.

Table 2.3. Popular Taiwanese snacks and Taiwanese cuisine

Taiwanese *hsiao-chih* (Taiwanese snacks, 台灣 小 吃)		Taiwanese *liao-li* (Taiwanese cuisine, 台灣 料 理)	
炒米粉	Fried rice noodles, *chao-mi-fen*	糖醋排骨	Sweet-and-sour spareribs, *tang-tsu-pai-ku*
蚵仔麵線	Oyster thin noodles, *ke-tzu-mien-hsien*	麻油腰花	Stir fried pork kidneys with sesame oil, *ma-yu-yao-hua*
割包 刈包	Steamed stuffed bun, *ke-pao, kua-pao*	脆皮肥腸	Crispy hog large intestines Crispy pork intestines, *tsui-pi-fei-chang*
潤餅	Spring rolls, *jun-ping*	五柳嘉臘魚	Red seabream (Japanese seabream) with five shreded ingredients, *wu-liu-chia-la-yu*
肉圓	Taiwanese meatballs, *jou-yuan*	煎虱目魚	Fried milk fish, *chien-shih-mu-yu*
碗粿	Steamed rice cake (pudding), *wa-kuei*	鹹蜆仔	Salty clams, *Guan-la-a*
吳豆腐	Stinky tofu, *chou-tou-fu*	小焦化生	Small fried fish with peanuts, *hsiao-yu-hua-sheng*
麻糬	Sticky rice cakes, *mua-chi*	煎菜脯蛋	Egg with dried & marinated white turnips, *chien-tsai-fu-tan*
滷肉飯	Braised pork rice, *lu-jou-fan*	魷魚螺肉鍋	Squid and conch meat with garlic hot pot, *yu-yu-lo-jou-kuo*
筒仔米糕	Glutinous tube rice cakes, *tang-a-mi-kou*	蔥油清燉石斑魚	Steamed grouper, *tsung-yu-ching-tun-shih-pan-yu*
粥	Rice porridge, *chou; mei*		
粽子	Glutinous rice dumpling, *tsung-tzu*		
蚵仔煎	Oyster omelet, *ou-a-chien*		
炸蚵嗲	Deep fried oysters, *cha-ou-tei*		
四神湯	Four spirits soup, *szu-shen-tang*		
豆花	Tofu pudding, *tou-hua*		

Source: Compiled specifically for this chapter from various cookbooks on "Taiwanese snacks" and "Taiwanese cuisine" published recently in Taiwan.

Contextualizing the "Taiwanese Cuisine" Movement

Two major forces lie behind the abovementioned resurgence of "Taiwanese cuisine" since the 1990s. One is the indigenization of political power sharing and democratization initiated and impelled by the grassroots Taiwanese. Democratization in Taiwan since the 1980s has had far-reaching impacts on various aspects of Taiwanese society and culture. A macro change has been the making of a new Taiwanese national identity, while micro changes can be seen in the reappreciation of Taiwanese history, culture, art, tea, and food. To take a symbolic example of such a mix of political and cultural changes that was actually unprecedented, figures 2.1 and 2.2 are the menus of the national banquets for the 2000 and 2004 presidential inaugurations after the DPP (Democratic Progressive Party) took central government power. From the list of dishes prepared in these two national banquets, one outstanding feature is that every one of them has a story to tell, either about its ethnic origins (Hakka or aboriginal) or local origins (Tainan, Ilan, east coast, Penghu islands, Dajia, Guanmiao, Linbian, Pintung, Taitung, etc.). All of these descriptions of who and where the dishes have come from really conveyed a strong and clear political message to the guests at the banquets and the wider public. To put it simply and directly, it is the new Taiwan identity that the menus wish to respond to.

The other major force behind the resurgent appreciation and popularization of "Taiwanese cuisine" has something to do with the impact of globalization from outside and the localization from inside in response. The rediscovery and resurrection of "Taiwanese cuisine" in today's Taiwan also reflects the search for Taiwanese identity and the search for Taiwan's rich and complex past, the com-

Figure 2.1. 2000 National Banquet for Presidential Inauguration.

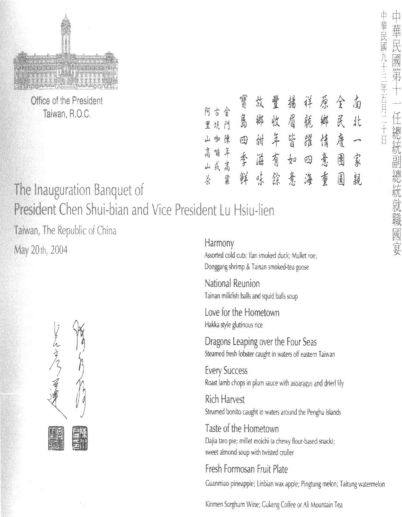

Figure 2.2. 2004 National Banquet for Presidential Inauguration.

position of its ethnic and cultural configuration, and its diverse food traditions and their coexistence and synthesis. Figure 2.3 is the text of the brief introduction of a DVD, *Taiwan's Rich Flavors,* produced by the DPP government's Council on Cultural Affairs and semi-governmental organization, the National Cultural Association, in 2008. In essence, the text calls the public's attention to the fact that the "Taiwan cuisine" has a long and diverse history, with its origins in immigration history, European influence, Japanese colonialism, and postwar Chinese refugees. The rich past of Taiwanese history has made Taiwanese cuisine rich and

Taiwan's Rich Flavors

As an island of immigrants and a maritime state, the food style in Taiwan is multidimensional and splendid. Over the last 100 years, immigrants from Fujian and Guangdong, European power, colonial rule and war refugees stepped on this land, one after another, and their cultures gradually fused with the earliest settlers from the Austronesian family. This has brought to the island a rich food culture that subsequently turned into surprising tastes.

People in Taiwan enjoy dining and even make friendship through dinning. There are the tastes of locals, the tastes of nostalgia, the tastes of fusion, the tastes of innovation, and after all, the tastes of strong human touch. The hospitable Taiwanese and the picky consumers make food in Taiwan more than just food but an extensive and profound culture of food and a creative and original art of food.

It is always a joy to eat in Taiwan. Either at midnight or in the early morning, in either cities or townships, there is always a magic marketplace, a friendly cook, a wonderful dish, a delicate dining table, and a red lantern which lights up the darkness waiting for you in the warm and hospitable steam, to seduce your tongue tip, to satiate your stomach and to warm your heart.

Figure 2.3. *Taiwan's Rich Flavors,* 2008.
Source: Taiwan True Colors: Cultural Documentation, by National Culture Association.

diverse. Taiwanese cuisine can be manifested in various forms, whether casual snacks or fancy official banquets. It even states that there are the local tastes, nostalgic tastes, the tastes of fusion, the tastes of innovation, and dishes that reflect a strong human touch. What the DVD tries to convey is that the national cuisine of Taiwan is still in the making, its configuration is the result of the nexus of the past and present, and it is also the reflection of the ongoing interplay of globalization and localization.

Conclusion

The historical developments of "national cuisine" in Malaysia and Taiwan show that politics indeed matter and play a very essential role in determining whose cuisine can be recognized as representing the nation. From our analysis in this chapter, it is clear that the development of the "national cuisine" of the two countries was greatly affected by their respective colonial governments. The British and Japanese colonial governments' attitudes toward their colonies' food and related local customs and cultures appear to have been very different, and that might reflect the different modes of colonial rule. The British colonialism was separatist in nature, through isolation or ignorance of the colonized Malayan society, while the Japanese colonialism was also separatist in essence, but with recognition or acceptance of the colonized Taiwanese culture. The different modes of colonial rule led to distinct results. The British ignorance of "Malaysian cuisine" suppressed the identification and development of local Malaysian culinary culture during the colonial period, while the Japanese recognition of "Taiwanese cuisine" helped the shaping and growth of local Taiwanese food culture.

It is interesting to note that both Malaysia's and Taiwan's experiences later also revealed different historical trajectories of "national cuisine" after colonial rule. Malaysia gained its independence after WWII, but in terms of food, there was no officially recognized national cuisine at the early period of the newly born nation. It was not until the bloody ethnic conflict in 1969 that the government realized the importance of ethnic unity and harmony, and the three principles of national culture were promulgated. Gradually, as we can see from the government's policies on cultural tourism, the variety of ethnic cuisine found in the country has been regarded as an additional asset to attract foreigners. However, each ethnic food that appears in official discourse of "Malaysian cuisine" seems to be *halal,* or food that Muslims can consume. In other words, one of the principles of national culture, the principle of Islam, is in fact the dominant determinant of what kind of ethnic food is to be appropriated in official discourse. The official or authority-defined Malaysian cuisine is multiethnic in nature by incorporation of and emphasis on the commonality of ingredients used and cooking styles among the various ethnic foods.

Unlike Malaysia, right after the end of WWII, the KMT Chinese government retreated in defeat to Taiwan and began to rule the island as outsiders. To eliminate the Japanese colonial legacy and suppress the development of local Taiwanese culture including cuisine, the KMT Chinese government began to propagate, through government-controlled schools and other social institutions, the idea "of the same language and the same race" between the Chinese mainlanders and local Taiwanese. Taiwanese cuisine, which had been fully supported and established during the Japanese colonial rule, was inevitably targeted by the KMT government. Through education and various forms of propaganda such as mass media, things related to Taiwan were despised and seriously discriminated against, including Taiwanese language, cuisine, and so on. This has resulted in not only the KMT Chinese government but also the local Taiwanese themselves holding "Taiwanese cuisine" in contempt. "Taiwanese cuisine" was downgraded to become only "Taiwanese dishes." In contrast, "Chinese cuisine" was promoted and upgraded to be the national cuisine of the Republic of China, the official name of the defeated Chinese mainland government in Taiwan. It was not until 2000, after two decades of indigenization of politics and democratization, when local Taiwanese elites got hold of political power, that "Taiwanese cuisine" as the national cuisine was resurrected. In the year 2000, a national banquet for the presidential inauguration offered a typical set of Taiwanese cuisine that was designated as having "national character." Taiwan's national cuisine is, however, still in the making and self-shaping and even self-reshaping. Yet, similar to Malaysian national cuisine, the Taiwanese national cuisine in the making will definitely also incorporate ingredients of culinary culture left by the Japanese as well as ethnic Chinese influences, and even the cultural globalization that has been taking place for more than two decades in Taiwan.

Notes

1. According to the population survey in 2000, of a total 21,889,916, there are 11,680,421 (53.4 percent) Malays, 5,691,908 (26.0 percent) Chinese, 1,680,132 (7.7 percent) Indians, 2,567,758 (11.7 percent) other indigenous people, and 269,697 (1.2 percent) others. See Jabatan Perangkaan Malaysia, 2008, 30.
2. Malaya or British Malaya was formed as a political entity through the incorporation of three different administrative units, namely the Straits Settlements (Singapore, Malacca, and Penang), the Federated Malay States (Perak, Selangor, Negeri Sembilan, and Pahang) and the Unfederated Malay States (Johor, Perlis, Kedah, Kelantan, and Trengganu) in 1926. The federation of Malaya was finally established in 1948. It was not until 1963 that the federation of Malaysia was formed by, among others, Singapore, Sarawak, and North Borneo (or Sabah as it is known now).
3. Singapore was finally expelled from the Federation in 1965 due to various irreconcilable political differences between the premier of Singapore, Lee Kuan Yew, and Malaysian Prime Minister Tunku Abdul Rahman.
4. In the 1969 general election, the ruling coalition party (the Alliance) lost its popular support. The humiliating election result sparked an intense party struggle in UMNO (United Malays National Organization), the dominant Malay party in the Alliance. The moderate leaders of the party were under fierce criticism from within. Tunku Abdul Rahman was forced to step down and a state emergency was declared. According to the official report of the incident published later, the communists, economic discrepancies between Malays and non-Malays in the country, and the lack of mutual understanding among different ethnic groups were blamed for the racial riots. See National Operations Council (1969).

5. See Ministry of Information, Communication and Culture, "Dasar Kebudayaan Kebang-saan," in http://kebudayaan.kpkk.gov.my/about/perkhidmatan/?c4=22&c3=40&click=1 (2 September 2009).

6. See Prime Minister's Office, "Rancangan Malaysia Ke Enam (1991–1995)," http://www3 .pmo.gov.my/RancanganWeb/Rancangan1.nsf/c830edf214b37444482567320023aab0/ 1318b5769bdae4b84825674b0031581c?OpenDocument (2 September 2009).

7. See Prime Minister's Office, "Rancangan Malaysia Ke Tujuh," http://www3.pmo.gov.my/ RancanganWeb/Rancangan1.nsf/e2eb45b5229534fe4825673100031def/6bd22ccf2d39 caa1482570a70030c21f?OpenDocument (2 September 2009).

8. See Prime Minister's Office, "Rancangan Malaysia Ke Sembilan," http://www3.pmo.gov .my/RancanganWeb/Rancangan1.nsf/fec3c825c96ab6be482571a20024010b/f68fdecb 4050cc46482571aa0004fe13?OpenDocument (2 September 2009).

9. The following materials are extracted from the website of Tourism Malaysia, which introduces the theme of Malaysia Truly Asia. See http://www.tourism.gov.my/en/about/ default.asp. (3 September 2009).

10. *Nasi lemak* is rice cooked with coconut milk and served with anchovies, roasted nuts, cucumbers, a slice of egg, a chili paste known as *sambal,* and a choice of curries and *rendang. Nasi dagang* is a kind of *nasi lemak* found in Trengganu and Kelantan. *Nasi goreng* is a type of fried rice, traditionally flavored with pounded mackerel, but also fried anchovies are used. *Nasi kerabu* is also a kind of rice that originates from Kelantan. Traditionally, the rice is tinted bright blue from the petals of a kind of blue flower (*Clitoria ternatea*). *Nasi kerabu* is normally a combination of fresh aromatic herbs, such as mint, basil, lemongrass, kaffir lime leaves, turmeric leaves, and raw vegetables (bean sprouts, long green beans, shallots, and cucumber) that are combined together with strongly flavored ingredients like salted fish, dried prawns, fish crackers, fried coconut, and other savory garnishing. *Nasi himpit* is a kind of rice usually served with peanut sauce or *satay. Ketupat* is a type of rice dumpling. It is usually eaten with *rendang* or served as an accompaniment to *satay. Bubur nasi* is porridge of rice.

11. *Lemang* is glutinous rice cooking in bamboo. *Rendang* is a dried curry made of beef or chicken. *Roti jala* is a lacy pancake; it literally means "net bread" due to its web-like appearance. *Laksa* is a spicy noodle soup. There are at least four theories to explain the origins of *laksa.* One theory traces it back to the Hindi/Persian *lakhshah,* which means a type of vermicelli. It may also been suggested that the word *laksa* is derived from the Cantonese word for "辣沙," meaning "spicy sand" due to the ground dried prawn that makes the gravy taste extremely sandy. The third theory states that the word *laksa* is similar to Hokkien's pronunciation of the word "dirty" (*la sam*) due to its appearance. The last theory suggests that the word *laksa* is derived from Sanskrit's *lakhsa,* which means "a lot"; it refers to its many ingredients and efforts in making the gravy. *Satay* is a dish consisting of diced or sliced barbecued chicken, mutton, and beef or other meat. Turmeric is a compulsory ingredient used to marinade *satay. Ais kacang,* or "red bean ice," is a dessert in Malaysia. It is also popularly known as *air batu campur,* or ABC for short. *Dodol* is a toffee-like food delicacy that is made with coconut milk, jiggery, and rice flour, and is sticky, thick, and sweet. *Pengat pisang* is a dessert made from tropical fruits cooked in coconut milk and palm sugar.

12. *Char kuay teow* (炒粿條, as pronounced in Hokkien) is stir-fried rice noodles with prawns, eggs, pork or chicken, chives, and bean sprouts. Curry mee (咖哩麵, or curry noodles) is

a bowl of thin yellow noodles mixed with rice vermicelli in spicy curry soup, dried tofu, prawns, cuttlefish, chicken, and mint leaves, and topped with a special *sambal*. Hainanese chicken rice (海南雞飯, *hai-nan-chi-fan*) is steamed chicken served with rice cooked in margarine or chicken fat and stock. *Yong tau fu* (釀豆腐) is a soup dish of Hakka origins; brinjals, lady fingers, fried bean curd, and chilies are stuffed with fish paste, rice flour, and flavoring. It can be served with rice, noodles, or rice vermicelli. *Joo hoo eng chai* (魷魚空心菜, pronounced in Hokkien) is made up of cuttlefish, water convolvulus, a sweet prawn-based sauce, and sprinkled with ground peanuts or toasted sesame seeds. *Popiah* (薄餅, pronounced in Hokkien) is a Hokkien or Teochew-style spring roll stuffed mainly with stewed jicama (known locally as *bangkuang*), shredded tofu, egg, pork mince, and sometimes lard residue. *Yee sang* (魚生, pronounced in Cantonese) is a Cantonese style of raw-fish salad. It usually consists of strips of raw salmon, mixed with shredded vegetables and a variety of sauces and condiments. *Yee sang* literally means "raw fish" but since "fish (魚, *yu*)" is commonly given symbolic value by its homophone "abundance (餘, *yu*)," *yee sang* (魚生) is interpreted as a homophone for Yusheng (餘升), meaning an increase in abundance, a symbol of abundance, prosperity, and vigor. Clay pot rice (or *Ngah po fan*, as it is locally called, 瓦煲飯) is a clay pot chicken rice dish. It is basically chicken rice cooked over high heat in copious amount of soy and oyster sauce topped with dried salted fish. Moon cake (月餅, *yueh-ping*) is a traditional Chinese pastry shaped to resemble the full moon. It is a must to celebrate the mid-Autumn festival or Moon Cake festival of the fifteenth day of the eighth lunar month.

13. *Bah kut the* (肉骨茶, pronounced in Hokkien) is a soup cooked with herbs, garlic, and pork ribs. It is believed that *bah kut teh* has medicinal properties. *Bah kut teh* is usually served with rice or yam rice in certain places. *Hokkien mee* (福建麵) is a dish of thick yellow noodles fried until crispy in thick black soy sauce and pork lard.

14. *Briyani* rice is made from a mixture of spices, basmati rice, meat/vegetables, and yogurt. The ingredients are ideally cooked together in the final phase. It is a time-consuming dish to prepare. *Naan* is a leavened, oven-baked flatbread. *Chapathi* is a type of bread originated from Punjab, which is usually eaten with vegetable curry dishes. *Roti parata* is a pancake bread originating in Pakistan and India. In Malaysia, *roti parata* is called *roti canai*.

15. *Nasi kandar* is plain rice or *briyani* rice served with other dishes of curry chicken, fish, beef, or mutton and also pickled vegetables. *Rojak mamak* is a variant of *rojak* consisting of substantial ingredients like boiled potatoes and hard-boiled eggs. *Mee goreng mamak* is a dish of fried noodles with flavoring (usually curry), vegetables, egg, tofu, and occasionally chicken. Curry fish head is a dish where the head of red snapper is semi-stewed in a thick curry with assorted vegetables such as okra and brinjals and usually served with either rice or bread.

References

Appadurai, Arjun. 1988. "How to Make a National Cuisine: Cookbooks in Contemporary India." *Contemporary Study of Society and History* 30: 3–24.

Belasco, Warren. 1999. "Food and the Counter Culture: A Story of Bread and Politics." In *Food in Global History*, edited by R. Grew, 273–292. Boulder, CO: Westview Press.

Carsten, Sharon A. 2005. *Histories, Cultures, Identities: Studies in Malaysian Chinese Worlds.* Singapore: Singapore University Press.

Chang, Yu-Hsin. 2008. "Exploration of the Term of 'Taiwan liao-li' (Taiwan Cuisine)." *Newsletter of Chinese Dietary Culture Foundation,* 14(1): 40–44.

Chen, Yu-Jen. 2008. "Nation, Class and Cultural Presentation: 'Taiwanese Cuisine' During Japanese Colonial Era and Early Post-War Taiwan," *Taiwan Historical Research,* 15(3): 139–186.

"Culinary Delights" (e-brochure), http://www.tourism.gov.my/en/ebrochure/index.asp?id=6f7 df8a8.

Cwiertka, Katarzyna. 2006. *Modern Japanese Cuisine: Food, Power and National Identity.* London: Reaktion Books.

Goody, Jack. 1982. *Cooking, Cuisine and Class: A Study in Comparative Sociology.* Cambridge: Cambridge University Press.

King, Victor T. 1993. "Tourism and culture in Malaysia." In *Tourism in Southeast Asia,* edited by Michael Hitchcock, Victor T. King, and Mike Parnewell, 99–116. London and New York: Routledge.

McIntyre, Kevin T. 2002. "Eating the Nation: Fish Sauce in the Crafting of Vietnamese Community." PhD dissertation, Department of Anthropology, University of Wisconsin-Madison.

Ministry of Information, Communication and Culture. "Dasar Kebudayaan Kebangsaan," http://kebudayaan.kpkk.gov.my/about/perkhidmatan/?c4=22&c3=40&click=1.

Mintz, Sydney W., and Christine M. Du Bois. 2002. "The Anthropology of Food and Eating." *Annual Review of Anthropology* 31: 99–119.

National Operations Council. 1969. "The May 13 Tragedy: A Report." Kuala Lumpur: National Operations Council.

Parasecoli, Fabio. 2008. *Bite Me: Food in Popular Culture.* New York: Berg.

Prime Minister's Office. "Rancangan Malaysia Ke Lima (1986–1990)," http://www3.pmo.gov .my/RancanganWeb/Rancangan1.nsf/18919c170a1dfba182567320023cc04/7c7c36dd b3e360134825674b0033aa29?OpenDocument.

———. "Rancangan Malaysia Ke Enam (1991–1995)," http://www3.pmo.gov.my/Rancangan Web/Rancangan1.nsf/c830edf214b37444482567320023aab0/1318b5769bdae4b84825 674b0031581c?OpenDocument.

———. "Rancangan Malaysia Ke Tujuh (1996–2000)," http://www3.pmo.gov.my/Rancangan Web/Rancangan1.nsf/e2eb45b5229534fe4825673100031def/6bd22ccf2d39caa14825 70a70030c21f?OpenDocument.

———. "Rancangan Malaysia Ke Sembilan (2006–2010)," http://www3.pmo.gov.my/Rancan ganWeb/Rancangan1.nsf/fec3c825c96ab6be482571a20024010b/f68fdecb4050cc 46482571aa0004fe13?OpenDocument.

Skinner, G. William. 1996. "Creolized Chinese society in Southeast Asia." In *Sojourners and Settlers: Histories of Southeast Asia and the Chinese,* edited by Anthony Reid, 51–93. Honolulu: University of Hawaii Press.

Stockwell, A. J. 1993. "Early Tourism in Malaya." In *Tourism in Southeast Asia,* by Michael Hitchcock, Victor T. King, and Mike Parnewell, 258–270. London and New York: Routledge.

"Tourism Malaysia," http://www.tourism.gov.my/en/about/default.asp.

Wilk, Richard W. 1999. "'Real Belizean Food': Building Local Identity in the Transnational Caribbean." *American Anthropologist* 101(2): 244–255.

Yeh, Chu-Hao, ed. 1903. *Taiwan Hall.* Taipei: *Taiwan Daily Newspaper.*

CHAPTER 3

Wudang Daoist Tea Culture

Jean DeBernardi

This chapter explores the promotion of tea culture at Wudang Mountain, a Daoist temple complex in Hubei Province that is a popular tourist destination. At shops in temples and market areas, vendors brand their teas as Wudang Daoist tea, emphasizing its health benefits and connecting their teas to the Daoist discourse of life-nourishing (*yang sheng*) practices. In their marketing materials and on their website, the management of the Eight Immortals Temple Tea Plantation further cites folklore and mythic history to claim profound local roots for Wudang tea culture. In so doing, this company echoes the memory narratives of more famous Chinese teas like Iron Guanyin and Dahongpao.

In China as elsewhere, convenient travel now puts people in contact with areas and peoples that a few decades earlier only a few non-locals explored. As a consequence of a global trend toward commodification, members of local groups, including distinctive ethnocultural groups, now seek to create distinctive local brands for a tourist market. These may include generic products like t-shirts emblazoned with name places and images, or ethnic styles of jewelry and clothing. But commonly local people lay claim to unique local delicacies that visitors may sample but also purchase for gifts or souvenirs. Corporations now regularly mine these local traditions to find items that they can transform into commodities for a wider market (Comaroff and Comaroff 2009).

Tea is a global commodity, but tea's history started in Asia, and majority and minority peoples in East, Southeast, and South Asia drink tea. Nonetheless, for many Chinese the art of tea drinking epitomizes Chinese identity. Chinese authors and tea-museum curators often claim China to be the homeland of tea, and trace its history back to the legendary Chinese emperor Shennong. This narrative claims five thousand years of history for Chinese tea drinking.

Wudang tea vendors may seek to promote their tea as having Daoist characteristics, but in the Tang Dynasty (618–907) itinerant Buddhist monks spread the practice of tea drinking, which they used as an aid to fasting and meditation

(Benn 2005). In this period, Japanese Buddhists who visited Chinese monasteries also learned of Buddhist tea culture, and introduced the tea plant and tea drinking to Japan. Lu Yu (733–804), the so-called tea sage who wrote the *Tea Classic*, himself was raised in a Buddhist monastery, and his master introduced him to Buddhist tea culture. In the *Tea Classic*, he introduced the methods of tea cultivation, preparation, and consumption to a wider public.

Much like Chinese popular religion, which blends elements of Confucianism, Daoism, and Buddhism, Chinese view tea culture as blending Confucian, Daoist, and Buddhist values and practices (Wang 2000: 51–68). For example, Wang Ling, in his popular *Chinese Tea Culture,* notes that the "social influence of Chinese tea culture is mainly reflected in Confucian thought, while its aesthetic viewpoint, skills and practical spirit are mainly influenced by Taoist thought" (2000: 58). He further observes that tea culture expresses the basic Daoist idea that the natural and the human are a unity; moreover, noting that the cultivation, brewing, and drinking of tea offered insight into natural law. He also notes that Daoists focus on health preservation (*yangsheng*), and that tea may be used to calm the mind and improve digestion (60–61).

The social act of sharing a cup of tea in an artful way broadly symbolizes Chinese identity, but diverse varieties of tea and tea culture are associated with diverse regional, ethnocultural, and religious identities. Oolong tea is produced in many regions of China and also in Taiwan, for example, but the most famous varieties are associated with specific areas of Fujian province, including Anxi (Iron Guanyin) and Wuyi Mountain (Dahongpao). Each of these teas is associated with historical narratives that pinpoint the discovery and/or creation of these varieties of tea and also the history of the tea's official recognition.

People explain the name of Dahongpao tea, which translates as "big red robe," for example, in light of several different stories. According to one version of this account, the Buddhist monks at the Tianxin Temple at Wuyi Mountain offered this tea to a scholar who fell ill on his way to the imperial examinations. He recovered and passed the examination. To show his gratitude, he sent red robes to Wuyi Mountain to clothe the four trees from which the healing tealeaves had been picked. Similarly, a story is told of Iron Guanyin that explains that the tea became well known when a scholar gave some as a gift to the Qianlong Emperor (Hai, Xie, and Luo 2010: 12).

Wudang Tea Culture

One of Hubei's richest tourism assets is the Daoist temple complex at Wudang Mountain, which draws pilgrims and tourists from China and Greater China. China's State Council identified Wudang Mountain as a National Key Scenic Area in 1982, and UNESCO named its ancient temples to its World Heritage list in 1994. The Chinese government has worked with the Chinese Taoist Association to develop Wudang's temples and pavilions, which are spread over 400 square kilometers of mountainous terrain, into a major tourist destination. The government tourist office promotes Wudang Mountain for its scenic beauty, its deep historical heritage, its religious culture, and famous martial arts.

In 2006, Wudang's ritual music and martial arts were placed on a list of National Intangible Heritage. Wudang's ritual performers and martial arts troupes often travel internationally to perform, and Wudang's martial arts academies attract international students and tourists taking martial arts tours of China (see DeBernardi 2008a, 2010).[1] Although its tea culture is less renowned, local tea sellers claim that Wudang teas have a deep history and Daoist qualities.

Wudang Mountain is in the Qinling Mountains, which is part of a larger chain of mountains that includes the Shennongjia nature reserve. Located in a subtropical zone, Wudang's trees are enormous and its plant life abundant.[2] The Yuan Dynasty South Cliff Palace is embedded in the side of a cliff, suspended over a deep forested ravine; its stone dragon incense burner faces across that ravine to the Golden Peak, whose small bronze temple, the destination of every pilgrim, sits atop the highest peak overlooking the mountain range in all directions.

Tourist literature stresses the great antiquity of the imperially sponsored temples at Wudang Mountain, whose development reached its zenith in the Ming dynasty (1368–1644), but which include temples dating to the Tang, Song, and Yuan dynasties. The patron deity of Wudang Mountain is Xuantian Dadi, also known as Zhenwu, a savior god who is supposed to have achieved enlightenment while meditating at Wudang Mountain. The third Ming emperor attributed his success at taking the throne from his nephew to Xuantian Dadi, and supported and developed the temple complex. The small temple on the Golden Peak was designed for imperial worship; it was opened to the public only in the Qing Dynasty. Veneration of Xuantian Shangdi became a national cult in the Ming dynasty, in part promoted by a vernacular novel, *Journey to the North* (see Seaman 1988).

Because he remains a popular deity, Wudang Mountain draws pilgrims from all parts of China and greater China, including Taiwan, Singapore, and Malaysia. Chinese in Southeast Asia make the pilgrimage to Wudang Mountain much as Christians might visit the Holy Land to see Biblical sites like Bethlehem (Lagerwey 1987). Pilgrims and visitors may climb on foot to the Golden Peak through three Heaven Gates or chose a swift gondola ride to the mountain summit. Pilgrims may pray for a good marriage partner, or children, or prosperity, and some may sponsor a ritual or throw numbered divination sticks at Zixiao Palace (see DeBernardi 2008b).[3]

At the gate and near the temples, these visitors encounter shops selling a variety of commodities that have a special relationship to Wudang Mountain, including *taiji* swords, books on Daoism, videos, tapes of ritual music, dried wild mushrooms, and medicinal plants. Wudang tea is among the commodities commonly offered to tourists for sale. Like wild mountain products, tea grown at Wudang Mountain is said to have a special *lingqi,* a term that suggests that the product is both spiritually efficacious and filled with a kind of natural energy absorbed from the soil, water, sun, and air of this spectacular mountain environment.

Some shopkeepers claim to sell wild tea that they have harvested themselves, while others whisper that these teas are purchased in bulk and then packaged as Wudang tea. Although the provenance of these teas is doubtful, the Wudang Scenic Area includes a tea mountain and tea factory. The Eight Immortals Tea Plantation offers visitors the chance to relax and enjoy their teas on a pavilion overlooking the rolling fields of tea, and produces green, oolong, and black teas for sale at its shop.

Wudang Tea: The Making of a Tradition

Wudang Mountain attracts Asian and international tourists, pilgrims, and martial artists. Whatever their diverse interests, many visitors seek out local foods including tender spring bamboo shoots (which were a prized tribute item from Wudang in imperial times),[4] wild vegetables, wild game, free-range chicken (raised surreptitiously in the forest), and local varieties of tea. They find Wudang tea sold at a number of locations, including small shops run by local people, a tearoom inside the temple complex at Crown Prince Slope and also an open-air pavilion overlooking the mountains next to the tea plantation.

Wudang Mountain has a system of buses that transports visitors from location to location. Most visitors and pilgrims visit Wudang Mountain's Golden Peak, and traditional pilgrims still follow a stone path up the mountain from Wuyaling or unmarked paths known only to local people. But most visitors are pressed for time, and many travel in groups. These will choose instead to ride a gondola to the peak. The bus going to the gondola station passes by the Eight Immortals Temple Tea Pavilion and tea store, and the driver will stop there on request.

The Eight Immortals Temple (*Baxian Guan*) is a small Yuan dynasty temple barely visible from the road. The temple is unrestored and neglected; to approach it the visitor must follow a dirt path through a field of tea trees and the front yards of villager's residences. Most who stop here seek instead the Eight Immortals Temple tea store and tea pavilion. This small settlement is called Eight Immortals Temple town; it includes a dormitory for workers and a small hotel and restaurant, and a handful of students also stay here to study at the Eight Immortals Martial Arts School. But the tea company with its store, pavilion, and factory dominates the narrow strip of buildings.

The teas sold at Crown Prince Slope Temple are not grown there; by contrast, Eight Immortals Teas are grown at Wudang Mountain in a plantation that carpets the mountain slopes surrounding the tea pavilion (see figure 3.1). Local peo-

Figure 3.1. Eight Immortals Temple and tea plantation, June 2010.

ple harvest and process these teas, which are sold through the company's store. According to one of their brochures, at present the plantation comprises 1,500 mu (approximately 247 acres), and produces 25,000 kilograms of tea per year. They have developed more than twenty tea products, including one prize-winning tea, Wudang Yinjian tea. They claim to have been certified organic by the European Union (*Wudang Organic Taoism Tea Series*).

The Wudang Mountain tea plantation is a modern enterprise launched by a retired soldier, Wang Fuguo in 1986, and a year later formed into a company. Wang was close to Wudang Mountain's abbot, Wang Guangde, who was a key figure in the restoration of Wudang Mountain as an active Daoist community and in developing international linkages.

Although this enterprise is relatively new, the Eight Immortals Temple Tea Plantation presents itself as having deep historic roots. Indeed, in conversation with me the manager claimed that the history of tea at Wudang Mountain was much older than that of Fujian Province, whose tea history only dated to the Yuan dynasty. A promotional article claims that "China is the birthplace of tea, and tea was discovered earliest at Wudang Mountain" (*"Wudang Daocha"*). Historians observe that the tea plant is native to the mountains of southwestern China and northeastern India (Gardella 1994: 9; Mair and Hoh 2009: 24), which suggests that Wudang Mountain is unlikely to have been the place of its discovery. But a widely repeated legendary history of tea suggests that Hubei Province played a role in China's tea history.

One source of this legendary history is the *Tea Classic,* a book written in the Tang dynasty, which as I note above is the period in which tea drinking became widely popular in China (Lu Yu 1974). The *Tea Classic* probably was the first book written on tea, a fact that many offer as evidence that China is the homeland of tea. Its author, Lu Yu was born in Jingling City (now named Tianmen) in Hubei Province, a fact that supports the plantation manager's claims regarding the antiquity of tea culture in this region. Today, tea merchants revere Lu Yu as the "saint of tea" and tea factories and museums commonly display statues of him.[5]

In the *Tea Classic,* Lu Yu claimed that Emperor Shennong, whom Chinese venerate as the founder of Chinese agriculture, first discovered tea as a drink. Shennong is said to have discovered tea in 2737 BCE in the course of tasting plants to discover their medicinal uses. Some of these plants were poisonous and he found that he could use tea to detoxify himself. But Shennong is undoubtedly a legendary figure, and the writings that are attributed to him date many centuries later.

Some identify the forests where the First Farmer (as Shennong is known) tasted one hundred herbs as being in Shaanxi not far from Xian, but others believe this location to be Hubei's Daba Mountains. Hubei's tallest peak is named after Shennong, and Wudang Mountain is not far from "Shennong's shelf" (*Shennongjia*), an area of high mountains that is listed on UNESCO's World Network of Biosphere Reserves. The history of Wudang Daoist tea as a named brand is recent, but its vendors claim deep roots for Hubei tea culture.

Although Hubei may have a connection with two important figures in China's tea history, and although Hubei produces a high volume of tea, Hubei is not among the most prominent of China's tea-growing areas. Lists of China's top ten teas vary, but typically they include the teas of coastal China (Fujian, Zhejiang, and Jiangsu) and southwest China (Yunnan), areas that produce the top teas offered for sale in China in tea shops, supermarkets, and airport stores and also exported.[6]

From an economic perspective, the top ten brands of tea in 2012 include West Lake Longjing (a variety of green tea), which according to a 2012 study had a brand value of 5.26 billion yuan, and Anxi Iron Guanyin (a variety of oolong tea), with a brand value of 5.2 billion yuan. Although Hubei teas did not rank in the top ten, remarkably Wudang Daoist tea ranked eighteenth with an estimated value of 1.27 billion yuan (US $202 million) (Zhang 2012).[7] By contrast with West Lake Longjing and Anxi Iron Guanyin, which are identified both by distinctive methods of processing the tea and by the place where these teas are produced, Wudang Daoist tea is identified only by place of origin.

The government has recognized Wudang Daoist tea as a "national geographic indications protection product" meaning that only teas from this region can be sold under the Wudang Daoist brand. This designation is a legal restriction widely used in the European Union and elsewhere to promote and protect agricultural products like Roquefort and Champagne, which can only carry these labels if they are produced in the designated region and meet standards of quality.[8]

Wudang Daoist tea may be the top brand in Hubei province, but to date this regional variety of tea is not widely sold internationally. One unique enterprise, Cha Tao the Way of Tea, sells organic teas from Wudang Mountain in Fort Collins, Colorado. According to their website, their founder is an ordained Daoist priest, Yun Xiang Tseng, who studied for ten years at Wudang Mountain but who is now based in Colorado. In addition to importing tea, Master Tseng (whose Daoist name is Chen) is also a martial arts teacher. He promotes Wudang Daoist culture through a personal website that explains Wudang Daoism and martial arts, and sells his books and DVDs through an online store.[9] He regularly leads "Journey to Enlightenment" tours to China. In 2009, the itinerary included a visit to Wudang Mountain and to his tea farm, and also to Wuyi Mountain, a tourist destination whose attractions include the Dahongpao mother trees.[10]

On the Cha Tao tea store website, Yun Xiang Tseng explains how he began to import Wudang Daoist tea to the United States. In 2000, he led a group of visitors to Wudang Mountain, and on the way to the Golden Peak, they stopped at a schoolhouse where they met a teacher and his students cultivating tea trees to support their school. He bought the tea crop from them, and after the school was relocated continued to grow tea there for export to the United States.

The store's website describes this plantation and claims to follow the traditional, non-mechanical method of processing their organic Sacred Mountain Green Tea, noting: "After the tea is processed, every pound undergoes a ritual of prayer and ceremony by Master Tseng's fellow priests at the Purple Cloud Temple [*Zixiao Gong*]. This ancient ceremony is intended to infuse each leaf with blessing of health, well-being and joy, and to pass-on the energetic blessings to the consumer."[11] The company further seeks to share the experience of enjoying high-quality teas and of "authentic tea culture" with the "extended global communities sharing the planet."[12]

Master Tseng appears to be alone in promoting Sacred Mountain Green Tea to Americans. By contrast, in China, the Eight Immortals Temple Tea Plantation partakes in a well-patronized effort to promote Wudang Mountain and its spirituous teas to tourists (see figure 3.2).

Performing Daoist Tea Culture

Wudang Mountain's Eight Immortals Temple Tea Plantation has created a form of tea culture that blends Daoist symbols, health claims, legends, history, and naming practices to produce a Daoist brand of tea and tea performance. Recog-

Figure 3.2 Preparation of "Daoist Tea" at the Eight Immortals Plantation Tea Pavilion, April 2009.

nizing their success, in 1999 the Ministry of Agriculture designated this business as the "original place of Chinese Taoism Tea Culture" ("Wudang Organic Taoism Tea Series"). Although it may not be as famed as Wudang martial arts, Daoist tea culture undoubtedly is one of Wudang's tourist attractions.

When I attended a conference in a Wudang Mountain town in June 2009, the organizers invited participants to a performance by the Wudang Gongfu and Art Troupe of China. In addition to impressive martial arts displays, two singers and a dance troupe entertained us. One of the dances celebrated Wudang tea culture. The female dancers performed in traditional black-and-white costumes decorated with yin-yang symbols, demonstrating a Daoist-style tea ceremony as the narrator explained it.

At the Eight Immortals Temple Tea Pavilion, young unmarried women make and serve the tea (see figure 3.3), wearing form-fitting *qipao*s emblazoned with the yin-yang symbol. At an after-hours party organized by the manager to entertain some Malaysian Chinese friends, three of the women prepared tea for us in a perfectly synchronized choreographed performance. As they prepared tea, another man and woman performed classical Chinese music for us, taking turns with one of the Malaysian guests, also a classical musician.[13]

A common expression, *chadao,* or the way of tea, describes the art of tea. At the Eight Immortals Tea Plantation, however, they reverse the characters and refer to their practice of the "way of tea" (*chadao*) as "Daoist tea" (*daocha*). They further brand their tea as Daoist through stories and the names they give different varieties of tea, and also relate the healthful qualities of their products to the Daoist practices of health cultivation (*yangsheng*) and to the spiritual potency (*lingqi*) of the Daoist mountain where their tea trees grow. Like the store in Fort Collins,

Figure 3.3. Young woman serves tea to visitors to the Eight Immortals Plantation Tea Pavilion, April 2007.

they stress that their products are organic, noting that the pristine water and ecological balance of the mountain environment in which their teas are grown.

In 2008, the company produced a promotional video with the assistance of Chris D. Neve, the president of Monarex Hollywood Corporation. Neve has recently made a number of documentaries under the Mysterious China franchise, including *Holy Mountain* (2009), which focuses on Wudang Mountain, and *Kung Fu Masters* (2009), which includes footage on Wudang martial arts. Their video is entitled "The Native Place of Chinese Daoist Tea Culture" (*Zhongguo Daocha Wenhuaji Xiang*) and includes footage of Neve filming young girls picking tealeaves as they sing a folksong.

The video shows spectacular aerial views of Wudang Mountain, followed by interviews with a number of experts on tea culture who describe Daoist tea culture as Chinese heritage. The video both cites classical sources on tea culture, and provides scientific testimony on the medical benefits of tea drinking. Many scenes include foreigners enjoying tea at their shop and pavilion. The film shows that their finest tea is offered to the god during rituals at Zixiao Palace, the main temple venue for ritual performances, but also includes photographs of prizes won when they exhibited their teas in Hubei, Hong Kong, Japan, and Malaysia.

In the video as well as the promotional literature for the Wudang Tea they explain the temple's name (and by extension the company's name) in light of its history. According to them, after the Eight Immortals crossed the sea they visited Wudang Mountain, where the Jade Emperor and Xuantian Shangdi welcomed them with tea. The Eight Immortals found the beautiful scenery and the tea attractive, and they lingered there. Because of their affection for the place, people built the Eight Immortals Temple to worship them.

In addition to these legendary connections, the tea factory asserts its connection with the Daoist context through the coining of tea names that allude to elements of Wudang Daoist culture. The Eight Immortals Temple Tea Plantation offers a Daoist tea series, including Wudang Yinjian (Silver Sword) tea, which takes its name from the Wudang sword so popular with tourists; Wudang Zhenjing (Needle Well) tea, referring to a place named for an episode in the story of the Emperor of the Dark Heavens as he sought enlightenment on Wudang Mountain; Wudang Taihe tea (*Taihe* is another name for Wudang Mountain, and means Grand Harmony), Wudang Qifeng (Miraculous Peak) tea, referring to Wudang's seventy-two peaks.

They also sell the King of Wudang Daoist tea, which they explain is Wudang's *Taijiquan* health-cultivating (*yangsheng*) *gongfu* tea.[14] As the brochure describes it, one of eighteen steps in making Wudang *gongfu* tea is to use a Great Ultimate Heaven and Earth (or Male and Female) ball (*Taiji Qiankun*), which they describe as one of Wudang's thirty-six skills. The video shows not tea-factory workers but three young men wearing Daoist robes, holding balls that they turn from top to bottom and bottom to top to shake the tea.

These teas range in cost from the relatively affordable (although local people consider them to be expensive) to the very expensive. A recent price list showed the cheapest teas (green tea and Wudang Qifeng tea) at 60–70 yuan per 500 grams (approximately one pound) or around US $9–$10. The most expensive teas (*Wudang Yinjian* and *Wudang Jinzheng*) are produced in very limited quantities and listed at 2880 yuan, or US $420, more than four hundred times more costly than the cheapest teas. When I asked who bought these premium teas, the company's secretary noted that wealthy people bought them, and the government purchased the finest teas for their receptions.

The tea producers promote their tea through the performance of so-called Daoist tea arts. They note: "The Wudang Daoist tea performance is unique in its combination of Daoist principles such as the union of the heaven and human, valuing nature and truth, and maintaining health, with the culture of martial arts, Daoist medications, and beautiful mountains and rivers" ('*Wudang Daocha*'). To further emphasize the Daoist identity of their teas, the packaging includes the Great Ultimate (*taiji*) yin-yang symbol surrounded by the eight trigrams. Among the products that they sell in their store are tea sets displaying this symbol on one side and the characters *Wudang Daocha* (Wudang Daoist tea) on the other. They use as their company's logo a modern interpretation of the yin-yang symbol that represents Wudang Mountain in other tourist brochures.

Conclusion

The Eight Immortals Temple Tea Plantation market their teas as Wudang Daoist tea, using history, legend, ritual, and sacred location to distinguish its green, black, and oolong teas from those produced elsewhere. Their development of Daoist tea culture has been concurrent with the development of Wudang Mountain itself as a location that uniquely represents the history and contemporary practice of Daoism and Daoist martial arts.

The tea connoisseurs whom I interviewed undoubtedly preferred to select teas by the look and fragrance of teas sold in bulk. But many tea companies, like the Eight Immortals Temple Tea Plantation, use modern marketing strategies, including illustrated brochures and books, eye-catching websites, promotional videos, and attractive packaging to engage the attention of potential customers.

Although the company has only begun to market its teas internationally, they enjoy an advantageous relationship with Wudang Mountain, which is a well-known tourist destination in China and Greater China.[15] China has many famous tea mountains, however, including Fujian's Wuyi Mountain and Zhejiang's Longjing Mountain, both of which are internationally recognized for the quality of their teas.

The Eight Immortals Temple Plantation seeks to valorize their teas through claims about the excellence of their growing environment (not unlike the terroir of a fine wine) and the historical depth of their tea history. They further use legend and mythic history to position their products, and associate their teas with Daoist traditions of health preservation, including martial arts. But they sell their teas in a competitive environment, and cannot reinvent the larger history of tea.

Those selling Iron Guanyin or Longjing green tea advertise that their teas were once tribute teas, enjoyed in imperial palaces. At the Eight Immortals Temple Tea Plantation they must turn to legend for a parallel distinction, claiming that when the Eight Immortals flew to the mountain, divine emperors—the Jade Emperor and the Emperor of the Dark Heavens—served them Wudang tea.

In *Ethnicity Inc.,* John and Jean Comaroff propose that "commerce has been instrumental either in crystallizing or in reproducing the sociological entities ('people,' 'nation,' 'community') in which cultural identity is presumed to inhere" (2009: 114). In particular, they conclude that people use identity-laden objects as a vehicle through which "ethnic consciousness is materialized" (33). They focus on the modern discourse of intellectual property rights, including competing national claims to trademark signature products (122).

Wudang tea vendors have used story, packaging, and performance to promote teas that evoke Wudang's history, local traditions, and landscape. They also claim that their Daoist teas (*Daocha*) have absorbed some of the spiritual energy of this numinous mountain. But the marketing of tea now unfolds in national and global markets where tea sellers and connoisseurs appreciate and repeat historical tea narratives and esteem high-mountain teas, but evaluate these teas on the basis of quality and taste (see Tan and Ding 2010).

Although the green, oolong, and black teas sold resemble those produced elsewhere in China, Wudang tea sellers stress that their teas grow in a numinous mountain environment that (they claim) imparts its spiritual energy to their teas. Hubei officials pay premium prices for the Eight Immortals Temple Plantation's highest-quality teas, but outside China, Wudang tea is not well known. Although it enjoys impressive sales, even within China, Wudang Daoist tea ranks much lower than better-known varieties of tea. As global awareness of this spectacular world heritage site grows, Hubei's Wudang Daoist tea series may find a place among the specialty teas now sold on the world market. But for now, Wudang Daoist tea is an innovative brand that symbolizes a heritage that is simultaneously imperial, national, Daoist, and deeply local.

Notes

I visited Wudang Mountain to study religious and cultural tourism in 2004 and 2007 with support from the Chiang Ching-kuo Foundation and the Social Science and Humanities Research Council of Canada. I returned in 2009 with support from the University of Alberta China Institute, and revisited the Baxianguan Tea Plantation. I especially thank the company's manager, Mr. Wang Fuguo, and secretary, Ms. Li Cui, for providing me with all the materials concerned. I thank Ms. Leilei Chen for commenting on a draft of this chapter. I also conducted a pilot study on tea culture in 2009 in collaboration with Professor Zeng Shaocong of Xiamen University supported by the Chinese Academy of Social Sciences and University of Alberta Mobility Program. In 2011, I continued that research in Fujian, Zhejiang, and Jiangsu provinces with support from the Chiang Ching-kuo Foundation. Special thanks are due to Kwang Ok Kim and the Institute of Cross-Cultural Studies at Seoul National University and the Foundation of Chinese Dietary Culture. I would also like to acknowledge the influence of Marshall Sahlins, whose perspective on the "indigenization of modernity" informs this chapter.

1. Wudang Mountain is also internationally famous in field of martial arts since one of its legendary figures, Zhang Sanfeng, is supposed to have invented *Taijiquan* at Wudang. When the Daoists revived its temples in the 1980s, a handful of martial artists gathered there to study.

2. The forest is the source of many wild plants, including a number that have been identified as having value as herbal remedies. According to a Wudang tourism website, a survey done in 1985 showed that there were 617 kinds of medical materials in the mountain. The tourism website notes in its overview on Wudang Mountain that "Li Shenzhen, a famous medicine scientist in the Ming Dynasty, especially went to Mt. Wudang to gather medical herbs and 400 species were recorded in his Compendium of Medical Materials. The Taoist priests of Mt. Wudang have been fully utilizing the plant resources and giving a full play to the special functions of the medical plants, especially Langmei fruit" (http://www.wudang.com/index3A3.htm, consulted 9 August 2009). A 1996 book that lists Wudang's herbal remedies includes fifteen recipes for herbal teas (Shang 1996: 172–174).

3. As well as being a historic site, Wudang Mountain is also an active Daoist community. Closed during the Cultural Revolution, the monastery at Zixiao Gong trains and supports Daoist priests and nuns. Some are highly trained ritual performers who conduct traditional rituals daily and also at major festivals in the third and ninth lunar months, the anniversaries of Xuantian Dadi's birth and enlightenment.

4. I thank Wudang historian Professor Yang Lizhi for this information and for his hospitality in Danjiangkou.

5. The manager of the Eight Immortals Tea Plantation claimed to have studied Lu Yu's *Chajing*, and also to have studied with Wudang Daoists and tea experts before establishing his business. He also brought in high-quality tea plants

6. On visits to tea markets and tea stores in Beijing and Shanghai (many of which are run by Fujianese), I noted that none displayed Hubei teas for sale, nor did I find any for sale in tea stores in Hong Kong.

7. The rating was done by the Agricultural Brand Research Center of the China Academy of Rural Development (CARD) of Zhejiang University, *China Tea* magazine, the Chinese Tea Office, and China Tea Net. The top ten 2012 brands were West Lake Longjing tea (Zhejiang Province), Anxi Iron Guanyin (Fujian Province), Pu-er (Yunnan Province), Xinyang Maojian (Henan Province), Dongtingshan Biluochun tea (Jiangsu Province), Fuding White tea (Fujian Province), Dafuo Longjing tea (Zhejiang Province), Anji White tea (Zhejiang Province), Wuyishan Dahongpao (Fujian Province), and Qimen Black Tea (Anhui Province) (Zhang 2012).

8. See for example "Fact Sheet: European Policy for Quality Agricultual Products" (January 2007). http://ec.europa.eu/agriculture/publi/fact/quality/2007_en.pdf (consulted 17 August 2012).

9. "Wudang Dao" (http://www.wudangtao.com/). The website includes a link to "Wudang Blog: The Master's Thoughts" (http://wudangtao.org/wudangblog/, consulted 22 August 2009).

10. http://www.wudangtao.com/announcements/index3.html, consulted 22 August 2009. In addition to leading tours to China, he also travels in the United States to hold Daoist workshops.

11. "Our Story" (http://www.chataotea.com/our_story.html, consulted 21 August 2009). According to Li Cui, the Eight Immortals Tea Plantation sells some of its teas through this store and also plans to visit them to help them promote Wudang teas.

12. "Our Tea" (http://www.chataotea.com/teas.html, consulted 21 August 2009).

13. Although he did not perform when I visited the tea pavilion, a poster displays and their promotional literature shows a young man performing tea *gongfu* using a long-spouted teapot; the video also included a short clip of this athletic performance.

14. The Crown Prince Slope Temple teashop also sold teas named for famous sites at Wudang Mountain: Taihe Mountain Sword Tea, Wudang Sword Tea, Crown Prince Sword Tea, Purple Empirium Clouds and Fog Tea, Wudang Maojian ("hairy tips") tea, and finally, the cheapest, Wudang Green Tea. The most expensive of these and their highest grade was 1,200 yuan, or US $175.

15. Around 2004, government regulations were changed to allow independent tea growers to export tea without going through the provincial government. As a consequence of this important change, many tea companies are now seeking to export their teas.

References

Benn, James A. 2005. "Buddhism, Alcohol, and Tea in Medieval China." In *Of Tripod and Palate: Food, Politics, and Religion in Traditional China,* edited by Roel Sterckx. 213–236. New York: Palgrave Macmillan.

Comaroff, John L. and Jean Comaroff. 2009. *Ethnicity, Inc.* Chicago: University of Chicago Press.

DeBernardi, Jean. 2010. "Wudang Mountain and the Modernization of Daoism." *Journal of Daoist Studies* 3: 202–210.

———. 2008a. "Wudang Mountain: Staging Charisma and the Modernization of Daoism." In *Chenghuang Xinyang* [City God Belief], edited by Ning Ngui Ngi, 273–280. Singapore: Lorong Koo Chye Sheng Hong Temple Association.

———. 2008b. "Commodifying Blessings: Celebrating the Double-Yang Festival in Penang, Malaysia and Wudang Mountain, China." In *Marketing Gods: Rethinking Religious Commodifications in Asia,* edited by Pattana Kitiarsa, 49–67. London: Routledge.

Gardella, Robert. 1994. *Harvesting Mountains: Fujian and The China Tea Trade 1757–1937.* Berkeley: University of California Press.

Hai Fan, Xie Wenzhe, and Luo Yanxiu, eds. 2010. *Anxi Ti Kuanyin (Iron Goddess of Mercy): The Legend of a Great Plant.* Jersey City: Prunus Press. English translation authorized by Beijing World Publishing Corporation and Post Wave Publishing Consulting.

Lagerwey, John. 1987. "The Pilgrimage to Wu-tang Shan." In *Pilgrims and Sacred Sites in China,* edited by S. Naquin and Chun-fang Yu, 293–332. Berkeley: University of California Press.

Lu Yu. 1974. *The Classic of Tea.* Introduced and translated by Francis Ross Carpenter and illustrated by Demi Hitz. Boston and Toronto: Little, Brown and Co.

Mair, Victor, and Erling Hoh. 2009. *The True History of Tea.* New York: Thames and Hudson.

Sahlins, Marshall. 1999. "What is Anthropological Enlightenment? Some Lessons of the Twentieth Century." *Annual Reviews of Anthropology* 28(1): i–xxiii.

———. 1998. "Cosmologies of Capitalism: The Trans-pacific Sector of the world System." Radcliffe Brown Lecture in Social Anthropology. *Proceedings of the British Academy* LXXIV: 1–51.

Seaman, Gary. 1988. *The Journey to the North: An Ethnohistorical Analysis and Annotated Translation of the Chinese Folk Novel Pei-Yu Chi.* Berkeley: University of California Press.

Shang Ru Biao. 1996. *Zhongguo Wudang Yiyao Mifang* [China's Wudang Medicines and Folk Remedies].

Sterckx, Roel, ed. 2005. *Of Tripod and Palate: Food, Politics, and Religion in Traditional China.* New York: Palgrave Macmillan.

Tan Chee-Beng and Ding Yu-ling. 2010. "The Promotion of Tea in South China: Re-Inventing Tradition in an Old Industry." *Food and Foodways* 18: 121–144.

Wang Ling. 2000. *Chinese Tea Culture.* Beijing: Foreign Languages Press.

Zhang Xiao. 2012. "'Wudang Taoist tea' is worth 1.27 billion yuan," edited by Fu Bo and Tom McGregor. *China Daily,* 27 April. http://wudang.chinadaily.com.cn/2012-04/27/content_15156855.htm.

CHAPTER 4

Rice Cuisine and Cultural Practice in Contemporary Korean Dietary Life

Kwang Ok Kim

Comparing Korea with other Asian countries where the staple food is rice, the present chapter pays special attention to the proliferation of rice cuisine as well as the distinctive dietary structures and modes of culinary service in Korea. Taking food as a genre of culture rather than a medico-nutritional sphere, this chapter analyzes the contents, forms, and consumption patterns of rice dishes in order to understand underlying meanings of diversification and invention of dishes as cultural commodities in the globalizing food market.

In China, at the end of a luxurious banquet, guests are served a main dish of plain steamed rice, fried rice, noodles, or dumplings. Plain rice and noodles are also staple foods in Japan. Similarly, cooked rice (*bap*) is the staple item in everyday meals in Korea,[1] with the traditional mode of serving in the form of set meals (*hanjeongsik*) and home-style meals (*gajeongsik*) in which all dishes are served at once, together with rice and soup (*guk*). Recently, some "modern" restaurants have adopted the Western custom of serving meals in courses, with different parts of the meal brought out at different times. In Korea, this practice has come to mean rice served at the end of the meal along with soup and *kimchi* (Korean fermented vegetable).

Here we see also proliferation of new kinds of *bap*, each of which has been invented as an individual dish. Items, forms, and quality of food, as well as their symbolic meanings, change through the processes of interactive encounters, competition, compromise, innovation, and invention (Gillet 2000; Watson 1997; Yan 2000). Also, food and cuisine should be approached in the context of the various social and cultural elements practiced both by producer and consumer.

Ethnographic discussion here focuses on the rice (*ssal*)[2] and grains (*gok*) that have traditionally been used as ingredients for the staple food, *bap.*[3] In addition to *bap,* grains including rice are also used to make confectionaries, cakes, and liquor.[4] In traditional Korea, cooked rice was the most prestigious staple and its consumption was an indicator of economic wealth for families, while porridge (*juk*) was regarded as inferior and an indicator of poor economic status.

In this chapter, I would like to show the fluctuation of the social position of the traditional staple foods, *bap* and *juk,* in the national cultural and historical context, and to examine the recent invention of various forms of *bap* as part of a changed lifestyle. I will discuss the importance of rice and grains in the field of food studies, which has been dominated by studies focusing on meat and specialty items in national cuisines.

Biography of Rice in Korea

There have been numerous discussions on the cultural meaning of rice in Asian nations. Although rice has long been a national symbol, reflecting the historical antiquity of its cultivation (Ohnuki-Tierney 1993; Kim 2006), it is only recently that rice has become commonly available to people of Korea, Japan, and North China. In pre-modern Korea, rice was a prestigious and expensive foodstuff, so most people lived on millet, barley, beans, corns, potatoes, and sweet potatoes. In China, while elderly people still have vivid memories of hunger, their children enjoy a typical peasant food, *wowotou* (steamed corn flour), as a nostalgia dessert at luxurious banquets. In Korea, a family was regarded as rich if its members were able to eat rice at each meal. During the Japanese colonial occupation of Korea (1910–1945), the government built the ports of Mokpo and Gunsan to export Korean rice to Japan to ensure their own food sufficiency. During World War II, in order to feed the Japanese soldiers, the government confiscated grain while locals kept themselves from starvation by subsisting on the industrialized remnants of bean and sesame supplied by the colonial government.[5] In shaman rituals, hungry ghosts lamented their miserable life of hunger while their fertile rice field was robbed by the Japanese (Kim 2006). After World War II, Korea was divided and devastated by the Korean War (1950–1953). Until the late 1960s, Koreans suffered shortages of grains and relied heavily on foreign aids, including Vietnamese rice and American corn. So in the past "rice with meat" was referred to as the index of wealth one might expect to achieve. North Korea's founder Kim Il Sung once said in a speech to his poverty-stricken people there would come a day when all would enjoy "*ipab-e gogiguk*" (rice and soup with meat), and Kim Jong Il reemphasized this idea of food security in his New Year address of 2010, saying he would realize his father's sixty-year-old dream.[6]

In order to solve the perennial shortage of rice, the government prohibited the industrial use of rice in the 1960s and organized a cultural campaign to eat rice mixed with barley or millet. Importing massive quantities of wheat from the

United States, the government also implemented a campaign to shift people's diet away from rice by popularizing flour-based foods. Medical doctors, nutrition scientists, and culinary professionals appeared in mass media to extol the positive aspects of flour food and the negative effects of excessive intake of carbohydrates such as rice in relation to health, disease, mode of physical growth, refinement of culinary life, convenience of food preparation, and a whole slurry of social issues. Under this government-manipulated science to invent the popular imagination of interaction between flour foods and physical as well as mental superiority, people gradually accepted wheat bread as a substitute for traditional staple food.

Traditionally, during the three-month spring famine from March until early May called *bori gogae* (literally, "barley hump"), grain shortages between the end of the winter stocks and the barley harvest caused widespread hunger. The development of a new, high-yield variety of rice called *tongilbyeo* ("unification rice") in the mid-1970s helped solve this problem. However, the government still attempted to diversify the populace's foodways to incorporate a wider variety of grains beyond rice. Medical and nutritional scientists warned of the dangers of "excessive" rice consumption, along with peppers and salt, which were blamed for a variety of diseases, as part of the effort to get more people to adopt a Western-pattern diet. Those born before the 1960s still express a strong conviction that flour does not afford the same level of physical energy as rice (*bapsim*).

Within modernity's theoretical framework, traditional meals consisting of rice, *kimchi*, and soybean paste (*doinjang*) came to be contrasted with Western meals of bread, milk, and meat. In this way, young urbanites' tastes began to be domesticated by the Western dietary structure despite the fact that a majority of Koreans insist that rice is their national staple food. Though traditional Korean meals predominate in rural regions, the consumption of rice has declined sharply since the 1990s, while meat consumption has rapidly increased.[7]

Sinto buri and the Culture of Well-Being

Old people still have nostalgic memories of now-disappeared restaurants such as Hanilgwan and Joseonok in Seoul where they tasted the economic growth with barbecued beef (*bulgogi*) and grilled beef ribs (*galbi gui*)[8] since the mid-1970s. At that time, young "salary men" used to spend hours in shabby restaurants drinking *soju* and eating cheap barbecued intestines (*gopchang gui*) or stewed beef intestines (*gopchang jeongol*).

Starting in the mid-1980s as part of preparations for the 1988 Seoul Olympics, the Korean government opened the markets to foreign material culture, especially Western imports, including food and fashion. Facing this increasing influx of foreign culture, a group of intellectuals organized a popular nationalistic cultural movement that used rice as a symbol of national identity and sovereignty. Despite such efforts by intellectuals, bread and meat continued to increase in popularity.

The late 1980s to 1990s can be seen as a period of competition between global modernity and local nationalism. Radical changes occurred in the foodscape of Korea during this period, including the appearance of a new breed of fancy restaurants, along with fast-food chains such as McDonald's and KFC and "family restaurants" such as T.G.I. Friday's and Coco's. Soda and instant coffee became "national drinks" until they were replaced by mineral water and "whole bean coffee" (instead of instant coffee) around 2000, when Italian restaurants began to challenge the popularity of McDonald's and KFC (Bak 2005). Many kinds of bread and delicacies have been introduced at luxurious bakeries, too. At present, the newly emerging urban middle class have bread and fresh coffee for breakfast at home or at neighborhood bakeries. Occasions to have meals outside the home have increased, and meals are mainly beef, chicken, or pork prepared in either Western or Korean style.

In the 1980s, some intellectuals displeased by such drastic changes in the foodscape organized various kinds of cultural activism to protect and preserve "national foods." The Agricultural Cooperative Federation adopted and popularized the idea of *sinto buri* ("Body and earth are one") from the philosophy of Cheontae Buddhism, which believes in the inseparability of the karma of a person and that of his surroundings (Kim 1994; Pemberton 2002; Walraven 2002). According to this philosophy, health is maintained only when human physiology maintains harmony with food, which is produced by the water, soil, air, wind, and sunshine in the land where the person lives. This is also connected with traditional idea of *pungsu,* the geomantic analysis of the relationship between human conditions and the physical arrangement of nature. Along with growing nationalistic fever, these movements earned popular acclaim as a form of resistance against the modernization and science that had promoted excessive use of chemicals and antibiotics in agricultural products. It was a countercultural movement against the expansion of Western modernity that many Korean people regarded to have destroyed traditional life and food systems, as well as the national agricultural economy.

Under the slogan "Ours is good," active members of the movement insisted that they should cultivate indigenous crops with traditional methods and technologies, while rejecting the use of chemicals and antibiotics. Agricultural goods thus produced are branded as *yuginong* (organic), are thus more expensive than conventionally produced goods, and are consumed by the urban middle class.[9] The idea of *sinto buri* is now a philosophy that dominates the foodways of Koreans as a whole. Eating rice, grains, and vegetables, as well as the roots, leaves, and fruits of wild plants gradually came into fashion among the middle class. Foods once rejected as backward by Koreans due to Western distaste have been reembraced due to advances in both food science and cultural nationalism: soybean paste, *kimchi*,[10] seasoned sesame leaves, and fermented condiments (*jeotgal*) of such seafood as shrimp, fish, and many kinds of shellfish. In spite of this, there has been competition between Korean traditional cuisine and various foreign foodways, often expressed in the generational gap and gendered culture.

At the start of the twenty-first century, a group of cultural entrepreneurs pursued food as an important cultural genre in which national or ethnic traditions compete with and challenge one another. They actively disseminated discourses on the superiority of Korean food, both in terms of nutrition and aesthetics. Among many cultural enterprises emerging at this time were restaurants and culinary experts who formulated various forms of *bap*. This return-to-tradition movement aligned with people's self-critique on the meat-centered gluttony they indulged in during the 1980s and 1990s. As the ideas of *sinto buri* and "well-being" gain converge, the consumption of rice, grains, and vegetables has begun to concomitantly increase.

"Well-being," a newly introduced English word, became popularized in everyday life of Koreans in the early 2000s. It carries multiple meanings of good/ideal quality of life, wealth, and a cultured lifestyle.[11] People who adhere to this philosophy enjoy food as another genre of aesthetics or art, rather than as a nutritive necessity. They appreciate the color, shape, taste, and fragrance of a dish, the atmosphere of the restaurant, and the manner of service. They try to find philosophy and cultural symbols in what they eat. These people enjoy traveling to fashionable restaurants and trying new dishes. It becomes part of middle-class people's "well-being life" to travel, take photos, enjoy wildflowers and landscapes, practice yoga, swim, golf, and exercise at fitness centers, visit Buddhist temples for meditation, attend cultural programs at museums, art galleries, and concert halls, visit traditional houses in the countryside, and participate in study trips to cultural heritage sites. They are focused on natural food, using local ingredients and prepared through traditional methods. Mostly interested in pseudo-medical science concerning health and bodily fitness, they are preoccupied with whether a food represents "nature." Not only ingredients but also taste and color should be all "natural," they insist.

Words such as organic, non-GM (genetically modified), clean and pure, natural, pollution-free, sunshine, water, air, wind, soil, environment, ecology, and sustainability are used to emphasize the superior quality of the individual foodstuffs. Other important words in the well-being movement are related with human values such as life, love, motherhood, family ties, mind or heart, sincerity, responsibility, and trust. For example, the photo, name, telephone number, and email address of the cultivator are printed on the bag or tag of a product to connote trustworthiness or sincerity. Agribusiness companies also adopt words that connote naturalness and purity, such as Chungjungwon (meaning "clean and pure garden"), Haechandle (meaning "field of sunshine"), Sannaedeul (meaning "mountain-brook-field"), and Pulmuone (meaning "garden of traditional wind blowers") in order to appeal to the consumer's imagination of nature and humanity.

Rice in Renaissance of Korean Culinary Culture

In reaction to the decades of west-oriented modernity that included an overall depreciation of Asian staple food, rice, as nutritionally inferior, there arose recently a rethinking of traditional culinary culture that once again highlighted the importance of rice to Korean people leading to many new inventions and reconstructions of rice-related dishes.

Bap *(Cooked Rice) as a Cuisine*

In traditional food service in Korea, all dishes are placed on the table at the same time, unlike Chinese or Western styles of food service in which entrees are served one at a time (see figures 4.1 and 4.2). At a traditional Korean banquet, individuals can sample several dishes according to their preferences so that at any given moment diners enjoy their own selection of tastes. Flavors are created through a combination of the chef's skills and diner's choices. Therefore, not only the quality of the chef but also the quality of basic condiments or seasonings, such as soy sauce, soybean paste, red pepper paste, and other supplementary sauces is important to the quality and taste of the food. The Korean table is a space where maker and consumer compromise creatively to define the taste of a dish.

In restaurants of relatively high fame today, many different kinds of *bap* made of varying grains appear as an independent or individual dish. Some restaurants that specialize in *bap* explain that they grow special breeds of rice and grains in

Figure 4.1. A Korean table setting, where all dishes are served simultaneously.

Figure 4.2. A scene where a foreign couple and a Korean couple enjoy a Korean table d'hôte.

specially designed fields, which are selected on the analysis of the geomantic arrangement of land, water, air, and sunshine.

Rice is cultivated in several colors in addition to the well-known white variety—including red, black, green, and yellow, which together with white are the five colors representing the five cardinal directions and five elements in Korean cosmology.[12] Koreans regard the color red as the most auspicious element to expel evil spirits, enhance life essence and fertility, and enrich fortune and happiness. Some folklore-oriented people explain the use of colored rice as being based on this symbolism. Colored rice is still produced only in small quantities and is thus expensive. Red and black rice are especially expensive, as these kinds of rice were once consumed exclusively by emperors and kings. Nowadays, colored rice grains are mixed with white rice when cooking *bap*; however, only cooked white rice (*me*) is offered at rituals for ancestors and spirits.

The brand name and place of production is usually printed on rice packaging, accompanied by advertising slogans such as "Odae rice is selected from the highest-quality rice, and cultivated by organic methods in Cheorwon in the pollution-free DMZ where the air, wind, water, and sunshine are all fresh," or "'His Majesty, the King's Rice,' is the same rice that was used exclusively for the king's meals in the past. The rice was cultivated in the very paddy in Yeoju that produced the royal rice and is strictly controlled by the County Agricultural Cooperation."

In contemporary Korea, *bap* is made with rice and grains including millet, sorghum, barley, and corn. It is also sometimes made with beans,[13] bean sprouts, potatoes, sweet potatoes, pumpkin, dried wild plants, mushrooms, or roots such as ginseng or balloon flower (*doraji*). Also, there are various types of cooked rice enriched with pine nuts, gingko, chestnut, jujube, and/or walnut. As a topping, some even use flower petals. In the past, people cooked rice in a large iron pot. Since the early 1980s, some restaurants have served *bap* in a small pot-shaped bowl made of special stone called *gopdol*. In the late 1980s, they began to cook rice in small, individual stone pots for each customer. As stone retains relatively intense heat for a prolonged period of time, it produces a scorched layer of rice crust called *nurungji*; diners will often pour water into the stone bowl to turn this layer into a broth called *sungnyung*. Restaurants that use electric cookers cannot make *nurungji* and so imported inexpensive scorched rice from China. However, food safety concerns were raised when some of the imported *nurungji* was found to have been coated with antiseptic chemicals, and consequently many restaurants have replaced *sungnyung* with tea or coffee.

Nowadays, it is common to see that the restaurateur or chef would come out to explain the special aspect of the *bap* the restaurant serves, i.e., the kind of rice, technical method and process of drying and husking the harvested rice, and the process of making *bap* (as a kind of industrial secret or intellectual property, it is usually mystified). Also, the quality of the water, amount of heat, ratio of grains, cooking time, and other factors are said to be important. In addition, some restaurants started serving *dolsotbap* (nutritious rice cooked in a stone pot) as well as a dish of rice steamed in bamboo, which adds a distinctive fragrance to the rice. Since bamboo is known to thrive in unpolluted soil and air, such rice is regarded as being particularly untainted. In this way, restaurants compete for people's imagination of nature, science, and philosophy on the one hand, and try to persuade people to recognize that the restaurant provides unpolluted, high-quality, and refined food as they treat customers as their family members.

Many local governments and the Agricultural Cooperative Federation have organized festivals to advertise the superiority of their local agricultural products. Rice is one of the main items to represent the locality. At the annual rice festival held by the county government of Icheon, one of the most popular programs is the competition for the title "Master of Rice Cooking" (*ssalbap myeongin*), where women representing their villages compete for top honors regarding the quality and taste of their cooked rice. They use their own secret methods and show off their skills in preparing rice and *nurungji*.

Recently, Koreans have enthusiastically embraced the new phrase *chinhwangyeong* (environmentally friendly) in terms of their locally produced rice. In the early 1980s, ethnically Korean Chinese agricultural scientists took rice seeds from Korea and successfully transplanted them in the northeast provinces of China, including Liaoning, Jilin, and Heilongjiang. This new breed, called "Northeast Rice" (*dongbeimi*), is regarded as the best in China, and began to be exported back to Korea in the 2000s. This "imported rice" is much cheaper, but is not popular because it is not organic, and thought to be polluted by excessive use of agricultural chemicals and preservative antiseptics. This Chinese rice is used for mainly for industrial food and liquor.

Bibimbap *(Mixed Rice)*

Mixed rice, *bibimbap,* has become so popular that it is now regarded as one of the representative items of Korean cuisine. The two most well-known types of *bibimbap* are Jeonju *bibimbap* and Andong *bibimbap* (also known as *heot jesabap*). Jeonju *bibimbap* consists of rice, vegetables of various colors to symbolize the five cosmological elements (Jeong 2007), raw seasoned ground beef, sesame oil, red pepper paste, and often a fried or raw egg. *Bibimbap* in Andong stems from Confucian ancestral rites and the rites held for important scholars. In addition to rice, the same vegetables used at these ceremonies, such as shredded turnip, boiled cabbage, bean sprouts, and fiddlehead ferns are mixed in, along with other ritual foods including fried tofu, and are seasoned with soy sauce instead of pepper paste. Seasoning is very restricted, as in the foods offered at ancestral rites and memorial services. Andong *bibimbap* is much simpler and more "Confucian" than the colorful and heavily seasoned Jeonju version.

The popularity of *bibimbap* is growing along with concern and interest in the "well-being" lifestyle. It also offers a taste of individuality, since diners can adjust the flavor of individual servings by adding pepper paste, sesame oil, or soy sauce in order to suit their preferences. *Bibimbap* is another cultural space where one can exercise choice and selection to create a distinctive taste rather than enjoying it as produced by someone else.

Ssambap *(Wrapped Rice)*

Another cooked rice dish that features a unique Korean way of eating rice is *ssambap.* In *ssambap,* lettuce or another large leafy vegetable is used to wrap up various combinations of meat, fish, rice, seasoning, and other vegetables. Koreans often wrap *hoe,* or raw fish similar to Japanese-style *sashimi,* and vegetables together in the same way.[14]

Eating vegetables with other food is ubiquitous throughout the world but it is unique in the Korean case of *ssam* in terms of methods of consumption. In the case of a hamburger, for instance, lettuce and/or sliced onion are put in between pieces of cooked meat inside of a bun, instead of putting individually selected food on top of a leaf of vegetable and wrapping it, as is done with the Korean *ssam.* The different ways of eating affect the taste. When we eat hamburgers, we first chew the flour-made bun before our tongue reaches the vegetables. In the case of Korean *ssam,* however, it is the vegetable that the teeth and sensory part of tongue first touch before they reach food inside. This means that Koreans taste fresh vegetables before they enjoy the taste of other components such as rice, meat, and fish. The Korean way of eating wrapped rice (*ssambap*) allows each diner the individual choice among many dishes placed on the table so that he/she may create a customized taste experience. The wrap is thought to have originated among poorer families that could not afford proper side dishes. This style of serving and eating became popular in the "well-being" movement as a result of its emphasis on fresh vegetables, which once were only seasonal leafy vegetables. But thanks to greenhouse cultivation and transnational market networks, choices have recently expanded.

As Korea entered a postindustrial era in the 1990s, the idea of "eating nature" began to spread in popularity. Restaurants with names like Gohyang (native town), Todamjip (house with mud wall), and Chogajip (thatched house) appeared, catering to the privileged urban middle class, as it allowed them to imagine their native home or countryside they left behind. These restaurants serve home-style peasant food that claims to spring from before the intensive economic growth of the postwar period. Soybean paste soup, steamed barley or millet, rice with bean sprouts, and home-style meals with various small side dishes are outstanding examples of this penchant for simpler, less ostentatious cuisine. Instead of plentiful *bulgogi* or *galbi*, diners consume broiled mackerel or saury, once considered cheap fish for the populace. Those relatively inexpensive food items are usually presented and commoditized as having been directly transported from the farmer or fisherman. Lettuce wraps, green pepper, garlic, spring onion, red pepper paste or soybean paste, and mixed *bap* with rice and millet, etc., are the primary items that trigger nostalgic memories of preindustrial Korea for an older generation (Kim 2001). Because of the nostalgic values these foods evoke, expensive restaurants that specialize in these foods have appeared, though they rely upon a middle- and upper-middle-class customer base.

Gimbap *(Seaweed Rice Rolls)*

Rice wrapped in seaweed is a popular food among many Koreans. The Japanese also wrap rice in seaweed for a kind of *sushi* called *norimaki* that usually features one or two food items, such as pieces of tuna or cucumber, placed in white rice. In contrast, Korean *gimbap* contains more ingredients, including a variety of vegetables and meat. It is convenient and contains a number of foods that normally appear as side dishes in Korean meals, making it popular on picnics and lunches. Office workers and students may grab one on their way to the office or school, or have it as a simple lunch when they do not have enough time to enjoy a proper meal.

Juk *(Porridge) and* Mieum *(Gruel)*

Another interesting new trend is the growing popularity of *juk* and *mieum*. In the past, gruel was mainly given to infants, the aged, and the sick who cannot eat solid foods. Since it was also a way of making a little bit of grain stretch by using more water, consuming porridge was considered a sign of poverty. For Koreans, "living on a bowl of barley porridge" was a common expression used to describe the miserable economic condition of a family.[15] On the other hand, wealthy Koreans, including members of the royal court, dined on gruel made from expensive grains; these various *juk* and *mieum* were considered a nutritious and prestigious meal for the privileged.

Since the early 2000s, many small chain restaurants specializing in porridge have appeared, serving porridge similar to the kind wealthy people used to enjoy in the premodern period. Basic rice or millet porridge is enhanced with green beans, red beans, sesame, pine nuts, mushrooms, vegetables, abalone, crab, shrimp, ginseng, meat, or fish. Pine nuts, sesame, walnuts, and peanuts are favored ingredients as a vegetable oil substitute for animal fat that is considered to be unhealthy due to its saturated fat and cholesterol content. Beans are considered very nutritious: green (meng) bean porridge (*nokdujuk*) is especially popular in summer because it is believed to keep the body cool, while red bean porridge (*patjuk*) is usually eaten during the winter, though it can also be enjoyed on summer days. Following Korean color symbolism, people make *patjuk* on the day of the winter solstice (*dongji*) and throw a little on the ground in order to expel evil spirits.

Porridge has likewise become an item common on "well-being" menus because it is simple to eat and full of natural ingredients. Simplicity and naturalness are two important elements in the well-being lifestyle. In the past, preparing a good lunch box for her children and husband was part of what was expected of a "wise mother and good wife," but nowadays in Korea, a good wife is expected to prepare a breakfast of fresh gruel with ingredients good for health and nutrition such as black sesame, pine, beans, and vegetables like carrots and pumpkins. Freshly made vegetable juice, full of minerals and vitamins, may be an alternative.

In the northeast provinces of China where Chinese Koreans have lived, sesame seeds and pumpkins have recently become one of the main items for export to South Korea, where they are used to make sesame seed porridge (*kkaejuk*) and pumpkin porridge (*hobakjuk*). In this way, the revival of traditional foodstuffs led to the construction of transnational networks for agricultural business between Korea and China.

Tteok *(Rice Cake)*

There are more than two hundred kinds of rice cakes in Korea. They are usually made from rice, other grains, vegetables, flowers, fruit, or other wild plants, and are often categorized based on the preparation methods used, including how the primary grain was processed, whether it was fermented, and what cooking methods were used, such as steaming or frying. It is generally a food for special occasions, such as rites of passage and holidays.

Steamed white rice cake (*baekseolgi*), cylinder-shaped white rice cake (*garaet-teok*), rice cake coated with bean powder (*injeolmi*), rice cake balls (*gyeongdan*), pan-fried rice cake (*hwajeon*), rainbow rice cake (*mujigaetteok*), and layered rice cake (*sirutteok*) are representative rice cakes. Steamed rice cake covered with red beans, called either *pattteok* or *sirutteok,* is believed to have special meaning since, as in the case of red bean gruel at the winter solstice, red is an auspicious color thought to expel evil spirits and enhance life essence and fertility, making it a ritual food for spirits or gods. The *gosatteok* is distributed among neighbors, establishing networks of relationships in the act of constructing community.

Since the 1980s, it has become customary to celebrate birthdays, weddings, and other congratulatory events with Western-style flour cakes. When compared with hand-made traditional rice cakes, mass-produced Western-style cakes are relatively cheap. The popularity of traditional rice cakes has declined in favor of soft, sweet, creamy, flour-based cakes decorated with chocolates, fruit, or whipped cream. However, an increasing number of people have for breakfast plain glutinous rice cakes such as *injeolmi, baekseolgi, jeungpyeon,* or glutinous rice cakes stuffed or topped with beans, pumpkin, chestnuts, or jujubes. Rice cakes for breakfast are perceived as being simpler and more convenient than a traditional breakfast, while still being healthier than bread.

Garaetteok is occasionally used in ritual offerings, such as ancestral worship (*jesa*) and sacrificial offerings to spirits (*gosa*). More recently, *garaetteok* has become popular among young kids in a dish called *tteokbokgi,* made by drenching *garaetteok* in a spicy-sweet sauce. Under the slogan, "Globalize Korean Food," a group of ambitious culinary professionals and government-supported organizations launched a special project to develop various forms of *tteokbokgi* as a representative item of Korean cuisine in the twenty-first-century global food market.

The contemporary food culture of Korea is understood in the context of a combination of ideas of *sinto buri* and the well-being lifestyle. This combination provides modern people with a space in which they can recall what they have abandoned for the sake of modernity. For those modernists, it is a symbolic experience of attempting a cultural conversion in their search for well-being through reappropriation of the premodernity of native place, time, and indigenous (backward) way of life (Moon 1997). Visiting restaurants to taste high-quality *bap* in this context is not a simple gastronomic tour by the leisure class, but a cultural pilgrimage to search for a mythic time and nature that they have lost or given up in the process of Western-oriented modernization. At their everyday table, they eat Western-style, meat-centered meals. From time to time, however, they depart from their routine to hold rituals that recall their (imagined) primordial sacred world of food.

The combination is also related with the rise of Asian localization to face globalization. Prior to 2000, the Western lifestyle was synonymous with modernity and associated with science, civilization, and culture. Recently, however, Asian/

Korean traditional cuisines have been more closely examined, particularly with regard to health benefits, obesity prevention, and effect on longevity. In Western countries such as the United States and parts of Europe, Thai, Vietnamese, and Indian cuisines have become popular, and Japanese *sashimi* and *sushi* have come to be widely savored. Both Western and Asian people have begun to adopt new perspectives on Asian Others, and culinary experiences provide an important space of understanding them. Globalization makes the transnational flow of cultures inevitable and people come to enjoy other cultures, especially in the field of food and fashion. While bagels and cream cheese and Jewish kosher foods are becoming fashionable among the Korean middle class, Korean restaurants for *ssambap* and *bibimbap* are becoming popular among New Yorkers.

The contemporary combination of the *sinto buri* and well-being concepts in Korea's food culture can also be understood in the context of a growing emphasis on aesthetics rather than cost, which focuses on the color, shape, decoration, and taste of a dish. In addition, anecdotal and scientific knowledge is stressed over nutritional analysis. At the same time, there is a new appreciation of national or local food. Also, the distinction between haute cuisine and peasant food has become blurred. As we see in the changes in the position of *ssam* and *juk,* some traditionally peasant foods have become high cuisine, while many items of haute cuisine are reinvented as royal cuisine and become popular dishes.[16]

The recent fashion in food described here can be understood in the context of globalization that leads to cultural encounters and competition between cuisines. It also explains how the tastes of Western people have changed to the extent that they have begun to appreciate and accommodate the tastes of Korean and Asian foods. Koreans also have begun to reconsider their attitude toward their food as the locus of cultural identity. It has become fashionable to enjoy anthropological examinations of their food culture and appreciate their traditional local cuisines.

Conclusion

In this chapter, I have reviewed how, in Korea, during the past half-century, people's foodways have gone through a great transformation in content, quality, and manner, focusing on the case of rice. One may call this change Westernization, depicting a general tendency toward increasingly casual table manners as well as consumption of meat and fast foods, while the consumption of vegetables and rice decreases, especially among the younger generations. However, I would like to point out that contemporary Korea can be said to be in a process of dynamic competition and compromise between the global process of multinationalization of foodways, rather than simple Westernization, and there has been a distinct renaissance of national culinary culture since the late 1990s.

The more Koreans come to enjoy diversified foods of foreign origin, the more they become conscious of the tradition or authenticity of their "national" foods and foodways. They have vigorously reproduced and even invented many items of "national" cuisine with amplified cultural and scientific theories of Korean food, and at the same time have talked about their idea of transnational expansion of Korean food in the context of globalization.

People have adopted a new perspective to reinterpret their traditional meals in which all condiments and dishes are served at the same time. At the Chinese and the Western table where dishes are served one by one, an eater has no other choice than to enjoy the taste of a dish as it is prepared. At the Korean table, however, diners can select among various condiments and dishes to combine with *bap* to create different personal tastes, although they sit at the same table. Also, *bap* and to some extent *juk* have become independent items of cuisine. The invention of *dolsotbap* accelerated diversification of rice cuisine through mixing different kinds of grains, beans, vegetables, and even meat and fish. *Bibimbap, ssam,* and *gimbap* are diversified to become additional representatives of popular cuisine. Another new fashion is to eat *tteok* for breakfast, and young people enjoy *tteokbokgi* to the extent that it has been chosen for the ambitious globalization project of Korean cuisine.

Koreans' affection toward rice as their "self" can also be observed in diversification in the industrialization and commodification of rice. In addition to a base for liquor and confectionaries, rice is used in many other industrial commodities such as soap, shampoo, and cosmetics. One may argue that Korean cultural nationalism is responsible for recent positive reinterpretations of rice and Korean dishes once seen as unsophisticated, including *kimchi,* soybean paste, and hot red pepper paste. However, it should be understood in a more complex historical and cultural context in which *sinto buri* and well-being converged in a way that made a traditional diet into a fashionable trend in the era of globalization.

It is in this context that we can understand the use of new vocabulary in the advertisements and brand names of agricultural products, as part of efforts to shape people's imagination of harmony between nature and culture and beyond the inhuman sciences and capitalism. Especially in the field of agricultural products, the term "domestically produced" (*guksan*) is seen as a way to guarantee its quality. Tofu is labeled as a "100 percent Korean product" (100 percent *guksan*) if it has been processed in Korea, although the raw ingredients are GM soybeans imported from the United States, and thus people are willing to pay higher prices. Also, words such as cleanness, purity, nature, sunshine, air, water, wind, non-pollution, indigenous, and purely Korean, as well as love, mind, Mother's hands, sincere mind, and other such phrases are used in advertisements.

To anthropomorphize agricultural commodities in this way is a countercultural response to the recent modernity that separates food from the world of humanity in the name of science and civilization. People taste their cultural imaginations and meanings through selection of foods. The widespread use of the term "eco-friendly" also reflects Koreans' rising consciousness regarding food-safety problems that may be caused by GMO (genetically modified organism) bioscience and the excessive use of insecticides, agricultural chemicals, fertilizer, antiseptics, and antibiotics. Many Korean and Japanese agribusiness companies produce their products in specially rented land in China, but they use exclusive organic technology or original equipment manufacturer (OEM) systems in order to minimize food safety problems.

The position of a food or dish changes incessantly. Especially as globalization brings various foods from across the world into our everyday meals, local foods once abandoned are being revived and (re)invented; these foods are valued not simply as a source of nutrition but rather as culture and aesthetics within an ideological amalgamation of *sinto buri* and well-being. The newly emerging genres of rice cuisine can be understood not only as an attempt to construct the cultural identity of the nation, but also as a postmodern lifestyle centered on enjoying local culture once abandoned in favor of the Western definition of modernity. It is not a competition between globalization and localization, but a compromise and conspiracy between the two. The renaissance of "national" culinary culture in contemporary Korea is meaningfully practiced only in its relation with growing multinationalization and globalization of foreign foods in people's everyday dietary lives.

Notes

An earlier version of the present article was published in 2010 in *Korea Journal* 50(1): 11–35.

1. *Bap* in Korean means a main food, mostly made of grains including rice. There are many kinds of *bap* such as rice, barley, foxtail millet, sorghum, and African millet. Rice is classified by methods of cultivation, such as wet paddy versus dry paddy, as well as the physical qualities of the rice, such as plain rice, glutinous rice, white rice, red rice, and black rice. It can be further enriched by adding chestnuts, walnuts, pine nuts, soybeans, lentils, red beans, bean sprouts, wild plants, and even pieces of meat or oysters to make a proper bowl of *bap*. At the First Full Moon Festival, for example, the Chinese eat a soup of *yuanshao* while the Koreans eat *ogokbap* (five-grain-*bap*), which is made of glutinous rice, millet, sorghum, black beans, and red beans, and often also includes chestnuts, jujubes, pine nuts, and gingko nuts.

2. In Korea, rice is classified as *byeo* (rice in the field), *narak* (rice harvested but not husked), and *ssal* (husked rice). Cooked rice for everyday consumption is called *ssalbap,* while offerings for the soul of the dead are called *me*. The honorific term for a meal set for a king is *sura,* that for the elderly is *jinji,* while *bap* is a term for general use and for people of inferior status.

3. For Koreans, the politico-economic importance of *bap* is expressed by their beliefs that *bap* is the Heaven, meaning that to have something to eat is as important as worshiping the God/Heaven. They also say that only after having a proper meal can one appreciate the (famous) beauty of Geumgangsan Mountain.

4. Rice is also used for medicines and in cosmetics such as soap, shampoo, skin lotion, and skin cream.

5. The war cabinet of Japan extracted oil from beans and sesame and fed Koreans with its leftovers.

6. *Ssal* (rice) is also called *ipssal; ssalbap* (cooked rice) is called *ipap.*

7. The government statistics reveal that the annual average consumption of rice per head has decreased in the following fashion: 93.6kg (2000), 88.1kg (2001), 87.0kg (2002), 83.2kg (2003), 82.0kg (2004), 80.7kg (2005), 78.8kg (2006), 76.9kg (2007), 75.8kg (2008), and 74.0kg (2009). See Statistics Korea (2000–2009).

8. These restaurants introduced the new custom of eating a bowl of cold noodles, *naengmyeon,* at the end of a meal of grilled meat. Alternatively, many of these also served *galbitang,* a soup made with beef ribs.

9. Grocery stores classify agricultural products in four categories: organic, transitory, nonagricultural chemical, and low-chemical agricultural goods. Products cultivated from fields that have not been exposed to chemical fertilizers for three years or more can be classified as "organic." If no chemicals have been used for more than a year, the products are considered transitory. If less than one-third of the recommended amount of chemical fertilizer is used, those products are labeled nonagricultural chemical goods, while products from the soil where half of the recommended quantity of chemicals were used are classified as low-chemical agricultural goods. The prices vary accordingly, with organic the highest and therefore most prestigious, and its consumption is associated with higher socioeconomic status.

10. See Han (1994) for more discourse on *kimchi.*

11. See Bornstein et al. (2003), Brim, Riff, and Kessler (2004), Mathews and Izquierdo (2009), and Nussbaum and Sen (1993) concerning a new philosophy of life as discussed in the Western world. In Korea, however, this word is used in mass-media advertisement for food and consumption without any clear idea of its origin. Some Koreans translate it into *chamsari* (true living).

12. Red represents the south, life essence, and summer, and is symbolized by a mythical animal called the red peacock. Black represents the north, land of death, and winter, and is symbolized by a black turtle with a dragon's head. Green or blue represents the east, spring, and youth, and is symbolized by the blue dragon, while white represents the west, pure land of eternal life for souls of the dead, and autumn, and is symbolized by a white tiger. Yellow symbolizes the center of the universe, ruler, and human being. As such, yellow, the color of gold, is the color of emperor and king. Water, iron, wood, soil, and fire are the five elements of the cosmos.

13. The most popular of these are soybeans, green beans, mung beans, black beans, and red beans.

14. Japanese would insist that they should eat *sashimi* as is without other additions in order to appreciate the pure taste of it. However, Koreans would insist that raw fish should be eaten together with natural vegetables so that they can enjoy a taste and fragrance produced by the combination. It is said in Korea that stomach cancer is higher among the Japanese who eat *sashimi* without vegetables than Koreans who eat *hoe* with vegetables.

15. Kwon O-sang, a member of Independent Movement Organization under the Japanese colonial rule, was tortured to death by the police. At his funeral, his mother served the guests with only a small bowl of millet gruel saying, "Our land has been robbed (by the

Japanese) and thus we have nothing to treat you properly. Only when we get our nation back can we serve you proper meals with white rice."

16. See Moon, chapter 1, this volume.

References

Bak, Sangmee. 2005. "From Strange Bitter Concoction to Romantic Necessity." *Korea Journal* 45(2): 37–59.

Bornstein, Marc H., et al. 2003. *Well-Being: Positive Development across the Life Course.* Mahwah: Laurence Erlbaum Associates.

Brim, Orville Gilbert, Carol D. Ryff, and Ronald C. Kessler. 2004. *How Healthy Are We? A National Study of Well-Being at Midlife.* Chicago: University of Chicago Press.

Gillette, Maris Boyd. 2000. "Children's Food and Islamic Dietary Restrictions in Xi'an." In *Feeding China's Little Emperors: Food, Children and Social Change,* edited by J. Jing, 71–93. Stanford: Stanford University Press.

Han, Kyung-Koo. 1994. "Eotteon eumsik-eun saenggak-hagie jotta—gimchiwa hanguk minjokseong-ui jeongsu" (Some Foods Are Good to Think: Kimchi and the Essence of Korean National Character). *Hanguk munhwa illyuhak* (Korean Cultural Anthropology) 26: 651–668.

Jeong, Hyekyoung. 2007. *Hanguk eumsik odisei* (The Odyssey of Korean Food). Seoul: Thinking Tree.

Kim, Kwang Ok. 1994. "Eumsik-ui saengsan-gwa munhwa-ui sobi: chongnon" (Production of Food and Consumption of Culture in Contemporary Korea: An Anthropological Overview). *Hanguk munhwa illyuhak* (Korean Cultural Anthropology) 26: 1–44.

———. 2001. "Contested Terrain of Imagination: Chinese Food in Korea." In *Changing Chinese Foodways in Asia,* edited by D. Wu and C. Tan, 201–217. Hong Kong: Chinese University of Hong Kong Press.

———. 2006. "Appropriation of Imagination: Cultural Politics of Rice in Globalizing Korea." Paper presented at the Center for Korean Studies, George Washington University, 28 October.

Mathews, Gordon, and Carolina Izquierdo, eds. 2009. *Pursuits of Happiness: Well-Being in Anthropological Perspective.* New York: Berghahn Books.

Moon, Okpyo. 1997. "Jeontong'-ui saengsan-gwa sobi" (Production and Consumption of "Tradition"). In *Hangugin-ui sobi-wa yeoga saenghwal* (Consumption and Leisure Life in Contemporary Korea), edited by Moon Okpyo. 9–74. Seongnam: The Academy of Korean Studies.

———. 2010. "Dining Elegance and Authenticity: Archaeology of Royal Court Cuisine in Korea." *Korea Journal* 50(1): 36–59.

Nussbaum, Martha, and Amartya Sen. 1993. *The Quality of Life.* Oxford: Clarendon.

Ohnuki-Tierney, Emiko. 1993. *Rice as Self: Japanese Identities throughout Time.* Princeton: Princeton University Press.

Pemberton, Robert. W. 2002. "Wild-gathered Foods as Countercurrents to Dietary Globalization in South Korea." In *Asian Food: The Global and the Local,* edited by K. Cwiertka and B. Walraven, 76–94. Abingdon: Routledge.

Statistics Korea. 2000–2009. *Hanguk tonggye yeongam* (Korea Statistical Yearbook), *2000–2009.* Seoul: Statistics Korea.

Walraven, Boudewijn. 2002. "Bardo Soup and Confucians' Meat: Food and Korean Identity in Global Context." In *Asian Food: The Global and the Local,* edited by K. Cwiertka and B. Walraven, 95–115. Abingdon: Routledge.

Watson, James L., ed. 1997. *Golden Arches East: McDonald's in East Asia.* Stanford: Stanford University Press.

Yan, Yunxiang. 2000. "Of Hamburger and Social Space: Consuming McDonald's in Beijing." In *The Consumer Revolution in Urban China,* edited by D. Davis, 201–225. Berkeley: University of California Press.

Food Practice across Cultural Boundaries

CHAPTER 5

Noodle Odyssey
East Asia and Beyond

Kyung-Koo Han

This is an attempt to use Japanese *ramen,* Chinese *lamian,* and Korean *ramyeon* to examine some of the major issues in the study of food and culture. East Asians are known to the West as ardent consumers of cooked rice, but they have been eating other cereals in many different ways. Noodle is one of them. As rice has been increasingly cherished and prized as the national food in modern Japan and Korea, much attention has been paid to rice (see Kim, chapter 4, this volume), resulting in the relative neglect and marginalization of noodles and other cereals. Let this chapter be a modest start to look at other traditions.

Korean *ramyeon* began to be produced with Japanese instant *ramen* technology, which was invented by Ando Momofuku to reproduce *sina soba* (Chinese noodles) sold at stalls and restaurants in Japanese cities. This *sina soba,* as the name suggests, came from China, most likely during the Sino-Japanese War of 1894–1895, and was further developed and became famous in Sapporo. In Japan, as in Korea, *ramen* and *ramyeon* not only came to find loyal consumers and occupy a significant place in the food cultures of both countries, but also began to cross national boundaries to find overseas fans and markets. You can find Japanese-style *ramen* restaurants in the streets of Beijing and Taipei, and in Chinese supermarkets Korean-style instant *ramyeon* is sold at much higher prices than in Korea. Whether Korean or Japanese style, *lamian* has come home, and its odyssey, a 100-year-long voyage home, deserves serious attention and study. However, I will limit my discussion in this chapter to Korean *ramyeon,* providing only a sketch of Japanese *ramen* and an even smaller mention of Chinese *lamian.* I hope to have a chance to study Japanese noodles and Chinese noodles systematically in the near future.

Here I would like to make the following three points: First, although virtually the same names are used, Korean *ramyeon* has become a different kind of global food, quite different from Japanese *ramen*. I seriously doubt whether we can put Korean *ramyeon* and Japanese-style *ramen* in the same category. *Ramyeon* in Korea means "instant noodles," while *ramen* in Japan are noodles sold at *ramen* restaurants, unless specifically labeled "instant *ramen*."

Second, Korean *ramyeon* is a class confuser. Sociological and anthropological studies of food (Appadurai 1986, 1996; Beadsworth and Keil 1997; McCracken 1990) have been fascinated with the ways food is used to assign distinction. Regional differences, as well as differences in social class, gender, and ethnicity, have been shown to be produced and reproduced by food. *Ramyeon*, however, seems to play the role of confusing and modifying class distinctions instead of delineating and reinforcing them. It seems that *ramyeon* sometimes integrates class differences.

Third, I would like to play on the concept of McDonaldization and introduce a new word, *ramyeonization,* to describe the social and cultural practices associated with the production, distribution, serving, and consumption of *ramyeon,* and its implications for society at large. Ramyeonization can be considered at least in three different fields: the increase in new forms of food sold in plastic packages that can be prepared and served almost instantly by boiling or adding boiling water and waiting a few minutes; the increasingly dominant taste of hot and spicy *ramyeon* soup in Korean cuisine[1]; and the individualization and fragmentation of meals and the resulting impact on family and society at large.

From *Ramen* to *Ramyeon*

Japanese *ramen* first appeared as *sina soba* (Chinese noodles) after the war with China from 1894 to 1895, before its name was changed into the more or less politically correct *chuka soba*.[2] Local variations began to develop, and with enthusiastic coverage on the part of mass media, *ramen* restaurants, as well as *ramen manga* and websites, are now significant players in Japan's tourist industry.

In postwar Japan, which suffered from severe food shortages, Chinese noodles, or *ramen,* began to attract people's attention. Okumura Ayao (2001) says that the popularity of *ramen* in the mid-1950s was part of the "swing from lean to fat" in the Japanese diet. Compared to "light" traditional Japanese soups, which used dried seafood such as *kombu* (dried kelp), *katsuobushi* (dried bonito), or *niboshi* (dried small sardines) as the base, *ramen* indeed seemed to be more fatty and nutritious. It is likely that *ramyeon*'s greasy soup was not as new to Koreans as it was to the Japanese. For many poor Koreans who could not afford beef-based soup, the taste of *ramyeon* soup, although largely artificial, was probably more than welcome. Japanese *ramen* is made with fresh noodles, while Korean *ramyeon* producers fry the noodle in either beef or vegetable suet. Many Japanese restaurants take great pride in making their own noodles, while no Korean *ramyeon* restaurants dream of making noodles of their own. It is said that the instant *ramen* invented in 1958 by Nissin Foods was initially rejected by Japan's food industry as "a novelty with no future." Japanese-style *ramen* is not only popular around the world, but according to a report from the BBC in 2000,[3] many Japanese believe instant noodles to be their country's most important invention of the twentieth century. Instant *ramen* earned higher marks than karaoke, Walkman personal stereos, computer games, and small cameras. Announcing the results of a survey of what the Japanese see as their best exports, Fuji Research Institute declared, "Instant noodles, representing 'Made in Japan,' are now not only just a national food but a global food." *Ramen* is now considered a proper Japanese dish that has gone through the process of adaptive evolution of more than a hundred years in Japan.

Making of Korean-Style Ramyeon

Jeon Jung-yung was the first to produce *ramyeon* in Korea. According to the official history of Samyang Ramyeon Co., he started as an insurance man and who occasionally had to visit Japan and Southeast Asia on business trips. He was deeply impressed with Japanese *ramen,* which began industrial production in 1958. One of the official reasons for the production of *ramyeon* in Korea was to deal with the shortage of food, especially of rice. *Ramyeon* was introduced in Korea to become the "second rice."

Samyang produced its first *ramyeon* in September 1963, with the help of Myosei Food in Japan. It was a great success, and soon others began to manufacture *ramyeon.* Samyang was the industry leader, enjoying 40 percent of the market share as consumption of *ramyeon* continued to increase during the 1980s. Samyang used second-rate beef tallow in producing its *ramyeon* soup powder and in frying the *ramyeon* noodles, and advertised that its *ramyeon* was made of beef, something fantastic to the ears of poor Koreans who could not afford to buy real beef. Since traditional Korean cuisine has long used beef and pork, there was no need for "a swing from lean to fat" (see below) as in Japan, whose citizens seldom ate beef and pork until the Meiji period. It was only because of poverty that Koreans could not eat beef, and *ramyeon* claimed to offer the chance to enjoy it at an affordable price. Visible bits of rendered beef fat floated in *ramyeon,* which could be served inexpensively and conveniently.

Samyang was doing well, but suffered a big setback in November 1989 when it was accused of using industrial tallow for its *ramyeon.* When the press reported this, the public was indignant. The concern and fear over the potential harm *ramyeon* may have had on their health seemed to have been justified.[4] Such worries had been an open secret ever since the consumption of the first *ramyeon* in Korea. The whole incident started with an anonymous report that *ramyeon* makers were using industrial suet for soap or lubricating oil. More than ten businessmen were arrested and boycott campaigns were organized. Samyang Ramyeon had to remove several million dollars' worth of its products from the market and close its factories for three months. Although Samyang's name was cleared by a belated "not guilty" decision of the Supreme Court in August 1997, seven years and eight months after the first accusation, it still has not recovered its market share. Now Nongshim enjoys more than 60 percent share of the market.

There has been widespread public concern for food safety and health ever since the introduction of *ramyeon* in Korea, although *ramyeon* producers have emphasized the nutritional value and taste of beef. Criticisms have been raised against *ramyeon* for the nutritional imbalance it can cause when eaten too often and in too great a quantity. *Ramyeon* has also been targeted for its high sodium content and the poor quality of palm oil or beef suet used in frying the noodles, as well as the excessive use of artificial flavoring or MSG (monosodium glutamate), and hot peppers. In fact, many nutritional scholars and opinion leaders have warned that a diet too dependent on *ramyeon* may lead to malnutrition. The cheap price of *ramyeon* seemed to underscore complaints that producers were using cheap, poor-quality materials. Also important is the criticism that *ramyeon* is not environmentally friendly; many *ramyeon* producers use palm oil, as well as receptacles and packages made of synthetic materials that may cause endocrine disruption. *Ramyeon* has also been held responsible for swollen faces, pimples, rashes, and obesity because of the use of trans fat and other additives. There are even many tricks that supposedly keep your face from swelling in the morning after having eaten *ramyeon* during the night before that are discussed widely online.[5]

Because of its cheap price and beginnings as a rice substitute, *ramyeon* was considered food for those who were too poor to buy rice, unable to cook properly, or those who happened to have too little time to prepare and enjoy regular meals. The Korean government's efforts in the 1960s and 1970s to promote the consumption of wheat flour, which the United States gave as aid, played a significant role in giving *ramyeon* an association with poverty and expediency.

It is not difficult to find stories of overcoming poverty and hardship that mention *ramyeon*. In a children's book *Huimang ramyeon sebongji* (Three Ramyeon Bags of Hope), two children from a poor family wanted to eat *ramyeon* and tried to coax their mother into buying some, but their mother was too poor. This desperate situation was solved by the appearance of another small girl living next door who happened to hear the lamentation. She brought three bags of *ramyeon* for her poor neighbors, and her kindness gave the poor children hope for the future.

It would be unthinkable for Koreans to eat *ramyeon* on their birthdays, although noodles are a traditional part of celebrations since they symbolically represent wishes for a long life. In fact, at the workshop I mentioned above, both Koreans and Japanese were shocked to hear that their Chinese colleagues eat *lamian* on birthdays. For Koreans, eating a surrogate dish of inferior quality and expediency, such as *ramyeon,* is one of the saddest things that can happen on a birthday.[6]

The symbolic and practical significance of *ramyeon* for the poor makes *ramyeon* one of the important indices of consumer prices in Korea. The government has made efforts to keep the price of *ramyeon* as low as possible in order to give the impression that inflation was under control. It was because of the image of *ramyeon* as food for the poor that the Lee Myung-bak government included *ramyeon* in its anachronistic plan to control the prices of fifty-two necessities, including gasoline, *soju* (a cheap alcoholic beverage), and cram school tuition in March 2008.[7]

As instant *ramyeon* is so cheap and convenient to serve, it also has the image of being an emergency food. Whenever there is an emergency situation, such as a natural disaster, huge quantities of *ramyeon* are sent as relief goods. That explains why panicked Koreans purchased *ramyeon* when North Korea announced its withdrawal from the Nonproliferation Treaty in March 1993.

Japanese-Style "Fresh" *Ramen* versus Korean-Style "Fried" *Ramyeon*

Korean *ramyeon* is based on Japanese *ramen,* but they have become quite different, as you can see in Table 5.1. In Japan, *ramen* can refer to both the noodles sold in restaurants and instant noodles sold in supermarkets, but it is possible that most Japanese associate it with the former. In contrast to Korea, where *ramyeon* is synonymous with the instant *ramyeon* sold in cups or plastic bags at supermarkets and is often regarded as insufficient to constitute a complete meal in itself, in Japan, *ramen* is considered a complete meal by itself and is sometimes consumed with *gyoza* (fried dumpling). In Korea, *ramyeon* sometimes can be eaten in place of a meal in times of necessity, but many people finish the noodles first and then eat the soup with steamed rice or *gimbap* (rice rolled in a sheet of dried seaweed and stuffed with other ingredients, such as meat or vegetables). This interesting difference between *ramen* and *ramyeon* is corroborated by the assertion on a *ramen* website that says, "There is no reason for confusion. 'Cooking *ramen* is easy. Unbelievable!'"[8] The site declares that it takes at least several hours to prepare *ramen.* It proudly adds that it takes a day or more for some shops to prepare just the broth. *Ramen* seems to have joined or been adopted into the so-called tradition of authentic Japanese cuisine. It is easy to find many Japanese websites making the claim that *ramen* is not an instant food.

Japanese-style *ramen* succeeded in securing its place in Japanese cuisine as a low-cost but still respectable dish with many local varieties. A vast number of cities and provinces now claim their own variety of *ramen* and the search for and development of new tastes in *ramen* is taken for granted. On the other hand, Korean-style *ramyeon* started as instant *ramyeon* and has remained so. Several different food companies began to produce *saeng ramyeon* (unfried *ramyeon*), but it is the instant *ramyeon* that is the dominant form produced, purchased, and consumed in Korea.

There are very few Korean-style restaurants in Korea that specialize in *ramyeon*. Together with *ramyeon,* they usually sell other simple dishes or snacks for students and office workers who want quick meals or need to eat between meals. Those Korean chefs at these shops have little room for improvement in taste since they have to work with instant *ramyeon,* which they have to serve at a much lower price than their Japanese counterparts can. Surprisingly, even so, some restaurant chefs continue to invent new ways of serving *ramyeon.*

Many chefs and devotees of Korean-style *ramyeon* are proud of their personal secrets for working with industrially produced *ramyeon,* but all of them use noodle and soup powder produced industrially by one of the food companies in Korea. This narrows their concentration to their cooking methods. One way to make a real difference is to add a variety of ingredients such as egg, kimchi, rice cakes, fish cakes, and other foodstuffs. Rarely are beef, pork, fish, or chicken used, probably because these are too expensive for such a cheap dish.[9]

Japanese *ramyeon* has to be understood in the system of Japanese cuisine, while Korean *ramyeon* should be understood in the system of Korean cuisine. Japanese *ramen* appeared in a society where the tradition of *udon* (thick wheat-flour noodle) and *soba* (thin buckwheat flour noodle) was already in existence. *Soba* could be described as the traditional fast food of the Edo period. One of the reasons why *ramen* became rapidly popular in postwar Japan was that it could provide a very rich soup for a cheap price.

In Japan, it was only after *ramen* became popular that instant *ramen* was invented. Instant *ramen* was, from the beginning, a substitute for the *ramen* sold at restaurants. When Momofuku Ando invented the instant noodle, his intent was to make it easy for people to reproduce the *ramen* served at street stalls and specialized restaurants. *Ramen* in Japan began to attract attention as a new item in domestic tourism. It has become quite common to watch TV programs devoted to visiting local cities to introduce the special variety *ramen* of that particular place. In addition to TV programs and magazine articles, *manga* also shows the efforts of a *ramen* chef to improve the taste of *ramen* in the same style of the traditional artisans, expending a tremendous amount of energy. However, in Korea, when instant *ramyeon* was introduced, it did not have a long tradition of urban noodle restaurants. Although noodles were expensive in Korea in the past, traditional Korean cities did not experience the urbanization and commercialization that provided the socioeconomic environment for specialized noodle shops to develop.

The nearest equivalent to Japanese *ramen* may be *kalguksu* (knife noodle, or noodles cut with a kitchen knife) or *jajangmyeon* (noodles with black bean paste sauce). There are some famous *kalguksu* and *jajangmyeon* specialty restaurants

Table 5.1. Comparison of Japanese *ramen* and Korean *ramyeon*

Japanese *Ramen*	Korean *Ramyeon*
Ramen sold at specialized restaurants and instant ramen in plastic packages	Instant *ramyeon* in plastic packages sold at supermarkets
"Fresh" noodles and *ramen* soup often made at the restaurants	Noodle and soup industrially produced (noodle fried in oil or fat)
Chefs' efforts to make difference; cooking *ramen* is "not easy"	Cooking *ramyeon* should be "easy"; inconvenient *ramyeon* is no longer *ramyeon*
Great variety in tastes and materials	Dominance of the hot and spicy flavors
A meal complete in itself, though often eaten with *gyoja* (dumpling)	Not a complete meal in itself, frequently supplemented with a bowl of rice; often eaten as snack
Existence of urban noodle restaurant traditions (*udon* and *soba*), which could become models for *ramen* restaurant; *ramen* became popular in street stalls and restaurants, followed by the invention of instant *ramen*	*Ramyeon* was introduced into Korea in the form of instant noodles; no independent *ramyeon* restaurant tradition exists

that take pride in their unique taste and secret recipes, many of which make their own noodles "in house." Like Japanese *ramen, kalguksu* and *jajangmyeon* can be consumed as a proper meal or as a snack.

One of the reasons why *ramyeon* has not attracted the same level of attention or effort in Korea as in Japan until recently is perhaps the low price of *ramyeon,* or rather Koreans' general perception of *ramyeon* as cheap food. Another reason might be the "less-than-full" meal status *ramyeon* occupies, stemming from its great convenience in preparation and serving. In the past, *ramyeon* has meant instant *ramyeon,* so *ramyeon* was identified as a cheap and handy substitute for a proper meal, not a full one. However, being cheap and convenient does not mean that there have not been efforts at developing various tips and tricks for making good *ramyeon* or improving *ramyeon*'s taste, only that such tips and tricks have not developed into a commercially rewarding pursuit. It is ironic that *ramyeon* does not enjoy a prestigious position in the hierarchy of Korean food despite the fact that many Koreans seem addicted to *ramyeon*.

Spiciness in Korean-Style Ramyeon: *A Blessing and a Curse*

Although instant *ramen* was first invented in Japan, Koreans consume and sell more instant *ramyeon* now. According to a report of the *Korea Times,*[10] Nongshim Ramyeon Co. exported 161 billion won worth of its spicy instant *ramyeon* to more than seventy countries, including China, Japan, and the United States. The most famous of the spicy instant noodles is Shin Ramyeon (produced by Nongshim Ramyeon Co.), which rose in 1986 to become the number-one seller in the Korean market despite being glutted with more than 150 different styles of instant noodle products. Shin Ramyeon has a unique spicy taste that Nongshim's officials claim to have developed through several years of research efforts in their lab.

Of course, there are different kinds of *ramyeon* in Korea, including some that are not spicy. However, spiciness seems to have become the quality that differentiates Korean *ramyeon*. In 2008, Shin Ramyeon (literally, "spicy-hot *ramyeon*") singlehandedly took a 23 percent share of a market in which some 160 different kinds of instant noodles are sold. Some netizens argue that Shin Ramyeon purchased in Korea actually tastes better than Shin Ramen purchased in Japan.

Some criticize that spiciness dominates and obscures other tastes so that one does not really know the flavor of what he or she is eating, while others say that it is the spiciness that attracts consumers, who are almost addicted to the hot taste. I will discuss this addiction later in detail.

Japanese Ramen *in Seoul*

In recent years, Japanese-style *ramen* shops have appeared in Seoul, Hong Kong, and Beijing, while Korean instant *ramyeon,* famous for its spicy taste, is very popular not only throughout East Asia, but also in Russia and Europe. Although the number of Japanese-style *ramen* restaurants is on the rise, it does not seem that they will ever pose a significant threat to Korean-style *ramyeon*. Many Korean students who have visited Japanese-style *ramen* restaurants said that they found the taste greasy, dull, and not spicy, while the price was rather expensive. Most of the guests who visit these Japanese-style *ramen* restaurants are young men and women. At the many Japanese-style *ramen* restaurants in Seoul, *ramen* is neither fast nor cheap.

Japanese-style restaurants in Seoul are different from their Tokyo counterparts. Many guests in Japanese-style *ramen* restaurants in Seoul do not immediately leave after finishing their bowls of *ramen,* but continue to occupy the seats and talk just as they would if they were in other restaurants. Many Japanese-style *ramen* restaurants also sell "Japaneseness" by decorating the walls with Japanese pictures, posters, and dolls. In some places they greet the customers in Japanese and/or repeat the contents of the order in Japanese. Some restaurants seem to try to teach "*ramen* culture" to their customers by placing information sheets that explain how to best enjoy *ramen*.

Approximately ten years ago, an attempt to introduce Japanese *gyudon* (a bowl of boiled rice topped with beef) in Korea failed. Yoshinoya Gyudon shops were strategically placed in Gangnam and Sinchon, which bustled with young people, but the attempt failed miserably. It was relatively expensive, but not very chic. The taste was a little too sweet. It is potentially very difficult for boutique *ramyeon* (Japanese style or Korean style) to enjoy major success in Korea. This is not because it is difficult to develop unique and tasty *ramyeon,* but because many Koreans love *ramyeon* for its convenience and price. It isn't reasonable in the minds of most people to sacrifice price and convenience, the greatest attractive points of *ramyeon,* for what they consider to be a meager improvement in taste.

What is more important is that many Koreans, as well as foreigners who have become lovers of Korean-style *ramyeon,* find it delicious precisely because of its hot and spicy taste. One Korean, who was asked whether he has ever tried to make *ramyeon* using the "fresh *ramyeon* noodles" produced by Pulmuwon, smiled and answered that it would deprive one of all the merits of *ramyeon.* You eat *ramyeon* precisely because it is so convenient. If you can bother to buy fresh *ramyeon* noodles and prepare the soup and everything, why would you eat *ramyeon?* You'd be better off cooking other dishes.

For some Koreans, there is a strong possibility of cognitive dissonance and emotional resistance if they have to put so much energy, time, and money into boiling a bowl of *ramyeon,* a dish that has always been cheap, fast, effortless, and bearably tasty. In other words, for many Koreans, expensive, time-consuming, serious *ramyeon* is a contradiction. Koreans are, in a sense, "addicted" to the taste of *ramyeon.* Many Koreans may enjoy Japanese-style *ramen* for a change, but it is unthinkable that they would forget the familiarity they developed with the taste of Korean *ramyeon* soup. The cheap Korean-style *ramyeon* continues to enjoy popularity in the face of the extremely rich, refined *ramen* made at boutique restaurants. It may well be impossible for Japanese-style *ramen* to dominate the Korean market, in spite of its short-term success.

Animals Are Good to Think with, But *Ramyeon* is Not: Distinction and Beyond

Sociologists and anthropologists have been fascinated with the ways in which people use food to distinguish themselves from one another.[11] Preparation and consumption of food is used to produce and reproduce regional differences, as well as differences in social class, gender, and ethnicity. However, *ramyeon* seems to play a role in confusing and modifying class distinctions instead of delineating and reinforcing them. It seems that *ramyeon* sometimes integrates class differences.

Ramyeon is usually associated with poverty and expediency now, but the noodle enjoys prestige in the traditional food system, with a history of more than a thousand years in Korea. Early records show that Koreans enjoyed noodles in the Goryeo period (918–1392), but they were rare and expensive at that time since wheat was not widely cultivated. One Chinese observer said that the Goryeo people cherish noodles, as wheat flour had to be imported from China and was very expensive. Buckwheat flour was much easier to produce and popular, as well. However, both wheat-flour noodles and buckwheat-flour noodles were special dishes served on birthdays and weddings because of their length, symbolically pointing toward long life.[12] People wanted their lives and marriage bonds to be as long as the noodles. When noodles are put in a bowl to be offered at ancestral rituals, special care is given to prevent the noodle from being cut into smaller segments.

Ramyeon, although technically a noodle, does not share the traditional prestige and symbolic meanings associated with other noodles. It is sometimes associated with poverty and is not considered to constitute a proper meal in itself. *Ramyeon* was something you had when you were too poor to have a proper meal of steamed rice.[13] The price of rice has fallen, but the image of *ramyeon* as food for the poor has not vanished. Sometimes, it is not simply the price but the lack of cooking time or facilities needed to prepare it that continues to suppress the image of *ramyeon.*

Instant *ramyeon* has also been consumed as-is by kids, just as if it were a confection or a snack. Kids tear open the plastic package, break up the dried *ramyeon* noodles into smaller chunks, pour the *ramyeon* soup powder over the broken chunks of *ramyeon* noodles, and enjoy. Taking notice of this practice, one food company developed and sold a special snack product called "Ppusyeo Ppusyeo," imitating this very practice.[14] Some call this practice "eating *ramyeon* fresh." This is one way of enjoying *ramyeon* that the Japanese have not incorporated.

During their years of schooling and military service, many Koreans eat a huge amount of *ramyeon* and develop strange ways of serving it. As so many people developed an addiction to *ramyeon* as children, students, and soldiers, *ramyeon* plays a role in modifying class distinctions, instead of delineating and reinforcing as food usually does. This class-bonding role in *ramyeon* consumption is very interesting.

In sum, almost all Koreans have been exposed to instant *ramyeon* since early childhood, and many of them have become addicted to its taste. Whatever the class background, Koreans have had plenty of opportunities to eat it during childhood: before or after cram school and private lessons; for lunch or snack; and during field activities and military service. They have many chances to eat *ramyeon* once they are employed, too. As such, Koreans from all different socio-economic backgrounds have eaten the same instant *ramyeon,* which leaves little room for assigning class distinctions. Many men and women of wealth, power, and high social status in Korea are presumed to be addicts of *ramyeon* who grew up eating it in many different ways. Of course, there are some that have not acquired the habit, and persons of some influence can engage themselves in the politics of food by showing off their love for *ramyeon* or consuming it in the company of their "lesser" friends. At the same time, those who don't eat *ramyeon* might be scoffed at as too highly born.

A legendary tale illustrates this point. When the infamous Korean Air flight took off from Rangoon after the North Korean bomb attack intended to assassinate the Korean president and his entourage on 9 October 1983, it was in such a hurry that it did not have time to load any meals on board. During the long flight to Seoul, the stewardess served instant *ramyeon,* which they happened to have on board. It was another classic case of *ramyeon* being served as food of emergency and expediency.

According to urban legend, one young *jaebeol* (conglomerate) president who succeeded his father, the founder president, refused to eat *ramyeon* because it was a low-class food. On seeing this, supposedly Mr. Jeong Ju-yeong, the founder and then president of Hyundai Group, took his neighbor's bowl and ate two servings with gusto. This idle gossip was usually repeated by white-collar workers and told with a certain fondness for old Mr. Jeong, who relished *ramyeon* because he started out in life very poor. Those who could not eat *ramyeon* (such as the young president) were often spoken of as having been brought up in a different world entirely. When the story is told, there is a sense of mild criticism for a leader so removed from mainstream Korean society because of his rich father, and thus not really qualified to lead. Admirals and generals, as well as captains and colonels have enjoyed sharing bowls of *ramyeon* with sailors and soldiers whenever they have the chance. Sharing the cheapest and most common food is one way of building solidarity in many hierarchical organizations. A community of *ramyeon* can be briefly created and experienced in this way. When President Kim Young-sam was inaugurated in February 1993, he began to practice "*kalguksu* politics." Instead of serving regular meals to the visitors to the Blue House, he had his cook serve his favorite noodle, indicative of his authentic "common folk" quality, an important trait of a truly democratic leader.

A Ramyeonizing Society?

Playing off the concept of McDonaldization, I've introduced the term *ramyeonization* to emphasize the social and cultural practices associated with the production, distribution, serving, and consumption of *ramyeon,* and the implications for society at large. Ramyeonization can be considered at least in three different fields: the increase of new forms of food sold in plastic packages that can be served instantly by boiling or adding boiling water; the increasingly dominant taste of hot and spicy *ramyeon* soup in Korean cuisine; and the individualization and fragmentation of meals and the resultant impact on family and society at large.

While the McDonaldization thesis (Ritzer 2004) is composed of four key concepts such as increase of efficiency, calculability, predictability, and control in society in general, ramyeonization is composed of three key concepts: increase in industrially produced instant food products, fragmentation of meals and family, and dominance of hot and spicy flavors.

Ramyeonization of Food in Korea: Increase of Ramyeon-*Style Food*

McDonaldization is focused on the increase of fast food and the sociocultural changes associated with it. I would like to focus on the increase of instant food and its sociocultural implications. Fast food is called fast because it can be ordered and received in a very short amount of time. Fast food can be eaten at the restaurant, but it can be taken out or delivered to the home or office. Instant food is even faster than fast food. The consumer does not have to travel to the fast food restaurant. Instead, it only requires the individual to retrieve it from the cupboard or refrigerator, remove the package, add boiling water, or put it in the microwave oven. Instant food is purchased at the supermarket and prepared at home, at the office, or in the field without bothering to visit or call fast food restaurants. Moreover, it gives the consumer some control in terms of preparation, including the addition of flavors or ingredients, as well as control over preparation time. As simple as the process is, it does allow for a certain degree of creativity on the part of the consumer. Consumption of industrially produced food at home is rapidly increasing. There is a significant increase in food products that can be prepared "instantly" at home.

Ramyeonization of food can lead to interesting jokes. Students who frequent convenience stores instead of fast food restaurants for instant food invented so-called 7-Eleven *jeongsik* (table d'hôte), which consists of a "cup *ramyeon*" as an appetizer, *gochu bulgogi gimbap* (triangular rice ball with hot and spicy pork in the center, wrapped with dried seaweed) as the entrée, a canned coffee, and a cup of fruit jelly as a dessert.

The slow food movement started in response to the rise of fast food, and celebrates cooking at home. However, we are now witnessing the rapid transformation of "cooking at home." Even though prepared and served at home, much of the cooking process is skipped because of industrial processing. Furthermore, as less and less is done at home, the promotion strategy of food producers tends to emphasize the home-like qualities of their products. Commercials emphasize such qualities as "just like homemade," "motherly love," "use of authentic, traditional methods," etc. At the same time, health, well-being, omission of MSG and food additives, and use of organic or natural ingredients have risen as new catchphrases.

Selling "mother" (Hochschild 2003), "nostalgia" (Boym 2001; Creighton 1997; Stewart 1988), "authenticity" (Bendix 1997), "tradition" (Ivy 1995), and terms like *health, well-being,* and *nature* seem to be the secret to marketing industrially produced food products in a world where one can find many different dishes that are not fundamentally different in taste. As tastes are standardized, we may be losing the ability to distinguish fine differences.

Ramyeonization in Taste: Dominance of Hot and Spicy Flavor

So many Koreans share memories from their youthful days when they used the contents of the soup bag they found in the *ramyeon* package to improve the taste of food they prepared during camping, mountain climbing, hiking, or any other such occasions when they had to prepare their own meals.

The hot and spicy flavor of industrially produced Korean *ramyeon* soup seems to be the most common denominator in making the taste a favorite for those around for meal preparation. Using the *ramyeon* soup for improving the taste of any soup-based dish has been an open secret among Boy Scouts, mountain-climbing societies, and other outdoor adventure seekers. It is no wonder that so many Koreans burst into laughter watching a pop singer use *ramyeon* soup as his secret to improve the taste of many different dishes he and his colleagues were expected to make on a popular TV program titled "The Family Is Out." After his addition of *ramyeon* soup powder, everybody said that the taste actually improved.

As mentioned earlier, *ramyeon* is generally considered to be a very low-class dish in Korea. It is very spicy, and notorious for profuse use of artificial seasoning. However, Koreans are accustomed   even addicted—to the taste. It can be compared to the great popularity of a certain food company's "banana milk," which has no natural banana in it. This artificial flavor and taste seem to be the correct banana taste and flavor to the extent that banana milks from other companies with real banana as an ingredient do not do well in the market. As the saying goes, there's no accounting for taste. Authenticity does not seem to help when one is already addicted to a certain flavor profile.

We can also see that the consumption of instant coffee has not decreased, even though other forms of coffee have become very popular as Starbucks and Coffee Bean coffee shops have begun to appear in Korea. Many Koreans who learned to enjoy the flavor and taste of regular coffee have not discarded their love for instant coffee. Many Koreans continue to ask for *japangi* (automatic vending machine) coffee or *dabang* (coffee shop) coffee. This means that Koreans might learn to like Japanese-style *ramen* with its exquisite taste and flavors achieved through elaborate preparation as well, but continue to indulge themselves in the pungent taste of cheap *ramyeon*. As many Koreans do not seriously compare drip coffee and instant coffee, so they may not compare Japanese-style *ramen* and Korean-style *ramyeon*.

Fragmentation of Meal, Fragmentation of Family

Ramyeon can be used in creating a sense of community, but it is quite often consumed alone and in a hurry, transforming the traditional idea of a family who eats from the same pot. Because of its convenience, *ramyeon* renders meal time meaningless. It can be eaten at any time, in any place, with or without company. In this way, *ramyeon* blurs the distinction between meals and snacks, between those who share meals and those who do not.

One of the most unique experiences of modern men and women may well be eating alone. Sharing food and communal dining have been regarded as normal ever since the appearance of hunting and gathering as a mode of subsistence. Eating alone was considered extraordinary: it was a mark of unhappiness, loneliness, being cast out, punishment, eccentricity, misanthropy, or worse. However, modern children often, out of necessity, learn to eat alone. Family members often have difficulty in finding time to sit together at the dining table. Not eating together is made easier by *ramyeon* and other instant foods; now, one begins to wonder whether fragmentation is not so much the cause as the result of the rise of *ramyeon* and instant food.

Conclusion

When I began my study for this chapter, I expected *lamian, ramen,* and *ramyeon* to provide a mirror for East Asians to reflect on the issues of food culture. One of the goals of my work was to compare and contrast Japanese *ramen,* Korean *ramyeon,* and Chinese *lamian,* and to use the insight and knowledge from this to understand East Asia and its foodways. I wanted to understand the relative importance and place of *lamian, ramen,* and *ramyeon* in the food culture of each nation. However, it has become clear that we have to be extremely careful in any such comparative study. While *ramen* in Japan includes both "boutique" *ramen* and instant *ramen* sold at supermarkets, *ramyeon* in Korea usually means instant food. If we think about the semantic domain of *lamian* in China, the picture becomes even more complicated.

At the same time, one embarrassing problem is raised by this study. It is the predicament faced by the Korean government in promoting globalization of Korean food. The Korean government is positioning Korean food as "slow food," "made using traditional methods," with "natural flavors and tastes." In other words, it is the food of the future, with a healthy and refined taste. However, modern Koreans seem addicted to the cheap and unrefined taste of instant *ramyeon* soup. I propose that modern Koreans have become rather insensitive to understanding the fine differences in taste because of the extremely hot and spicy food to which they have grown accustomed. *Ramyeon* in Korea seems to be one of those dirty little secrets that might be called cultural intimacy (Herzfeld 1997).

Further study on Chinese *lamian,* as well as the consumption of Japanese *ramen* and Korean *ramyeon* in China, is needed to complete this odyssey of the noodle. We have seen that the rise of *ramen* in Japan and *ramyeon* in Korea would never have happened without war, modernization, US aid, rice shortages, rapid economic growth and the subsequent increase of female workers, internationalization, concerns for health and food safety as well as environmental conservation, traditional food culture, nostalgia business, and other related matters. Also noteworthy is the new trend in the consumption of *ramyeon* in Korea, with significant efforts made not only to make *ramyeon* "chic" and high class, but also to cultivate niche markets.

In short, *lamian, ramen,* and *ramyeon* provide the mirror for East Asians to reflect not only on the issues of food culture but also on the modern history of each nation-state and of the region as a whole.

Notes

An earlier version of this chapter was published in 2010 in *Korea Journal* 50(1): 60–84.

1. For a discussion on the "hot and spicy" in Korea, see Han (2000).
2. The early history of ramen in Japan is not clear, but Shin-Yokohama Ramen Museum exhibited an alleged replica of the first ramen dish ever eaten by a Japanese citizen, Tokugawa Mitsukuni (better known as Mito Komon), who was ruler of Mito Domain in the seventeenth century. The first newspaper ad for Chinese noodles (called "Nanking soba") appeared in 1884. In 1906, *ramen* or "*sina soba*" became popular, and in 1910 the first regular ramen shop (Rairai-ken) opened in Asakusa, Tokyo.
3. "Japan Votes Noodle the Tops," http://news.bbc.co.uk/2/hi/asia-pacific/1067506.stm (consulted 12 December 2000).
4. For a discussion of Koreans' sensitivity toward health and food-safety issues, see Han (2011).
5. One trick is rather simple: add milk to the *ramyeon* as it cooks, or don't drink any water during the night. Refer to: http://cafe.daum.net/ramyunheaven; http://blog.naver.com/sphere4u?Redirect=Log&logNo=50073389556; http://cafe.naver.com/18886.cafe?iframe_url=/ArticleRead.nhn%3Farticleid=1728.
6. Dr. Park Dong-Sung, who had a chance to read and discuss my first draft, pointed out that this "shock" on the part of Koreans and Japanese might be due to the sacredness they find in rice. Many Chinese do not eat rice as their staple food, and thus find no problem in eating something other than rice on birthday.
7. According to the report by *Korea Times* staff reporter Yoon Ja-young, "Prices of *ramyeon,* gasoline, *soju,* and cram school tuition will be monitored and controlled by the government. … The ministry said it has picked 52 daily necessities whose prices will be monitored and controlled to stabilize the livelihood of the working class amid global inflation pressures. The measure comes after President Lee Myung-bak's remarks that the prices of daily necessities should be controlled. … The government said the selection was based on

an analysis of shopping and spending habits of households making an average of 2.47 million won or less each month. They often buy such items, spending a considerable portion of their income on them. Consumer groups also gave advice in selecting the items. It first chose 26 items that had increased in price by over 5 percent over the last year. Included in the list are wheat, *ramyeon*, Korean cabbage, radish, tofu, garlic, red pepper paste, vegetable oil, eggs, apples, snacks, detergent, gasoline, subway and bus fares, cram school tuition, shampoo, and daycare center fees, among others. … The National Statistical Office will monitor price changes of these 52 items every 10 days, and they will be released with consumer prices statistics every month, the ministry said" ("Prices of 52 Daily Necessities Under Control," *Korea Times*, 25 March 2008).

8. The website says: "Since the word 'Ramen' reminds you of instant noodles, many seem to have mistakenly thought that cooking 'Real' ramen is easy as well. This is a complete misunderstanding. It takes at least several hours. Some shops take a day or longer to prepare just the broth. Moreover, the temperature, moisture levels, and conditions of ingredients will affect the taste and flavor, so close and unremitting attention is required to keep each serving reliable in taste. It is said that it requires years-long practical training to become a master ramen chef" (http://freeforumzone.leonardo.it/discussione.aspx?idd=3679049, consulted October 2009).

9. There was a report that pork cutlet *ramyeon* appeared recently in Korea, signifying an interesting change in Korean *ramyeon* making.

10. Jane Han, "Lotte Gum No. 1-Selling Product Overseas," *Korea Times*, 19 April 2009.

11. See Appadurai (1986, 1996), Beadsworth and Keil (1997), and McCracken (1990).

12. This comes from a story of a birthday party for an ancient Chinese emperor.

13. Reading a draft of this chapter, Dr. Park and several others pointed out that it might not be universally correct to say that the price of *ramyeon* was cheap. *Ramyeon* was cheap in the eyes of middle-class Seoulites, but not to most poor peasant families. Many families found the price of *ramyeon* rather expensive, and some families would buy several bags of *ramyeon* and increase the quantity they could serve by adding cheaper ordinary noodles (*guksu*).

14. Ppusyeo Ppusyeo (literally, "break-break") produced by Ottugi Food Co. has a *ramyeon*-noodle shape and a bag of soup mix, and is available in six different flavors.

References

Anon. 2009. "Life Surrounded by Ramen." http://www.worldramen.net/ABC/Life Surround/LifeFlame.html (consulted 1 October 2009).

Appadurai, Arjun. 1986. *The Social Life of Things: Commodities in Cultural Perspective*. Cambridge: Cambridge University Press.

——. 1996. *Modernity at Large: Cultural Dimensions of Globalization*. Minneapolis: University of Minnesota Press.

Beadsworth, Alan, and Teresa Keil. 1997. *Sociology on the Menu: An Invitation to the Study of Food and Society*. London and New York: Routledge.

Bendix, Regina. 1997. *In Search of Authenticity: The Formation of Folklore Studies*. Madison: The University of Wisconsin Press.

Boym, Svetlana. 2001. *The Future of Nostalgia*. New York: Basic Books.

Creighton, Millie. 1997. "Consuming Rural Japan: The Marketing of Tradition and Nostalgia in the Japanese Travel Industry." *Ethnology* 36(3): 239–254.

Han, Kyung-Koo. 2000. "Some Foods Are Good to Think: Kimchi and the Epitomization of National Character." *Korea Social Science Journal* 27(1).

———. 2011. "The Kimchi 'Wars' in Globalizing East Asia: Consuming Class, Gender, Health, and National Identity." In *Consuming Korean Culture in Early and Late Modernity: Commodification, Tourism, and Performance,* edited by L. Kendall. 149–166. Honolulu: University of Hawaii Press.

Herzfeld, Michael. 1997. *Cultural Intimacy: Social Poetics in the Nation-State.* New York and London: Routledge.

Hochschild, Arlie Russell. 2003. *The Commercialization of Intimate Life: Notes from Home and Work.* Berkeley, Los Angeles, and London: University of California Press.

Ivy, Marilyn. 1995. *Discourses of the Vanishing: Modernity, Phantasm, Japan.* Chicago: University of Chicago Press.

Kube, Rokuro. 1999/2009. *Ramen hakkenden* (The Ramen King). Tokyo: Shogakkan.

McCracken, Grant. 1990. *Culture and Consumption: New Approaches to the Symbolic Character of Consumer Goods and Activities.* Bloomington and Indianapolis: Indiana University Press.

Miller, Daniel. 1995. "Consumption and Commodities." *Annual Review of Anthropology* 24: 141–161.

Ritzer, George. 2004. *The McDonaldization of Society.* Rev. ed. Thousand Oaks, London, and New Delhi: Pine Forge Press.

Stewart, Kathleen. 1988. "Nostalgia: A Polemic." *Cultural Anthropology* 3(3): 227.

CHAPTER 6

Cultural Nostalgia and Global Imagination

Japanese Cuisine in Taiwan

David Y. H. Wu

The ubiquitous Japanese foodways and cuisine in Taiwan become an integral part of today's Taiwanese culture and society. This chapter is an attempt to investigate the Japanese foodways in Taiwan in the cultural context and political economy of the island's history, including Japanese colonization and cultural assimilation of Taiwan between 1895 and 1945; postwar Chinese Nationalists' anti-Japanese cultural policy on the island; and underground Taiwanese nostalgic expression of Japanese culture between 1945 and 1990. Powerful representation of Japanese foodways in Taiwan can be further explained in connection with the global resurgence of Japanese capitalism since the late twentieth century. Food and cuisine serve to indicate intensified Japanese capitals beginning in the early twenty-first century, bringing renewed global cultural connection with Japan, hence visible cultural resurgence of Japanese representation on the island nation of Taiwan.

The present chapter aims to discuss, in the broad sociocultural context of the practice, the imagination, and the nostalgia of Japanese culture as observed in Taiwanese foodways. Nostalgia is referring to versions of historical experience and collective memory of Japan and Japanese culture in Taiwan, while imagination concerns contemporary adoption and reinvention of new styles of Japanese food in day-to-day lives among the Taiwanese. Due to the particular political history and contested national identity of Taiwan, Japanese cuisine and restaurants also become recent sites for public contestation and nostalgized discourse. As Japanese food or Japanese style of food being one of the most popular eating-out choices, I conducted research in terms of anthropological participant observation. From 2007 to 2011, I lived on the island each year for at least three consecutive months, and my research was carried out mainly in the Japanese restaurants, Japanese departmental stores, and new Japanese-style food courts in major train and subway stations in Taipei as well as in Hsinchu City in north Taiwan. I also visited supermarkets, sidewalk cafes, and small restaurants in the rural areas. In addition, I interviewed food consumers. For data analysis, I also relied on my personal memory of eating Japanese food in Taiwan since my early childhood in the 1940s.

Theoretically speaking, I realized that sociopolitical issues of Taiwan can be demonstrated and explained when we investigate the current state of Japanese food and cuisine. The anthropological study of food pushes us closer to understanding social history and political issues of ethnic identity, cultural nationalism, formation of social class, and local vs. international politics (to cite but a few recent works: Y. Chen 2008, 2010; Caldwell 2001; Wilk 1999; Watson 2005; and Wu 1998, 2004, 2006, 2008, and 2010). In this chapter I will look into the social history of Japanese cuisine on the island; discuss the mundane Japanese food items consumed in the past as well as those domesticated or reinvented locally; and document more recent importation of Japanese restaurants from Japan and their social impacts. At the end of this chapter, I wish to conclude by forwarding my arguments that: there was an obvious contrast in postwar cultural ideologies on Taiwan between the government policy and cultural practice among the local Taiwanese people; and an alternative modernization of Taiwan can be observed as far as the culture of food is concerned. I shall now proceed to portray the physical settings of Taipei City and Taiwan at large.

Behind the Local and Global Japanese Cuisines

Until recently, flying into Taipei, Taiwan, meant usually arriving at the Taoyuan international airport. Fredric Jameson (1991: 44) portrays the long passenger corridors and duty-free shops at the airport as representations of the modern and globalized aspects of Taiwan. He argues that the airport displays a "late capitalist Taiwan hyperspace," where passengers walk by large photographic billboards in glass windows that advertise (Western-style) skin care, fitness (weight loss), as well as Formosan aboriginal ethnicity. Traveling to the capital city of Taipei, the almost completed subway networks symbolize the coming of age of Taipei as a global city (Lee 2009). International travelers may be overwhelmed by the skyscrapers, including the new 101 Building (completed in 2007 in the attempt to rival the height any building in Asia), Japanese department stores, the Japanese-style subway, the Japanese-built bullet train, and the luxury high-rise condominiums standing along multilane boulevards in the newly developed East Taipei.

The postmodern phenomena of globalized food and restaurants in Taipei are even more dazzling for foreign travelers or visitors from south Taiwan (considered more rural and less cosmopolitan). Taipei is such a cosmopolitan city if we consider the thousands of restaurants of foreign (or exotic) food, including American, African, European, Japanese, Russian, South Asian, Southeast Asian, Formosan aboriginal, mainland Chinese minority, and even Middle East Muslim. Among all these, many upscale Japanese restaurants served the most expensive food in town.

In an interesting twist to what Japanese food or cuisine means in Taiwan, one may also find Japanese cuisine hidden among down-to-earth Taiwanese eateries—the so-called little eats (*xiaochi*) on the side streets, in the sidewalk cafes, and at food stalls inside huge night markets that supposedly serve "indigenous Taiwanese food."[1] In addition to these food markets or sidewalk cafes, the local Taiwanese "low cuisine," which includes many traditional Japanese food items (to be discussed later), would also be available side by side with spaghetti, pizza, and hamburgers sold at food court stalls on the basement floor of huge Japanese department stores such as the Pacific Sogo, the Mitsukoshi, and the newly (2011) opened Hankyu Taipei. However, in a reversal, Taiwanese low cuisine has also recently surfaced as repackaged Japanese high cuisine that could be found in the most expensive and upscale restaurants, where one can enjoy contemporary Japanese-European chic in decor and service. Thanks to official and commercial promotions of tourism, especially since the opening of Taiwan in 2008 to mainland Chinese tourists, Taiwanese low cuisine of *xiaochi* (little eats) was singled out and privileged in the national discourse of the "unique" and representative Taiwanese food that can best be promoted to the tourists. This started in 2000 when the new president, Chen Shui-bien, a Taiwanese who advocates for Taiwan independence, introduced Taiwanese little eats, or Taiwanese nostalgia food, to the "national" menu of the presidential inauguration banquet.[2] Mundane food attributed to traditional rural Taiwanese culture thus emerged to display a new consciousness of Taiwanese cultural nationalism (Hsiao and Lim 2011).

We shall continue in the following section to review a culinary history on the island that reveals the origin of colonial Japanese cuisine as well as postcolonial nostalgia for cultural Japan.

From Forbidden Nostalgia to Ultramodern Japanese

Under the Japanese colonial rule during the Meiji, Taisho, and early Showa eras, Taiwan went through a process of westernization and industrialization initiated by the Japanese. Other than a major sugar industry in the central and southern parts of the island, the Japanese introduced other new agricultural industries, including, for example, British Assam black tea to the mountain area of Nantou, Central Taiwan (F. Chen 2009). At the turn of the twentieth century in Tokyo, for instance, drinking Taiwanese black tea with Taiwanese sugar gave the Japanese a new pleasure and pride at becoming colonial masters of Taiwan.[3] One can also imagine at the same time the Japan-educated Taiwanese elites sipping Japanese-British afternoon tea and eating the Nagasaki Castella cake (sponge cake introduced by the Portuguese to Japan in the sixteenth century), which also became available in the Taiwanese bakeries after 1895. The Castella cake is today still available at Bunmeido bakery/cafe in Ginza, Tokyo, where I yearly visited and enjoyed since the 1970s. I noticed that during the same period the cake was popular, it was also available during the 1980s in Japanese-style (luxury) tea saloons and bakeries in Taipei. When Japanese-style curry dishes were introduced to Taiwan in the early Japanese colonial era, native Taiwanese opened curry restaurants in Taipei, first by the end of the eighteenth century, marking the beginning of Japanese-style Western cuisine (C. Chen 2003).

Since the Meiji era and by the end of the nineteenth century, hundreds of Japanese restaurants—the *ryoriya* (in Japanese)—opened in Taiwan to serve three types of cuisine: (1) Japanese cuisine or *Nihon ryori* (Japanese cuisine); (2) Taiwanese high cuisine (Taiwan *ryori*); and (3) Japanese Western cuisine (*yoshoku*) (Y. Chen 2008: 149; 2010). These restaurants enjoyed the same status as the most upscale and expensive ones in today's Japan. In those early days inside the *ryoriyas* the Japanese colonial elite and elite Taiwanese businessmen entertained guests in an environment of Japanese-style entertainers and geishas. Yu-jen Chen (2008) argues that the Japanese term of *ryori* (cuisine), that has today in Taiwan linguistically transformed into a common Mandarin term *liaoli,* represented high class, whereas the Chinese Mandarin term *cai* (dishes or cuisine), that applied to ordinary Taiwanese food, became low-class cuisine or "no-cuisine" (not qualify to be treated as a cuisine). Thus it begins a class differentiation on the island between Japanese cuisine and Taiwanese no-cuisine (or low cuisine) in the traditional food industry and among consumers. Japanese cuisine also helped to create a class distinction among Taiwanese people on the basis of one's social, economic, and educational standing. Those Taiwanese who were knowledgeable about and could afford to consume Japanese food would gain enormous cultural capital. We must also keep in mind, however, that during the Japanese period and up to the postwar era of the late 1940s (as I have personally observed), most on the island were peasants, and their rural diets had little to do with either the Japanese or the Chinese high cuisines. As I have pointed out elsewhere (Wu 2004), the Mandarin Chinese terms *taicai* (Taiwanese cuisine) in and *taicai fanguan* (Taiwanese restaurant), due to their low esteem in the eyes of both the colonial Japanese and the China refugee Chinese after the war, were unknown in Taiwan until after the 1960s (see also Hsiao and Lim 2011). The point is that by the end of Japanese rule, as food habits and cuisines are concerned, Japanese culture was regarded as high class (or *haikara* in Japanese) in Taiwanese society, enjoyed by Japanese-educated Taiwanese elites. We can say the same for the arts, modern theatrical performance, and music (such as Western-style music, including Jazz, and Eu-

ropean classical music). This colonial legacy of class consciousness in the embodiment of Japanese culture is still obvious in contemporary Taiwan, especially
among the Taiwanese families whose elders (including either living or deceased
grandparents who belonged to the so-called Japanese speaking generation, or *Nihongo Sedai* [Igarashi 2011: 185]) had received higher Japanese education before
1945.

There was a long period of time (forty years) in postwar Taiwan when nationalist authorities forbade demonstration of nostalgia for cultural Japan. The
KMT (or Guomindang) government launched a national project to promote
China-oriented Chinese nationalism and, at the same time, a cultural "de-Japanization" policy during the 1950s and 1960s to "re-educate" the Taiwanese (to
become Chinese). Under the martial law in the 1950s, the bureau of censorship
for movies closed the doors to importation of Japanese films (it later, by the end
of the 1960s, changed to allowing a quota of five Japanese films per year), while
Japanese music disappeared from radio broadcasting.[4] Due to the popularity of
the Japanese movies and music in the 1950s, a clear indication of cultural nostalgia on the part of native Taiwanese, the censorship was put in place in part for
the protection of a budding Chinese film industry in Taiwan that manufactured
political propaganda films representing Taiwan as an "authentic cultural China"
(as opposed to the "fake cultural China" created by the new Communist regime
on mainland China) (Wu 1998). I have in the 1990s argued, on the basis of
an anthropological conceptualization of landscape, that the Republic of China's
capital city of Taipei was very Japanese. The city was full of major landmarks
(including the present Republic of China's Presidential Palace, which was the
site of the Japanese governor general's office in colonial Taiwan until 1945) that
symbolized Westernized cultural Japan since the Meiji, Taisho, and early Showa
eras. In other words, side by side with the old Japanese architecture, by the 1980s
Japanese restaurant food culture, as well as the newly imported Japanese cafe
culture known in Mandarin as *kafeiguan,* symbolized a strong undercurrent of independent Taiwanese national identity that surfaced in public politics after 1990
(Wu 1998). It is interesting to call attention to two styles of *kafeiguan:* the *kisaden*
(a Japanese term for café, and in Taiwan a luxurious European-style coffee house),
known in Mandarin as *chunchicha* ("pure tea house"), which stood in contrast to
the local Taiwanese *"Cha-shi,"* meaning tea room in Mandarin, or *deidiama* in
Taiwanese colloquial. The latter offered hostesses to serve male-only customers,
keeping them company or providing extra sex services.

Only by the 1990s did the (Nationalist) government officials finally realize
how badly the cultural China policy and the de-Japanization project had failed,
whereas a new generation of the youth population (the grandchildren of prewar-
born Taiwanese and mainland-born Chinese who came to Taiwan after 1945)
became *"Harizu,"* fanatic fans of Japanese culture. They pursue Japanese fashion
and youth popular culture in all forms, including *manga* comics, pirated Japanese

TV shows and movies, and modern Japanese restaurant food.[5] Ming-Tsung Lee (2003) told the story of how during the late 1990s and early 2000s the Taiwan government (under the Taiwanese-dominated new party) made efforts in Japan to promote Taiwan tourism in order to attract former Japanese (colonial) expatriates. All the media attention and publicity focused on Japan, however, generated reverse tourism among Taiwanese youth through a new "fever" for visiting Japan that continues still today.

When we shift our gaze toward twenty-first-century Taiwan, we can see the active presence in Taiwan of Japan capitalism and Japan-oriented Taiwanese transnational corporations at work (most conspicuous in the capital city of Taipei). Ultramodern Japanese eateries were newly opened; I noticed at least five types of eating places that did not previously exist in Taipei. They included the contemporary *izakaya* (traditional Japanese bar, with a sign in Japanese characters that in Mandarin would translate to "living in the wine house"); *shokudo* (cafeteria, or *shitang* in Mandarin); upscale Japanese restaurants; novel Japanese Italian restaurants (their décor and setting are different from indigenous Taiwanese European-style bistros that were in business in Taipei a decade earlier); and Japanese-style bakeries that also serve Western-style light meals. Newly developed on every corner of the island nation were also tens of thousands of inexpensive restaurant chains of *shabu shabu* (Japanese-style hot-pot eateries called *shuanshuanguo* in Mandarin, or "shabu-shabu-pot") and *yakiniku* (*kaorou*, or "grill meat" in Mandarin). Many of these new food businesses were joint ventures between the largest Japanese food corporations and big Taiwanese companies of food manufacturing and processing. New Japanese restaurants also included additional small-chain restaurants operated both under the Japanese capital and management, and the locals as well. Travelers in Taipei today who use the public rapid transit system are confronted with postmodern cultural Japan, represented by Japanese "food cities" inside the Taipei Train Station or on top or close to some of the new subway stations, such as the Banquao station and the Gongguan (across from the entrance of the National Taiwan University, where the main gateway structure as well as several old buildings on campus were constructed during the early Showa era of European-style architecture, similar in style the old buildings in the Imperial [today's National] Tokyo University). The settings and decors of these multistory food courts so much resembled (or were identical to) those in Japan that when one eats inside these "Japanese" food courts a bowl of Japanese *ramen* noodle, a plate of Japanese-style spaghetti, or even a bowl of Taiwanese *danzimian* (street hawker's soup noodle, originated in the country side of south Taiwan), it might satisfy the consumer's imagination (or illusion) of sitting at a modern train station or underground shopping city in Tokyo or Osaka, Japan.[6] Inside these food courts, there were also small restaurants serving "Taiwan *niuromian*," a beef soup noodle dish that arguably became the national dish, invented in the 1950s by the *waishenri* (mainlander refugees who migrated to Taiwan after 1949). Taiwan official tourism authorities promoted *niuromian* since 2000 by holding annual national contests for the best Taiwan beef noodle dish. Mass media reported comments from even the president of Republic of China praising the best (or most delicious) national noodle dish in the nation, claiming that it finds no rivals elsewhere in the entire world.

Since 2008, I have also noticed a new style of Japanese bakery/cafes that serve Japanese-style pastries and light Western meals (such as spaghetti, curry rice, and sandwiches), concentrated and mushrooming in the busy restaurant district of East Taipei. In interviews, some of the owners admitted to having learned of the concept (both the style of food and the garden-patio décor of the store) when they traveled to Japan to seek inspiration. These bakeries included many all-you-can-eat cake shops (*chidaobao dangaodian* in Mandarin), targeted at young and female consumers mainly considered as belonging to the *Harizu* (literally, the tribe who flatter Japanese).

When I look into Japanese-style Taiwanese companies with an established history, I further notice the historical continuity of Japanese influence in food processing and production. One Taiwanese bakery and wedding-cake shop, now a huge corporation of chain stores (I-Mei), used to be (since the 1950s when I shopped there) well known among the ethnic Taiwanese consumers for traditional Taiwanese ceremonial cakes. The cakes for gift giving at marriage betrothals or wedding parties were very big, usually as large as a medium-sized pizza, and contained filings of the unique "Taiwanese flavor" of being both sweet and salty at the same time. Prior to the 1970s, the bakery also had the reputation of being *the* cake shop for social gift giving among affluent ethnic Taiwanese who bought boxed Japanese *wagashi* (Japanese traditional sweets, including fancy rice cake *omochi* and bean jelly cake *yokan*) and Japanese-style European pastries. After the 1980s, Japanese-style French cookies and chocolate candies were in favor and replaced the traditional Taiwanese wedding cakes for prestigious and ceremonial gift giving. The taste and style of these traditional Taiwanese cakes were in apparent contrast to the mainland Chinese cookies and sweets reinvented in Taiwan after the 1960s (for instance, cakes, candies, and beef jerky sold at chain shops of Xindongyang). However, today's gift-box cookies, sold at airport duty-free shops for tourists (especially targeting the Japanese) to bring home as special gifts from Taiwan, have lost their ethnic distinctions in terms of taste and shape when compared with common Western cookies. Euro-American-style cookies under the guise (and the name, such as "pineapple cakes") of traditional Taiwanese gift cookies (known as the *omiyage*, a Japanese word that has been adopted in both Taiwanese dialect and Mandarin) are sold under many new brands. However, these new style confectionaries taste foreign to someone like me who has been away from Taiwan for forty years and still remembers the flavors of the authentic traditional ingredients. To me the new Taiwanese *omiyage* (the word was recently replaced by a new official Mandarin translation of *banshouli* [carry-by-hand gifts]) today taste the same as Euro-American short cakes or butter cookies.[7]

Just like the prewar or postwar period in Taiwan where wealthy, Japanese-educated, elite Taiwanese families sought class distinction by consuming Japanese-style food, and in contrast to the later-arrived China-born elite Chinese who favored American-style products, even consuming the daily "bread" helped to create ethnic segregation in terms of food taste. While in the 1950s and 1960s, the Taiwanese bought Western bread in the name of "bun" (Portuguese word for bread adopted first in Japan in the sixteenth century and then introduced to Taiwan in the early nineteenth century) from Japanese-style bakeries, elite ethnic Chinese *Waishenrin* bought *mianbao* (Western bread in Mandarin) and (Jewish) bagels at selective Shanghainese bakeries in Taipei.

In 2008, Taipei city saw the opening of a Japanese French bakery located at the intersection of Ren-ai Road and the posh South Dunhua Boulevard (a grand European-style traffic circle, where luxury condominiums and large commercial companies are located). Following its opening, there were daily lines of customers stretching out of the shop and sometimes into the street. I went there a couple of times to buy bread and observe the scene. The two young bakers in the shop were Japanese nationals. My Taiwanese friends in town told me that the customers were predominately elite Taiwanese who waited for the so-called natural-yeast bread that came out of the oven only twice a day (the store also advertises that all other ingredients of their bread, mineral water included, were imported from France). When the bakery first opened, each batch of freshly baked bread sold out quickly at a price of around US $20 per loaf. However, when I passed by the bakery again in late 2011, I did not see any line stretching out the door. A friend commented that the reduced number of customers just showed how Taipei people are mostly in the habit of following trends or fads. In 2009, another France-based Japanese baker, Aoki, opened his first Japanese "Paris"-style bakery at the new Mitsukoshi Department Store of the fashionable newly developed East district of Taipei. The French Japanese bakery caused a media sensation, while the New-East-Taipei district became a new location of food consumption for distinction among affluent Taiwanese (thanks to anthropologist Guo Pei-yi for information about this particular episode).

In any event, the Japanese bakery seems to become another example of modern Taiwanese upper-class consumption of the European chic à la Tokyo that continues with the Meiji tradition of Taiwanese Westernization, elitism in consumption, and Japanized globalization (Shoji 2009). I would argue that these Japanese bakeries, being strong examples of Japanese global capitalism, symbolize colonization and the commodification of "Japanized European culture" in Taiwan. In 2006, I learned that operating in Japan were already some twenty "French" bakeries. When I visited one in Osaka in 2011, it appeared to me to be of no particular distinction in size or specialty as compared with many other Western-style bakeries in Japan. I also noticed that most of the bakeries used French names. In Taipei, however, once the bakery claims or is known to be Japanese, it commends exceptional admiration and prestige for customers.

New Japan Craze and Japanization of Taiwanese High and Low Cuisine

The post-modern conceptions of transnationalism and cultural deterritorialization (see Adrian 2003; Appadurai 1996; Huang 2009: 5–11; Jameson 1991; and Wang and Guo 2009) are quite useful in the explanation of current Taiwanese Japanese foodways. We shall continue to demonstrate the shift of cultural meanings and social standings when local food becomes Japanese, or vice versa.

The Japanese department stores continue to present or represent modern cultural Japan to Taiwanese consumers through the introduction of new merchandise, food, and cuisine. This coincides with the development of a twenty-first-century commercial center and luxury residential area in the east end of Taipei city the so-called new Hsinyi neighborhood. Newly constructed were huge shopping complexes that housed new Japanese stores: Sogo Pacific, Mitsukoshi, and the huge bookstore called *Chengpin* (Elite flagship). A few blocks away to the east side of an older section of the city stood another new shopping center of luxury stores known as the Breeze (*Weifeng*, which housed the largest Japanese bookstore of Kinokuniya in Taiwan). In the Breeze, for instance, shoppers crowded the new "Japanese" supermarket to select local "organic" produce as well as imported Japanese fruits, vegetables, meats, and canned goods. They also shopped for fresh-made *heguozi* (a Mandarin phrase meaning "peaceful fruits," but the characters actually make up the Japanese words for *wagashi,* or Japanese sweets and cakes, in contrast to *yokashi,* or Western sweets), Japanese bread, and Japanese "French" pastries. There were large signs in Japanese on top of the sweets counters, while all the Taiwanese workers clayed in Japanese pastry chefs' costumes. In great contrast to shopping at traditional Chinese wet markets or ordinary supermarkets, such a practice of "consuming Japanese" in luxury department stores commends social prestige, and certainly a demonstration of, in Bourdieu's words, "consuming for distinction" (1984).

During 2009, in Hsinchu city, on the top floor food court of Pacific Sogo and Mitsukoshi, I saw the opening of many new Japanese fast food restaurants (or stalls), each specializing in a certain type of popular Japanese food, such as *omuraisu, tongkatsu, shabushabu,* and *teppanyaki.* They are considered in local Chinese standards to be upscale restaurants that are popular with children and young customers who ate Japanese *danbaofan* (Mandarin for ketchup omelet-on-rice; in Japanese it is called *omuraisu*); *zhazhupai* (Mandarin for the deep-fried pork chop known as *tonkatsu* in Japanese); *zhupaifan* (the Japanese *katsudon* or *tonkatsu* on a bowl of rice); *rishi huoguo* (Mandarin phrase meaning Japanese-style hot-pot); and *tiebanshao* (grilled steak or *tebbanyaki*).

Mass media and commercial advertisements for food, restaurants, and local cultural tourism all helped in the promotion to the general public of a contemporary cultural Japan that goes beyond food. It is worth taking note of how media generated popularization of Japanese vocabularies adopted in daily (especially youth) Chinese language (in Mandarin, not the local Taiwanese). Among many adopted new words or phrases I have heard translated into Mandarin are *renqi, darenqi, oishi, kawai, zhai, zhai nan, zannian, dianzhang,* and *xinfamai.* A literal translation of these Chinese words (in the above order) into English produces amusing results: "human odor" (actually "popularity" in the original Japanese); "adult odor" ("very popular"); "delicious"; "cute"; "residence," as in Mandarin adoption of *zhai jibian* (*takkyuben* in original Japanese for express delivery to homes); "man of the house," or handsome and desirable man; "leftover thoughts," meaning "regrettable or pitiful" in the original Japanese phrase; "store elder" or "manager"; and new distribution or new merchandise on sale.

We have so far presented case after case of the transformation of Japanese food and cuisine into a local Chinese cultural world in Taiwan. However, parallel to this development, due to the popularity and class distinction of Japanese cuisine and restaurants, there was the reverse development of the other side of the coin—the Japanization of traditional Taiwanese high and low cuisines. One famous restaurant of Taiwanese cuisine that has established a reputation for fifty years opened a new branch, upscale and very expensive, in 2008 in the above-mentioned new shopping center, the Breeze. I visited when it first opened. On its black glass doors was a huge sign with the store's name in both Japanese and English—Aoba—while there were no Chinese characters on the door. When I stepped into the restaurant I mistook it for a Japanese restaurant. Both the décor and manner of service were distinctively modern Japanese, but the dishes reflected reinvention of the traditional Taiwanese dishes that used to be served on sidewalk little-eats places. If one (who needs to know Japanese) translates the Japanese store name into Chinese, it would reveal the restaurant's original name in Chinese, *Qingye* or Green Leaf, which interesting enough, by late 2011, when I visited the restaurant again, had been added to the door. By then the restaurant had already established a reputation of being one of the most expensive places for enjoying "traditional Taiwanese little eats," for which only the Japanese tourists and the wealthy could afford. Another example of the elevation of traditional little-eats food from low to high cuisine was found, for example, at a five-star hot-spring resort hotel north of Taipei catering to Japanese tourists. A local Taiwanese dish of *rouzaofan* (minced and braised pork on a bowl of rice), which if sold at small sidewalk cafes would cost about NT$30 (US $1) per bowl, was listed at the price of NT$450 (US $15).

Domestication and Sinicization of Japanese Food and Cuisine

If we examine a few common Japanese food items, we discover their long history and popularity in Taiwan at different times, whether colonial and postcolonial, or postmodern global. One must understand the intriguing linguistic transformation of the food names in their Japanese origins in order to decipher the contemporary Chinese names in Mandarin. I shall discuss the four most popular Japanese food items: sushi, sashimi (raw fish slices), *oden* (hot pot dish with fishcakes and vegetables), and *bendo* (Chinese corruption of the Japanese word, bento, lunch boxes). My research started by interviewing a number of young people between the ages of twenty and forty by asking them the following simple questions: What comes to your mind if I ask you to name some Japanese food items? When was the first time you had that food? Where did you have it? Their answers demonstrate the problematic and contested definition of Japanese food. Sushi, sashimi, *chawanmushi* (steamed salty egg custard in a ceramic tea cup), and *oden* (known in Taiwan as *Guandongzhu,* or in Japan as *kantohni* or *kantodaki*) were among the popular answers. These interviewees predominately experienced such food items for the first time in their early childhoods when either their mothers made it at home or they had it in a "Japanese" restaurant. However, some told me that they had no idea that sashimi is Japanese, or *tonkatsu,* or tempura for that matter. In the United States, these Japanese words have almost become standard household terms. Most in Taiwan, however, did not recognize the Japanese words, either spoken or in writing, because the terms have been transformed into Mandarin vocabularies. Even Taiwanese-speaking persons had to order these foods in Mandarin, as if they were Chinese food items introduced from China. I shall now provide a short history of these food items in Taiwan.

Shousi, Shoujuan, *and* Yufantuan *(Sushi,* Temaki, *and* Onigiri*)*

One informant in his sixties recites a silly children's rhyme he learned in Tainan city when he was young: in Taiwanese (*Minnan* dialect), "*Tailang Miendo sushi*" (which relates to how convenient it is to execute a man without using knife [or sword]). The rhyme is just to repeat in corrupted Japanese pronunciation a phrase of "*bendo* and sushi of Tainan city." The rhyme shows that bento (Japanese box lunch) and sushi had for a long time become popular food items for local Taiwanese people.

Several young informants I interviewed remembered eating *shousi* (Mandarin for sushi) for the first time when they were very young and were told that it was "Japanese" food. Interestingly enough, only those whose mothers are ethnic Taiwanese would have experienced Japanese meals or *shousi* at home, not the children of mainland Chinese mothers. Today one can buy *shousi, shoujuan* (hand roll or *temaki*), and *fantuan* (rice ball in Mandarin, meaning *onigiri*) al most anywhere; at food stalls and small eateries, school cafeterias, and convenient stores. I once saw a commercial sign in Japanese kanji that read "*onigiri*" on the wall along a Hsinchu street. If read in Mandarin the words would be "*yufantuan*" (honorable rice ball). The triangle-shaped rice balls were mass produced by the largest food company on the island and sold twenty-four hours a day anywhere throughout the nation.

When a popular food writer describes traditional Taiwanese "little eats," he mentions a small sushi shop in the southern town of Pingdong (Shu 2007: 286–289). The sushi shop is said to have been in business for some seventy years, first opening in 1938 (under the Japanese rule). The author praised the good taste of two kinds of sushi sold at the store: "*Haidai* [kelp] *shousi* and *Doupi* [tofu skin] *shousi*" (both in Mandarin, the latter indicating *inarizushi* in Japanese). The author named the individual sushi in Mandarin as "*haidai shousi*," meaning kelp sushi. The added word for kelp may mean seaweed, and the Sinicized term becomes redundant since sushi would usually be wrapped in a thin sheet of baked seaweed. If the author is referring to the sushi roll or *makizushi,* the Taiwanese version would contain fried egg, preserved minced pork (*rousong*), and Taiwanese baby cabbages (*xiao baicai*)—all items not typically used in the traditional Japanese *makizushi.* Today there is plenty of room for *shousi* imagination, for chefs or consumers, in varieties of shape, color, and ingredients, much like with sushi in Japan or elsewhere around the globe. All the sushi sold in Japanese convenient stores, such as 7-Eleven and Family Mart, sell new styles of sushi (started a decade ago) with added sauces such as mayonnaise, ketchup, hot spicy sauce, as well as toppings including fried rice and fried noodles. It is not surprising that the sushi sold in the Taiwanese convenient stores copies the temporary food fashions of Japan, rather than represent local invention by Taiwanese restaurant owners.

Shengyupian *(Raw Fish Slices) or Sashimi*

Today one can purchase packaged sashimi at supermarkets and convenient stores or sidewalk stalls. It used to be expensive and not so common. By the 1980s, following the economic boom in Taiwan, sashimi became an essential appetizer (or *toupan,* the first dish) at a Chinese banquet, whether in the countryside or in upscale Chinese restaurants in the cities. In the early 1990s, one of the sidewalk cafés at a little-eats night-market of the oldest section of west Taipei opened on the (posh) east side of Taipei a most luxurious Taiwanese cuisine restaurant (*taicaiguan*). It was known not only for its food specialties, but also for serving food exclusively in containers of chinaware made in Germany under the auspices of the high-fashion brand *Versace.* I remember the first course of the dinner banquet being a generous serving of *maguro* (tuna) sashimi. In 2008, when I dined at a new branch store of this renowned and expensive restaurant of Taiwanese cuisine, I noticed the restaurant's Japanese-style décor, Japanese-influenced methods of cooking, and Japanese-style service. The dishes were hardly authentic for traditional Taiwanese. For instance, other than the Japanese-style cooking and service, the live fish (freshly picked from the restaurant aquarium) was cooked and served Hong Kong–style of Cantonese or Tiochew origin (Chaozhou, a city in east Guangdong).

Oden

Oden, a nostalgic food of Japan (in Japan, it often invokes the image of an old man with a steaming pot on his street cart on a winter night), becomes *olian* or "black wheel" in Taiwan. It is written in the two Chinese characters of *heilun*, but pronounced in Taiwanese or Minnan (south Fujian) dialect and thus produced the phonetic sound in Taiwanese meaning black wheel. A popular food item in the pot is *tian-bu-la* (the three characters read in Mandarin mean sweet but not spicy hot). *Tian-bu-la* is actually Japanese-style fishcake tempura stick cooked in *oden*-style soup.[8] In south Taiwan, if one asks what little eats can be a representative food item for the southern port city of Kaohsiung (or the city of Takao during the Japanese era), they would say, in Taiwanese, "*olian*" (black wheel). *Olian* is corrupted pronunciation of the Japanese word *oden*—food cooked in a large pot of soup (of dried *bonito,* fish and kelp stock). In Mandarin, *oden* is also called *Guandongzhu* (or the soup dish of the Kanto [Tokyo] area of Japan). *Oden* has become one of the most common fast foods (or cooking style) popularized by the 7-Eleven stores during the 1990s, and it is now also readily available in most of other convenient stores as well as school cafeterias. The Taiwanese 7-Eleven chain is said to be a Taiwanese corporation of Japanese franchise. The twist in the case of *oden* is found in the variation and Taiwanization. Most food items in the *oden* pot are different from that of the traditional *oden* items in Japan, and they may be beyond recognition by Japanese visitors. In particular, one essential Taiwanese item is the black rice cake *chushiegao*—blood cake, which is prepared by socking rice cake in pork blood. However, in Japan, I have observed a reverse diffusion of *oden* items in the 7-Eleven shops in the Osaka area, with the only exception being the black-colored blood cake.

One informant told me that Taichung city also has many sidewalk *olian* stalls that charge customers a higher price than in other cities of Taiwan. When I was a high school student in Taichung some fifty years ago, I saw street peddlers who carried large *oden* pots on bicycles. Gambling was one Chinese cultural element that was introduced to attract (mostly youth) customers (a customer can choose to throw a dart toward a spinning wheel to determine the size and numbers of fishcake stick that he can get for paying the basic price of one stick). In the *oden* pots, the most popular item was the fishcake roll that today becomes "*Tianbula.*" In Japan or the United States, the word *tempura* invokes the image of battered and deep-fried shrimp and vegetables. This kind of tempura in Taiwan is now called *Tianfuluo* (written on vendor's banners in the old kanji or Chinese characters of "sky, woman, and gong"). One informant I interviewed told me that he had no idea that shrimp tempura came from Japan, as he only knew it as *zhashia* (fried shrimp). He said the same thing about *zhazhupai* (fried pork cutlet), and had no knowledge of the Japanese term *tonkatsu*.

Biandang

Biandang (Mandarin; derived from *obento* in Japanese) or *bendo* originates in Taiwan's prewar railway system; they were lunch boxes sold at train stations the same way as "*ekiben*" was in Japan. Parents then, just like in Japan, prepare *bendo* for their children when they go on annual outings (*ensoku*) or participate in sports contests (*untokai*). For my generation (and the next generation in their forties or fifties), *bendo* in Taiwan brings back fond memories of childhood for those that I have interviewed. When I was in elementary school and traveled by train from Taichung to Taipei (in the late 1940s and early 1950s), the most anticipated and rewarding part of the trip was to get to eat a Japanese bento at Hsinchu or Chunan station, most famous at that time for their delicious bento. When the train pulled into the station, a railway employee in a black uniform (carrying a tray with belts rested on his shoulders) would shout out slowly, in Japanese, "*benn ... do ... , benn ... do*," to attract potential buyers on the train. And the *bendo* and cash were exchanged through the train windows. All the *bendo* sold at the stations from north to south Taiwan were almost standardized in a thin, rectangular wooden box containing half of a hard-boiled *shoyu* egg, (Japanese-style) shredded red-colored cuttlefish or braised hard tofu cake, and *takuon* slices (Japanese picked sweet radish), served on a thin layer of rice. The bento box was thin and small (in contrast to later mainland Chinese–style large metal box), made of paper-thin wood slices (almost the same material used for making matchboxes). Interestingly enough, several mainlander friends of my generation who lived in northern Taiwan had never heard of such Japanese-style bento, although they too had traveled on trains. The bento serves as a clear ethnic marker, as the following stories can testify.

Today the word *biandang* is standard Mandarin vocabulary in daily usage that denotes "a meal in box." The Chinese in China do not recognize that this term originated in Japanese characters that would in Chinese mean "convenient." They instead call it "*he fan*," or boxed rice. People in Taiwan on average eat *biandang* several times a week. *Biandang* stores or vendors are everywhere in any cities, small towns, and villages. I would consider it Chinese fast food, as the price for a *biandang* (less than US $2) may be lower than the price of a hamburger. A *biandang* includes cooked Chinese food, such as Shanghai-style (often greasy) pork chops or chicken thighs, and sautéed vegetables, on top of rice. In school cafeterias and street shops around universities as well as at street-level residential high-rises, you can go to a small *biandang* store to make your own by picking up desirable Chinese dishes on a buffet table, putting them in a paper box, and paying for it either by items or by weight. *Biandang* makers also deliver them to workplaces. It is a common practice for the host of a conference or office meeting to provide *biandang* at lunchtime to the attendants.

The Sinicization of railway bento started in the late 1950s and early 1960s when the trans-Taiwan (north–south) train was modernized with added luxury-class train, introduced as the Guanguanghao (tourist-class super-express train) by the Taiwan Provincial Railway Bureau. At the same time, to new passengers of social elites, many who were ethnic mainland Chinese, they invented and introduced *paigucaifan* (Shanghai-style fried pork-chop on rice cooked with shredded green cabbage [in the United States known Shanghai bok choy), packaged in a round and thick aluminum box (about twice the size of an old Japanese train bento mentioned earlier). In October 2008, the newly elected President Ma entertained a group of foreign dignitaries by serving them (Chinese) metal-box *biandang* of his nostalgic "*huoche biandang*" (in his own words, the *biandang* of the train).[9]

Clearly, the Mandarin *biandang* originates with the Japanese lunch box, bento or *obento*. However, the postwar history of *biandang* can serve as a symbol of de-Japanization in popular culture. In Taiwan schools during the 1950s and 1960s, students carried their own lunch boxes to school. *Bendo* in schools signified a clear ethnic marker. Students of ethnic Taiwanese background carried to school Japanese-style (tiny, rectangular) *bento,* while mainlander (*waishenren)* students carried large Chinese (sometimes round Shanghainese-style) *fanhe* (literally, rice box). As the two groups of students carried lunch boxes containing different ethnic dishes, they often exchanged food items to satisfy their curiosities (as confirmed even by younger informants only in their forties). Unlike the Japanese, who eat *obento* cold (so did most Taiwanese students in the past), the schools (dominated with ethnic *waishenren* teachers and students) were obliged to collect student *biandang*s in the morning, send them to the school kitchen, and steam them in huge steamers so that the students could enjoy a steamy hot meal at lunch time.

In some stores in Taipei, they served "traditional" *obento* (in Mandarin as *rishi-biandang* [Japanese-style *biandang*]). This is often repackaged Chinese and Taiwanese food put in a (imagined) Japanese-style (compartmentalized) container. The lunch box makers no longer put into the so-called Japanese bento box the traditional *tsukemono* (Japanese pickled radish or cucumber), and instead put in Sichuan-style pickled cabbage. It seems to me that the entire issue of *biandang* in Taiwanese food and culture history warrants some future dissertations.

Conclusion

We have reviewed the practice, the imagination, and the nostalgia for Japanese culture as demonstrated in the Taiwanese foodways in a social history of over a century. Taiwan has become an intriguing "crossroads" for various state cultural projects that involved the Japanese government, the states of ROC and PRC, and the imagined independent Taiwan as a nation. As convenient symbols—although obvious products of both local invention and international travels and tourism—food and cuisine have played important roles consciously or unconsciously in the domestic and regional politics of ethnic and national identity. When we investigate the foodways in Taiwan, the issue of the meaning of Taiwanese identity started during the era of Japanese colonial rule, went through some fifty years of the Chinese Nationalists' authoritative governing, and recently surfaced in public expression among grassroots Taiwanese (Chuang 2010). As mentioned in the beginning of this chapter, contemporary Japanese foodways in Taiwan can be studied to demonstrate postmodern conceptions of transnationalism and cultural deterritorialization. My research also documented contemporary new waves of Japanese restaurants, cafes, bakeries, luxury supermarkets, and departmental stores arriving on the island. The contemporary consumption of Japanese food for distinction can be understood in connection with a continued cultural imagination of Japan, and has a significant impact on the island ethnic differentiation and social class formation.

New waves of Japanese capitals connected to the twenty-first-century international food and restaurant business also marked intensified imagination of commercialized cultural Japan in a postmodern world of globalization. In this chapter, I have reviewed a social history of Japanese cuisine since the colonial time of the later eighteenth century. It is most interesting to also note that in the period immediately following the Second World War, after the departure of the Japanese colonists on the island, Japanese culture was a target for the Chinese Nationalist government's official project of de-Japanization, which parallels the promotion of China-oriented nationalism. However, contrary to the government's intentions, local Taiwanese people displayed a grassroots, albeit underground, "Taiwanese nationalism" that continued to evoke Japanese culture. We also found that local Taiwanese low cuisine became a space for symbolic representation of the contemporary new Taiwanese identity and national culture.

In this chapter, we also investigated the social history of some of the most common Japanese food items that have become global household words: they include *sashimi, tempura, oden, shabu-shabu, yakiniku,* and the lunch box of *obento.* We realized how these food items have been absorbed into Sinicized foodways and adopted into the Chinese cuisine in Taiwan.

Taiwanese cuisine as a site of commoditized cultural material can also serve a more important purpose if we consider the meaning of modernity in the postmodern world. With the coexistence of the Japanese high cuisine and the down-to-earth Japanese cum Taiwanese low cuisine in night markets and sidewalk cafes, I would argue that Japanese cuisine in Taiwan presents a paradoxical cultural awareness for the Taiwanese consumers, making it familiar but exotic, ancient but new, old but young, masculine but feminine, high class but low class. I introduced in the beginning of this chapter the physical settings of Taipei city as being ultramodern, global, international, and cosmopolitan. However, in the meantime I would characterize the entire country to be rural and traditional when restaurant culture in terms of eating out is considered. When we use Japanese cuisine as a lens to look into Taiwan's modernity, the culinary culture in Taiwan may appear to be global and transnational. The little-eats culture that dominates people's day-to-day meal habits makes Taiwan down-to-earth local, traditional, and rural. It is also noted that the local "little-eats" have become a place for cultural practice of the Taiwanese national identity to the eyes of the mainland Chinese tourists. The low cuisine, in contrast to the high Chinese cuisine, at the same time continues to represent the longings for an imagined local cuisine as a symbol of ethnic and national identity, be it Taiwanese, Chinese, or Japanese.

Finally, to discuss Japanese foodways in Taiwan may also offer the opportunity of engaging in the theoretical dialogue of global modernity. We can ask the essential question of whether foodways in Taiwan demonstrate an alternative modernity or an alternative Asian modernity. Taipei, as a major capitalist city in Asia, is often portrayed as being a postmodern, transnational, global city. However, I wish to emphasize that it is a city full of traditional Chinese peasant culture originated from south China. To conclude, one thought comes to mind: "Japanese cuisine" played such a prime role in the understanding of the process of Taiwan's national and global cultural imagination and nostalgia, yet it may continue to generate complicated new twists and ironies that would render Taiwan a haven for Japanese traditional foodways that are eventually disappearing in their original homeland.

Notes

For this chapter, I have benefited from various forms of support from the Foundation for Chinese Dietary Culture, Taiwan, and Seoul National University, Korea. From 2008 to 2011, I was a visiting professor at the National Taiwan University, National Tsing Hua University, and National Chao-tung University in Taiwan supported by the National Science Council that funded this research. I am most indebted in receiving research assistance from Chen Chung-min, Chen Hsiang-shui, Chang Yu-hsin, Han Pu-yin, Huang Yu-han, Li Yih-yuan, Lin Shu-jung, Tsai Ying-chun, Wu Yen-ming, Guo Pei-yi, and Midori Hino.

1. In Taiwan, whether in the cities, rural townships, or villages, the low-cuisine outlets remain the most popular for daily consumption of food outside of the homes. They originated from rural peasant markets or temple faires. Hundreds of thousands of the mobile or semi-permanent "little-eats vendors" (*xiaochitanfan*) in the past were housed in illegal

squatter shelters or illegally stationed stalls that occupied the sidewalks outside of condominiums or commercial buildings or sometimes set against the outer walls of residential compounds or schools. Many are now "hole-in-the-wall" family restaurants.

2. Anthropologist Guo Pei-yi reminds me of President Chen's "*Guo-yen*" (national banquet) that initiated the national discourse of *xiaochi* (little eats) in terms of Taiwanese national identity. I recall the media reports at that time on how the chef in charge of the banquet claimed to have attempted 250 times to cook an old desert recipe before he could create (or reproduce) the perfect texture and flavor of the desert dish *wa-gui* (cake in a bowl). The dish was a popular rural Taiwanese street food, sold by peddling vendors for NT$0.10 a bowl when I was a child. My grandmother would occasionally make it at home, to be served either sweet or salty.

3. I am grateful to Professor Naomichi Ishige for speaking to me about colonial Taiwanese black tea and sugar. He further commented that the postwar-era (reverse) nostalgia food for Japanese expatriates from Taiwan was *bihong* (rice noodles), which is now known in Mandarin as *mifen*.

4. When I was conducting ethnological field research in a coastal village of an aboriginal tribe in northeastern Taiwan in the late 1950s, the Japanese-speaking mayor (like most of the Japanese-speaking villagers of aborigines at that time) regularly tuned his home radio to listen to Japanese (actually Okinawan) radio stations. One of the reasons for tuning in to Japanese stations rather than the major Chinese stations in Taipei was the fact that the Central Mountain Range blocked radio waves from Taipei and thus caused poor reception in many pockets of the east coast. He usually tuned the radio to a high volume so it could be enjoyed by all his neighbors. One day the mayor accidentally tuned to Beijing Central Radio Station, which was even clearer than the Japanese station. He was not aware of what he was listening to, as his Mandarin was poor in any event. When I pointed out what he was listening to, he panicked, turned off the radio, and apologized profusely for unintentionally listening to "the bandit's" radio broadcast. I found it all very amusing, but if someone had reported him to the authorities, he may have been arrested.

5. I visited Taichung city, where I grew up, for the first time in over ten years in 2008 and I could not believe the enormous expansion of the city, with modernized roads, highways, and high-rise buildings. What surprised me more was an encounter with a commercial promotional street show in front of the *Chengpin* (Elite flagship) bookstore. All the young singers and dancers on stage were dressed in the ultramodern fashion of Japanese *manga* characters, as if they had just come from the Sunday youth gatherings of Harajuku Ward of Tokyo, Japan. The young performers sang and danced on stage surrounded by a large crowd of young audience who sang along or shouted excitedly.

During my visits to Taichung I frequently used taxi cabs as my mode of transportation. I was shocked on one taxi ride when I encountered a middle-aged Taiwanese male driver and learned how cultural Japan still was alive today among the (elderly) working-class Taiwanese. When I recognized the songs from a tape he was listening to as belonging to that of the Japanese postwar popular singer Misora Hibari (sort of a Judy Garland of Japan in the 1950s), he began to converse with me in a combination of Taiwanese and Japanese. He proudly proclaimed to me, "a fellow country man," that only "we [fellow] Taiwanese" got "*kurasu*" (class, he said with Japanese pronunciation), so "we" can enjoy the "classy" music such as Hibari's and (other) "*jatsu*" (jazz music; again he said this in a Japanese manner). He also emphasized in Taiwanese that "we" do not enjoy the "Chinese stuff" (he used the term *Dionggoklang'e,* that referred to the popular ethnic mainland Chinese music in Taiwan).

6. By early 2012, only three years after its opening, I found that the entire three-story "Japanese" food court near the National Taiwan University had been closed, with all the restaurants going out of business.

7. In Hawaii one can buy Japanese confectioneries (*senbei, yokon, annban, omochi,* and varieties of Japanese traditional candies) at the supermarkets or Japanese *depado,* such as the Shirokiya. These Japanese sweets and candies always bring back my childhood memories of Taiwan. They also demonstrate how the Taiwanese could be more Japanized then the descendants of the Japanese immigrants in Hawaii. The small print on candy wrappers reveals that many "traditional Japanese sweets" sold in Hawaii are actually manufactured in Taiwan by companies such as the I-Mei. This means that Taiwan has been helping to globalize Japanese food by means of transnational trade. Also, the Bunmeido of Honolulu, specializing in Castella cake and omochi for fifty years, closed down in 2008. In the United States, Chinese restaurants in Hawaii also helped to popularize Japanese food (Wu 2008). In many Taiwanese-operated Japanese restaurants in the United States, some owners or chefs may personify a Japanese identity behind the sushi counters, as Bester (2005) reports.

8. I appreciate Hino Midori's comment regarding different terms used in two major urban areas of Japan to refer to the same *oden* food items. While the Osaka/Kyoto-area (Kansai) residents refer to *oden* as *Kantoni* (meaning, the *oden* food of Tokyo area), the Tokyo people themselves would not use such a term for *oden.* Also, the term *tempura* (inside the *oden* pot), actually a fried fish cake (*tien-bu-la* in Mandarin phonetic translation in Taiwan), is popular only in western Japan, such as in Kyushu. Tokyo people would not refer to the fish cake as tempura. This probably indicates that most of the chain convenience stores and food items served in Taiwan were introduced by Japanese corporations of the Kansai area, where there is a large population of Chinese descendants that originally came from Taiwan.

9. Lin (2009: 16–17) discusses the case of the participation of Taiwanese "train *bendo*" in 2003 at an "*ekiben* [train station bento] fair" of the Tokyo Keiyo Departmental Store (I speculate that it could be at the Shinjuku branch store). The Taiwan *tielu biandang* (railway bento) sold out in fifteen minutes upon the store's opening. Lin attributes this to Japanese customers who exemplified postmodern, global cultural schizophrenic identity. Because the Japanese train bento from Taiwan supposedly satisfies the nostalgia for colonial cultural Japan in Taiwan. Lin's source was a Chinese newspaper article (in Lianhebao, the *United Daily*) published in Taipei. Obvious errors can be found with careful examination of the newspaper photos of the "nostalgic Taiwanese colonial Japanese railway *bendo.*" While the Taiwan *bendo* on sale at the Tokyo fair were supposedly reproduced *ekiben* of the Japanese colonial-period Taiwanese train station, the photo in the sensationalized article actually shows a reproduced round metal rice box of the mainland Chinese–style *fanhe* sold after the late 1950s onboard the Guanguanghao express train. The Chinese-style "metal boxed lunch" was the same type I have mentioned in this chapter that was served (under the KMT regime) to the first-class train passengers, many of them elite Nationalist Chinese. Therefore, interestingly enough, the reportedly sold-out lunch boxes at the Japanese store in Tokyo were not at all reproductions of Japanese colonial or postcolonial

ekiben remembered by the Japanese, or imagined by elderly ethnic Taiwanese or the "Japanese-speaking-generation" Taiwanese.

References

Adrian, Bonnie. 2003. *Framing the Bride: Globalizing Beauty and Romance in Taiwan's Bridal Industry.* Berkeley: University of California Press.

Appadurai, Arjun. 1996. *Modernity at Large: Cultural Dimensions of Globalization.* Minneapolis: University of Minnesota Press.

Bester, Theodore C. 2005. "How Sushi Went Global." In *The Cultural Politics of Food and Eating,* edited by James L. Watson and Melissa L. Caldwell, 13–20. Malden: Blackwell.

Bourdieu, Pierre. 1984. *Distinction: A Social Critique of the Judgment of Taste.* Cambridge, MA: Harvard University Press.

Caldwell, Melissa L. 2001. "The Taste of Nationalism: Food Politics in Postsocialist Moscow." *Ethnos* 67(3): 295–319.

Chen, Chien-yuan. 2003. "The cultural implications of curry in Taiwan and Japan: Its localization and globalization." Unpublished MA thesis, National Taiwan University.

Chen, Fang-yi. 2009. "Any Chance to Success in Organic Farming? The Adaptive Changes of Black Tea Production in Yuchih" (in Chinese). Unpublished MA thesis, National Tsing Hua University.

Chen, Yu-jen. 2008. "Nation, Class and Cultural Presentation: 'Taiwanese Cuisine' during Japanese Colonial Era and Early Post-war Taiwan" (in Chinese). *Taiwan Historical Research* 15(3): 139–186.

———. 2010. "Bodily memory and sensibility: Culinary preferences and national consciousness in the case of 'Taiwanese Cuisine.'" *Taiwan Journal of Anthropology* 8(3): 163–196.

Chuang, Ya-chung. 2010. "You meng zue mei: Zuqun rentong yu chengren zhengzhi" (It is most beautiful to have dreams: Ethnic identity and Cognizant of Politics). *Taiwan Journal of Anthropology* 8(2): 3–35.

Hsiao, Michael H. H., and Lim Khay-thiong. 2011. "The history and politics of Malaysian and Taiwanese 'National Cuisine.'" In *Overseas March: How the Chinese Cuisine Spread?* edited by David Y. H. Wu, 297–334. Taipei: Foundation of Chinese Dietary Culture.

Hsu, Ching-wen. 2009. "Authentic tofu: Cosmopolitan Taiwan." *Taiwan Journal of Anthropology* 7(1): 3–34.

Huang, Lan-shiang. 2009. "The architectural historians in Taiwan under Japanese colonial occupation." *Taiwan Wenxian* (Taiwan Gazettes) 62(2): 276–305.

Igarashi, Masako. 2012. "Japan in the language of the Japanese Speaking generation (in Taiwan)." In *Concerning the "Colonial" Experience of Taiwan: The Emergency of Recognition of, Change, and Break Away from Japan,* edited by Ueno and Yuko Mio, 185–214. Tokyo: Fukyosha.

Huang, C. Julia. 2009. *Charisma and Compassion: Cheng Yen and the Buddhist Tzu Chi Movement.* Cambridge, MA: Harvard University Press.

Jameson, Fredric. 1991. *Postmodernism, or the Cultural Logic of Late Capitalism.* Durham, NC: Duke University Press.

Lee, Anru. 2009. *Subway as a Space of Cultural Intimacy: Mass Transit System in Taipei. China Journal* 58: 31–35.

Lee, Ming-Tsung. 2003. "Zheli xiangxiang, nali shijian" (Imagine Here/Practice There: The Japanese TV Drama Tour and the Cross-Cultural Identities of Taiwanese Youths), Meijie Niexiang (Journal of Media Imagination) 2: 42–73.

Lin, Hsuta. 2010. "Houzhimin Taiwan de huaijou xiangxiang yu wenhua bianxi" (The Nostalgic Imagination and Cultural Manipulation in Postcolonial Taiwan). *Sixiang* (Thoughts) 14: 111–137.

Shoji, Kaoji. 2009. "Bread as fashion, Tokyo-style." *The New York Times.* http://www.nytimes.com/2009/11/fashion.

Shu, Guo-zhi. 2007. *Taipei Xiaochi Zhaji* (Notes on Taipei's Little Eats). Taipei: Crown Press.

Tanaka, Chizuru. 2006. "Talking about the phrase of 'Colonial Taiwan.'" *Reading and Decoding Legends about Hatta Yoichi.* Tokyo: Fukyosha.

Ueno, Hiroko. 2009. "Routine Life of Taiwan and Japanese Education: From Students' Families of a Girl's High School." In *Concerning the "Colonial" Experience of Taiwan: The Emergency of Recognition of Change, and Break Away from Japan,* edited by Hiroko Ueno and Yoko Mie, 141–184. Tokyo: Fukyosha.

Wang, Hong-zen, and Pei-yi Guo, eds. 2009. *Liuzhuan Kuajei: Kuaguo de Taiwan, Taiwan de Kuaguo* (To Cross or Not to Cross: Transnational Taiwan, Taiwan's Transnationality). Taipei: Center for Asian Pacific Area Studies, Academia Sinica.

Watson, James L. 2005. "Introduction." In *Golden Arches East,* edited by James L. Watson, 1–25. Stanford: Stanford University Press.

Wilk, Richard. 1999. "Real Brazilian food." *American Anthropologist* 2: 244–256.

Wu, David Y.H. 1998. "Invention of Taiwanese: A Second Look at Taiwan's Cultural Policy and National Identity." In *From Beijing to Port Moresby: The Politics of National Identity in Cultural Policy,* edited by Virginia R. Domingues and David Y. H. Wu, 115–132. New York, London, and Australia: Gordon and Breach Publishers.

———. 2002. "Cantonese cuisine in Taipei and Taiwanese Cuisine in Hong Kong." In *The Globalization of Chinese Food,* edited by David Y. H. Wu and Sidney C. H. Cheung, 86–99. Hong Kong: Chinese University of Hong Kong Press.

———. 2006. "McDonald's in Taipei: Hamburgers, Betel Nuts, and National Identity." In *Golden Arches East,* edited by James L. Watson, 110–135. Stanford: Stanford University Press.

———. 2008. "All you can eat buffet: The evolution of Chinese Cuisine in Hawaii." *Journal of Chinese Dietary Culture* 4(1): 1–24.

———. 2011. "Introduction." In *Overseas March: How the Chinese Cuisine Spread?* edited by David Y. H. Wu, 1–10. Taipei: Foundation of Chinese Dietary Culture.

Yasuda, Toshiaki. 2010. *Karera no Nihongo: Taiwan "Zanryu" Nihongo Ron* (Their Japanese Language: On the "Residual" Japanese in Taiwan). Kyoto: Jinbun Shoin Press.

CHAPTER 7

The Visible and the Invisible

Intimate Engagements with Russia's Culinary East

Melissa L. Caldwell

Accounts of the dramatic culinary and cultural transformations taking place across the formerly Soviet world over the past twenty years have consistently emphasized the influence of global trends and flows originating in the West. From the arrival of McDonald's inside "the Iron Curtain," first in Yugoslavia in the late 1980s and subsequently in the Soviet Union itself in 1990, to the more recent arrival of avant-garde international cooking trends such as dining in the dark, molecular gastronomy, and the creative experimentation promoted by Spain's *El Bulli* restaurant (Shectman 2009), post-Soviet culinary traditions have undergone profound changes inspired by Western trends and methods. Coinciding with these profound changes in culinary styles and cooking techniques has been a dramatic expansion in the variety of foods that are available for purchase in supermarkets and restaurants. Not only have the recurring food shortages of the Soviet era disappeared with the consistency and diversity of goods for sale in the supermarkets and hypermarkets that now dot the landscape of both urban and rural areas, but the diversity of available dishes and ingredients has expanded beyond the cultures of the formerly Soviet world to represent a more culinary internationalism: Italian, French, Irish, Scandinavian, Mexican, Indian, Thai, Tibetan, Middle Eastern, Australian, Brazilian, and South African, to name just a few.

These changes did not happen all at once, but rather occurred in two distinct waves. The first, initial wave occurred during the 1990s with the "importation" of Western food products, cuisines, and restaurants that accompanied the larger dynamics of Western economic redevelopment in the former Soviet Union (Lankauskas 2002; Patico 2001), followed by a second wave in the late 1990s marked by the expansion of post-Soviet ethnic cuisine and experimentation with Asian foods and restaurants: Chinese, Thai, Tibetan, Mongolian, and, most notably, Japanese restaurants (Caldwell 2006). The proliferation of restaurants serving sushi, stir-fried rice dishes, and noodle soups flavored with miso, bean sprouts, and seaweed across Russia's urban and rural landscapes alike is matched only by the proliferation of domestic restaurant chains offering Japanese, Chinese, and other Asian dishes.

Both geographically and politically, Russia's position at the nexus of Western and Eastern global flows has long made it a node within global circulations of cultural trends and culture brokers. These flows have cultivated within Russia a vibrant cultural diversity, despite representations that have emphasized nationalist orientations and cultural homogeneity as markers of Russian culture (Humphrey 1995; Khazanov 1997). The multiple transecting global flows that converge on and through Russia highlight the difficulties of locating Russia within geopolitical classifications that divide the world into West and East (Caldwell 2011; Creed and Wedel 1997; Escobar 1995).[1] Despite Russia's location in the midst of global currents, accounts of the impact of globalization on Russian culture have typically prioritized Western trends and Russians' alternately antagonistic and welcoming attitudes toward them (Crowley 2000; Kelly 1998). By highlighting a very particular set of cultural dynamics between Russia and its West, these accounts have effectively positioned Russia as the de facto "East" in these relations of globalization.

Far less attention has been given to Russia's relationships with its own cultural East. Within Russia's culinary culture, the arrival of Western food cultures has been accompanied, and in some cases preceded, by the arrival of Eastern food cultures. Korean and Chinese immigrants who had come to Russia by the second half of the nineteenth century (Um 2000: 123–125; Kho 1987) brought with them their own cultural practices, including recipes and food preparation techniques. These immigration patterns have continued into the post-Soviet period, as Korean and Chinese arrivals have more recently been accompanied by migrants from Japan, Vietnam, India, and the Philippines, among other countries, who have similarly brought their own culinary traditions. Yet the "Easternization" of Russian food cultures has been received relatively quietly. Unlike the global media frenzy surrounding the opening of the first McDonald's in Russia in 1990 and the opening of the first Starbucks almost twenty years later in 2008 (Caldwell 2004; 2009), the opening of the first international coffeehouse in Moscow in the early 1990s by the Japanese chain Doutor scarcely attracted any attention beyond the small group of North American and European expatriates living in Moscow who craved a cup of brewed coffee and a quiet place to sit and read.[2] Similarly, Moscow's vibrant community of Korean restaurants was known primarily by word of mouth among residents who knew where to find it near a major market on the edge of the city. Hence while the Westernization of Russia's cuisine has been highly visible both in public awareness and public spaces, Russia's experiences with culinary Easternization have been far less apparent until relatively recently.

The presence of "Eastern" culinary trends in Russia presents an instructive alternative to the persistent privileging of the West in accounts of Russia's cultural transformations. Russian consumers have received Eastern culinary traditions in different ways, revealing intriguing degrees of sociopolitical visibility and acceptance of "Easternness" in Russian daily life. This visibility, in turn, shares some puzzling similarities with recent public and popular attitudes toward the countries of Korea, China, and Japan and their peoples. Attention to Eastern food cultures in Russia thus offers a lens for considering the growing importance of economic and cultural relations between Russia and its Asian partners and, ultimately, broader cultural attitudes about Russia's stakes and position within global flows of capital and immigration between West and East. Tropes of space and visibility are critical for exploring these issues, as spatial presence and absence—both actual and imaginary—reveal how distinctions between local and global are constituted, as well as how and when particular local and global forces are alternately made visible or invisible. In the particular case of food, the placement and circulation of dishes, ingredients, and culinary styles through spatial registers creates both geographies of edibility or palatability (Kirshenblatt-Gimblett 2004: xiii) and geographies of inedibility.

In the discussion that follows, I explore the spatial arrangements of Easternization in Russia through comparison of Chinese, Korean, and Japanese cuisines. This analysis will illuminate what Easternizing processes of globalization reveal about cultural orientations toward Russia's relationship with its Eastern neighbors, as well as about the dynamics of globalization itself and the geopolitical work that globalization performs. I first provide a brief overview of how Russia's culinary cultures have been embedded in particular forms and flows of globalization, before discussing these three different trajectories of Korean, Chinese, and Japanese culinary traditions. This analysis is based on long-term ethnographic fieldwork in Russia since the mid-1990s, as I have tracked the impact of global food trends on domestic food practices and cultural values.

Tasting Culture: Culinary Zones of the Public, the Peripheral, and the Popular

Russians' culinary sensibilities are oriented both to the spatial location of foods and food consumption areas and to the gustatory, olfactory, and visual sensations evoked by these foods (Caldwell 2006)—what one anonymous Russian food writer has described as a "geogastronomic" sensibility that captures how topographical arrangements of food are informed by the visceral experiences they evoke (Anonymous 1998: 8). The relationship between space and sense is a reciprocal one, so that at the same time that the emplacement of foods evokes particular bodily sensations, the sensory qualities of foods also evoke particular locales, both actual and imagined, thereby imbuing Russians' food practices with qualities of mobility (Caldwell 2006).

Attention to the simultaneous emplacement and mobility inherent in Russian food practices is significant for understanding how reconfigurations of Russian cuisine in the post-Soviet period are tied both to shifts to an international, cosmopolitan culinary lifestyle and to the continuation and preservation of distinctive regional identities across the formerly Soviet landscape. At the same time that some anthropologists have reported that post-Soviet citizens have described their embrace of foreign cuisines and food products as the desire to signal their departure from a "backward" Soviet lifestyle and their movement to a more "modern," even "normal" lifestyle (Fehérváry 2002; Lankauskas 2002; Jung 2006; Rausing 2002), other anthropologists have documented how post-Soviet consumers have appropriated foreign food trends as means for celebrating indigenous culinary traditions and elevating them to the international level as legitimate participants in global *haute cuisine* trends. For instance, Stas Shectman (2009) has documented how Russian chefs and cooking schools draw on the standards and institutions of international cooking competitions and media to elevate Russian cuisine to the level of an international cuisine and to make it internationally visible. Still other anthropologists have reported that foreign cuisines have provoked a domestic backlash in which post-Soviet consumers demonstrate their patriotic and nostalgic sentiments through a return to Soviet-era "traditional" foods (Klumbytė 2009).

Such accounts foreground globalization as the primary context and mechanism through which post-Soviet consumers first access foreign food cultures, then make sense of these new trends, and ultimately attempt to articulate a compelling narrative of authentic local cultures that successfully accommodates these new, foreign trends, even if by rejecting them. Acknowledging the spatial dimensions of globalization that are inherent in Russians' food practices elucidates the economic, political, and cultural structures that facilitate encounters with foreign cultural trends and reveals the shifting parameters of distinctions between local and foreign. In turn, this attention to the fluid dynamics informing local/foreign juxtapositions creates opportunities for probing why consumers choose to engage with the foreign cuisines that they do and how they experience these encounters.

Culinary tourism is an instructive lens for examining these fine-grained cultural dynamics of engagement and mobility. As a form of globalization, culinary tourism offers consumers possibilities for traversing physical, virtual, and even imaginary global boundaries. As Lucy Long argues, "culinary tourism is more than trying new and exotic foods" but rather entails "a perception of otherness, of something being different from the usual" (2004b: 1). Culinary tourism is also a deliberately participatory experience that arises when consumers perceive the "otherness of the foodways" and then that "[perception of] otherness elicits curiosity" (Long 2004a: 21). For Long, the dynamics of perception that characterize consumers' roles in these encounters are neither passive nor unreflexive, but are instead active and intentional; and it is this active intentionality that shifts foods to the category of the Other (2004a: 22). Hence as foods are made Other, or foreign, through practices of awareness and categorization, discrete classifications of "local" or "indigenous" versus "non-local" or "foreign" become problematic. In a statement that echoes Arjun Appadurai's critique (1986) of "authentic" local foods in which he notes that "authenticity" is less a marker of an absolute quality than it is a normative discourse, Barbara Kirschenblatt-Gimblett observes that it is "not authenticity, but the *question* of authenticity, [that] is essential to culinary tourism, for this question organizes conversation, reflection, and comparison and arises as much from doubt as from confidence" (2004: xii).

Underlying these perceptions and experiences of Otherness are cultural values of comfort and familiarity. Exploration can be dangerous, as both categories of local and Other may become confused and as participants move outside familiar zones of aesthetic and sensory propriety. While "culinary tourism creates opportunities to find, test, and push the threshold of the unfamiliar" (Kirschenblatt-Gimblett 2004: xii), it also anchors culinary tourists in a clear sense of "home" or "local" that allows them to imagine and experience cultural difference from a position of both safety and critical evaluation (Molz 2004; cf. Caldwell 2006). Yet as food scholars have observed, identifying what constitutes "home" and "familiar" as distinct from "Other" and "exotic" through aesthetic or sensory perceptions of taste preferences can be difficult, precisely because larger cultural dynamics of familiarization and domestication can familiarize the formerly exotic (Long 2004a: 32–37; Mankekar 2002; Turgeon and Pastinelli 2002), thus emphasizing that "the local" is never a static state but rather a process of continuous adjustment (Appadurai 1996). Considering the intersection of taste and space evoked in culinary tourism offers possibilities for identifying where and when societies not only recognize and delineate the local from the foreign, and the familiar from the unfamiliar, but also assign normative values of desirability and undesirability. Consequently, practices of alternately making invisible or making visible are intrinsically normative processes of demarcating the ordinary from the out-of-the-ordinary (Rosaldo 1993).

Russians' practices of making Korean, Chinese, and Japanese cultural trends alternately invisible and visible also show that this dynamic is not a linear one between states but rather a more complicated process in which invisibility may in some moments be associated with familiarity and ordinariness and in other moments be associated with disdain, and where visibility can alternately be associated with desirable exoticness or with excessive ordinariness. Eastern cultural trends are largely invisible when they are ordinary and have been fully integrated as normal components of Russian daily life, as is the case for Korean foods. But Eastern cultural trends and brokers are also being made invisible and shifted to the peripheries of Russian daily life as a way to demarcate their Otherness and undesirability, as is the case with Chinese foods. In still other cases, Eastern cultural trends are deliberately made visible, both to highlight their Otherness and to capitalize on their popularity to bring other more-ordinary food cultures, including traditional Russian foods, to the fore, as is the case for Japanese food trends. As these differences show, states of visibility must be understood in terms of their placement in public, private, or on the periphery. In the following sections, I will address these issues by examining two extremes of Russians' attitudes toward Eastern cultural trends, where Korean cultural trends have been most readily made familiar and Chinese trends have been most distanced as exotic, and then analyze how Japanese trends are changing the dynamics of exoticness, familiarity, and desirability.

Tasting the Self versus Tasting the Other: Degrees of Culinary Intimacy and Distance

In the spectrum of invisible versus visible as markers of familiarity or exoticness, the invisibility of Korean culinary trends reveals the extent to which they have been integrated and normalized in Russian food practices and have thus become part of a collectively held public heritage. Korean food trends are identified most readily by a tremendous diversity of pickled salads, and virtually every food market and grocery store offers a selection of Korean salads made from carrots, cabbage, mushrooms, tofu, seaweed, and noodles. Most salads come in both "spicy" and "not-spicy" options to appeal to Russian taste sensibilities, with "spicy" being a relative quality. The salads are prepared by Korean-Russians who work in several processing centers in large cities and then distributed to salad stands operated by Korean-Russian vendors. In large supermarkets, Korean salads are generally dispensed from a common "salad section," where they are typically arranged alongside Russian-style salads with little to distinguish them from one another. When buying prepared salads, Russian consumers might mix up their selections, so that they purchase spicy carrots and kimchee along with salads made from smoked herrings and sour cream, and from beets and olive oil or mayonnaise. In other words, Korean salads occupy the same spaces as Russian salads, both in terms of their physical placement in shops and in their place on the table. Korean salads are, in many ways, integrated with more traditional "Russian" foods, and consumers describe them as "Korean" merely to designate a style of preparation rather than a particular cultural system.

Korean foods sold outside markets and grocery stores are typically available in intimate, largely informal commercial spaces that are known only by word of mouth among customers. Over the past fifteen years, my attempts to locate a formal Korean restaurant in Moscow have failed, and informants who are otherwise knowledgeable about restaurants have admitted that they, too, have never encountered a formal Korean restaurant. Korean meals are offered primarily in small, intimate cafeterias tucked away in neighborhoods where Korean-Russians live and work. With their simple menus, minimal furnishings, and word-of-mouth advertising, they resemble the small cafeterias and restaurants that offer basic Russian menus for neighborhood residents. Until recently, with the emergence and spread of several chain restaurants offering a stereotypical selection of Russian dishes, Russian food was most available in small cafes and pubs located in small, discretely marked sites, often outside highly commercial districts.

Such examples suggest that it is perhaps not appropriate to classify Korean foods as entirely separate from Russian foods. While the styles and flavors of Korean foods are recognizably different from traditional "Russian" foods, they are not viewed as anything exceptional or obviously different. In fact, Korean foods have quietly become "domesticated" (Caldwell 2004) over the past several decades, such that they are an unremarkable, ordinary, and even expected part of everyday Russian food habits. In the late 1990s, long before Asian vegetables and soy products were available in Russia's supermarkets or restaurant culture and during a period of heightened nationalism when foreign foods were under attack by culinary patriots, I attended a worship service at a Korean-Russian church and observed elderly ethnic Russians eagerly taking sacks filled with bean sprouts and tofu from their Korean-Russian friends. Within a cultural context in which the older generation, and particularly elderly women, occupy a social position of cultural superiority from which they can judge norms of social, cultural, and moral propriety, the fact that elderly ethnic Russians were eagerly divvying up bean sprouts and chunks of raw tofu for themselves is a remarkable testament to the very ordinariness of these foods.

In addition to the familiarization of Korean food in Russian daily practice, Korean-made food appliances offer another example of the extent to which Korean food styles have been brought directly into the most intimate spaces and ordinary activities of people's lives. Unlike the futuristic, highly computerized technologies associated with Japanese food appliances (such as vending machines that can prepare hot and cold foods, talk, or communicate with consumers via computer chips embedded in cell phones or wristbands), the Korean appliances available in Russia are more ordinary domestic appliances that enhance the efficiency and quality of home food preparation: for instance, microwaves, juicers, mixers, blenders, and coffee makers. These are not appliances that are new or exotic for Russians, but are the sorts of ordinary items that Russians might already have at home, although Korean-made appliances are believed to be of better quality than Russian-made appliances.

While price may put particular Korean-made goods out of reach of many Russian consumers, the appliances themselves are perceived as familiar, ordinary, and part of a "normal" middle-class lifestyle (Patico 2008). The normalcy of these appliances in domestic life became apparent when I attended church with an elderly Russian friend in Moscow.³ The minister of the church and the majority of the congregation are Korean-Russian, a detail that my friend, an ethnic Russian, dismissed as insignificant.

By way of invitation to the church service, my friend had related that her favorite part of the church service was the fellowship hour, when congregants gathered to drink coffee and visit with one another. The highlight of this time was the special coffee machine that the church had installed. The machine was a simple automated coffee machine that dispensed instant coffee, instant espresso, and instant cappuccino for a small fee. A pensioner on a very small, fixed income, my friend carefully planned for her coffee time by making sure that she had several of the necessary coins to insert in the machine, and she proudly told me that she could finally treat me to proper coffee, rather than the instant coffee she made when I visited her at home.

As my acquaintance repeatedly expressed her delight with the coffee maker, it became apparent that she did not find the mode of preparation particularly innovative or unusual. In fact, she compared the machine to Soviet-era beverage dispensers but suggested that this new machine was better because it dispensed servings of coffee into individual cups rather than the Soviet machines that dispensed drinks a serving at a time into a common glass shared by everyone. Even though my acquaintance laughingly told me that she could not read the instructions printed in Korean, it was clear from the way her fingers flew over the various buttons and dials that she had familiarized herself with the system and was comfortable using the machine and making the appropriate adjustments to ensure that her coffee arrived in just the manner she intended. Drinking coffee from the automated machine was obviously a pleasure that was made only more special because her limited pension would never enable her to purchase an electric coffee maker of any sort for herself.

The extent of this domestication is further evident in global Russian food cultures, particularly Russian grocery stores such as the ones that exist in Northern California. Like the Indian grocery stores in Silicon Valley that Purnima Mankekar has described (2002), these small Russian shops offer a wide selection of both imported and domestically produced Russian and East European foods, beverages, medicines, and other household items. For homesick Russian and East European émigrés, these products offer the familiar and comforting tastes and smells of home. Nestled in the refrigerated cases alongside fresh Russian-style yogurts, butter, and cheese, are the Korean salads: spicy julienned carrots, spicy marinated diced tofu, and marinated mushrooms. On a recent visit to one of the local Russian grocery stores in my city, I spied the carrot salads just as I was about to pay for my purchases. I quickly extricated a container of carrot salad from the refrigerator and placed it on the counter with the rest of my purchases. The Russian saleswoman asked me if I knew what the salad was, as if she suspected that I, as a non-Russian, might not have sufficient knowledge about Russia to know which food products to select. When I replied "*Koreiskii salat*," she smiled and nodded approvingly, as if to acknowledge that I had passed some kind of test of knowledge about authentic Russian food. After that exchange, we spoke to one another in Russian and she helped me find the other *authentically* Russian food items I was looking for but were not readily apparent on the store shelves, rather than urging me to buy the Americanized versions of those products.

Korean foods are thus imbued with qualities of "normalcy" in Russia. They are found in ordinary places where ordinary people go: neighborhood grocery stores, markets, cafeterias, churches, and private homes. It is this ordinariness that makes Korean foods familiar and comfortable. Among Russians who do not like Korean foods, the most common explanation is that they do not like spicy foods, not that they dislike the cuisine itself. From this perspective of familiarity and desirability, these foods are invisible both because they are so ordinary and taken for granted (Rosaldo 1993) and because they have been so seamlessly incorporated into the most intimate spaces of Russians' daily life: the world of the private and the personal.

Russians' treatment of Chinese culinary cultures presents an intriguing counterpoint to their encounters with Korean culinary trends. When compared to other global ethnic cuisines, Chinese foods are relatively uncommon in Russia. Although there are several Chinese restaurants in big cities like Moscow or St. Petersburg, these restaurants are primarily located in close proximity to major tourist centers and hotels, and are oriented primarily to foreigners, especially Chinese tourists, rather than to local residents. For instance, one Chinese restaurant in St. Petersburg was recognizable by the large buses filled with Chinese tourists parked outside. Non-Chinese guests were rare during my visits over several years, a detail that was confirmed by a waitress who expressed surprise whenever my non-Asian friends and I visited and demonstrated our familiarity with the dishes available on the menu. During a summer that I lived in Tver, a medium-sized city between Moscow and St. Petersburg, I visited the city's one Chinese restaurant once or twice a week and rarely encountered any other customers.[4]

Spices and ingredients used in Chinese cooking are also comparatively difficult to find in ordinary grocery stores, unlike ingredients for Thai and Japanese dishes. Where spices and ingredients for Chinese dishes are available, they are most likely to be found in the specialty supermarkets that serve foreign diplomats and businesspeople living in Russia. Even in regions of Moscow where large numbers of Chinese citizens live, Chinese food is surprisingly absent. During summer 2009, when I rented an apartment in a building located adjacent to the Chinese embassy and residential compound (and near Moscow State University, the largest and most international university in Russia), I expected that the proximity would yield opportunities for enjoying Chinese dishes. Intriguingly, my search for a Chinese restaurant or shop selling Chinese food or ingredients in the larger region was in vain. Not only were there no Chinese restaurants in the area, but none of the many grocery stores and hypermarkets in the larger neighborhood region carried any food products that would be appropriate for Chinese cuisine.[5] The only visible marker of the presence of Chinese traditions in the area was a faded sign for Chinese take-away food that hung over a barricaded walk-up window to a former sidewalk shop. Judging from the rust on the sign and the locks, the shop had clearly been closed for a while.

When Chinese food does appear visibly in Russian shops and markets, it is in the form of foods and other goods that have been processed and packaged in China: for instance, frozen seafood, canned vegetables, hygiene products, and cleaning supplies. Because of concerns over tainted foods from China, however, Russian consumers are hesitant to buy these items. Most commonly, Chinese cuisine is reduced to simple dishes that are sold from small commercial take-away food kiosks located along city sidewalks and inside the food courts of shopping malls. The incredible diversity of Chinese cuisine is reduced to a few simple selections of rather bland-tasting dumplings and rice and noodle dishes. None of the food is freshly prepared. Instead, the food is prepackaged into paper or Styrofoam boxes that an employee removes from a freezer and then pops into a microwave. Consequently, the food that is sold at these kiosks represents not Chinese cuisine but industrial efficiency.

These stands are not typically located in prime pedestrian spaces where kiosks selling Russian and other foreign foods are located, but are instead set aside in less heavily trafficked areas along the edges of neighborhoods and food courts. Rarely are there customers, much less lines, at these stands, unlike at other fast food trucks. In one revealing example from a densely occupied neighborhood located just outside central Moscow and alongside a busy market, the sidewalk leading from the metro station to the market was completely full with kiosks, small food shops, and restaurants offering an incredible diversity of cuisines: American-style sandwiches, sushi, shwarma, pizza, soups, salads, fresh pastries, and Russian dishes. The food shops were aligned evenly next to one another, so that their entrances and window fronts were each at the same position on the sidewalk, presenting an unbroken line down the sidewalk. The one noticeable exception to this spatial positioning was that of a small kiosk selling warmed-up Chinese dumplings and noodles. The kiosk was positioned at the very end of the line of food shops at a distance from its neighbor and behind an automated kiosk that accepted payment for cell phone services and other utilities (see figure 7.1). Even though I walked past this stand several times every day for months, I rarely noticed any activity. By spring 2010, the stand had been replaced by a kiosk selling sandwiches.

Such techniques of spatial distancing and concealment signal the lower position that Chinese foods occupy on Russia's culinary and cultural hierarchy. The physical emplacement of Chinese food at the peripheries of Russian society and culture reveals its subordinate position on the culinary hierarchy of creativity and desirability. From the perspective of Russian informants, the relative invisibility

Figure 7.1. This Chinese food truck is tucked away along the sidewalk alongside other, more established and more heavily frequented food stands. The most activity I have ever witnessed at this stand occurred at the blue computer terminal where residents make payments for their cell phone and internet service.

of Chinese cuisine is correlated not with its familiarity but rather with its exoticness and even dangerousness. For consumers who question the safety of Chinese foods, spatial distancing becomes a marker of Otherness and lack of desirability.

If Chinese and Korean foods are relatively invisible in Russia, albeit for very different reasons, Japanese foods are far more publicly visible, as restaurants serving sushi, tempura, and other Japanese dishes are now ubiquitous throughout both large cities and small towns. Public sidewalks are crowded with male restaurant employees dressed in samurai costumes and acting as living advertisements for their respective employers. Signs advertising "sushi" are ever-present on billboards, window fronts, and the free advertising flyers distributed as promotional materials. So popular are Japanese restaurants that throughout Moscow and St. Petersburg, it is common to find multiple competing chains located next to one another (see figure 7.2).

The popularity of Japanese cuisine is a relatively recent development from the late 1990s, when Japanese cuisine first entered Russia's culinary scene through a few very expensive and very exclusive sushi restaurants. In Moscow several of the very first sushi restaurants were located inside nightclubs that catered to wealthy foreign businessmen and Russian mafia. The gradual introduction of sushi restaurants coincided with the introduction and spread of the other "hot" food trend of that period, the coffeehouse. These two trends did not happen in isolation from one another but were deliberately paired, so that new restaurants offered both coffee and sushi in the same space. Very quickly over the span of just a few years, both sushi and coffee have emerged as the most popular and viable food options in Russia, with scores of chains and thousands of outlets.

While sushi is still the main attraction for Russian consumers, Japanese restaurants have expanded their offerings to include a wide variety of hot and cold noodle dishes, rice dishes, grilled meats, and salads. Pickled ginger, wasabi, udon and soba noodles, and seaweed are now standard fare in both large supermarkets and tiny neighborhood grocery stores, as are the bowls, chopsticks, rolling mats, and other implements needed to prepare and serve Japanese cuisine. Increasingly, grocery stores are offering packages of freshly made sushi. The popularity of this trend has quickly caught on across Russia and beyond, so that Japanese restaurants and foods are appearing well beyond major cities like Moscow and in smaller, provincial towns, far removed from global transit hubs. More significantly, Russia is home to a burgeoning industry of Japanese-themed restaurant chains that originated in Russia and have expanded abroad, such as the popular Yakitoriia chain that was created in Russia in the late 1990s and is now serving customers in other countries of the former Soviet Union.

For Russian diners, sushi and other Japanese foods are appealing precisely because of their cultural difference, most notably their exoticness. Japanese foods, and sushi in particular, have become so desirable that they have displaced French fries, Russia's most popular foreign food trend following the arrival of McDonald's in the early 1990s. Increasingly, sushi and Japanese noodle dishes have emerged as part of the main menus in restaurants and take-away food stands as essential accompaniments to pasta, pizza, and hamburgers.

Yet even if Japanese cuisine is still appealing because of its difference, it is no longer fully Other. Rather, Japanese foods are in the process of becoming domesticated and perhaps even showing signs that they have already become integrated as part of Russia's local culinary and cultural repertoire. Striking evidence for this appears in the prevalent use of sushi not just to promote Russian food but also to guarantee the legitimacy and authenticity of Russian cuisine and restaurants. One noteworthy example of the symbolic power of sushi to anchor Russian cuisine appears in an advertising brochure for the restaurant Matreshka.[6] While the front side of the advertisement features the restaurant's specialty—a smorgasbord—and lists the restaurant's hours of operation, the reverse side of the flyer contains pictures of individual entrées from the menu, with three of the five illustrations occupied by Japanese dishes: seafood sushi rolls, miso soup, and a deep-fried seafood patty. Equally intriguing is that the Russian-owned chain of Japanese restaurants called Yaposha recently expanded its menu options to offer

Russian dumplings, labeling them "antisushi" as a paired opposition to "sushi," as if to signal that it is now possible to use sushi to entice consumers to try Russian foods.

A third intriguing variation appears in the menu options available at the Russian pizza restaurant Nasha Pitstsa, which translates to "Our Pizza." Drawing on the nationalist linguistic cue *Nash* (Our) to signify local, domestic, and familiar cultural trends, this restaurant opened in the late 1990s as an explicitly domestic alternative to foreign pizza restaurants such as Il Patio and Pizza Hut. Not incidentally, Nasha Pitstsa assumed the restaurant space formerly occupied by Pizza Hut after the latter was forced out of Russia in the wake of an economic downturn and heightened nationalist fervor in the late 1990s. The main attraction on Nasha Pitstsa's menu is now sushi, and a separate sushi bar counter was installed adjacent to the counter where pizzas and other fast food items are ordered and prepared. Finally, by summer 2010, even Ëlki-Palki, the quintessential Russian-themed restaurant chain that promotes its authenticity through deliberate deployment of peasant-themed decorations, was offering sushi as part of its menu of traditional Russian dishes.

Perhaps most intriguing of all is the symbolic power of Japanese food to make other foreign cuisines familiar and normal, as is occurring with the inclusion of

Figure 7.2. Further along the same sidewalk as the Chinese food truck depicted in figure 7.1 are two competing Japanese restaurants and a coffeehouse.

sushi on the menus of Italian, Brazilian, and even Central Asian restaurants in Moscow. More significant is the extent to which Japanese food is used to market Chinese cuisine. Chinese restaurants are increasingly starting to offer sushi and Japanese-style noodle dishes. The lunch menu at a Chinese restaurant in suburban Moscow includes two possibilities: "Chinese lunch" and "Japanese lunch," as well as an à la carte menu with sushi. Consequently it appears that in order for Chinese cuisine to move along the path of domestication into Russian culture, it requires translation by other, more familiar and desirable cultural trends, such as by association with Japanese cuisine or even in the case of a Chinese shopping center and restaurant that are anchored by McDonald's. Like McDonald's, because Japanese cuisine is associated with quality, taste, desirability, and trustworthiness, it has become a persuasive conduit for Chinese cuisine to gain respectability and appeal.

Domesticating Foreignness: The Presumed Safety and Dangers of Particular Others

How are we to make sense of these three very different food trends? While it might be tempting to suggest that it is the newness of Japanese foods that has made them so enticing to Russian consumers, this conclusion does not go far enough in explaining how Korean, Chinese, and Japanese foods have met with such very different responses from Russian consumers. A more fruitful lens is potentially offered through consideration of how Russia has treated the brokers of these cultural trends from Russia's East—namely, persons from Korea, China, and Japan. In the current historical moment, Russia is experiencing profound internal debates about how to deal with multiculturalism, including whether and how the state should incorporate foreigners and foreignness. At issue are numerous concerns with determining whether foreignness, as embodied in foreign cultures and foreign peoples, poses a threat or a benefit to the Russian nation and a Russian way of life. Such debates and concerns are playing out both at the national level of state policies and on more personal, individual levels among ordinary Russian citizens. Hence, attention to Russia's relationships with its Eastern neighbors and Russians' attitudes toward individuals from these three countries will perhaps shed light on how some Asian cultural trends have been perceived as more or less desirable and comfortable than others.

For the case of Korean foods, the perspective that Korean foods are domesticated foods—that they are part of Russian cuisine itself—is instantiated in how people from Korea have been integrated within Russian society. As a result of several waves of migration from Korea to the Soviet Union during the twentieth century (Kho 1987; Um 2000), Korean immigrants have become assimilated into Russian society as yet another indigenous minority ethnic population.

Most Koreans living in Russia are Russian citizens, and many are in fact second- and third-generation Russian citizens. Most Korean-Russians have Russian first names and patronymics (i.e., middle names), and there is intermarriage between Korean-Russians, ethnic Russians, and Russian citizens from other ethnic groups. While Korean-Russians are phenotypically visible as members of a distinct ethnic community in Russia, they are nonetheless included as legitimate members of Russia's indigenous Asian populations.

The extent to which Korean-Russians have become integrated in Russian society is evident in the reverse migration patterns of elderly Korean-Russians who have resettled in Korea. As anthropologist Dorota Szawarska (personal communication) has documented in her work with elderly Korean-Russians who have migrated to Korea after retirement, these persons are so Russified that after they have arrived in Korea they complain about the food and not being able to eat in the manner to which they have been accustomed. These Korean-Russian immigrants to Korea then demand Russian grocery stores where they can buy familiar foods, set up Russian-style vegetable gardens so that they can grow and prepare their own Russian foods, and return home to Korea from visits to Russia with suitcases filled with familiar, Russian foods.

In terms of contemporary movements of Korean citizens to Russia, Koreans occupy a very particular position within global economic flows to Russia. Koreans are visible primarily as professionals who move to Russia to work as managers and experts in Korean companies that have established Russian facilities and as professional clergy in Korean-Russian religious congregations. Thus, Koreans who come to Russia are depicted as well educated and unproblematic—in other words, as individuals who are unquestionably "normal," "familiar," and even desirable.

There are similarities with Russia's treatment of Japanese persons. Although there are far fewer Japanese immigrants to Russia, individuals who come to Russia do so primarily as professional businesspeople. In the post-Soviet period Japanese companies have invested heavily in Russian companies, and the Japanese government has been extremely generous in providing humanitarian aid to Russia (Akaha 1997). Consequently, Japanese culture represents both economic and technological advancement, and the cultures of Japan, and by extension Japanese citizens, occupy a more privileged, favored status in Russia.[7]

These favorable attitudes toward Koreans and Japanese are not matched by the treatment afforded Chinese citizens and Chinese products. Attitudes toward Chinese are far less positive, and a growing popular sentiment in Russia depicts China and Chinese citizens as threats to Russia's economy. In this logic, whereas Japan and Korea represent Russia's economic advancement, China is popularly associated with Russia's economic decline. In 2007, Russia celebrated "The Year of China in Russia," which was intended as the beginning of a two-year cultural and economic exchange between the two countries. However, the promise of this partnership and the positive promotion of China deteriorated following the preliminary festivities as Russia fell into a severe economic depression in which prices for domestic goods escalated and many people lost their jobs. The effects of this economic depression on Russian companies and Russian workers were compounded by the fact that over the past ten years, Chinese migrants have moved to Russia to work as laborers in the construction industries and as vendors in the markets, and as Chinese consumer goods have saturated the Russia market as cheap alternatives to Russian- and European-made goods, further pressuring Russia's domestic industries.

These economic constraints have prompted Russian consumers to reevaluate their views of Chinese products, Chinese citizens, and China itself. In the past several years, conversations with acquaintances and reports in the media reveal pervasive concerns among Russian consumers, businesspeople, and state officials alike that Chinese industry is undermining the ability of Russian factories to compete and stay solvent as well as fears that the allegedly poor quality of Chinese goods threatens Russian standards of quality and safety. These fears about the quality, safety, and productive benefits of Chinese products have informed public attitudes about Chinese citizens, as Chinese laborers are routinely subjected to harassment by local officials and residents, and graffiti at construction sites in Moscow reveals harsh anti-Chinese sentiments.

Such attitudes escalated in the summer of 2009 with several high-profile closures of public markets in Russia. The closures were directed primarily at removing foreigners, Chinese and Vietnamese vendors in particular, from these markets. At the end of June 2009, Moscow authorities closed the Cherkizovskii Market, one of the largest outdoor markets in Moscow, and began demolition of the structure in mid-August. This was initiated by then-Prime Minister Vladimir Putin's demand for criminal convictions in the case of US $2 billion worth of goods that had allegedly been smuggled in from China in 2008 (Krainova 2009: 3). The closure and demolition of the Cherkizovskii Market prompted tremendous outcry throughout Moscow, particularly among the thousands of Asian and Central Asian vendors and laborers who found themselves out of work and locked out their stalls, and in many cases separated from their legal documents. In response to the outcry, Moscow Mayor Yurii Luzhkov replied that helping "our friends from China is not our job" (Krainova 2009: 3). After many Chinese laborers found work at other Moscow markets, local authorities distributed pamphlets written in Chinese that provided instructions for proper hygiene in public commercial spaces. The message was clear: Chinese laborers were neither clean nor capable of proper, civilized behavior without direct instruction.

With the removal of Chinese workers from markets, the destruction of Chinese goods, and the enforcement of particular sanitary and hygiene regulations directed at Chinese workers, Russian authorities publicly engaged in tactics of spatial cleansing (Herzfeld 2006) to eliminate polluting and dangerous elements from public view. With the physical relocation and cultural sanitizing of Chineseness, Russian authorities were attempting to secure the safety of the nation. These protectionist measures reflect the simultaneous movement of Chinese foods to the peripheries, or outside altogether, of Russia's culinary topographies. By cleansing national spaces, Russian authorities are also cleansing the national palate.

Tasting the Places of Desire and Disdain

Russians' differential treatment of Eastern cuisines reveals a complicated conceptual and sensory topography of desire and disdain. The differential placement of Japanese, Korean, and Chinese culinary traditions expresses both symbolically and materially qualities of familiarity, difference, desirability, and undesirability. Space and taste are mutually informed so that the values and experiences associated with particular foods are contingent upon the places in which they exist—whether it is in public, in private, or on the periphery. In contrast to Japanese foods, which are very deliberately afforded heightened visibility in the public spheres as a marker of their desirability and difference, both Korean and Chinese foods are largely out of public view. Yet Korean and Chinese foods occupy very different non-public spaces that evoke different sensibilities of desire. While Korean cuisines have been effectively domesticated by being brought into the most intimate and private spaces of Russians' personal lives, thereby indicating their place as a normal and acceptable part of Russian culinary tastes, both Chinese foods and the migrants that are associated with them have been expelled beyond the private and the public and into a different invisibility of the periphery, thereby marking their status as undesirable.

   In this respect, consideration of location and visibility as separate but intrinsically related aspects of sensory experiences of edibility is productive for rethinking the nature of intersecting processes of globalization and localization. At the same time that categorical distinctions between the local and the global, the Self and the Other, and the familiar and the exotic demarcate the larger fields of difference in which cultural trends circulate, they also invoke models in which globalization and localization are depicted as two ends of the same spectrum with interactions between the global and the local always positioned along that spectrum (Long 2000a; Rosaldo 1993). While such approaches are useful for demarcating the field in which these encounters occur by assigning cultural forces to one position or another and for identifying places at which those distinctions are in flux, they are less helpful for capturing how certain trends marked as "foreign," "Other," and "exotic" can retain their position of difference while simultaneously being used to promote "the local," "the familiar," and "the edible." Nor are they helpful for recognizing when and how particular cultural trends marked as "foreign" may get displaced altogether from the relational spectrum of "foreign" versus "local." Consequently, attention to the intersections of the spatial and the sensory illuminates how qualities such as edibility and palatability are not simply the symbolic products of cultural preferences but are also themselves organizing frameworks that shape how and where individuals navigate and live their lives.

The varying correlations among symbolic and actual qualities of visibility and invisibility on the one hand, and familiarity, desirability, and disdain on the other, that are made apparent in Japanese, Korean, and Chinese food trends in Russia also shed light on how diverse processes of Easternization are playing out so differently from one another and from more familiar narratives of Westernization. As a particular form of globalization, Easternization is not a monolithic process but rather one that is embedded in vastly diverse systems of economic, political, and cultural needs, expectations, and obligations that are not always aligned with the dynamics identified with Westernization processes. By repositioning Russia vis-à-vis its Eastern cultural interlocutors, this alternative geopolitical orientation creates both an alternative topography and an alternative hierarchy of value within the conceptual terrain of Self and Other that is evoked by globalization. At the same time that Russians' differing appreciation of Korean, Japanese, and Chinese cultural trends highlights a Russian ordering of the values of these cultures in relationship to one another, these attitudes also reveal how Russians envision their own place within a global hierarchy of value.

Easternizing modes of globalization have also called into question the subordinate, responsive positioning of Russia as the Eastern Other that has occurred with Westernizing trends, whereby Russia's two options are either to incorporate Western trends as a means to advance and lose its Otherness or to reject those trends and insist on cultural distinctiveness. Instead, Russia's differential treatment of Eastern cultural trends shows possibilities not just for articulating new forms of local, but also for using the Other to articulate a new local. Easternizing trends illuminate how global processes may require the mediation of other global trends, as with Japanese foods becoming conduits for Chinese, Italian, and other food cultures, at the same time as they call into question conventional culinary orders of internationally recognized cuisines. In the Russian case, Chinese cuisine cannot stand on its own merits as a discrete, international cuisine but must be "brought up" to international standards through association with other foreign cuisines. At the same time, the deliberate appropriation of Japanese foods in Russian culinary culture might signal a way for Russia to position itself as a viable international cuisine. It is this shifting stage of creative appropriations and partnerships that allows Russians to move beyond simplistic Self-Other constructions to more complex positions within a global order of both cuisine and migration. Ultimately, as taste is made manifest through visual markers, gradations of visibility, familiarity, and desirability signal the changing parameters of both the personal and the cultural palate.

Notes

1. Other classificatory systems such as North and South; First World, Second World, and Third World (and even Fourth World), and Developed, Developing, and Undeveloped are equally problematic (Escobar 1995).
2. Ironically, the space formerly occupied by the Doutor coffeehouse is now a Starbucks.
3. This was a different church from the one previously described.
4. I must confess that my reasons for eating so frequently at this restaurant were both because the food was good and because this was one of the few restaurants in the city that was not crowded with other customers. It was not until much later that I learned from my Russian friends and colleagues about their ambivalence, or even dislike, of Chinese food and gained insight into why this restaurant was so underutilized despite the quality and portion size of the dishes.
5. In fact, the largest and most popular restaurant in the vicinity was a Japanese restaurant.
6. *Matreshka* is the word for the traditional Russian nesting dolls.
7. Informally, I have heard personal accounts that suggest that Japanese and Japanese-American citizens living in Russia enjoy a more privileged position than Chinese citizens. In one case, a Japanese businesswoman living in Russia was a frequent target of racial slurs about Chinese. In most cases when her accusers learned that she was in fact Japanese, they stopped and immediately apologized for their mistake. In another case, a Japanese-American man shopping at a market was stopped by the police and loaded in a van with other presumably undocumented "Chinese" laborers. When the police eventually got around to checking documents several hours later and discovered that he was Japanese-American, they immediately released him and scolded him for not identifying himself—and his difference from the other men in the van—earlier.

References

Akaha, Tsuneo, ed. 1997. *Politics and Economics in the Russian Far East: Changing Ties with Asia-Pacific.* London: Routledge.

Anonymous. 1998. "Moskva na ostrie shampura" (Moscow on a sharp skewer). *Restorannye Vedemosti* February 1: 4–10.

Appadurai, Arjun. 1996. *Modernity at Large: Cultural Dimensions of Globalization.* Minneapolis: University of Minnesota Press.

———. 1986. "On Culinary Authenticity." *Anthropology Today* 2(4): 25.

Caldwell, Melissa L. 2011. "Assistance Migrants in Russia: Upsetting the Hierarchies of Transitional Development." In *Global Connections and Emerging Inequalities in Europe,* ed. Deema Kaneff and Frances Pine, 145–162. London: Anthem Press.

———. 2009. "Tempest in a Coffee Pot: Brewing Incivility in Russia's Public Sphere." In *Food and Everyday Life in the Postsocialist World,* ed. Melissa L. Caldwell, 101–129. Bloomington: Indiana University Press.

———. 2006. "Tasting the Worlds of Yesterday and Today: Culinary Tourism and Nostalgia Foods in Post-Soviet Russia." In *Fast Food/Slow Food: The Cultural Economy of the Global Food System,* ed. Richard Wilk, 97–112. Lanham, MD: AltaMira Press.

———. 2004. "Domesticating the French Fry: McDonald's and Consumerism in Moscow." *Journal of Consumer Culture* 4(1): 5–26.

———. 2002. "The Taste of Nationalism: Food Politics in Postsocialist Moscow." *Ethnos* 67(3): 295–319.

Creed, Gerald W., and Janine R. Wedel. 1997. "Second Thoughts from the Second World: Interpreting Aid in Post-Communist Eastern Europe." *Human Organization* 56(3): 253–264.

Crowley, David. 2000. "Warsaw's Shops, Stalinism and the Thaw." In *Style and Socialism: Modernity and Material Culture in Post-War Eastern Europe,* ed. Susan E. Reid and David Crowley, 25–47. Oxford: Berg.

Escobar, Arturo. 1995. *Encountering Development: The Making and Unmaking of the Third World.* Princeton: Princeton University Press.

Fehérváry, Krisztina E. 2002. "American Kitchens, Luxury Bathrooms, and the Search for a 'Normal' Life in Post-socialist Hungary." *Ethnos* 67(3): 369–400.

Herzfeld, Michael. 2006. "Spatial Cleansing: Monumental Vacuity and the Idea of the West." *Journal of Material Culture* 11(1/2): 127–149.

Humphrey, Caroline. 1995. "Creating a Culture of Disillusionment: Consumption in Moscow, a Chronicle of Changing Times." In *Worlds Apart: Modernity through the Prism of the Local,* ed. Daniel Miller, 43–68. London: Routledge.

Jung, Yuson. 2006. "Consumer Lament: An Ethnographic Study on Consumption, Needs, and Everyday Complaints in Postsocialist Bulgaria." PhD dissertation, Harvard University, Cambridge, MA.

Kelly, Catriona. 1998. "Creating a Consumer: Advertising and Commercialization." in *Russian Cultural Studies: An Introduction,* ed. Catriona Kelly and David Shepherd, 223–244. Oxford: Oxford University Press.

Khazanov, Anatoly. 1997. "Ethnic Nationalism in the Russian Federation." *Daedalus* 126(3): 121–142.

Kho, Songmoo. 1987. *Koreans in Soviet Central Asia.* Helsinki: The Finnish Oriental Society.

Kirshenblatt-Gimblett, Barbara. 2004. "Foreword." In *Culinary Tourism,* ed. Lucy M. Long, xi–xiv. Lexington: University Press of Kentucky.

Klumbytė, Neringa. 2009. "The Geopolitics of Taste: The 'Euro' and 'Soviet' Sausage Industry in Lithuania." In *Food and Everyday Life in the Postsocialist World,* ed. Melissa L. Caldwell, 130–153. Bloomington: Indiana University Press.

Krainova, Natalya. 2009. "City Starts Razing Cherkizovsky." *The Moscow Times,* 19 August, no 4213: 3.

Lankauskas, Gediminas. 2002. "On 'Modern' Christians, Consumption, and the Value of National Identity in Post-Soviet Lithuania." *Ethnos* 67(3): 320–344.

Long, Lucy M. 2004a. "Culinary Tourism: A Folkloristic Perspective on Eating and Otherness." In *Culinary Tourism,* ed. Lucy M. Long, 20–50. Lexington: University Press of Kentucky.

———. 2004b. "Introduction." In *Culinary Tourism,* ed. Lucy M. Long, 1–19. Lexington: University Press of Kentucky.

Mankekar, Purnima. 2002. "'India Shopping': Indian Grocery Stores and Transnational Configurations of Belonging." *Ethnos* 67(1): 75–98.

Molz, Jennie Germann. 2004. "Tasting an Imagined Thailand: Authenticity and Culinary Tourism in Thai Restaurants." In *Culinary Tourism,* ed. Lucy M. Long, 53–75. Lexington: University Press of Kentucky.

Patico, Jennifer. 2008. *Consumption and Social Change in a Post-Soviet Middle Class.* Washington, DC: Woodrow Wilson Center Press; and Stanford: Stanford University Press.

————. 2001. "Globalization in the Postsocialist Marketplace: Consumer Readings of Difference and Development in Urban Russia." *Kroeber Anthropological Society Papers* 86: 1127–1142.

Rausing, Sigrid. 2002. "Re-constructing the 'Normal': Identity and the Consumption of Western Goods in Estonia." In *Markets & Moralities: Ethnographies of Postsocialism,* ed. Ruth Mandel and Caroline Humphrey, 127–142. Oxford: Berg.

Rosaldo, Renato. 1993. *Culture and Truth: The Remaking of Social Analysis.* Boston: Beacon Press.

Shectman, Stas. 2009. "A Celebration of *Masterstvo:* Professional Cooking, Culinary Art, and Cultural Production in Russia." In *Food and Everyday Life in the Postsocialist World,* ed. Melissa L. Caldwell, 154–187. Bloomington: Indiana University Press.

Turgeon, Laurier, and Madeleine Pastinelli. 2002. "'Eat the World': Postcolonial Encounters in Quebec City's Ethnic Restaurants." *Journal of American Folklore* 115(456): 247–268.

Um, Hae-Kyung. 2000. "Listening Patterns and Identity in the Korean Diaspora in the Former USSR." *British Journal of Ethnomusicology* 9(2): 121–142.

CHAPTER **8**

Experiencing the "West" through the "East" in the Margins of Europe[1]

Chinese Food Consumption Practices in Postsocialist Bulgaria

Yuson Jung

We just want to be normal. Not backward, not communist, not in transition, just to live like they do in *normal* countries. ... Just look back. We
have always been in some mess, either under Ottoman control, clients
of Germans, part of the communist camp, and now in transition. And
what is this transition? During my whole life we have been in some kind
of transition: the transition to socialism, the transition to communism,
and now the transition to capitalism. We are always in transition. The
goals change, but we stay in transition. This is our fate, to always be on
the road to someplace we never reach.—Bulgarian villager (quoted in
Creed 1998, 1; emphasis added)

In postsocialist Sofia, Bulgaria, red lanterns have become the symbolic markers
of the globalization that came with the democratic changes and capitalist market
economy. Just as McDonald's became the emblem of capitalism and the visual
evidence of the drastic social change that followed the collapse of the socialist
regime in 1989, so did the red lanterns that were hung in the entrance of every
Chinese eatery in Bulgaria. But unlike McDonald's golden arches, which could
be spotted only in major downtown areas or along major highways, the red lanterns gradually permeated the local urban landscape throughout Sofia, the capital
city of Bulgaria. By 2002, it was not unusual to observe red lanterns in many
neighborhoods (and often in unexpected places) of Sofia.[1]

This chapter explores the phenomenon of globalization, and its impact on consumption practices and identity formation through the lens of Chinese food consumption in postsocialist Bulgaria. By tracing the changing practices of Chinese food consumption in Bulgaria over the past decade, I show that the experience of eating "other" cuisines is not simply to imagine and romanticize the experience of the "Other." Neither is it about localizing or domesticating foreign food against the homogenizing effects of globalization and rendering different meanings to the locals, a popular anthropological interpretation on food and globalization (e.g. Watson and Caldwell 2005; Phillips 2006; Nutzenadel and Trentmann 2008). Rather, I argue that Bulgarians use Chinese food consumption practices to evaluate and affirm their sociocultural position within the global hierarchy of geopolitical and economic order during intensive social transformation (cf. Herzfeld 2004). This approach offers an alternative understanding to the global spread of diverse food traditions that have been the center of the globalization/localization debates. To many Bulgarians, Chinese food was considered a symbol of a "normal life" they felt they were deprived of during state socialism. In addition, it was a novel experience with which they were familiar only through Western films (mostly American) and second-hand accounts from those who had traveled to the West. Thus, Chinese food became an emblem of globalization, and its consumption was understood as a "Western" experience, regardless of the cultural label it apparently carried.

As is the case with modern consumption practices around the world (e.g. Campbell 1987; Slater 2000), novelty has been a major element that draws curious consumers into "exotic" food experiences. In the case of postsocialist Bulgaria, "normalcy" became another important factor of appeal because Chinese food consumption came to be understood as a "normalizing" practice, namely something that reminded them that life was becoming "normal" (that is, Western). In other words, the presence and accessibility of Chinese eateries in postsocialist Bulgaria made Bulgarians feel that they were no longer "lagging behind" and afforded a sense of global belonging. At the same time, the consumption of Chinese food was not simply a fad associated with new consumption practices. As Chinese food has started to lose its novelty and indeed become part of everyday consumption practices, the "authenticity" debate has sparked off and Bulgarian consumers have started to engage in the practice of distinction (Bourdieu 1984). This practice also places one in the global hierarchy by means of cultural capital, in this case, through the ability to distinguish "authentic" Chinese food. Bulgarian consumers are increasingly commenting on the differences between "authentic" and "inauthentic" Chinese food. The ability to differentiate them is used as a way of demonstrating identity and consumer status in the constantly changing global world.

The meaning of *ordinary* or *normal* here should not be confused with either localized or domesticated practices of Chinese food consumption: "localized" indicates the local adaptation of global products and practices where the salience of the "foreign-ness" or "globality" is not erased. In comparison, "domesticated" refers to a similar process where the boundaries between foreign and domestic are blurred (Caldwell 2004, 6).[2] The articulation of "normalcy" or "ordinary-ness" through consumption practices, on the other hand, does not point to the dichotomies of "foreign/domestic" or "theirs/ours." Rather, they reflect the frame of references that govern one's sense of identity in the global era. Thus, the process of normalization has different implications from that of localization and domestication: the former evokes a hierarchy of values and status, the latter does not. In addition, while the localization and domestication of "global" food implies the importance of the "taste" of the food, the normalization is not premised upon the taste discussion; taste becomes an issue after the normalization is achieved. This complex process, I argue, cannot be explained properly through the framework of global/local, which has become the dominant interpretation to counter the seemingly homogenizing effects of globalization (e.g. Caldwell 2004; Watson 2006). While such approaches provide insights into the diverse local interpretations of global foods in the everyday practices, they overlook how food practices are also intimately related to positioning oneself and one's citizenship within the larger global context of space and time. In this sense, new foods and food practices in the era of globalization are not merely a result of adapting to local cultures or reinventing the local, but signify identity formation of the consumers in the rapidly changing world. I argue that while non-Western commodities and practices become global symbols, their meanings are filtered through a Western lens that offers the hegemonic standards (points of references) of modern consumption practices. Chinese food consumption practices, therefore, become a symbol through which Bulgarians evaluate their political economic position in the global hierarchy.

Note on Chinese Immigration in Bulgaria

Is Chinese food simply incidental in representing the phenomenon of globalization in postsocialist Bulgaria through which Bulgarians derive a sense of normalcy? Could any other type of cuisine have fulfilled a similar role? What are the similarities and differences between Chinese immigration in postsocialist Bulgaria and similar cases in other parts of the world?

A brief history of Chinese immigration in Bulgaria might be useful in addressing these questions. Chinese people in Bulgaria have started to become visible only in the past decade as part of an immigration influx to Eastern Europe after the collapse of the socialist regimes in 1989.[3] The most recent influx of Chinese migrants is considered the fifth wave of Chinese migration to Europe, a region where Chinese migrants started to settle from the nineteenth century and increasingly after the Second World War (Benton and Pieke 1998; Nyiri 1999, 2007; Nyiri and Rostislavovich 2002). Compared with other Eastern European countries, such as Hungary, the Czech Republic, and Romania, the number of Chinese people in Bulgaria is relatively small (about 3,000 people in 2002, and much less in 2009).[4] They are predominantly involved in the restaurant business and trading of consumer goods in open-air markets. These were the market niches in the aftermath of state socialism when there was great consumer demand for cheap, novel, and exotic goods and services. Unlike in other Western European countries, however, almost none of the Chinese immigrants in Bulgaria have labored in workshops or small factories. Furthermore, as per the general trend of the fifth wave of Chinese migration in Europe, the immigrants have come mostly from mainland China (especially the northern provinces of Jilin, Liaoning, Heilongjiang, and Zhejiang). They are also first-generation migrants, many of whom arrived without kinship ties in the Chinese overseas community.

According to my Chinese informants, they decided to come over because they believed that it was easier to compete with 8 million Bulgarians than with 1.27 billion Chinese in China.[5] Their migration is economically motivated and reflects the predominant pattern of Chinese migration in Eastern Europe, where immigrants tend to show greater mobility compared with their counterparts in Western Europe. In other words, many of them do not consider Bulgaria as their final destination or home of their migration journey. In Bulgaria, Chinese are considered the "new immigrants" (Krasteva 2005). Since Bulgaria joined the European Union in 2007, however, it has become more difficult for the Chinese population in Bulgaria to grow. Although they are considered immigrants, many of them aspire to return to their homeland, and some of them have already done so. In this regard, they could be understood more as "sojourners" than immigrants.

Like elsewhere in Eastern Europe, Chinese immigration in Bulgaria is still in the making, so communities do not exhibit the characteristics of Chinese communities in Western Europe where they have become rooted, organized, and formed a transnational migration network through kinship ties (Watson 1975; Benton and Pieke 1998). At the same time, unlike in Western Europe or North America, Chinese restaurants in Bulgaria have not become saturated to the point of driving down prices and/or inspiring the introduction of prestige brands or Asian-fusion cuisine. Rather, as I will discuss below, the sudden influx and subsequent decline in the number of Chinese restaurants has started the debate on authenticity among Bulgarian consumers.

Against this backdrop, it should also be noted that in Bulgaria, new "global" cuisines such as Chinese and Japanese food are *not* promoted in terms of "ethnic" food, as is the case in the United States, for example, but rather as "exotic" food, indicating lower familiarity, novelty, and social changes. Indeed, "ethnic food" does not exist as a meaningful cultural and linguistic category in Bulgarian. As state socialism deprived ordinary Bulgarian consumers of diverse world cuisines and food practices, the introduction of Chinese food carried the connotation of a global/Western experience rather than an "ethnic" one. The result is that the practice of Chinese food consumption in Bulgaria is akin the McDonald's experience elsewhere, where the chain became the symbol of modernization and globalization (e.g. Krasteva-Blagoeva 2001; Caldwell 2004; Watson 2007). Chinese food has also become emblematic of a Western lifestyle as a result of the experience of socialist consumers with American films. My Bulgarian informants repeatedly noted how such films had contributed to their imagination of ordinary and normal life in the West, where take-out Chinese food appeared as part of everyday life. Although Chinese food has not been the only commodity from which many postsocialist consumers have derived a sense of normalcy, neither has it been incidental in representing aspects of a normal life as in the West.[6] The following section will further elaborate the connection between Chinese food and "normal life" through an ethnographic examination of Chinese food consumption in Bulgaria.

Kitaiska Hrana (Chinese Food) and "Normal Life"

On a Sunday in July 1999, I went with my host family to a Chinese restaurant called Aziya in Sofia that was considered by the local people as one of the "best" and "most affordable" Chinese eateries. Bulgaria had just gone through another economic crisis in the winter of 1997–1998, and the official average monthly income per person was estimated at around US $150. Despite the material abundance with which Bulgarians now surrounded themselves, ordinary people's living standards had plummeted compared with socialist times, and many Sofians felt deprived of basic "needs" such as free education and healthcare, or even the seaside summer vacation they regarded as part of a "normal life" during the socialist era (Jung 2007). Consequently, price was one of the most important standards governing everyday consumption practices. Chinese food appealed to ordinary Sofians for several reasons under these circumstances: it was novel ("exotic"), relatively cheaper than most Bulgarian eateries, and restored their sense of "normalcy." The following ethnographic example from Aziya will illustrate this point.

Upon entering a modestly decorated space with metal frame tables and chairs covered with vinyl covers, the first thing one would notice at Aziya was the vast amount of food served on the table, along with a big loaf of bread. It was quite a contrast to the scene outside where impoverished elderly often rummaged through garbage containers. The restaurant had a distinct smell that many locals immediately associated with something "exotic"—most likely from unfamiliar Chinese spices, sauces, and dried ingredients such as the *kitaiski gubi* (black Chinese mushrooms) that came to symbolize Chinese food. The portions of the dishes at the restaurant were indeed large. It seemed at least twice the amount of what would be served in a Chinese restaurant in the United States. People ate as much as they could, with usually about half the dishes wrapped up and taken home—these so-called doggy bags being common for Chinese restaurant customers. This also became a point of attraction for the local people who were not used to such take-out practices. The restaurant was crowded with Bulgarians eating with family and friends. There were even some older couples, perhaps better-off pensioners, who were enjoying their meal there.[7] It was not a fancy place and definitely not touristy; except for the two Chinese waitresses and the Chinese host behind the bar area, I was the only Asian and foreign visitor. There was a pattern to the dishes that were being ordered: fried rice and at least one fried chicken dish. The fried rice was typically served with eggs and vegetables and seasoned with soy sauce. The chicken dishes varied from sweet and sour chicken to a version of Kung Pao with diced carrots, celery, onions, and lots of peanuts stir fried with some soy sauce and oyster sauce, as well as chicken with Chinese mushrooms and vegetables served in a thicker oyster sauce. Another popular choice was the sesame chicken, which was crispier fried than the sweet and sour chicken and coated with a sugar and soy sauce mixture and sprinkled with toasted sesame seeds. No one ate with chopsticks, and on some tables a loaf of bread was present along with the Chinese dishes.

My host family, a couple who taught at a university in Sofia,[8] was very excited about this outing because they rarely went out to eat. When we were seated and had finished ordering, my landlady (in her mid-forties) remarked with a deep, happy sigh, "This is how a normal life should be! Being able to eat normal food like in the West!" My landlord (in his early fifties) added: "Yes, this is really nice. Finally, we also get to taste some 'different' food. Under socialism, only basic ingredients were available for ordinary people. All the good stuff was exported. Now you can find all kinds of ingredients in the market. Look at the Chinese mushrooms here. We had no idea what Chinese mushrooms were like. Now, you can find a lot of these kinds of new items in the stores—like in the West." This comment pointed to socialist Bulgaria's practice of primarily exporting agricultural products in order to import gas and other natural resources for the national economy. My landlady further commented: "Well, I can't say that all these people here are having a happy life because life is really hard here, but at least they can forget the anxieties of life momentarily by eating out and trying something new! Look around! This was unimaginable—so many normal Bulgarians in a *Chinese restaurant*." When our dishes were finally served, my host family insisted on having me teach them how to eat with chopsticks. They wanted to become culturally competent. While I was teaching them, our table received quite a bit of attention from the surrounding tables, although none of them actually followed our lead by asking for chopsticks.

My host family's comments on relating Chinese food with a "normal life" were echoed by other Bulgarian informants throughout my fieldwork between 1999 and 2002. Gradually, Chinese food became normalized; Bulgarian consumers considered it as part of their ordinary life. It was at this point when authenticity debates became meaningful in Chinese food consumption practices. The following section documents the changing Chinese food consumption practices in Bulgaria in the past decade.

Changing Chinese Food Consumption Practices in Bulgaria, 1999–2009

For many ordinary Bulgarian people, going out to eat is in itself a relatively "new" postsocialist experience; during socialist times, home or cafeterias at work were the primary locations for food consumption. If one dined out, it was for special occasion banquets or for casual fare, mostly with *kebabcheta* and *kyufteta,* grilled sausages and meatballs made from ground meat that were served in plain grill places. When I first visited Sofia in 1998, there were hardly any signs of Chinese restaurants in the urban landscape. There were a few frequented by foreign diplomats, but ordinary Bulgarians did not have access to Chinese food. When I asked around and finally located one Chinese restaurant by the British embassy near the Cultural Palace building in Sofia, my Bulgarian host, a graduate student, and her family asked me what "Far Eastern food" or "Asian food" was like. They had seen it in American movies, but they had never tried it before. I took my host to the Chinese restaurant that the locals at that point had only heard of.

The restaurant itself was not big, with about seven or eight tables in the main hall decorated with red walls, Chinese-style paintings, and some sculptures of lions and dragons. There was a relatively "luxurious" bar area where a Bulgarian bartender was cleaning the glasses facing the dining hall and against a small wall with a display of various alcoholic beverages. Including ourselves, there were four customers, and after we placed our order with the Bulgarian waiter, an Asian (presumably Chinese) chef came out to take a look at me (by simply staring at me) and went back to his kitchen to make the food.[9]

My host was excited because it was such a novel and fascinating experience for her. We both liked the food—it was decent and, in my opinion, quite "authentic." According to my host, it was spicy, tasty, and exotic. A middle-aged Bulgarian couple occupied the other table; they appeared to have ordered only a salad, which they shared, and a common local brandy *rakiya* (a typical way to start a meal in Bulgaria). We left the restaurant very content, but my host said she would probably not be able to come back because she could not afford it. By Western standards it was not very expensive, but for the locals after a heavy economic crisis, it was not considered to be an affordable meal.

In 1999, the local landscape in itself did not seem to have changed much except for the fact that people were occasionally taking me out to Chinese restaurants or simply pointing them out. It was still regarded as a rather "luxurious" and "exceptional" experience to consume Chinese food. On those occasions when my Bulgarian friends and I ate Chinese food or discussed it, they made it very clear that they ate this kind of food only on special occasions. Even though they enjoyed the taste—it was something "new," after all—it was just too expensive. In the summer of 1999, the price of a meat dish in a Chinese restaurant was between 3.80–4.50 lev (US $1.90–2.30). This was about 1–1.50 lev (US $0.50–0.75) more than the price of the dishes offered by the average Bulgarian restaurant.[10]

By 2000, however, Chinese restaurants had become highly visible. I was amazed how, literally, every other corner in Sofia had a red lantern, indicating a Chinese food place. This color was a notable addition to the city's gray concrete socialist architecture. According to a local media report in June 2000, there were at least 150 Chinese restaurants in Sofia (which has a population of approximately one million). The restaurants were run primarily by Chinese from China, although some were also run by Bulgarian entrepreneurs. The store signs read "*Kitaiska Hrana*" (Chinese food) or "*Kitaiska Kuhnia*" (Chinese kitchen) and there were also Chinese take-out businesses from which patrons were served a type of fast food in Styrofoam containers.

Whenever I expressed my astonishment at this development, Bulgarians reacted in a rather aloof manner: "Oh yes, there are a lot of Chinese restaurants in Sofia." Maria, an informant in her mid-forties, while nodding seriously, said, "Every [neighborhood] block has one now." Another male informant in his early fifties sarcastically remarked, "At least there are some changes *even* in Bulgaria!" Unlike in the previous years, most people were aware of Chinese food and had tried it at least once. If they had not tried it yet, they still knew about it through friends, families, neighbors, colleagues, and so on. Moreover, most of them expressed how much they enjoyed the *vkus* (taste) of Chinese food, and several people explained that they especially liked it because it was "lighter" than Bulgarian food and thus "healthier" (because the frying process in Chinese cuisine is faster and done with higher-temperature oil than in Bulgarian cuisine, it was often considered healthier and less fattening). The price of the dishes had increased slightly from the previous year, but in relative terms, dishes became more affordable given inflation and the gradual increase of income.[11] In addition, the generous portions that were symbolic of Chinese food made the outing to a Chinese restaurant both economical and attractive, as many could share the food or take the leftovers home.

It appeared that the consumption of Chinese food in Sofia was no longer seen as a luxury. In fact, only those places around the upscale downtown area were perceived as a little "expensive," but even those were not outrageous on account of the portion sizes. Certainly, these restaurants were no more expensive than nice Bulgarian restaurants. At this point, authenticity of taste was not a big issue; rather, it was the novelty of the food that was important. To underline this, those who had consumed this particular novelty all agreed that the time had at last come for Bulgaria to have some variety in its diet (after all, socialism was over and they no longer had to export all the good stuff abroad).

During my yearlong doctoral fieldwork in Sofia between 2001 and 2002, I frequented Chinese restaurants with my friends and colleagues. Chinese restaurants had become part of the mainstream dining culture in Sofia. Many more special occasions, such as birthdays, name days, and Students' Day, were celebrated at these establishments. Three of the more popular Chinese restaurants were owned by a Mrs. Zheng and her husband, Mr. Chu, with whom I had become very close. Mrs. Zheng and Mr. Chu were from China's Jilin Province, where they also ran a small restaurant business. They came to Bulgaria in 1999. Having tasted some Bulgarian food, Mrs. Zheng saw an opportunity to make a living in Bulgaria. She and her husband gradually brought over their family members from China, and within the next couple of years, they had opened these three restaurants in downtown Sofia.

Once my Bulgarian informants discovered that they would be served a different kind of Chinese food or off-menu dishes whenever they went with me to eat at Mrs. Zheng's restaurants, they began to question whether what they usually ordered was "authentic." At the same time, some of their friends, who had traveled to the United States and Western Europe and tried Chinese food there, assured my local friends that Chinese food in Bulgaria actually tasted *more* authentic. Indeed, as far as the taste was concerned, I did agree that Chinese food in Bulgaria tasted less Westernized, meaning the flavor profile did not seem compromised with the addition of nontraditional ingredients such as chicken bouillon cubes for soup and ketchup for sweet and sour dishes. Yet, I also knew from Mrs. Zheng that the more successful Chinese restaurants in Sofia compromised authenticity by preparing food in a more Bulgarian style. At times, they would cook with more sugar and vinegar to exaggerate what Bulgarians considered a typical sweet and sour Chinese sauce. They also avoided using more "exotic" Chinese sauces (beyond the basic soy sauce or oyster sauce) to appeal more to popular and familiar taste. I noticed that when Mrs. Zheng brought us the more authentic versions, which utilized less-known foodstuffs such as hoisin sauce, star anise spice, or black bean paste, for instance, my Bulgarian friends and colleagues said that those tasted a bit too exotic for their tastes.

In the spring of 2007, when I returned to Bulgaria after some years of absence, I learned that Mrs. Zheng had just moved back to China after spending eight years in Sofia. Her stepdaughter told me that Mrs. Zheng had always planned to return to her homeland once she had made a certain amount of money. Although Mrs. Zheng would occasionally complain that Bulgarians were poor and she would never make enough money, it appeared that she must have done okay for herself. Given the reduced number of Chinese restaurants now in Sofia, it seemed that some of her compatriots had also followed in her footsteps. Others, I was told, had attempted to move further west, especially as Bulgaria's EU membership in January 2007 facilitated mobility. In part, the closing of some Chinese restaurants in Bulgaria from 2003 to 2007 was considered symptomatic of a general trend in restaurants, with newer restaurants opening and competition becoming more saturated. Older non-Chinese restaurants were also closed in favor of newer restaurants. The novelty of Chinese food seemed to have faded a bit among Sofians, and it was certainly no longer considered "cool" or "hip." Instead, Chinese food was now associated with "cheap" and "fast" food choices as well as for take-out, indicating that a normalization process had taken place with Chinese food in Bulgaria. It was especially popular among young people catering for guests. Rarely did my friends suggest going to a Chinese restaurant for a meal. They claimed that the food quality had gone downhill; the food did not taste as authentic as before; and that the atmosphere of the restaurants had also deteriorated. In my observation, the Chinese restaurants' ambiance had remained the same, but other food places in Bulgaria had changed in the meantime, with more creative and posh-looking environments making Chinese restaurants look dirtier, cheaper, and less attractive.

During the longer periods of my fieldwork between 2008 and 2009, it was clear that Chinese restaurants had indeed lost most of their novelty appeal. As I walked and drove around my familiar places in Sofia, I was surprised that many of the red lanterns had disappeared without being replaced. When I inquired about where to find a good Chinese restaurant or suggested going to a Chinese restaurant, all of my friends from various ages and diverse socioeconomic backgrounds advised that if I wanted good food, I would be better trying something else, such as an Armenian restaurant or Serbian grill (*surbskata skara*). They also suggested some new sushi places that were currently popular in Sofia (although they added that I might not approve of their authenticity given my Asian background). Chinese food in Bulgaria, according to my friends and acquaintances, simply no longer tasted as good or authentic.

Globalization, Localization, and Domestication of Food

Do these changes in the consumption of Chinese food in Bulgaria indicate that Chinese food was simply a consumer fad? Or can they be explained in terms of the globalization/localization framework? One of the major contributions of anthropological studies to the globalization debate has been to refute claims that homogenization was an inevitable consequence of the globalization phenomenon (e.g. Wilk 1999; Watson and Caldwell 2005; Phillips 2006; Watson 2007; Nutzenadel and Trentmann 2008; among others). Scholars of globalization have often argued that the circulation of goods and services through an increasing global and transnational network results in a homogenized lifestyle and landscape (e.g. Tomlinson 1991; Waters 1995; Bhagwati 2004). In other words, the golden arches of McDonald's, the swoosh of Nike, and more recently the green letters of Starbucks—now seen across diverse global communities—have had a homogenizing effect on modern social life. George Ritzer (1993; 2004) has termed this the "McDonaldization" of society, where the organizing principles of social life are becoming increasingly standardized. He recognizes the division between the cultural form and the cultural content, however, and argues that whereas the forms may be homogenized, the contents are context-specific. Hence localization and globalization go hand in hand. Furthermore, as Melissa Caldwell (2004) rightly points out in her examination of McDonald's French fry consumption in Moscow, the weakness in the global/local paradigms is the assumption that there is an "authentic and unquestionably indigenous local." She argues that the local itself is reinvented through processes of "domestication," which goes beyond the cultural form/content analysis in globalization studies. In other words, although social processes of localization may be culturally specific, the content of local culture is continually invented, thereby blurring the boundaries between the familiar and the unfamiliar or foreign and domestic (2004, 6). The local is not a given but a process.

While these approaches have been productive to the discussion of food and globalization, and have certainly contributed to how the idea of globalization has been nourished through food (Philips 2006), I wish to move beyond the analytical framework of globalization/localization to explore the case of Chinese food consumption in Bulgaria. As Theodore Bestor reminds us with his study on global sushi, "globalization does not necessarily homogenize cultural differences nor erase the salience of cultural labels" (2000, 59). Here, Bestor uses the concept of brand equity to explain the globalization phenomenon of sushi; specifically, he argues that it is thanks to its brand equity that sushi is able to reign as a symbol of "prestige cuisine." On the one hand, sushi has become globalized, as witnessed in the popular and standardized sushi establishments (sushi can now be found anywhere from high-end restaurants to supermarket chains as well as airport eateries); on the other hand, it has become neither "localized" nor "domesticated" where the boundaries of the global/local or foreign/domestic become blurred. In other words, despite the flourishing of nontraditional maki rolls (such as California rolls and Philadelphia rolls) suggesting a form of "localization" in terms of the taste adaptation of sushi, sushi is not identified as "ours," as is the case with the McDonald's style of French fries in Russia (Caldwell 2004). Global sushi continues to keep the salience of the Japanese cultural label associated with superior cultural capital.

One might question whether global brands such as McDonald's can be likened to the "ethnic" branding to which both Chinese and Japanese foods point. I would argue that such comparison is possible because the seemingly "global" branding of McDonald's, for instance, also carries the culturally salient label of an American food (the hamburger; see especially Bak 2006 for the Korean case; Wu 2006 for the Taiwanese case; and Krasteva-Blagoeva 2001 for the Bulgarian case), in addition to symbolizing "global" and "modern" consumption practices. Furthermore, the category of "ethnic food" is in itself a cultural expression that is not used in certain cultural contexts such as in Bulgaria, as discussed previously.

Chinese food in Bulgaria has certainly not erased the salience of cultural labels. It is a foreign cuisine. Unlike Japanese sushi, the brand equity of Chinese food is not that of prestige cuisine. Rather, it has been identified as part of an "ordinary" life in "normal" countries—indicative of normalcy. Such a perception places one in a certain social position in the global hierarchy of political economy because the reference point of normalcy is in the West. In other words, having access to Chinese restaurants as in the West reflects a "normalization" of daily life in postsocialist Sofia. Therefore, Chinese food in Bulgaria has been associated with the sociocultural changes in the era of globalization, but its consumption practices are not so much emblematic of localization or domestication. Rather, Bulgarians use Chinese food consumption practices to evaluate their political economic position within the global hegemonic order. What makes the case under discussion more complex, however, is the fact that Chinese food becomes a further means of social distinction in which the ability to recognize "authentic" and "inauthentic" tastes reflects not only the individual's cultural capital, but also the political economic position of the nation-state in the global era. The following section attends to the two reference points, normalcy and authenticity, that enable Bulgarian consumers to use Chinese food consumption as a lens to evaluate their sociocultural position within the global hierarchy of geopolitical and economic order and to confirm their sense of global belonging.

Normalcy and Authenticity Debates in Chinese Food Consumption

As shown in the ethnographic account at the beginning of this chapter, the notion of normalcy (in the Foucauldian sense) was often brought up by Bulgarians when discussing general consumption attitudes in postsocialist Bulgaria. This notion of normalcy is not unique to the Bulgarian context—other anthropologists working in diverse postsocialist settings have reported similar attitudes and commentaries on normalcy in relation to new consumption practices after the political/economic changes in 1989 (e.g., Creed 1998; Fehervary 2002; Rausing 2002; Patico 2008). *Novelty* and *normalcy* were key words in the daily consumption practices in postsocialist Bulgaria. Likewise in Bulgaria, anything new, including the visibility of Chinese restaurants in Sofia, marked a change (or became a symbol of "transition"), and this led to a more "normal" state when compared with an "abnormal" past. Although novelty is hardly a surprising factor in modern consumption behavior (e.g., Campbell 1987), its connection to the concept of normalcy, and how these concepts further relate to identity formation in post-socialist Bulgaria, provide an interesting vantage point for further exploration: the concept of normalcy itself, as used in the Bulgarian context, reveals "the close association with Western standards of normalcy" (1998, 2), as Gerald Creed's quote in the beginning of this chapter also elucidates so vividly.[12]

This aspect then puts Chinese food in Bulgaria in an interesting position. It is unambiguously a "foreign" and "exotic" cuisine. At the same time, despite the fact that Chinese food is produced by native Chinese and often served by them,[13] the consumption of Chinese food in Bulgaria is associated with a Western experience. I suggest that the brand equity of Chinese food that has been established in Bulgaria stems primarily from Bulgarians' observation of American films in the socialist era as well as accounts of travel to the Western world by Bulgarians who were allowed such privileges (see also Fehervary 2002 for similar observation on the role of American films and popular magazines in Hungarians' imagination of the West). Two Bulgarian entrepreneurs who started a Chinese food eatery chain in Sofia in 1999, for example, reconfirmed other informants' reference to American films when explaining their initial encounter with Chinese food through American films that were aired during the socialist era. Indeed, their stores' establishments used cube-shaped take-out boxes that were inspired by those movies. Having seen how seemingly "ordinary" Americans were getting their take-out Chinese food in those cartons, they associated them with an ordinary and normal life in the West. They said that because they had patented this cube-shaped take-out box in Bulgaria, other Chinese restaurants and eateries could not use such boxes and had to resort to Styrofoam or plastic containers.[14] Interestingly, even though non-Western commodities and practices also become global symbols, their meanings are filtered through a Western experience because they offer the hegemonic points of references for modern consumption practices.

Chinese food also offered a break in a routinized life and provided a visible sign of the social changes. As my host families and informants remarked, being able to eat different kinds of food ("other cuisines") itself restored a sense of normalcy to Bulgarian consumers. Unlike in some places, such as in the United States or Western European countries, consuming Chinese food in Bulgaria is not so much related to an imagined "exotic" Other and the desire for experiencing the Other through food. Thus, it is hard to conclude that the consumption of Chinese food in Bulgaria provides an opportunity to experience Chinese culture. Moreover, this suggests an explanation for why the issue of authenticity (authentic cuisine/taste) did not really enter the discussion around Chinese food in Bulgaria until very recently, as I will discuss more below. When it did enter the discussion, the focus was more around cultural distinction to affirm their political economic position in the global hierarchy than around the experience of Chinese culture through food. Ironically, the cultural contact (between Chinese food and Bulgarians) in this case has produced stereotypes of a Western lifestyle exemplified in expressions such as "normal life."

This brings us to another interesting point: the notion of Western lifestyle among Bulgarians living with the legacy of socialism. Talal Asad mentions that terms like *modernity, liberal-democratic culture, advanced/late capitalism, the developed nations,* and *civilization* have served as partial equivalents of *Europe* and were understood as such (1997, 719; see also Herzfeld 1987). Although socialism in Eastern Europe was essentially an attempt to find a shortcut to modernity,[15] the collapse of socialism brought about the realization for Eastern Europeans that they were still in many ways behind their Western European counterparts, thus reminding them of their *nenormalno minalo,* or "abnormal past." As Talal Asad points out, the West has hegemonized the non-European world through transforming people's ways of living (1997, 720). I would further add that even within the geographically defined Europe there are people in "non-Western" regions such as Bulgaria that use Western standards to evaluate their ways of living. In this regard, *Europe* and *the West* are not necessarily interchangeable terms. As Bulgaria develops into a more consumerist society, Bulgarian consumers are further reminded of the invisible social distinction (Bourdieu 1984) that puts them into a certain position in the global hierarchy of geopolitical order.

In 2008, after I learned that my Bulgarian friends stopped frequenting Chinese restaurants because of their suspicions regarding "authenticity," I became curious about how they understood the concept. Anthropologists have long argued that discussions on authenticity tell us more about the locals than the "authentic" Others (e.g. Spooner 1986; Lindholm 2008). Moreover, through which or whose standards the authenticity is judged is debatable. In this regard, Arjun Appadurai has made three insightful observations on culinary authenticity, where he defines authenticity as "the degree to which something is more or less what it *ought* to be" (1986, 25; original emphasis). He suggests first that culinary authenticity is usually not the concern of the native participants in a culinary tradition except when they are far from home. Hence, it is the problem of the outsider and reflects the yearning as outsiders. At the same time, he points out that authenticity often is suggestive of quality, which is typically the insider's concern. Appadurai's question here is this: Can food be both authentic and of poor quality? Finally, he remarks how authenticity as a criterion seems to emerge after its subject matter has been transformed, and questions whether it is possible to create a dynamic criterion of authenticity. This is similar to Caldwell's (2004) argument about how the "local" continuously reinvents itself and thus one cannot assume an "authentic" local. Appadurai's observations aptly describe and support the Chinese food case under discussion here. The authenticity debates about Chinese food in Bulgaria emerged only after Bulgarian consumers started to notice the difference in the quality and taste of the Chinese food. The debates also reflect Bulgarians' yearning for a certain position in the global hierarchy of political economy, pointing to my argument that Chinese food consumption in postsocialist Bulgaria was not simply a matter of experiencing and romanticizing the Other.

My informants still went to Chinese restaurants occasionally to get take-out, something they enjoyed, but they also knew that they were not getting an authentic experience. When I asked them what they meant by "authentic Chinese food," a close friend, Darya, said:

> Something that is not so watered down, I mean it's difficult to say whether this is really Chinese or something else—it seems to have lost the identity. I don't think they will offer this kind of food in the Western [European] countries. I am not sure about America, but I certainly think that the authenticity is lost here. [With a big grin] This is Bulgaria. I think we had better Chinese food five or six years ago. It's definitely gone down [the quality]. Do you know that the best Chinese restaurants have actually closed down?

Given that my successful Chinese restaurateur friend Mrs. Zheng had moved back to China, and several other popular Chinese eateries had closed in the past three years, the locals' speculation that "good, authentic Chinese food" had not taken root in Bulgaria might not have been completely unfounded. At the same time, as mentioned before, Mrs. Zheng also told me that she was not serving what she saw as authentic Chinese food in Bulgaria, as she would have in China. What was most striking, however, was the constant comparison with the West and the equation of Bulgaria with inferior ("inauthentic") Chinese food compared with its Western counterpart. Authenticity, in this regard, is imagined and compromised both by its producers and consumers, but it is less of a concern by the Chinese producers (culinary insiders) than by Bulgarian consumers (culinary outsiders). This then points to the fact that Chinese food becomes a means of social distinction in which the ability to recognize (the imagined) "authentic" and "inauthentic" taste reflects not only the individual's cultural capital, but also the political economic position of the nation-state in the global era. Chinese food has also become a means to demonstrate one's identity in the rapidly changing world. Although Bulgaria became a member of the European Union in 2007, which enhanced its political economic status since the changes in 1989, it remains the poorest EU member state. The increased mobility of Bulgarians likely contributed to the evaluation of the authenticity of Chinese food served in Bulgaria, but such mobility remains limited as direct cultural exchanges between China and Bulgaria by means of tourism and business have not increased between 1999 and 2009.

Global Citizenship through Food and Eating

The consumption of Chinese food in Bulgaria reflects Bulgarians' ideas of their past, present, and future. Their ultimate desire to *finally* achieve a normal life is

deeply related to how they would like to formulate their identities in the postsocialist era. Bulgarians' attitudes toward the consumption of Chinese food thus offer a different interpretation on "ethnic" (non-Western) and increasingly "global"
food consumption in the modern world.

Modern consumption behaviors are governed by insatiable wants closely associated with novelty. The processes of globalization have intensified the notion of
"global citizenship" (a sense of a rightful global belonging; cf. Ong 1999; Tsing
2005) and consumption practices have become important sites on which to evaluate one's social, cultural, political, and economic position vis-à-vis the others.
In this regard, Chinese food consumption practices in Bulgaria show the close
relationship of food and globalization and point to the cultural significance of a
"food citizenship" in evaluating one's place in the world. Ultimately, this kind of
belonging in global consumer culture also becomes important in understanding
the complex process of identity formation in the era of globalization.

In a broader sense, Chinese food is an Eastern product in that it has traveled
from the Far East to Europe (the West). Ironically, Bulgarians perceiving themselves as the inferior "East" within the European context, experience the "West"
through Chinese food. In other words, in the current postsocialist context where
the consumption of Chinese food practices is perceived as a Western experience,
Chinese food serves as a tool that enables Bulgarians to become more "Western"
with a more "normal life." This enables them to position themselves in the global
hierarchy of political economy by engaging in the practices of social distinction.
Food is only one of the sites on which we can examine the notion of normalcy
in the postsocialist context of Bulgaria. Yet it is a very telling example because
practices around food reveal many aspects related to power relations, the legacy of
socialism, and identity formation in the postsocialist era and beyond.

Notes

The author acknowledges *Food, Culture, and Society: An International Journal of Multidisci-
plinary Research* (Bloomsbury) for permission to reprint this chapter from where it originally
appeared (15[4]: 579–598).

1. While there are Chinese restaurants outside of Sofia, they are still very few in number and
   rarely run by Chinese. I observed a couple of Chinese restaurants in a resort area by the
   Black Sea in 1999 and 2000, and in Plovdiv, the second largest city in Bulgaria, between
   2008 and 2009. Thus, the analysis of this chapter is primarily based on the Chinese food
   consumption practices in the urban environment of Sofia, Bulgaria.

2. For example, McDonald's becoming a location for social hangouts in East Asian countries,
   and not merely as a place to consume fast food, is a result of a localized practice of the
   global where McDonald's is considered a foreign food (Watson 2006). In Russia, however,
   McDonald's long and thin French fries have usurped the traditionally thicker and shorter
   fried potatoes, and are no longer considered "foreign" as they were when they were first
   introduced. Rather, they are regarded as "ours [Russian]" (Caldwell 2004).

3. See Nyiri (1999, 2007) for more detailed information regarding the history and pattern of Chinese immigration to Eastern Europe.

4. While official statistics were unavailable from the Bulgarian side in 2002, this number was provided by a Chinese informant who had close ties with the Chinese embassy in Sofia. It was also reported in a local newspaper article (Dimitrova and Rudnikova 2001). As Nyiri (2002, 2007) argues, contradictory official data combined with the high mobility of Chinese in Eastern Europe make it highly problematic to assign a figure to the number of Chinese migrants. When I had a chance to meet a Chinese diplomat informally at a dinner party, the diplomat confirmed the estimate of 3,000. All of these resources agree, however, that the number is always an estimate because of the fluctuating nature of the Chinese population in Bulgaria. The 2009 number was not officially confirmed, but one Chinese informant suggested that it was not more than 2,000. Given that the Chinese restaurants that I knew in 2001–2 were not replaced by other Chinese restaurants, and few new restaurants were visible, the suggested number seemed probable.

5. These Chinese people are mostly on a "resident permit" status that allows them to conduct business in Bulgaria. Some of them have married locals and became naturalized citizens. Local newspapers (such as the daily newspapers *Trud* and *24 Chasa*) also occasionally report on "illegal" Chinese in Bulgaria; indeed, some locals suggest that there are perhaps many more Chinese in Bulgaria than the official statistics indicate.

6. See, for example, Fehervary (2002), where the American kitchen and luxury bathrooms also symbolize a "normal life," as well as Rausing (2002), where the construction of the "normal" in the consumption of Western goods is central in postsocialist Estonia.

7. Pensioners in Bulgaria are regarded as having the toughest life after the changes, because they have spent their lifetime under the socialist system without knowing a different life-style. Now that there is a new world, they cannot afford the "new" experiences as a result of financial constraints. Between 1999 and 2002, the average pension was about US $50 per month and my informants suggested that these pensioners had likely saved for a few months before coming out to eat at the Chinese restaurant. Following Bulgaria's accession to the European Union in 2007, the official minimum pension increased to about €90 (approximately US $130).

8. My host family was an average middle-class (locals would refer to them as "ordinary folks") couple, both of who taught at a university in Sofia. Salaries for academics were low in Bulgaria. In 2000, an assistant professor's salary was about US $100 per month, while an associate professor's salary was $140 per month in Sofia. In addition to my rent for the room, my landlord supplemented her income with private tutoring. Right after the changes in the early 1990s, when private tutoring was not an option, to support her family she had to supplement her income with a second job as a cleaner for wealthy people.

9. My Asian background seemed to bring about different sets of reactions and sometimes dishes from the Chinese restaurant owners and chefs, raising questions about how "authenticity" is measured. On this occasion, the Asian-looking man (presumably the chef) came out and quickly looked at me. I think he wanted to see whether I was Chinese. It was not clear whether this resulted in serving us a more authentic kind of Chinese food, but the dishes that we were served, in my opinion, tasted quite authentic.

10. According to the Bulgarian National Institute of Statistics, the average annual income per capita was 1,587 lev in 1999 (exchange rate: 1 lev = US $0.50), and 3,867 lev in 2009 (exchange rate: 1 lev = US $0.70). While incomes have increased over the past decade,

so had the average cost of living. Locals complained that, with the entry to the European Union in 2007, they lived on a Bulgarian salary while paying European prices.

11. According to the National Institute of Statistics in Bulgaria, the inflation rate in 2000 and 2001 was 6.8 percent and 10 percent respectively (Bulgarian National Institute of Statistics 2000, 2001).

12. Discussions on normalcy (normality) in everyday practices of the postsocialist world have been widely documented in postsocialist ethnographies. See especially Fehérváry (2002), Humphrey (2002), Rausing (2002), and Patico (2008).

13. Most of the Chinese restaurants in Sofia have Chinese cooks. Even if the restaurants are actually owned and run by Bulgarians, they hire Chinese cooks for the kitchen. On the other hand, although a lot of Chinese restaurants do have a few Chinese waiters or waitresses, there are a lot of local waiters or waitresses serving Chinese food to the customers. There was once an occasion when I went out to a Chinese restaurant with a Bulgarian friend and we ordered a tofu dish. The Bulgarian waiter who served us asked whether we knew what tofu was and told us that it was "Chinese cheese" (because it looked similar to Bulgarian feta cheese) but did not taste good and therefore we should not get it. I insisted on getting it and, in fact, it was very good. This was another example that Bulgarians were not yet too keen on experiencing an "authentic" or "exotic" taste when they first started to experience Chinese food.

14. I was not able to verify the patent, but I never observed these containers (quite common in the United States, for example) in other Chinese restaurants or eateries in Bulgaria.

15. Lecture by Maria Todorova, Harvard University, spring semester, 1999.

References

Appadurai, Arjun. 1986. "On Culinary Authenticity." *Anthropology Today* 2(4): 24–25.

Asad, Talal. 1997. "Brief Note on the idea of 'An Anthropology of Europe,'" as part of "Provocations of European Ethnology," by Asad et al. *American Anthropologist* 99(4): 713–730.

Bak, Sangmee. 2006. "McDonald's in Seoul: Food Choices, Identity, and Nationalism." In *Golden Arches East: McDonald's in East Asia*, 2nd ed., edited by James L. Watson, 136–60. Stanford: Stanford University Press.

Bestor, Theodore. 2000. "How Sushi Went Global." *Foreign Policy*, November, 54–63.

Bhagwati, Jagdish. 2004. *In Defense of Globalization*. New York: Oxford University Press.

Bourdieu, Pierre. 1984. *Distinction: A Social Critique of the Judgement of Taste*. Cambridge, MA: Harvard University Press.

Bulgarian National Institute of Statistics. 2000. *Statisticheski Cprabochnik* (National Statistics Yearbook) 2000. Sofia: Bulgarian National Institute of Statistics.

———. 2001. *Statisticheski Cprabochnik* (National Statistics Yearbook) 2001. Sofia: Bulgarian National Institute of Statistics.

Caldwell, Melissa. 2004. "Domesticating the French Fry: McDonald's and Consumerism in Moscow." *Journal of Consumer Culture* 4(1): 5–26.

Campbell, Colin. 1987. *The Romantic Ethic and the Spirit of Modern Consumerism*. Oxford: Blackwell Publishers.

Creed, Gerald. 1998. *Domesticating Revolution: From Socialist Reform to Ambivalent Transition in a Bulgarian Village*. University Park: Pennsylvania State University Press.

Dimitrova, Milena, and Iva Rudnikova. 2001. "Bulgarskiyat Chainataun" (Bulgarian China-town). *Kapital,* 1 December, 37–39.

Fehérváry, Krisztina. 2002. "American Kitchens, Luxury Bathrooms, and the Search for a 'Normal' Life in Postsocialist Hungary." *Ethnos* 67(3): 369–400.

Herzfeld, Michael. 1987. *Anthropology through the Looking-glass: Critical Ethnography in the Margins of Europe.* Cambridge: Cambridge University Press.

———. 2004. *The Body Impolitic: Artisans and Artifice in the Global Hierarchy of Value.* Chicago: University of Chicago Press.

Humphrey, Caroline. 2002. *The Unmaking of Soviet Life: Everyday Economies after Socialism.* Ithaca, NY: Cornell University Press.

Jung, Yuson. 2007. *Consumer Lament: An Ethnographic Study on Consumption, Needs, and Everyday Complaints in Postsocialist Bulgaria.* Unpublished PhD dissertation, Department of Anthropology, Harvard University.

Krasteva, Anna. 2004. *Imigraziyata v Bulgaria* (Immigration in Bulgaria). Sofia: Mejdunaro-den Zentur za Izsledvane na Malzinstvata i Kulturnite Vzaimdeistviya.

Krasteva-Blagoeva, Evgenia. 2001. "Bulgarians and McDonald's: Some Anthropological Aspects." *Ethnologia Balkanica* 5: 207–218.

Lindholm, Charles. 2008. *Culture and Authenticity.* Medford: Blackwell Publishers.

Nutzenadel, Alexander, and Frank Trentmann, eds. 2008. *Food and Globalization: Consumption, Markets and Politics in the Modern World.* Oxford and New York: Berg.

Nyiri, Pal. 1999. *New Chinese Immigrants in Europe.* Aldershot: Ashgate.

———. 2007. *Chinese in Eastern Europe and Russia: A Middleman Minority in a Transnational Era.* Oxford: Routledge.

Nyiri, Pal, and Igor Rostislavovich. 2002. *Globalizing Chinese Migration: Trends in Europe and Asia.* Aldershot: Ashgate.

Ong, Aihwa. 1999. *Flexible Citizenship: The Cultural Logics of Transnationality.* Durham, NC: Duke University Press.

Patico, Jennifer. 2008. *Consumption and Social Change in a Post-Soviet Middle Class.* Washington, DC: Woodrow Wilson.

Phillips, Lynne. 2004. "Food and Globalization." *Annual Review of Anthropology* 35: 37–57.

Rausing, Sigrid. 2002. "Re-constructing the 'Normal': Identity and the Consumption of Western Goods in Estonia." In *Markets & Moralities: Ethnographies of Postsocialism,* edited by Caroline Humphrey and Ruth Mandel, 127–142. Oxford: Berg.

Ritzer, George. 1993. *The McDonaldization of Society: An Investigation into the Changing Character of Contemporary Social Life.* Thousand Oaks, CA: Pine Forge Press.

———. 2004. *The Globalization of Nothing.* Thousand Oaks, CA: Fine Forge Press.

Slater, Don. 2000. *Consumer Culture and Modernity.* Oxford: Polity.

Spooner, Brian. 1986. "Weavers and Dealers: The Authenticity of an Oriental Carpet." In *The Social Life of Things: Commodities in Cultural Perspective,* edited by Arjun Appadurai, 195–235. Cambridge: Cambridge University Press.

Tomlinson, John. 1991. *Cultural Imperialism.* Baltimore: Johns Hopkins University Press.

Tsing, Anna. 2005. *Friction: An Ethnography of Global Connection.* Princeton: Princeton University Press.

Waters, Malcolm. 1995. *Globalization.* London: Routledge.

Watson, James J., ed. 1975. *Emigration and the Chinese Lineage: The "Mans" in Hong Kong and London.* Berkeley: University of California Press.

————, ed. 2006. *Golden Arches East: McDonald's in East Asia*, 2nd ed. Stanford: Stanford University Press.

Watson, James, and Melissa Caldwell, eds. 2005. *The Cultural Politics of Food and Eating: A Reader*. Malden, MA: Blackwell Publishing.

Wilk, Richard. 1999. "Real Belizean Food: Building Local Identity in the Transnational Caribbean." *American Anthropologist* 101(2): 244–255.

Wu, David Y. H. 2006. "McDonald's in Taipei: Hamburgers, Betel Nuts, and National Identity." In *Golden Arches East: McDonald's in East Asia*, 2nd ed., edited by James L. Watson, 110–135. Stanford: Stanford University Press.

CHAPTER 9

Exoticizing the Familiar, Domesticating the Foreign
Ethnic Food Restaurants in Korea

Sangmee Bak

A food connoisseur whose job allows him to travel abroad frequently, Mr. Lee telephoned an Indian restaurant near a university in Seoul to make a reservation for dinner with a group of colleagues. He had dined there once previously, and found the place satisfactory. The restaurant was charmingly decorated with an Indian theme, the food was delicious, and the manager and staff appeared to be Indian. Everything was in line with his expectation of what a proper ethnic restaurant should be: a place where one can dine on authentic ethnic food as part of a cultural experience. However, as soon as he began conversing with the manager on the phone, he thought something was wrong. Instead of the Indian manager he met on his previous visit to the restaurant, a "Korean" man identified himself as the manager. Mr. Lee was extremely disappointed, thinking that the management of the restaurant has changed. He decided to confirm: "I think I met an Indian manager the other time. Has there been a change?" The person on the line replied, "Oh, I am that manager. I am an Indian myself. You must have met me!" As he was eagerly clarifying the situation, this Korean increasingly gained a distinctively Indian accent. The reservation was made, and when the group arrived at the restaurant, they found that the manager was a native of India with a high level of proficiency in Korean. This anecdote illustrates the constructive processes of the meanings and roles of ethnic food restaurants in today's Korean society. It shows the dynamic negotiations and compromises engaged in by Koreans and the operators of ethnic food restaurants. Together they define what ethnic food restaurants are supposed to be in Korean society.

This chapter is based on anthropological fieldwork on the meanings and positions of ethnic food restaurants in contemporary Korean society. It represents an attempt to understand how Koreans experience the process of globalization by focusing on ethnic food. When we use food culture as the lens through which to observe the process of globalization, we can find concrete and useful illustrations of several key concepts in the discourse on globalization: homogenization (standardization), heterogenization (localization or fragmentation), and hybridization.

Consumption of ethnic food is not only an expression of identities by the diverse ethnicities residing in Korea, but it is also a way for Koreans to construct their identities through consuming exotic food and the accompanying culinary culture. In this chapter, interviews were given and observations were made in various contexts where ethnic food is consumed in Korean society. Most of this took place in Seoul, but some fieldwork was also carried out in Ansan, a city about one hour's drive from Seoul, where a distinctive community of multiethnic immigrants is located. Both restaurateurs and consumers were interviewed, along with specialists in food production and consumption.

Ethnic Food and Ethnic Food Restaurants

Ethnic food,[1] if one defines it as a nondominant food practice, has been part of human history as long as people have been moving to locations remote from their birthplaces. Ethnic food has enriched local food cultures by introducing new ingredients and recipes. While ethnic food increases variety in local food culture, a form of standardization (homogenization) occurs when a cuisine is introduced as ethnic food to other cultures. For example, the cuisine of the Chinese, whose variety and depth of culinary sophistication are almost limitless, has been more or less standardized when it is served for American consumers. Except for exclusive upscale restaurants and, of course, restaurants catering to the Chinese immigrant population, only a limited number of dishes became widely available in the ubiquitous Chinese take-out restaurants in the United States. These include various combinations of stir-fried meat, seafood, and/or vegetables, fried noodles or rice, fried meat or seafood in egg batter, spring rolls, and dumplings. One could expect practically the same array of Chinese food whether in California, New York, or Minnesota. These processes of homogenization and standardization can also be found in the cases of Mexican and Thai restaurants in the United States. In other words, there is great variety among diverse ethnic cuisines, but within the individual cuisines, one can find a high degree of similarity from restaurant to restaurant within particular contexts.

In recent years, ethnic food has received more attention in the context of globalization as people became more alert to the possibility that the domination of Western culture will further accelerate. Valuing the diversity of local traditions also enhances people's appreciation of ethnic food. Malcolm Waters (2001) argued that one of the results of the globalization is the realization that all ethnic identities are legitimate. These identities include those without nation/state status. The increase of ethnic-food restaurants has been most notable in Western societies. Roland Robertson (1995) called this a "universalization of particularism," meaning that various kinds of ethnic cuisines have become popular in many different locations of the world.

Ethnic Food Restaurants in Korea

The production and consumption of ethnic food in Korea has a close relationship with class status. Food in general is an important marker for "distinction" (Bourdieu 1984), and Jack Goody (1982) also attempted to analyze the relationship between cuisine and class in historical processes. Consumption of food carries powerful meanings because food becomes a part of one's physical self. The close relationship between food and identity is clearly shown in the examples of Jewish dietary rules and the avoidance of beef among observant Hindus. Those food-related rules are not simply dietary rules but strong components of who they are and who they are not. Arjun Appadurai (1988) argued that a newly created "middle-class Indian cuisine" significantly contributed to the construction of a new collective identity in India after independence from the British colonial rule. The publication of cookbooks to establish and standardize the new national cuisine was pivotal in this process. Emiko Ohnuki-Tierney (1993) conducted a historical study on the central position of rice in defining Japanese national identity. Kyung-Koo Han (2000) and Yeong-ha Ju (2000) have both argued that kimchi might be the Korean equivalent of a defining food like rice for Japan. Eun Kyung Park (1994) examined how Chinese residents in Korea have adapted Chinese cuisine to suit their customers' palates and in the process established an overseas Chinese identity within Korea.

Expectations and Adaptive Strategies in Ethnic Food Restaurants

Ethnic food restaurants in Korea satisfy the expectation for exoticism while still remaining within the comfort zone of such expectations. It is a guarded and safe form of exotic experience, to a certain degree custom-made for Koreans.[2] These characteristics are expressed in the interior decoration, the selection of menus, and the modification of original recipes to cater to the palates of average Korean customers. In this way, ethnic restaurants dutifully carry out their role, akin to the object of "tourist gaze" (Urry 2002). The experience that Korean customers have is that of a distinctively unusual yet comfortable form of exoticism.

Since the majority of Indian restaurants in Korea are operated by Nepalese immigrants—not Indians—Nepalese owners strongly argue that there is in fact no significant difference between Indian and Nepalese cuisine. The Nepalese restaurant operators argue that they can provide authentic Indian cuisine without much difficulty. To support this argument, they enthusiastically emphasized that the relationship between the Indians and the Nepalese has always been amicable. Otherwise, they asked, how could the Nepalese have survived when they are surrounded by India in all directions?

The restaurateurs I interviewed were obviously proud of their food. For example, the owners of Indian restaurants maintained that Indian food is the healthiest cuisine. As evidence of this, restaurateurs mention that their signature dish, tandoori chicken, is put into an oven after removing all the fatty skin, their dishes use a plethora of vegetables and fruits, and many ingredients of Indian food, such as turmeric, have medicinal qualities. But even with this pride that they have in their original recipes and ingredients, they are ready to adjust their recipes to attract more Korean customers. In this way, the restaurateurs are negotiating the notions of authenticity with their customers.

The managers of Delhi Indian Restaurant in two locations told me that they are preparing their dishes sweeter than the versions popular in India because they believe that Koreans nowadays like their food sweet. They make their curries and a variety of nan bread sweeter by adding sugar or honey. However, some diners already familiar with Indian food strongly dislike these additions, and complain that the sweetness and Indian spices simply do not harmonize on the palate. In this way, efforts to please one group of customers may alienate others due to the different backgrounds and expectations of customer groups. An attempt to modify the original may seriously harm the expected authenticity of the cuisine and restaurant, which can in turn negatively affect the establishment's appeal for some customers.

The Popularity of Ethnic Food in Korea

There are several factors that have contributed to the popularity of ethnic food restaurants in Korean society. Most importantly, Koreans have become much more globalized in recent years. They are more informed about other cultures, and more willing to experiment with the less familiar. An increasing number of Koreans have traveled abroad and want to experience global cultural diversity in Korea as well. The increased availability of information on food and restaurants, and particularly the sharing of knowledge via websites on cuisine or tourism (for example, menupan.com or wingspoon.naver.com), have also allowed Koreans to experience exotic cuisines without putting in too much time and effort. Koreans have been dining out more frequently with increasing economic affluence and more women working outside the home. As one possible destination for such exploratory culinary excursions, ethnic restaurants have gained popularity. The ethnic restaurant business really started to take off after the 1988 Seoul Olympics, when Koreans began to seriously look outside their society and sought a global identity. Before this, the few ethnic restaurants available in Korea mainly catered to foreigners who already had experienced these cuisines prior to their arrival in Korea.

People who run restaurants in the same ethnic food category are obviously competitors, but also collaborators who exchange information with one another on the Korean market and try to promote their particular cuisine. They strive to increase the number of Korean customers who enjoy their cuisine. These efforts have significantly enhanced the visibility of ethnic food restaurants in Korea.

Categories of Ethnic Food Restaurants and their Customers

There are a significant number of inexpensive restaurants located in commercial districts and college neighborhoods where customers can satisfy their curiosity and appetite for ethnic food at a cost similar to ordinary Korean-style eateries. The majority of the owners of these establishments are Koreans, but the number of owners/managers who are from the original sources of those ethnic cuisines is on the increase. Some restaurants in this category provide customers with so-called authenticity in food and other related cultural experiences. The cooks of restaurants in this category are almost always professional chefs who have appropriate visas and come to Korea through personal networks. Many of them boast that they used to work at major restaurants in their native countries, and supervised a large number of chefs and staff. The price level at these places tends to be moderate or low.

Another significant cluster of ethnic food restaurants is located in Itaewon, where a distinctive foreign community has existed since the Korean War. In fact, the highest concentration of ethnic restaurants in Korea is found in this neighborhood. Nowadays, more than half of the customers who patronize the ethnic restaurants in this area are Koreans, and the rest are foreigners who are not necessarily from the region where the particular ethnic cuisine originates. Some restaurants sell religiously appropriate dishes (particularly halal foods for the Muslims). Ethnic cuisines popular with Western residents in Korea, such as Turkish or Thai, have more than one establishment in this neighborhood. Regardless of the variety of cuisines, most places offer service in English as well as in Korean.

The third category is that of ethnic restaurants in the areas where such immigrant communities have been established with the influx of a large-scale foreign work force starting in the 1990s. For example, the city of Ansan, about an hour's subway ride from Seoul, has a well-established district where immigrants who work in nearby factories come in order to satisfy their nostalgia for home. These restaurants tend to serve dishes that are regularly eaten as part of ordinary meals in their home countries. The food is relatively cheap and the menu is not very extensive. Some restaurants in this category also sell groceries from countries of origin, along with mobile phones, network services, and international telephone cards. Other examples of ethnic enclaves include the Korean-Chinese community in Garibong-dong, the historic cluster of Chinese restaurants in Incheon, and the community of Mongolian and former USSR nationals in Dongdaemun District.

The fourth category includes upscale ethnic restaurants in affluent neighborhoods. Naturally, prices tend to be higher in these restaurants. In some cases, the price for the same dish may be twice as much as what the customers would pay in restaurants in other locations. Their price ranges sometimes surpass those of upscale French or Italian restaurants. The ethnic restaurants in this category have sophisticated interior design and tend to carry lengthy wine lists. The owners are without exception Koreans, while the serving staff may be either Koreans or immigrants from the cuisine's original area. The cooks are almost always from the cuisine's country of origin. Some dining establishments were influenced by the Japanese style of cooking ethnic dishes, as some chefs come to Korea after working in Japan, which has a longer history of ethnic restaurants. Restaurants in this category include those in Garosugil, Cheongdam-dong, Samcheong-dong, and Hannam-dong.

There are large franchise restaurants for some popular ethnic cuisines such as Thai, Vietnamese, and Indian. Many dishes are Koreanized and standardized. For example, the use of coriander (cilantro) leaves is minimized, or provided only when the customers asks for them specifically. The food tends to use fewer spices and limit the use of oil. The restaurants in this category are not clustered in a particular area, but can be found in major commercial areas or near universities, where they can expect a steady flow of customers.

Cases

The following restaurants illustrate the different types of restaurants described earlier. Anthropological fieldwork, including participant observation and interviews was the primary means of obtaining information used here. The names of the restaurants were changed by the author.

Bombay

Bombay[3] is an Indian restaurant located near the front gate of a university in the northeastern part of Seoul. At the time of my first interview with the owner, the restaurant had been in business for about one-and-a-half months. They have only one cook, who came from India and for sixteen years had supervised a thirty-person staff as a head chef before moving to Korea. The owner is from the Punjab region of India. For both the owner and the chef, Bombay is their first restaurant business experience in Korea. A mutual acquaintance introduced them to each other, and the cook obtained a working visa for chefs before coming to Korea.

The food at Bombay is northern Indian, reflecting the hometowns of the owner and the chef. The owner claimed that neither of them could even eat south Indian food, since it is so different. The owner came to Korea in 2000 to export used PCs from Korea to India, but the price of new Indian PCs had dropped significantly and used ones from Korea were no longer a bargain for Indian consumers when compared to newly made domestic ones. It was at that point that he decided to convert to the restaurant business.

The most popular dishes at Bombay are tandoori chicken (14,000 won for a whole chicken, usually shared by two people), butter chicken (10,000 won for a serving for two), and chicken curry. The "whole chicken" served at Indian restaurants is smaller than that of other cuisines because Indian restaurants normally do not use the wings. Customers usually try well-known dishes first, before moving on to other, less familiar menu items. The owner claimed that he tried to put the lowest possible price on the dishes that Bombay serves so that even students can visit without worrying too much about money.

Bombay buys Indian basmati rice[4] from small-scale traders. One kilogram of rice costs 11,000 won. It is much more expensive than Korean rice varieties, but has a distinctive nutty fragrance and soaks up sauces better, making the food taste more like the food served in India. They hope that once the regulation on the import of rice for individual consumption is lifted, Indian restaurants will be able to lower the cost. They buy Kingfisher Beer (a well-known Indian brand) at 4,500 won a bottle from the wholesale importer, and sell them at 5,500 won. The owner asserted that he does not make much money from the sale of Indian beer, but carries them for customers who might want them, and believes that a proper Indian restaurant has to serve Kingfisher. They also have Italian wines on the beverage list, but so far no one has ordered them. Students do not usually drink beer or wine there, probably because of their tight budgets.

The owner said that one or two customers a day have problems with the coriander in their food, but others seem to really love it and would consider Indian food without coriander unthinkable. They make sure to ask their customers if coriander is desired when they take their orders. There is a wholesale fruit and vegetable market in Guri, a town northeast of Seoul, where the restaurant regularly buys their coriander.

Bombay has made some changes to make their food more palatable for Korean tastes, including toning down the spice. According to them, Korean food's spiciness only comes from chili peppers, but Indian food gets its distinctive taste from a combination of many different spices, which some Koreans dislike. As Koreans also tend to express distaste for "oily" foods, the chef mixes the oil with other ingredients during cooking, so the final dish looks less oily on the surface even though the amount of oil remains the same.

The owner confided that he had opened his restaurant at the current location because he has lived in this neighborhood for the last five years while engaging in the used-computer trade. Some Indians live there because there is a bus line that runs to the Sikh temple in Gwangneung. All in all, he likes running his restaurant in Korea because the business has been lucrative and he sees a bright future here.

One of the interesting characteristics of Bombay is that there are very few overtly "Indian" components in the interior of the restaurant. The place just looks clean and modern, and could be a restaurant of any variety. When asked about this, he said he did not want to decorate his restaurant in typical Indian style, so he just made it look modern.

About 60 percent of his customers are the students at the nearby university, and the rest are residents who live in the neighborhood. According to him, the number of those among his customer base who have visited India is still very small and does not make up a significant group of visitors to the restaurant. Most of his customers come as couples that can have a meal for 13,000–14,000 won per person. This price is a little higher than that of the cheapest meals near campus, but still quite affordable for many students.

The owner likes to compare his restaurant and the food with that of Chinese restaurants, which are also numerous in the area. Eating at Chinese restaurants is one of the least expensive options for students. The owner said that when he sees the food sold at Chinese restaurants here, it looks like the restaurant spends less than 1,000 won on raw material to make a 5,000 won dish, while in contrast, he declares, it is very costly to prepare Indian dishes. For instance, cashew nuts, used in large quantities in some Indian dishes, are very expensive in Korea, and the average cost for 100 grams of spice is 4,000–5,000 won. The only main ingredients they can source locally are the vegetables. He expressed concern that the price of vegetables would go up with the advent of winter.

The owner and the chef argued that Indian food uses only what is good for human body. For example, wild turmeric, one of the main ingredients in Indian curries, used to be picked by old people in the Himalayas, and was very good for health. Nowadays turmeric is cultivated. In the past, people used to drink ghee (clarified butter) in large quantities because they needed the calories for strenuous physical work. Now people do not engage in as much physical labor and do not drink ghee, but ghee, turmeric, and lassi (yogurt-based drink) are still important components of Indian cuisine.

The customers of Bombay that I interviewed, including university faculty and students, seemed to think of the restaurant as one of the places that added to the cosmopolitan composition of eateries around the campus. While the majority stated that they would not dine at Bombay every day because it would be excessive to eat Indian food so often, they were definitely willing to patronize the restaurant once in a while to diversify their meal choices. Some of the characteristics of Indian restaurants in general, and those of Bombay in particular, seemed to bother some customers, who disliked the fact that, by Korean standards, the kitchen was too slow. This is partly due to the fact that there is only one chef (although the restaurant is small, with only five tables), but also reflects the characteristics of Indian cooking style. Most customers order nan, a distinctive flat bread, as part of their meal, which must be baked right before it is served. Some foods, like curry, can be prepared in large quantities in advance, but the popular tandoori chicken should be cooked after the order is made so that it does not dry out from overcooking. Korean customers are used to having their food ready on the table almost immediately after ordering. Complaining over the wait for food is almost a regular part of Korean customers' dining experience; therefore, they would expect similar experiences at other ethnic food restaurants in Korea.

Delhi on Garosugil: An Indian/Nepalese Restaurant in an Upscale Neighborhood

Delhi opened in August 2009 on Garosugil, arguably the most chic neighborhood in Seoul at the time of research. Delhi is the second Indian restaurant on that street. The first one is a branch of a popular and upscale Indian restaurant chain that has other branch restaurants in Cheongdam-dong and Samcheong-dong, both areas known for upscale restaurants and cafes.

The managing owner of this restaurant is a forty-year-old man from Nepal who came to Korea as a student and later engaged in the export trade between Korea and Nepal. The main business for him was to export Korean merchandise to Nepal, which included blankets and knit sweaters. As Indian food gained popularity among younger Koreans, he resolved to open a restaurant. Although he is from Nepal, which has similar cuisine to India, he decided to open an Indian restaurant first, with plans to include Nepalese dishes later. He says that Nepalese cuisine is too exotic for ordinary Koreans to enjoy regularly, but he plans to include some spicy and soupy dishes from Nepal because Koreans seem to like having spicy soup to recover from hangovers.

The managing owner compared the business strategies of this establishment with that of another branch restaurant near a university (the third case in this chapter). He said that the strategies of the two locations would be quite different given the difference in clientele. In their Garosugil restaurant, they sell more wine and have higher prices, while the restaurant near the university tries to provide a less expensive menu. The interior decoration also reflects the difference in customers' socioeconomic background. More ornate and expensive furniture and objects outfit the Garosugil branch, and management was confident that Delhi is probably the most elegantly decorated Indian restaurant chain in Korea. They brought hand-carved furniture and ornaments from Nepal, and the restaurants are, in a way, display rooms for these items. If so inclined, customers can order such decorative items for purchase.

When I interviewed the customers of this restaurant, they first pointed out a disparity between the food prices and the level of wine on the list; the food was fairly expensive reflecting the overall price level in the area, but the wine list was too limited and inexpensive, although they admitted that spicy Indian food and delicate wines may not go well together. However, customers of restaurants on Garosugil expect a wine list to be included as part of the dining experience. They said the restaurant operators needed to spend more time putting together a solid wine list after rigorous research on good pairings between Indian food and wine. The customers also mentioned that the niche market of Indian restaurants on Garosugil may have some identity issues; most restaurants on that street double as cafes during the daytime, selling pricy drink menus with simple lunches as a means of dealing with the high rent in the area. For most Korean customers, having a drink at an Indian restaurant does not sound very appealing. Indian restaurants are places to eat food with strong flavors rather than cafes where one can enjoy an elegant cup of tea or coffee. Selling an inexpensive lunch menu is not sufficient to meet the rent for spaces on Garosugil.

Delhi, Near a University in the Northeastern Part of Seoul

When I approached the manager of this restaurant, they were still engaged in a renovation project and due to open the fourth Delhi restaurant near the subway station in front of the university. The restaurant will occupy the second and third floors of a four-story building. The third floor is designed to accommodate fifty to sixty people and host private parties. The restaurant was set to open in about ten days, once they acquired the necessary permits from the relevant city and district authorities.

The first Delhi restaurant opened in 1991 near the Dongmyo subway station. It started as a combination of a trading-firm office and a small restaurant for the Nepalese expatriates in Korea. Slowly, the number of local customers increased, and they opened their second restaurant in the Jongno Tower Building, a major center of commercial activities in a central office district. The third one opened on Garosugil in Gangnam district, a sophisticated and affluent part of Seoul, populated by galleries and upscale cafes and restaurants.

The differences among the four locations called for adjusting the menu, price level, and nature of service to suit customer characteristics. Dongmyo also serves as a retailer of spices and other imported goods, while the Jongno branch is for mostly young, white-collar workers, and the university neighborhood branch is for college students and local residents. The Garosugil branch is the most upscale among the four, as a result of the affluent and trendy neighborhood. In this branch, they plan to have a lengthier wine list and imported beers to comply with customers' demands. The interior of all Delhi restaurants are decorated with wooden latticed doors and carvings imported from Nepal, which can be purchased by customers at the restaurant's headquarters in Dongmyo. According to the Indian owner of Bombay restaurant, Delhi is a well-known success story among the Indians and Nepalese who do business in Korea.

The most popular dish is tandoori chicken. Various kinds of curries (including the spicy vindaloo) are popular as well. Mr. Bogati, the manager of the fourth restaurant, said that Koreans are learning that there are more than yellow, turmeric-based curries (modified and introduced by the Japanese to Koreans). Mr. Bogati believes that Indian food will be increasingly popular among Koreans because of turmeric's preventive effects on Alzheimer's disease. The generous use of fresh vegetables and skinless oven-baked chicken will also enhance Indian food's popularity among health-conscious Koreans.

As is the case in other Indian, Vietnamese, and Thai restaurants in Korea, the only problematic ingredient is fresh coriander, which is frequently mixed in or put on top of finished dishes as garnish. Some Koreans dislike the strong flavor of the herb. The staff routinely asks their customers whether to include coriander in the dish when they take the order. All raw materials except fresh vegetables and fruit come from Nepal or India. One problem, however, is that they cannot legally import the long-grained basmati rice eaten in Nepal and India. Using Korean rice significantly changes the texture and flavor of Indian dishes. Basmati rice is fluffier, nuttier, and more porous, which lets the rice soak up more liquid. For now, they are using basmati rice purchased from merchants who bring it into Korea in small quantities. The price is quite high, about 11,000 won for one kilogram of rice.

Due to the location of the restaurant near the university, they expect the customers will be half college students and half local residents. Since the price is relatively low (a lunch or dinner without drink costs about 4,000 won), they think they can attract price-conscious young people who want to satisfy their taste for the exotic. They hope to establish a friendly relationship with the university's student organizations and participate in the university's spring and fall festivals to familiarize the students with Indian food.

Contrary to what is reported in the mass media, the number of customers who seek out these restaurants because of prior travel to the region is still too small to be taken seriously. Most customers experience the cuisine for the first time in Korea, and slowly grow to enjoy it. The owners of the newest branch said that they know the person who runs Bombay and even have had tea with him. The owner believes the pool of potential customers is large enough for the survival of both restaurants, but the owner of Bombay confided that he is a little worried about the scale of the new restaurant, which takes up two floors of a building on a major street. He said he might have to compete by lowering the prices, and is thinking of opening a buffet-style restaurant in the basement of the same building his restaurant is currently occupying.

Some of the potential customers of Delhi, the faculty and students at the university, were not sure whether the third-floor banquet hall of the new restaurant would be utilized as the owners intended. The students said that the two main reasons they often gather in Chinese restaurants is that those restaurants provide an appropriate space for a reasonable price, and most students have no strong objections to Chinese food. Indian food may encounter stronger opposition from some students. The faculty also said that they might try Indian food once or twice with people who are similarly inclined, but would be reluctant to have a department gathering there because it would be a problem if even one member does not like it. Indian food is still too exotic to be used for such functions.

Ghandi in Itaewon: Indian/Pakistani Restaurant

This is a large-scale Indian restaurant with outdoor seating that is frequented by many foreigners. A buffet and grilled meat, which are commonly available in many restaurants of the neighborhood, are also popular dishes here. It is relatively upscale compared to other Indian restaurants in Seoul, and has an extensive wine and beer selection. Among the Indian restaurants included in this research, Ghandi seemed to have the largest percentage of family groups. The restaurant's facilities, including a garden and barbecue, make it ideal for family dining. The owner seemed to be very comfortable with customers of diverse ethnic backgrounds, reflecting the location of the restaurant.

This restaurant opened in 1984, making it one of the oldest Indian restaurants in Korea, and represents itself as a place where one can dine on royal palace cuisine. It has a full bar for drinks, including a wide array of cocktails, and an outdoor tandoor pit. The spacious garden has a glass partition that can be opened on warm days for better ventilation.

Many customers like to use the outdoor tables, which are not very common in Korea. Those who do not have much background knowledge of Indian food often prefer to dine from the buffet table. Although the price is not cheap (20,000 won for lunch, and 25,000 for dinner, excluding drinks), they like to see the food before making their own selections. Many customers, especially young people, order fruit-flavored lassi. Older customers, however, expressed the opinion that sweet drinks before or during the meal spoil the appetite.

The restaurant Ghandi has established itself as one of the main "ethnic" establishments in Itaewon. It also seems to enjoy good business with both Korean and international customers.

Annapurna in Shinchon

This restaurant has a primarily Himalayan theme, and is frequented by students of Yonsei University. Prices are low, and the food tends to be much spicier than other Indian restaurants in Korea. Consequently, customers say that the food at this restaurant tastes more "authentic."

One of the distinctive characteristics of this restaurant is that take-out is an important part of sales. At all the other restaurants observed for this research, most customers dine in, and except for the few customers who bring leftover food home, almost no take-out orders were made. Except for the home delivery of certain foods (inexpensive Chinese food, pizza, and fried chicken), Koreans seem to prefer eating in at a restaurant rather than taking out food for consumption elsewhere. This could be related to Koreans' preference for eating food right after the food is prepared, when it is still fresh and hot. Koreans also seem to think that the price of food at restaurants includes the cost for using the restaurant space.

Annapurna is located in a narrow back alley near the university, and is not particularly visible from the main street. The restaurant is very well known among young people who frequent restaurant and food websites, and has received very good reviews from amateur food critics online. Many writers commented that Annapurna is a place for those who are familiar with Indian cuisine and enjoy the distinctive spices, but not a place for novices in ethnic dining. The manager of the restaurant confirmed that he does not try to modify the original recipes because he already has enough loyal customers who like his restaurant's food as it is. He said that some customers eat at the restaurant and order the same food for take-out, to be eaten later.

Persian Dream: Iranian Restaurant

The owner of this restaurant first came to Korea as a student in medicine and psychology before he opened the restaurant near a university in central Seoul. The restaurant specializes in Iranian curry and meat dishes, and is located inside an obscure back alley. The interior of the restaurant is heavily decorated with Persian objects. Full of information on Iranian food culture and manners, the menu devotes significant space to highlighting press coverage of the establishment. However, many customers commented that the restaurant's food is very similar to Indian cuisine, and told me that they cannot distinguish one from the other.

The customers are mainly young people. The most popular dish is fried chicken in curry-flavored gravy. Except for the manager, all the people serving in the hall are Koreans who work there part-time. The restaurant does not sell any alcoholic beverages. When customers inquire, the serving staff explained that Iran is a Muslim country, and they serve good tea instead of alcoholic beverages.

A Cambodian Restaurant in Ansan

A Cambodian restaurant is located on the main street of Ansan's commercial and residential district for foreign workers. The restaurant does not have a large

Korean signboard; instead, the sign is written in Cambodian with Korean translation below in a small script. The outside of the restaurant is not indicative that it serves food, and the windows are covered with dark cellophane. Inside, the walls are covered with photographs of the Angkor Wat and other Cambodian tourist sites. The overall appearance gives the impression that it is not actively seeking Korean customers.

The owner is a Korean who is engaged in a trading business with Cambodia. He also sells mobile phones and other goods to ethnic Cambodians living in Korea. About half of his restaurant space was devoted to the display of these goods, including Cambodian food products.

The menu was very simple, with a limited selection of beef, pork, chicken, and fish with rice served with Korean kimchi and Cambodian hot sauce. When I ate the shrimp fried rice and pork, the owner suggested that I mix the sauce with the food to make it spicy enough for Korean tastes. Each plate of food costs about 5,000 won, except for some specialty dishes like whole fish. They only carried domestic beer and used Korean rice.

Overall, the restaurant did not seem to be intended as a place for sophisticated Cambodian cuisine, but the customers can at least fill their stomachs with Cambodian flavors. The chef used to work at the Cambodian Embassy in Korea and is a very well-respected chef according to the Korean owner of the restaurant. However, the menu is too limited for him to utilize his full culinary abilities. In addition to the chef from Cambodia, the restaurant also has one part-time female waitress from Cambodia. She is attending a local university, and works at the restaurant to support herself. The owner said that the majority of his customers are Cambodians who work in the area, along with occasional visits by Cambodian women married to Korean men.

Ethnic Food Restaurants and Identities

When the food of one ethnicity or nation food is introduced in other parts of the world, the cuisine undergoes standardization and modification to adapt to the receiving culture. This process helps construct its global identity. Indian cuisine, for example, is offered in buffet style at inexpensive prices in the United States. American customers have certain expectations of Indian restaurants. In the Korean case, the identity of Indian cuisine is still actively being constructed. The restaurateurs and their (potential) customers are actively engaged in negotiating and compromising on what Indian food should be in Korea. How Indian food is positioned in Korean food culture will be another component of the global identity of Indian cuisine. In this process, cultural homogenization (Indian food is available everywhere in the world), fragmentation (localization of Indian food), and hybridization (Indian mixed with Korean cuisine when they enhance the satisfaction of both) can all be observed.

A Korean restaurateur who is operating a successful Thai restaurant says that one of the remarkable characteristics of Korean customers at ethnic restaurants is that they are predominantly women. She said that the busiest day of the year at her restaurant is Valentine's Day, when couples make reservations to dine out. In most cases, according to her observation, it is the woman who makes the choice of the restaurant. She also said that while it is common to see groups of women eat at her restaurant, she rarely sees groups of men. Similar observations were made at other ethnic restaurants in my research. Women tend to be more flexible and willing to experiment with new cuisine. Many Koreans who have lived abroad testify that Korean women adapted to local food much sooner than men. Consumption of ethnic food and command of related knowledge as cultural capital seem to be highly gendered in today's Korean society.

The process for an ethnic cuisine to acquire a global identity can be applied to the much-discussed issue of the globalization of Korean food. The Korean government and related experts ask the following questions: Which Korean dishes will be most popular among the consumers outside Korea? How should we change to make them more popular? Should we stick to what is traditionally Korean, or modify recipes to suit the tastes of foreigners? Interestingly, it is always assumed that the "global consumers" are Westerners. Koreans attempt to identify what hinders Westerners from fully enjoying Korean food, and experiment with Western course-style Korean food in an effort to find the perfect match between wine and Korean food. In this context, economic concerns and nationalistic sentiments are prevalent. Many Koreans are frustrated to find that Korean food is not as popular as it should be. They also worry that some popular Korean dishes are being introduced to Westerners by the Japanese, thereby compromising the food's Korean identity. Through these complex discussions of Korean food and its identity, the cuisine is slowly gaining its global identity. There is no question that the global identity of Korean cuisine will be an important component of Korean people's identity throughout this process. Whether in consuming various ethnic foods within Korea or in promoting Korean food globally, diverse groups of Koreans located in different positions within Korea engage in the dynamic process of negotiating, competing, and contesting the nature of relationship between food consumption and their identities.

Notes

An earlier version of the present article was published in 2010 in *Korea Journal* 50(1): 110–132.
  1. Ethnic food is widely used in America to mean many different cuisines, but primarily used as a category for non-European cuisines nowadays.
  2. This is comparable to what Starbucks Coffee shops provided American consumers who wanted a European (Italian) coffee-drinking experience in the comfort of a familiar environment. In this case, Italian-style coffee drinking is filtered through the expectations of middle- and upper-middle-class Americans (Bak 2005).

3. The names of the restaurants in these case studies have been changed to protect their identities.
4. A long-grained rice favored in Indian cuisine.

References

Appadurai, Arjun. 1988. "How to Make a National Cuisine: Cookbooks in Contemporary India." *Comparative Study of Society and History* 30(1): 3–24.

Bak, Sangmee. 2004. "Negotiating National and Transnational Identities through Consumption Choices: Hamburgers, Espresso, and Mobile Technologies among Koreans." *Review of Korean Studies* 7(2): 33–51.

———. 1997. "McDonald's in Seoul: Food Choices, Identity, and Nationalism." In *Golden Arches East,* edited by James L. Watson, 136–160. Stanford: Stanford University Press.

———. 2003. "Mat-gwa chwihyang-ui jeongcheseong-gwa gyeonggye neomgi" (Crossing the Boundaries between Flavor and Taste Identities). *Hyeonsang-gwa insik* (Phenomena and Perceptions) 27(3): 54–70.

———. 2005. "From Strange Bitter Concoction to Romantic Necessity." *Korea Journal* 45(2): 37–59.

Bourdieu, Pierre. 1984. *Distinction,* translated by R. Nice. Cambridge: Harvard University Press.

Counihan, Carole M. 1999. *The Anthropology of Food and Body.* New York: Routledge.

Douglas, Mary. 1971. "Decipherng a Meal." In *Myth, Symbol, and Ritual,* edited by Clifford Geertz, 36–54, New York: W. W. Norton and Company.

Goody, Jack. 1982. *Cooking, Cuisine, and Class.* Cambridge: Cambridge University Press.

Han, Kyung-Koo. 2000. "Some Foods are Good to Think: Kimchi and the Epitomization of National Character." *Korea Social Science Journal* 27(1): 221–236.

Ju, Yeong-ha. 2000. *Gimchi, hangugin-ui meokgeori gimchi-ui munhwa illyuhak* (Kimchi, Koreans' Staple Food Cultural Anthropology of Kim-chi). Seoul: Konggan.

Kim, Kwang Ok. 1994. "Eumsik-gwa hyeondae hanguk sahoe: chongnon" (Foods and Contemporary Korean Society: A Brief Overview). *Hanguk munhwa illyuhak* (Korean Cultural Anthropology) 26: 1–44.

Mintz, Sidney W. 1996. *Tasting Food, Tasting Freedom.* Boston: Beacon Press.

Ohnuki-Tierney, Emiko. 1993. *Rice as Self: Japanese Identities through Time.* Princeton: Princeton University Press.

Park, Eun Kyung. 1994. "Jungguk eumsik-ui yeoksajeok uimi" (Historical Significance of Chinese Food). *Hanguk munhwa illyuhak* (Korean Cultural Anthropology) 26: 95–115.

Robertson, Roland. 1995. "Glocalization: Time-Space and Homogeneity-Heterogeneity." In *Global Modernities,* edited by M. Featherstone et al., 25–44. London: Sage.

Urry, John. 2002. *The Tourist Gaze.* London: Sage Publications.

Waters, Malcolm. 2001. *New World Chaos: Globalizing Cultures.* London and New York: Routledge.

CHAPTER 10

Serving Ambiguity
Class and Classification in Thai Food at Home and Abroad

Michael Herzfeld

Anthropologists have long argued a direct correlation between formal social structure and the elaboration or simplicity of food presentation and consumption (Douglas 1966, 1970; Goody 1982). These arguments are today further complicated by two factors. First, ethnography often celebrates indeterminacy and ambiguity as its most promising grounding (e.g., Malaby 2003; Steedly 1993; Tsing 1993). And second, renewed interest in taste and smell (e.g., Bubandt 1998; Seremetakis 1993) changes the conceptual context in which we understand the capacity of food to create as well as to cross social boundaries.

Ambiguous Explosions

Where better to conduct such an ethnographic investigation of these matters than in Thailand? This is a nation-state that claims never to have been a colonial possession but that often appears to follow the dictates of the Western political and cultural economy quite subserviently; that claims as its own "Thai pepper" (*phrik thai*) the acidic black peppercorn, which, by contrast to the alkaline chili brought to Southeast Asia around the sixteenth century by Portuguese and Iranian traders, is virtually the only form of pepper that is *not* generally seen by foreigners as typically Thai; that boasts both the remnants of a feudal system predicated on an authority structure the legal roots of which are as much Western as Thai (Loos 2006) and a flourishing tradition of radical agrarian and urban protest; and that also boasts a code of etiquette (*marayaat*) that conceals, much as do the elaborate manners of Italian *mafiosi,* a surprising amount of structural violence. Thailand is also the home of one of the spiciest cuisines in the world, as well as of a Buddhist ethic that decries intense tastes of any kind as being excessively appetitive in a material sense—but here we move straight into another paradox, the remarkable this-worldliness of Thai Buddhism (see Byrne 2009; Taylor 2008).

There are other countries to which these or similar descriptions might apply. In Italy, for example, although that country is now a republic, we meet ideals and styles of etiquette that are grounded in older aristocratic modalities and, not co-incidentally, are associated with elaborate food traditions. But the emergence of a distinctive Thai cuisine on a global level, resting (as a restaurateur might remark) on a bed of a Chinese-derived noodle dish known as "Thai stir fry" (*phad thai*), offers more grist to the mill of my present discussion, in part because, generally speaking, Thai cooks are more willing to experiment than their Italian counter-parts. They will even adapt Italian pasta to Thai sauces, remodeling, for example, the ever-popular "drunken noodles" (*kweitiaw phad khii mao,* a dish flavored with searingly hot green peppers [*phrik khii nuu,* "mouse-shit peppers"], garlic, fish sauce, and basil) as "drunken spaghetti" (*sapaketii phad khii mao*); it would be hard to imagine an Italian cook producing pasta with a correspondingly Thai flavor.[1] Since Thai attitudes to food are overtly flexible in ways that we do not encounter in the relatively conservative and highly regionalized Italian foodscape, Thai cuisine should allow us easier access to the underlying cultural and social processes now under way. The very notion of an Italian cuisine appears to have grown out of the production of cookbooks in a process of "entextualization" that was tantamount to an exercise in national solidarity building analogous in certain respects to what Arjun Appadurai (1988) reports for India.[2] Globalization has also brought its own peculiar effects; even without former Thai Prime Minister Thaksin Shinawatra's aggressive campaign to export Thai cuisine overseas on a grand scale, globalization seems to have standardized the canon of Thai cuisine worldwide. The global expansion of interest in Thai cooking has certainly led to simplification and streamlining in the internationally recognized Thai culinary repertoire without significantly damaging the range and variety of dishes obtain-able in the country itself.

Because a significant part of my argument concerns indeterminacy, I will have to risk provoking some serious salivation among my readers. Culinary experi-mentation and elaboration flourish in situations where flair is also appreciated in social interactions, and where the mastery of splendid courtesy may sometimes conceal a deep sense of social inequality—in other words, where manners are a matter of serious play, much of it ironic. Because food is not directly translatable into the language of respect and insult—and indeed may serve, as hospitality so often does (Herzfeld 1987), to reverse unequal roles by placing the nominally superior host under a serious social obligation—the ways in which it is offered and reinvented can serve as vehicles for quite complex negotiations of position.

Thus, I propose to begin with what I hope will be a mouthwatering descrip-tion of the complex gastro-symphony of Thai food, with its decided likeness to a complex firework display. (It may indeed be far from coincidental that Thais enjoy pyrotechnics, which themselves engage an intriguing tension between the official, public nature of many such events and the nagging sense of something disreputable associated with the manufacture and sale of the fireworks themselves.[3]) I will then contrast the seemingly unseemly intensity of Thai food experiences with the stately regulation of table manners, as well as with the ease and frequency with which that etiquette is breached. I will suggest that the game of table manners reflects the same paradoxical dynamic as so many other aspects of Thailand's "crypto-colonial" (Herzfeld 2002) condition, and I will conclude by sketching an argument—still necessarily preliminary—to the effect that Thailand's continuing domination by Western (and increasingly by Chinese) political and economic interests has now amplified Thai self-consciousness about what constitutes "Thai cuisine" to the point of self-parody, reflecting and paralleling the crisis of political legitimacy that has accompanied the emergence of a cosmopolitan Thai middle class.[4]

A few words about hierarchy and egalitarianism in Thailand, then, will help to set the context of the discussion. Thai life is marked by a constant tension between these two stances, marked by phrases and actions that often seem deliberately used to obscure its presence. Notable among these expressions in the term *phii nawng* (literally "elder siblings / younger siblings") used by political leaders to emphasize both their communal, quasi-familial membership but also their presumed superiority in terms of education and power (Herzfeld 2012: 149–150). In the Bangkok community of Pom Mahakan, where I have been conducting fieldwork for some years, these tensions are powerfully experienced, since the effective president of the community is a largely undisputed boss of quite aggressive style who harangues the residents about the importance of, paradoxically, making their criticisms of his leadership felt and heard. But in the segmentary world of Thai politics, the same phrase is used by politicians even at the national level; the whole polity is suffused with the same ineradicable tension, which has resulted in recent years in dizzying political instability and that also reflects the uncertainty that must accrue to any polity that both enforces fierce laws against *lèse-majesté* and yet promotes local forms of democracy (*prachaathipatai*) and civil society (*prachaasangkhom*) as quintessentially Thai. Indeed, the community president managed to capture something of the same logic when, in raising community support for the victims of the tsunami, he said that Thai tradition meant that one should not discriminate between Thai and foreign victims, or between Buddhists and non-Buddhists, thereby managing to elevate Thainess to a supreme virtue at the same time as, with the affectation of modesty that is the hallmark of Thai etiquette, he inveighed against the very idea of such invidious distinctions. Food that is both extraordinarily elaborate in preparation and yet served all at once would seem to express a very similar tension between, and yet also merging together, of opposites.

To begin the discussion of the food, then, let us turn first to the (literal) appetizers. Let us particularly consider peppers. I will not elaborate on the many varieties, but it is worth specifically noting the small green chili known as "mouse-shit pepper" (*phrik khii nuu*), which is the booster rocket for many spicy Thai dishes and in some ways the template for the way in which Thai food often seems to change taste in the mouth (having a long and variable aftertaste). Sliced into fish sauce (*naam plaa*) to produce the commonest of all condiments (*phrik naam plaa*) along with the equivalent made with vinegar (*naam som*), this chili ornaments even the most innocuously bland-seeming dishes. When the sauce mixture appears, as it usually does, Thai masculinity demands the equivalent of a "bottoms up," tipping of the entire explosive little dish of this sauce onto the main food item (see figures 10.1–3). It may be relevant that the same masculine ethos often demands very heavy drinking of spirits accompanied by much raucous banter. I am thus providing a comparison that might help to understand the explosive force of the "mouse-shit pepper." Phenomenologically, it is very difficult to know whether people experience such tastes in the same way, though the visible discomfiture of some of the uninitiated when they first encounter these fierce peppers suggests that, at least to some extent, the immediate effects are indeed widely shared. But the lingering doubt, an external realization of experiential indeterminacy, allows much space for conceptual play. A gustatory poetics therefore provides a particularly rich arena for the contestation of contested and ambiguous social meaning, notably including the significance of rank.[5]

In describing Thai cuisine, I find it useful to use the metaphor of the firework display in part because of the rapid changes in taste that often follow the initial explosive encounter with the "mouse-shit pepper." In this regard, Thai food is significantly different from most Chinese cuisines. I once cooked a Sichuan meal for a Taiwanese colleague whose brother is a noted chef. Also present was a Thai graduate student. The Chinese colleague told me that, while she liked my cooking, there was something un-Chinese about it. Asked to be more specific, she first commented on the texture of one of the meats, and then said that she could not

Figures 10.1–2. *Nam plaa phrik* (Pom Mahakan).

Figure 10.3. Anticipating taste in Pom Mahakan.

understand why the taste of each dish tended to change. At that point the Thai student began to laugh and remarked that I had obviously spent too much time in Thailand. This anecdote nicely illustrates the key difference, which ensures that Thai food often does not have a single, clearly defined, and fixed gustatory effect.[6] What is certain, however, is that usually it will be highly spiced, and, more often than not, will produce the pyrotechnic sensation of variegated colors falling to earth in one's mouth.

Justifying Taste: Buddhism, Chinese Identity, and the Intensity of Chili Peppers

There are Thais who decry the obsession with spicy food, and even some who claim not to like it. In the latter category are many who use their descent from Chinese immigrants to justify what might seem otherwise to be an attitude at odds with the stereotype of the fire-eating Thai. Those who simply criticize the desire for strong food as unseemly, on the other hand, do so on two grounds: that it is un-Buddhist, and that it is lower class. The pairing of these two "explanations" is in no sense coincidental; the aristocracy's claim to collective merit rests in part on its formal observation of Buddhist precepts, and it may be that the conspicuous nonconsumption of high spice could have served as a demonstrative performance of class authority. Fortuitously, then, the Chinese self-stereotype of preferring milder food coincides with the symbolic self-representation of the high-class Thai Buddhist. The Chinese, many of whom entered Thailand as merchant clients of the monarchy, were for long despised and debarred from entry into such areas of national life as the military officer corps. Yet their distinctive touch has pervaded ritual, architecture, and commerce to a sometimes-astonishing degree. What is equally important in the present context, however, is that the borrowing has clearly been reciprocal in culinary matters; thus, for example, supposedly Chinese food—at feasts held by "Chinese" communities to celebrate "Chinese" deities—often included spicy Thai soups such as *tom yam* (see figure 10.4).

The association of spiciness with working-class identity is more complex. It is always tempting to associate high spice with an ideology of masculine pride, and it is certainly true that even in places with relatively bland cuisines—such as Greece—the appearance (in the baggage of an anthropologist, for example) of intense spiciness quickly develops into a test of masculinity, while women claim be horrified by the very idea of eating anything so hot.[7] But there is no necessary biological connection between spiciness and masculinity, and it is not clear that such associations are found in all human societies. Nonetheless, it is worth noting that Thais will often remark of someone who likes to eat very spicy food, especially if that person is a Caucasian foreigner (*farang*), that this individual is *kaeng* (excellent)—a term that applies to skill in anything from sports to languages,

Figure 10.4. A "Chinese" feast in Bangkok (Thaa Phra-Chan).

and implies both dexterity and strength as well as intelligence. In most Thai restaurants in the United States, it takes a lot of persuasion—even speaking Thai does not always suffice—to convince waitstaff to ask the kitchen to prepare the food with sufficient spiciness. Insisting on using a spoon and fork at least lets the wait staff know that next time one will be expecting a full taste range.[8] And on one occasion a waitress wrote "*khon thai*" (Thai people) on the order chit when I insisted that we wanted the food "Thai style" (*baep thai,* that is, in spiciness). This last experience also verified the rumor that many Asian restaurants in the United States maintain duplex standards of cooking, often, it seems, for fear that American customers would not only be unable to handle the very hot food but would actually become quite angry when they discovered this.

That the term *kaeng* is used for the ability to eat highly spiced food is indicative of its social significance. The ability to eat spicy food is seen as socially praiseworthy even though it may conflict with Buddhist exhortations to forsake the passions of the world and especially of the plate. It is, for this Buddhist society, a mark of cultural intimacy in the technical sense in which I intend that term (Herzfeld 2005): that is, as that area of disreputable comportment that nonetheless marks true belonging to the (in this case, religious) polity. One might recall that in southern Europe being a "Christian," for example, is socially defined as being socially friendly and therefore something of a rogue—an amiable sinner rather than an impossibly lofty saint. The eater of spicy food in Thailand is, in this social sense, as good a Buddhist as the *mafioso* is a good *cristiano*. And that principle applies even to those of whom one would least expect it. Thus, there are both relatively aristocratic individuals and people of Chinese descent who enjoy highly spiced food. The rhetoric that revolves around the question of spiciness is perhaps little more than a form of self-identification, possibly coupled with a sense that, if *farang* are unlikely to be able to eat spicy food *baep thai* (Thai style), it might concomitantly be a mark of high status, of being *hai-so* (high society), to prefer bland and even Western food.

But the precise meaning of such choices remains both ambiguous and indeterminate—ambiguous because no one will admit to the existence of such a precise calibration of status with food habits, and indeterminate because again that relative silence signals a refusal of rigidity that is also apparent in Thai attitudes to grammar ("we have none") and social codes (the emphasis on relative indifference when another person has failed to measure up, marked by the phrases *mai pen rai,* "it doesn't matter," and *chaang man thoe,* "let it go").

Etiquette and Power

The same ambiguity attaches to the rules of table manners. Technically, Thais (unless they are northeasterners and eat with the right hand, dipping sticky rice into the more liquid dishes and folding it around more solid morsels) eat with spoon and fork, and are supposed never to place the fork in the mouth—a rule that usually puzzles Americans, who, unlike many Europeans, tend to eat with only that one utensil in hand. The spoon and fork appear on tables in restaurants (see figure 10.5), whereas chopsticks (*takiab*) are usually only to be found at noodle shops or in specifically Chinese establishments and feasts (see figure 10.6). Americans are frequently very surprised to discover that Thais only use chopsticks in a few contexts; orientalism reigns supreme in a restaurant business that strategically panders to it. Bangkok people are occasionally fastidious about eating with their hands, although, in the search for authenticity, they will sometimes handle sticky rice in Isaan-style (northeastern) restaurants, often commenting on the food with an authoritative-sounding Isaan-dialect *saep* (very tasty) instead of the more usual central Thai *aroi* (delicious). Eating sticky rice (*khao niaw*) with the right hand is somewhat like the American use of chopsticks in Chinese restaurants, an assertion of cultural competence in an "ethnic" setting. But it is also a social equalizer. Even in a central Thai feast of some formality, however, we encounter the same tension between egalitarian and hierarchical principles: the dishes are all laid out together, in no particular order, but they represent a wide variety of (mostly intense) tastes of the kind that marks, for Jack Goody in particular, a complex social order (see figure 10.7).

Figure 10.5. The tools of cosmopolitan *marayaat* (Rajdamnoen Avenue).

While many Bangkok Thais do indeed follow the formal practice of eating two-handedly with spoon and fork, and of consuming a little rice before proceeding to the tastier items as a sign of respect and modesty, and especially of being a "neat" (*riab roi*) person, one often encounters flagrant violations of these rules. Being *riab roi* is clearly an attribute of middle-class respectability, which in this case

Figure 10.6. Chopsticks at the feast (Thaa Phra-Chan).

fastens on practices usually attributed to the Westernizing and deeply revered monarch Rama V (Chulalongkorn).

This is not the place to explore in detail the cultural *embourgeoisement* of the Thai monarchy in the nineteenth and twentieth centuries (but see Peleggi 2002). Suffice it here to point out that the price of the highly conditional independence allowed to the Thais by the colonial powers depended on the adoption, not only of reduced territorial claims (further constricted by clearly demarcated territory, with proper, *riab roi* borders), but also of the accoutrements of being "civilized" (*siwilai*)—which, unlike the more nativist term *aariyatham,* implied the mim-

Figure 10.7. Quantity and order (Pom Mahakan).

icry (Bhabha 1994) of Western colonial models.[9] While the explanation usually accorded to the king's decision not to adopt the knife was that in his wisdom he saw that the prior preparation of Thai food rendered the knife entirely otiose at the table, we may also interpret this etiology as yet another example of the uncompromising rationalism that was so much a part of the desire to be *siwilai* (on which, see Thongchai 2000).

Be that as it may, I have noticed that those who, often ostentatiously, break the spoon-and-fork rule, usually by forking up their food with the right hand, are young, often well-educated or from the upper middle class, and sometimes of intentionally rebellious disposition. These are people who do not like the constraints of being *riab roi* but who are more likely to express their disaffection from the highly constructed and partly Western-derived exercise in "Thainess" (*khwaam pen thai*) by such small acts of rebellion rather than through political action. Using the fork in the right hand is a way of distancing oneself both from the formality of Thai etiquette and from the presumed low status of a non-Western style, and this combination makes it especially common among those with a relatively high level of education. It was very noticeable, for example, that the poor residents of the community of Pom Mahakan would pay much more attention to the formal Thai rules than do the academics and students with whom they have forged an alliance. Perhaps this is only to be expected; they, after all, are the ones who want the practical support of their educated friends as they struggle against the constant threat of eviction but have notably less freedom than these friends to defy the rules. Their careful observation of *marayaat* is of a piece with their assiduous temple worship, their extremely careful interpersonal manners (see figure 10.8) and formal address usages in the presence of the powerful and well educated, their energetic support and apparently deep reverence for the monarchy, and a constant and specific emphasis on their identity as Thai citizens.

Although most male residents (and many women) in Pom Mahakan like their food spicy, therefore, they eat it with strict adherence to the rules of etiquette.

Figure 10.8. The community president greets a *phuu awuso* (respected elder) (Pom Mahakan).

Here again we see the play of multiple possibilities in action. Precisely because the people of this community have been (mendaciously) accused of harboring drug addicts and dealers, and because this calumny has been used as part of a campaign to dispossess them of their dwelling area (which is scheduled for development as part of an ambitious plan of "historic conservation" and gentrification), the residents of Pom Mahakan are extremely careful to present themselves as respectful of authority and of the hierarchy that still subsists in their dealings with the bureaucratic world of municipality and state. They are especially careful to show deep respect to the institutions of monarchy and religion, giving alms to the monks in elaborately staged rituals of obeisance. None of this has interfered with their general preference for spicy food (nor, to the best of my knowledge, are there any vegetarians in the community). Commensality is an intimate space, even when it is staged for outside consumption or when a visitor, such as the anthropologist, is treated to a special feast; and the residents are proud of their working-class identity. It is here that the *social* dimensions of being *kaeng* are part of the shared, embodied, and ultimately irreducibly experiential world of community belonging.

There is a close parallel here with the logic of drinking. When I arrived at the community one New Year's day, I was invited by a group of men to join in their drinking. First I was handed a glass of cloudy white spirits and told to drink it; I did not find it exceptionally overpowering, and the men applauded. Then they handed me a second variety, mauve in color, and asked me to try that as well. I did so, although I found the taste of the second drink considerably less pleasant. When they asked me which one I preferred, I told them that I liked the white drink better. They applauded wildly again—and it emerged that the mauve drink was considered a women's drink. So I passed that test as well as the test of eating intense spice.

Yet the strength of the taste is not the only criterion of excellence. Thai cooking employs a huge variety of spices, and the complexity that accompanies the explosive force of the food is no less important. Indeed, this is the source of the pyrotechnic effect: the different temporalities of the various spices create a sense of brightly lit streams of taste that drift to earth at their respective, distinctive paces.

Complexity and Ambiguity: Fruitful Comparisons

The complexity of Thai taste, moreover, is a highly effective metaphor for the ambiguity of social relations. One need think only of the habit of dipping fruit into a reddish mixture of chili, sugar, and salt—a combination that, to most Westerners, would suggest an excessive confusion of categories (see figure 10.9). Awareness that it is significantly different from the generally bland food of both much of China and the West and that it takes a socially recognizable skill to be able to eat it, moreover, plays into the crypto-colonial dynamic, as does the adoption of an idiom of table manners that both apes and yet also reverses the West (and permits vast mockery of Westerners who fail to grasp its principles). In the same way, we see that the absorption into local cuisine of Western cookies (sometimes called *kukii*; see figure 10.10) and breads as well as pasta, for example follows the similar absorption of Chinese elements, reversing some of its stereotypical characteristics in order to make them part of a "Thai cuisine" now also related to a nostalgically recalled era of family-based commensality (see, e.g., Parichart 2005).

Ultimately, then, the moral high ground lies with recovering a presumed Thai essence from the diversity (*khwaam laak laai*) of complex sources.

Figure 10.9. Spicing fruit (Pom Mahakan).

That hypothetical quality is both a self-attributed feature of the national image of Thailand and a strategic asset of the Pom Mahakan community. Heterogeneity creates social risk—the essence of a viable social poetics. Being *kaeng* thus means an ability to adapt to new tastes and ways of being, and, as such, it becomes the criterion for judging those who come as guests, whether in the literal sense or in that of foreigners visiting Thailand. Being *kaeng* is a matter of being "adept" in the face of the unanticipated and the demanding, whether in mastering the rules of etiquette or in the ability to consume fiercely spicy food without obvious discomfort—to smile gastronomically, as it were, in the face of a pleasurable but intense assault on the digestive tract as well as the throat and eyes. There is a generic context for this requirement; to avoid "losing face" (*sia naa*), one smiles in response to any threatening or insulting gesture. In a word, the social poetics of *khwaam pen thai* (Thainess) lies above all in managing the risk to "face" (*naa*). Only those Thais who wish to risk attempting an alternative poetics by emphasiz-

ing how Western (or Chinese) they have become (or have always been) are likely to admit to disliking such powerful taste sensations, or to violate the standardized rules of table etiquette. Thus, in a double paradox, it is the lower-class flavor (favored by some bourgeois and especially by left-leaning academics[10]) and the upper-class table manners (so easily abandoned by those who can claim such privileged sta-

Figure 10.10. *Khukhii* from Pom Mahakan.

tus) that perform the same labor, that of identifying who is either truly Thai or a worthy guest at the Thai table.

In bringing this analysis to a close, I would also like to return to the thought of Mary Douglas. In one unpublished comment, made privately to me, she expressed the view that punning (word play on homonyms), generally despised as the lowest form of humor in bourgeois Britain, was much enjoyed by just two groups: workers and aristocrats. The inference was clear: that these were the two groups that stood outside the dominant bourgeois structure.[11] In like vein, the poor and the aristocracy in Thailand share with each other their opposition to the emergent, Chinese-dominated, and Western-leaning bourgeoisie. Instead of a fixed cuisine with little space for inventiveness, however, Thais enjoy a very flexible culinary tradition. Moreover, lacking the blunt confrontational style that often marks social and especially political interaction in Britain, Thais instead resort to elaborate displays of etiquette, deference, and condescension—a rich and, one might almost say, spicy array of social codes that permits the maintenance of a great deal of ambiguity about what is actually being said. It is hardly surprising that their cuisine manages to be wildly spicy and delicately nuanced at one and the same time.

Notes

1. There is something of a debate among Romans as to whether *bucatini*—a kind of thick spaghetti with a hole running through each strand—are truly the "traditional" pasta for this relatively spicy dish; some insist that it should be made with the thicker *rigatoni*. There are similar arguments about the kind of grated cheese that should be sprinkled over it, with diehard traditionalists insisting that one should use *pecorino romano* rather than the commoner (and non-Roman) *parmigiano*. Such discussions about gastronomic authenticity are much rarer in the Thai context.
2. On entextualization as a device of colonial ranking of subordinate populations (notably in India), see especially Raheja (1996).
3. This dynamic was noticeable in connection with their availability at the "illegal" settlement of Pom Mahakan where I conducted research, and on which see *infra*.
4. At the time of going to press, the Thai government had just announced that it would introduce a "robotic taster" to standardize Thai food abroad (see Fuller 2014). While the announcement provoked considerable merriment, it demonstrates that the military-based government, which is mainly supported by middle-class elements, takes the question of food and its role in the representation of Thai culture at least as seriously as the government it deposed.
5. I am using "gustatory poetics" here in the very technical sense that I have argued for "social poetics" (Herzfeld 2005: 183–199), an approach—based on Roman Jakobson's (1960) famous work on the "poetic function" as well as on the writings of J. L. Austin (especially 1975)—that seeks to find explanations of cultural change and conservatism in the pragmatic play between invention and convention. While I would be the first to describe an outstanding meal as a poem, I do want to emphasize that in the present context I am using the term "poetics" in a narrowly analytic sense.

6. Chinese food in Thailand, as in many other places, has changed in adaptation to local expectations, including the significance of the hierarchy of dishes. See Thanes (1999).

7. There may be an implicit parallel here with the convention that men drink fiery spirits while women prefer sweet liqueurs; see Cowan (1990).

8. In the United States, Thai restaurants often provide either knife and fork or just a fork, which is consistent with American eating conventions; Americans regard eating solid food with a spoon as undignified, rude, and childish. In Britain this is not the case, although recently Indian restaurants—which used to offer spoon-and-fork place settings—have turned to the knife-and-fork convention; and British customers now often eat with a fork in the right hand alone, something that was very unusual during my youth. In Australia, many Thai restaurants maintain the Thai convention, although again non-Thais there often do use the fork solo.

9. Indeed, the term itself ironically instantiates that of which it speaks, since it is clearly derived from the English *civilized*—a use of linguistic iconicity that shows how deeply the crypto-colonial condition had entered the Thai self-image.

10. A parallel instance is that of Chang (Elephant) beer, which has a higher alcohol content than the better-known lager-style beer of the Singha brand, and is generally associated with rough working-class habits and the strident masculine nationalism that often accompanies them—but is also much favored by (mostly more left-leaning) intellectuals. Buddhist campaigns against the breweries have not significantly blunted the enthusiasm of these groups for Chang beer.

11. No wonder Douglas so detested Margaret Thatcher, whose ascent marked the full *embourgeoisement* of Britain and the end of the caste-like "class" system of the traditional order.

References

Appadurai, Arjun. 1988. "How to Make a National Cuisine: Cookbooks in Contemporary India." *Comparative Studies in Society and History* 30: 3–24.

Austin, J. L. 1975 [1962]. *How to Do Things with Words.* 2nd ed. Edited by J. O. Urmson and Marina Sbisà. Cambridge, MA: Harvard University Press.

Bhabha, Homi K. 1994. *The Location of Culture.* New York: Routledge.

Bubandt, Nils. 1998. "The Odour of Things: Smell and the Cultural Elaboration of Disgust in Eastern Indonesia." *Ethnos* 63: 48–80.

Byrne, Denis. 2009. "Archaeology and the Fortress of Rationality." In *Cosmopolitan Archaeologies,* edited by Lynn Meskel, 68–88. Durham, NC: Duke University Press.

Douglas, Mary. 1966. *Purity and Danger: An Analysis of Concepts of Pollution and Taboo.* London: Routledge & Kegan Paul.

———. 1970. *Natural Symbols: Explorations in Cosmology.* London: Barrie & Rockliff / Cresset Press.

Fuller, Thomas. 2014. You Call This Thai Food? The Robotic Taster Will Be the Judge. *New York Times,* 28 September. http://www.nytimes.com/2014/09/29/world/asia/bad-thai-food-enter-a-robot-taster.html?_r=0.

Goody, Jack. 1982. *Cooking, Cuisine, and Class: A Study in Comparative Sociology.* Cambridge: Cambridge University Press.

Herzfeld, Michael. 1987. "'As in your own House': Hospitality, Ethnography, and the Stereotype of Mediterranean Society." In *Honor and Shame and the Unity of the Mediterranean,* edited by David D. Gilmore, 75–89. Washington, DC: American Anthropological Association, 1987; Special Publications # 22.

———. 2002. "The Absent Presence: Discourses of Crypto-Colonialism." *South Atlantic Quarterly* 101: 899–926.

———. 2005. *Cultural Intimacy: Social Poetics in the Nation-State.* New York: Routledge.

———. 2012. "Paradoxes of Order in Thai Community Politics." In *Radical Egalitarianism: Local Realities, Global Relations,* edited by Felicity Aulino, Miriam Goheen, and Stanley J. Tambiah, 146–157. New York: Fordham University Press.

Jakobson, Roman. 1960. "Linguistics and Poetics." In *Style in Language,* edited by Thomas A. Sebeok, 350–377. Cambridge, MA: MIT Press.

Loos, Tamara. 2006. *Subject Siam: Family, Law, and Colonial Modernity in Thailand.* Ithaca, NY: Cornell University Press.

Malaby, Thomas. 2003. *Gambling Life: Dealing in Contingency in a Greek City.* Urbana: University of Illinois Press.

Parichart Sthapitanonda. 2005. *Samrab kab khao: khrobkhrua Sathapitanon.* Bangkok: Anurin Publishing.

Peleggi, Maurizio. 2002. *Lords of Things: The Fashioning of the Siamese Monarchy's Modern Image.* Honolulu: University of Hawaii Press.

Raheja, Gloria Goodwin. 1996. "Caste, Nationalism, and the Speech of the Colonized: Entextualization and Disciplinary Control in India." *American Ethnologist* 23: 496–513.

Seremetakis, C. Nadia. 1993. "Memory of the Senses: Historical Perception, Commensal Exchange and Modernity." *Visual Anthropology Review* 9(2): 2–18.

Steedly, Mary Margaret. 1993. *Hanging Without a Rope: Narrative Experience in Colonial and Postcolonial Karoland.* Princeton: Princeton University Press.

Taylor, James. 2008. *Buddhism and Postmodern Imaginings in Thailand: The Religiosity of Urban Space.* Farnham: Ashgate.

Thanes, Wongyannava. 1999. "Localization of Chinese Haute Cuisine in Bangkok: A Preliminary Study." Paper presented at 7th International Conference on Thai Studies, Amsterdam, The Netherlands.

Thongchai Winichakul. 2000. "The Quest for '*Siwilai*': A Geographical Discourse of Civilizational Thinking in the Late-Nineteenth-Century and Early-Twentieth-Century Siam." *Journal of Asian Studies* 59: 528–549.

Tsing, Anna Lowenhaupt. 1993. *In the Realm of the Diamond Queen.* Princeton: Princeton University Press.

PART

III

Health, Safety, and Food Consumption

CHAPTER 11

Well-Being Discourse and Chinese Food in Korean Society

Young-Kyun Yang

Since the early 2000s, a craze for "well-being" has spread throughout Korean society. We can find this phenomenon in various spheres of society. Such a keen interest in healthy living by the public is not a special characteristic unique to Korean society. Many societies, especially those with developed economies, exhibit high public interest in well-being. However, in the Korean case, public interest in well-being has grown very swiftly due to the Korean ability for collective effort, most notable in Korea's rapid economic development and political democratization. The speed with which the concept has penetrated society is also closely related to the tendency of Korean people to be easily swept along by fads. Nevertheless, while the well-being phenomenon may have looked like a passing fad in the beginning, the fever has not abated. Indeed, the fever appears to be spreading to more people and more spheres of society.

The term *well-being* is used in a wide range of contexts with various meanings. The array of bestsellers with the keyword *well-being* shows how diverse its usages are. Nonetheless, most such books focus on health, broadly divided into two categories: dietary life (food, diet, nutrition, etc.) and physical fitness and healing (exercise, alternative medicine, massage, yoga, etc.). Another common book topic is leisure activities, including travel, recreation, and hobbies. Also falling under the *well-being* label are books on subjective feelings or attitudes that include positivity, happiness, and humor, as well as books that relate well-being with real estate, marketing, business, jobs, prayer, and so on. Such a wide range of use clearly reflects the fact that Korean people are highly interested in well-being, and publishers and authors intend to take advantage of people's interest for marketing purposes. The diversity of book topics can also be attributed to the fact that the concept of well-being has not been codified. I will delve into this point later.

In this chapter, I focus on how food, especially Chinese food, has been seen within well-being discourse. In popular discourse, food is an important part of well-being. People have shown a great interest in well-being or healthy food, which encompasses organic food, slow food, and Korean traditional food. As a result, people's perceptions and consumption of food began to change, including their perceptions of Chinese food, which has long been very popular in Korean society. This chapter intends to collect and analyze data on people's perceptions of Chinese food, as well as consumption patterns of Chinese food in connection with well-being discourse. In particular, these questions seek to determine people's perceptions of well-being, their opinions of Chinese food when considering well-being, and occasions when they do (or do not) consume Chinese food. The other important topic this chapter addresses is the responses of Chinese restaurants to these changing circumstances. Since Chinese food tends to be regarded as "unhealthy," and Chinese restaurants have a bad reputation for "uncleanliness" and "oldness," the inquiry into the restaurateurs' strategies for adapting to these changes has been very interesting. The responses include renovations, modifications in some ingredients and cooking methods, and the development of new dishes with healthy ingredients.

Previous Studies on Chinese Food and Well-Being

Anthropologists have long been engaged in the study of food from a multiplicity of perspectives, as it is indispensible to human life. Those studies can be divided into two categories: research on human biology and food nutrition, and research on the sociocultural aspects of food and diet.[1] Anthropological works about Chinese food and cuisine belong to the latter category. Earlier works such from K. C. Chang (1977) and Eugene Anderson (1988) focus on the history of Chinese cuisine and foodways in Hong Kong. Later works address the impact of changes inside and outside Chinese society.

The most remarkable feature of Chinese food since the eighteenth century is the global diffusion of Chinese food culture through the changes wrought by Western capitalism and colonialism. When hundreds of thousands of Chinese left southeast China, primarily Fujian and Guangdong, and arrived in Southeast Asia, Oceania, and North and South America, they brought with them not only Chinese ways of cooking but also new ingredients. In recent decades, Chinese restaurants have sprung up in countries that previously did not have substantial Chinese populations (Wu and Cheung 2002). The successful localization of Chinese food has brought about the global diffusion of Chinese food.

Recent works (e.g., Cheng 2002; Cheung 2001, 2002; Su 2001; Wu 2001, 2002b; Zhuang 2002) more or less examine changing foodways in China that are influenced by internal, regional, and global forces. Other research investigates the process of localization of Chinese food in other societies. Two subcategories appear in this research area: the localization of Chinese food by Chinese people who are ethnic minorities in larger non-Chinese societies, such as Malaysia, Singapore, and Indonesia (e.g., Chua and Rajah 2001; C. Tan 2001, 2007; M. Tan 2002; Fernandez 2002); the other is the incorporation of Chinese food into foodways by non-Chinese, such as Chinese food in Korea, Japan, Hawaii, and Australia (e.g. Cheung 2002; K. Kim 2001; Tam 1997; Tamotsu 2001; Wu 2002a).

The list of anthropological studies of Chinese food in Korean society is relatively short. Eun Kyung Park (1994) traces the shifting meanings of Chinese food in Korean society through the changes in Chinese restaurants owned by Chinese Koreans (*hwagyo*). Kwang Ok Kim(1998) examines the meanings of historical experiences of Koreans projected on Chinese food; and Yeong-ha Ju (2000) tries to understand Chinese people and society through Chinese food in Korean society. These studies mainly address the meanings that are attached to Chinese food localized in Korean society. Meanwhile, Young-Kyun Yang (2005) examines the changing position of Chinese restaurants as popular places to eat out, and the diversification of Chinese restaurants in response to the globalization of Korean society. Since the early 2000s, well-being has become a key word in the dietary life of Korean society and no restaurants can avoid the effects of this trend. Therefore, this chapter attempts to explore people's perceptions of the well-being trend and its relationship with the consumption and production of Chinese food.

Before reviewing research on well-being, let me start with an examination of the concept of well-being. The origin of well-being as an idea is closely related with the concept of health as defined by the World Health Organization (WHO) established in 1948. According to the WHO Constitution, "Health is a state of complete physical, mental, and social well-being and not merely the absence of disease and infirmity." The concept of well-being includes mental health as well as physical health, and later became an even more comprehensive concept that encompasses true happiness of life. One standard dictionary definition of the term is "the state of being healthy, happy, or prosperous." Well-being refers to any of these attributes, but the three are interconnected, and thus it includes the positive state of one's body, finances, and mind (Mathews and Izquierdo 2009: 2–3).

Though *well-being* is not as common a term as *happiness*, its usage has increased since the 1980s. Studies on well-being show a similar pattern of growth, with usage in the social sciences also increasing.[2] The academic fields that have produced more research in relative terms are economics, public health, and psychology. Economists realized that criteria such as income traditionally used to measure standards of living cannot fully tell us about the quality of life, and thus turned their attention to well-being. Medical professionals also came to realize that in the era of highly developed medical technology, to keep people alive is not enough, and individuals' overall well-being should be taken into account. Psychologists have also recently moved from research solely on mental illness to research on mental health. In other words, their interests are shifting from "ill-being" to well-being (Mathews and Izquierdo 2009: 3).

In the field of anthropology, well-being has not been a trendy topic. We can hardly find the term in popular anthropology textbooks and encyclopedias. This, however, does not mean that anthropologists have no interest in the concept. Even though research has not been systematic or continuous and the term *well-being* has not been used explicitly, there are studies that address the meanings of well-being. Raoul Naroll (1983) investigates cultural pathology and well-being, and the works of Oscar Lewis (1959, 1961, 1966), which delve into the culture of poverty, also are concerned with cultural well-being. In addition, Philippe Bourgois's research (1995) on life in a New York City crack den, and David Plath's (1980) account of the meaning of maturity in Japan, are also related to cultural well-being to a certain degree.

Anthropologists' passive approach to the research of well-being can be attributed in part to cultural relativism and field research methods that are greatly stressed in the discipline. Anthropologists have been negative toward the idea that a society or culture can be evaluated in terms of well-being because they believe such a stance is at odds with cultural relativism. It is also difficult for anthropologists who lay great stress on indigenous viewpoints to use the term *well-being* in their research because it is not actually used by indigenous people (Colby 2009). However, some scholars, including anthropologists, have incorporated well-being into their work as a major topic since the 2000s.

Research on well-being, as I indicated earlier, used to be centered on cultural pathology, and thus was mainly based on the concept of well-being defined as the state of being normal; in other words, not unhappy. In contrast, well-being has been recently redefined as a more positive state (Thin 2009). Well-being, however, has various meanings in various contexts. Especially in anthropological studies of well-being, it is apparent that its meanings are closely intertwined with each culture in which the concept is employed. Some case studies demonstrate the culture-dependent meanings of well-being, such as Carolina Izquierdo's (2009) analysis of well-being among the Matsigenka Indians of the Peruvian Amazon, who struggle to maintain their sense of wellness in opposition to outside forces, especially the Peruvian state and multinational oil companies. Even though objective measures show their physical health is improving, their sense of well-being is declining, as evidenced by an upturn in accusations of sorcery. Daniela Heil (2009) reveals that Australian Aborigines' relational concept of well-being stresses relationships with significant, mostly kin-related others and absorption in a tight network of social obligations and responsibilities, unlike the Australian government's individual concept of well-being. These two essays describe how the well-being of small-scale societies is being threatened by encroachment by the state and outside world and how such communities struggle to maintain their own well-being.

At the level of nation-states, much research has been conducted on well-being in China and India. William Jankowiak (2009) finds that well-being in Chinese society is rapidly rising due to the increase in individual free choice in the post-Mao era. In contrast to such individualism, according to Steve Derné (2009), young, middle-class Indian men prefer following parental guidance in choosing marriage partners, rather than making such choices on their own. In China, although the cultural orientation has shifted from state-centric into individual-centric, India still remains socio-centric, at least among middle-class young men. In other words, the meanings of well-being are different and somewhat contrary when comparing China and India. Scott Clark (2009) examines physical pleasure in the context of well-being by looking at bathing in Japanese culture. Thomas Weisner (2009) investigates well-being and family routines among American families with children with disabilities, and regards the idea of sustainability as key to well-being.

It is evident that the meanings of well-being are culturally particular; in other words, people from different cultures define well-being differently. Furthermore, the scope of well-being is quite broad, ranging from physical pleasure to familial routines and from individual freedom to social relatedness. In this chapter, well-being also has meaning particular to contemporary Korean culture, whose characteristics can be summarized as globalized, urban, and trend-sensitive.[3]

Practices of Well-Being

Since the concept of well-being possesses diverse meanings, it can be and is realized in various forms. We can find several lifestyles that fit the meanings of well-being, some of which existed well before the popularization of well-being discourse, while others can be seen as the realization of recent discourse. These well-being lifestyles include vegetarianism, the "Slow City, Slow Food Movement," and LOHAS (Lifestyle of Health and Sustainability). Dating back to the mid-nineteenth century, vegetarianism[4] values health, love for animals, and protection of the environment. Therefore, even if vegetarianism is not directly associated with well-being today, the basic ideas are very similar. The Slow City, Slow Food Movement, which started in Italy in the mid-1980s, aims for a life in harmony with nature and values traditional foods and cooking methods over fast food. This movement is closely related to recent well-being discourse in that it values a quiet and relaxed life over a busy and tension-filled life. Popularized in the 1990s, LOHAS stresses health, environment, and sustainable development of society and is directly related to the current discourse on well-being (Kim and Kim 2005).

Well-being has become a part of alternative social movements that consider people's health and environmentally friendly development. In this context, well-being has slowly taken root in Europe and the United States. In Korean society, however, the well-being trend began rather abruptly, thanks to the active role of mass media in introducing and spreading the well-being concept of Western societies. Enterprises that actively use well-being in their marketing materials have also played a major role in the rapid spread of well-being discourse in Korea.

The spirit or discourse of well-being can be falsely represented when it is combined with marketing or consumer culture in general. This sort of phenomenon is easily found in Korean society. Just as well-being is actively used in promoting books, it is also used to market many other commodities. For instance, clothing companies advertise their products as well-being clothes that are made with natural materials, fabrics that contain vitamins, or silver-nano textiles, all of which are claimed to be good for the body. Vacuum cleaners, washing machines, dishwashers, air conditioners, bidets, water purifiers, and many other appliances with additional functions are advertised as well-being items. Using the concept of well-being, services such as foot massage, lower-body bathing,[5] aromatherapy, yoga, and meditation are also promoted.

Nonetheless, it is food that receives the most attention in well-being discourse. The most representative case is environmentally friendly agricultural products including organic, transitional organic, pesticide-free, and low pesticide agricultural products classified according to the amount and application of pesticides and chemical fertilizers.[6] The popularity of environmentally friendly agricultural products can be ascertained in various ways. One method is to look at the output. The volume of environmentally friendly agricultural products (except for livestock products) certified by the government amounted to 87,279 metric tons in 2001, but jumped to 2,188,311 tons in 2008, nearly a 28-fold increase. In the case of livestock products, the volume of environmentally friendly products increased from 256 metric tons in 2005 to 137,079 tons in 2008 for a 535-fold increase.[7] Specialty stores and departments that stock environmentally friendly agricultural products and food, especially organic food, have substantially increased their numbers. We can find such sections in almost every large supermarket and department store, conglomerate-run chain stores that sell organic food and products, smaller-scale shops, and internet-based stores.

Another remarkable phenomenon is the flood of functional foods for health that are advertised to contain such ingredients as glucosamine, omega-3 fatty acids, gamma linolenic acid, spirulina, ginseng, and similar substances. Various foods made of beans, such as soy milk, bean curd, and simulated meat made of textured soy protein, have also been popularized. Green tea is also widely known to contain healthy ingredients and its range of uses has grown astronomically in recent years. The uses of green tea are not limited only to foods such as beverages, ice cream, various sweets, noodles, and other foodstuffs, but extend also to skin and hair care products, detergent, underwear, and other myriad items. The rapid growth of wine consumption is also linked with well-being discourse (Bak 1993; J. Kim 2008; Ko 2007; Yang 2005).

In many cases, well-being is combined with marketing and used to nudge consumers into opening their wallets. However, the effects of these so-called well-being products are mostly unproven and are significantly more expensive than similar products that sell without a focus on well-being. Furthermore, this phenomenon has been criticized for aggravating the evils of the consumer culture of capitalist industrial societies that people try to overcome through well-being (Seo 2005; Yun 2006). The wide dissemination of well-being discourse in Korean society exerts considerable influence on the consumption patterns of people. Some of my interviewees clearly and critically recognized that the virtue of well-being and the effect of well-being products were sometimes exaggerated. Nevertheless, they confessed that they were affected by well-being discourse and advertisements and so often ended up buying well-being products.

Interviewees' perceptions of well-being show the inclusiveness of the concept. Informant L[8] said, "Well-being is the combination of physical health and mental health. The important things in physical health are exercise and a balanced diet. The important things in mental health are to not get stressed and to be optimistic." Informant K[9] stated, "The important things in well-being are healthy food, clothing, and shelter and to not get stressed." However, the well-being practices of both of these informants concentrated on physical health, especially on food and exercise. They try to use less MSG and buy environmentally friendly products, however, such products are usually too expensive. L buys organic vegetables and fruit, but not organic rice or milk. K buys products made from locally produced wheat and organic vegetables, but not organic eggs. Yet another respondent, S,[10] said that she used to buy organic food for her kids when they were babies, but after they turned three, she rarely bought organic food because she could not afford to do so. Interviewees also engaged in exercise, such as hiking, swimming, *gi* training, and working out at fitness centers.

Well-Being and Chinese Food

Dietary life is affected by well-being discourse, and dining out is no exception. As the economic and social conditions for Korea's food industry improves, specifically through rising incomes, increase in leisure time, increase in double-income families, and other changes in lifestyle, domestic and foreign food service enterprises are actively entering the Korean market. The food-service sector is growing very rapidly, with an annual growth rate of approximately 10 percent. The percentage of family income spent on dining out more than doubled and the number of restaurants more than tripled over the past decade (Kang 2007; Kim,

Yeom, and Jo 2003). However, the importance of Chinese food in Korean dietary life has declined since the 1970s.

Chinese food was introduced to Korean society through the formation of an overseas Chinese community that began in the late nineteenth century. Since the vast majority of early Chinese residents in Korea were male, Chinese restaurants catered to this single male population with simple food. As the number of Chinese residents in Korea grew, Chinese restaurants increased and diversified.[11] In 1922, there were about 650 Chinese restaurants in 11 cities and around 30 percent of Chinese Koreans were engaged in the restaurant business, where most customers were also Chinese Korean. With the end of Japanese colonial rule and the establishment of a post-liberation Korean government, the Chinese in Korean society, whom mostly came from Shandong province, were severed from their homeland. Furthermore, their economic activities came to be concentrated in the restaurant sector because the Korean government restricted foreigners' engaging in trade. Even though the number of Korean Chinese decreased after independence, the number of Chinese restaurants greatly increased, as the market expanded to include Koreans as consumers. In the 1950s and 1960s, although Chinese restaurants were mostly owned by Chinese, the majority of customers were Koreans,[12] for whom Chinese food became a favorite treat. In the 1970s, Koreans began to participate in the cooking of Chinese food and management of Chinese restaurants. Around 65 percent of Chinese restaurants were managed by Chinese Koreans in the mid-1970s, but the percentage declined to 6 percent by 1993.

Over the past few decades, Chinese food has so successfully been localized that Chinese restaurants became a very familiar place for ordinary Koreans, and almost the only place for Koreans to enjoy exotic food in the 1970s. Meanwhile the high-end, large-scale Chinese restaurants provided a location for business meetings, family dining for the upper classes, or banquets for Korean Chinese.

However, the popularity of Chinese food has declined since the 1990s. While the market share of Korean restaurants increased from 56.7 percent in 1983 to 75.7 percent in 2003, that of Chinese restaurants decreased from 20.4 percent to 8.4 percent during the same period. The percentage of Korean restaurants in the food service sector soared to 83.9 by June 2009. This increase can be explained by several factors, one being the spread of well-being discourse. As the importance of slow food is increasingly emphasized, Korean food is perceived to be healthier than fast food. It has also been said that Korean traditional food is much better than foreign food because of an abundance of vegetables, little meat, and many fermented ingredients.[13] Research indicates that the consumers who seriously take well-being into account tend to prefer Korean restaurants.[14]

Interest in well-being can be found in consumers' choice of dishes and restaurant preferences. As customers increasingly order based on health considerations, this facilitates the development of new menu items (Ahn and Cho 2006; T. Kim

2002). Many kinds of restaurants are developing new menus in order to keep up with the craze for well-being. Fast food restaurants, although far from the embodiment of well-being, are no exception and have developed so-called well-being menus that can be characterized as low-cholesterol, low-fat, low-sodium, and incorporating vegetables and cereals.

Chinese restaurants also give the impression that they do not fit the well-being trend in many aspects. One source of such impressions is mass media, which generated an onslaught of negative news reports about Chinese food and restaurants. Some representative headlines include: "Pickled Radish in *Gimbap* and *Jajangmyeon* ... Lots of Industrial Additives?" (*Medical Today,* 16 April 2009); "Chinese Food Contains Lots of MSG; Two Times as Much as Food in Korean Restaurants" (*Munhwa Ilbo,* 16 October 2007); "National Teams in Olympic Games, 'We Don't Trust Chinese Food'" (*Maeil Business Newspaper,* 27 June 2008); "Chinese Food Syndrome" (*Busan Ilbo,* 18 October 2006); "Detecting Lead Eight Times the Safety Level in Chinese Preserved Eggs" (*Yonhap News,* 3 November 2005); "Terrible Sanitary Condition of Chinese Restaurants, 'You Can't Eat Food If You Know the Cooking Conditions'" (*Newsis,* 24 March 2009); "Chinese Restaurants, Lacking Sterilization" (*Yonhap News,* 16 February 2005); "Wondering If There Are Cockroaches in Chinese Food" (*Newsis,* 8 January 2009).

According to my field research, the most mentioned off-putting characteristic was that Chinese food was too greasy.[15] In another study, the most popular answers by college students about the image of Chinese food were that it is high in calories and greasy (Min and Oh 2002). It is clear that Chinese food is perceived as being distant from well-being food.

The representative image of Chinese restaurants was also negative. Chinese restaurants were said to be dark, crowded, dirty, and overall unattractive. Interviewee H[16] told me that Chinese restaurants were associated with cockroaches, but she also confessed that she had never seen one in a Chinese restaurant. However, interviewees did not perceive Chinese restaurants to be homogeneous. They broadly classified Chinese restaurants into two types: small, dirty, and cheap or big, clean, and expensive. The examples of the latter include Chinese restaurants in luxury hotels, usually in city centers and used for business meetings, banquets, and dining with coworkers and friends. However, a majority of Chinese restaurants are located in residential areas or the outskirts of towns, and depend largely upon delivery and casual dining for their sales. This is the main source of the negative image of Chinese restaurants.

The pervasiveness of well-being discourse is an important factor causing a crisis for Chinese restaurants and Chinese food. Chinese restaurants, however, are attempting to emerge from this predicament and take advantage of the well-being trend. This chapter will examine several different cases.

M restaurant was a fusion Chinese restaurant whose menu included a considerable number of fusion dishes as well as traditional Chinese dishes.[17] During my research in 2003, when the well-being trend was first taking root, the restaurant tried to distinguish itself from other Chinese restaurants by placing great emphasis on health. It tried to minimize the use of MSG and lowered calories by eliminating the use of batter when deep frying prawns. In addition, it encouraged customers to consume wine through a large selection of wines that were widely considered to be good for health. They also enclosed the kitchen with glass to allow customers to see the sanitary conditions of the kitchen for themselves. In this way, M restaurant addressed almost all the perceived weaknesses of Chinese restaurants from the standpoint of well-being.

U restaurant claims to be a well-being Chinese restaurant, as indicated by the signboard in front of the store.[18] It specializes in seafood such as sea cucumber, abalone, adductor muscle of shellfish, and vegetables, instead of meat. For example, the Congxiang Sea Cucumber dish is prepared very similarly to Congxiang Beef, and chicken is replaced with adductor muscle in Fried Adductor Muscle. The menu also includes Well-Being Chicken in Lettuce and Chinese-Style Well-Being Soybean Paste Noodle (*welbing jajangmyeon*). Most dishes taste very light, and are prepared with a minimum of MSG and fresh oil. According to the manager, when the restaurant first opened, the dishes were more bland and lighter, but more seasonings have been incorporated in response to customers' requests. However, the dishes still did not suit the tastes of young people, or those who expected or preferred ordinary Chinese food. The menu items appealed instead to middle-aged people who preferred light flavors and those who cared greatly about their health. The manager also informed me that they changed the oil for deep frying every day, unlike other Chinese restaurants, which are often criticized for reusing oil over and over again. The other thing he emphasized was that they cleaned the kitchen two or three times a week. In conclusion, U restaurant is making an effort to overcome negative images such as "Chinese food is too oily, high in calories and MSG" and "Chinese restaurants are dirty." This is unmistakably an effort to take advantage of the well-being trend.

C restaurant also claims to be a well-being fusion Chinese restaurant and was advertised as "a restaurant for those who look for well-being Chinese food with light and intense flavors, using healthy oil (high-grade canola oil)."[19] The manager was very proud of the fact that they discarded such expensive oil on a daily basis to keep the food light and clean. He was also proud that they cleaned the kitchen with chemical disinfectants every two days, in contrast to ordinary Chinese restaurants, which, he asserted, cleaned their kitchens in such a fashion only once a year. According to the manager, the clean, hygienic environment and the healthy menu and cooking style have made the restaurant so popular among young mothers that the restaurant provides a "first birthday celebration" special menu.

Y restaurant is another fusion Chinese restaurant that emphasizes well-being.[20] This is evident in the menu, which features several steamed dishes such as Steamed Eggplant Stuffed Shrimp Paste with Chili Sauce, Steamed Tofu & Scallops with Crab Meat Sauce, and Steamed Grouper with Y Soy Sauce. Dishes such as Fried

Minced Shrimp Ball (*saeu nanja wanseu*) and Deep Fried Minced Beef Ball (*soegogi nanja wanseu*) are usually first deep fried and then stir fried, but the owner said that Y restaurant lowers the greasiness by only deep frying to maintain the ball shape and then steaming.[21] There are also some dishes that are transformed to fit the well-being concept, for instance Seafood & Vegetable with Sesame Sauce, Spicy Chicken in Endive, Fresh Yam with Oyster Sauce, Asparagus with Pine Mushroom, Braised Puffer Fish with Garlic Sauce (*kkanpung bogeo*), and Noodles with Grape Seed Oil Soy Bean Sauce (*podossiyu jajangmyeon*). In order to lower calories, the restaurant actively makes use of steaming, rather than deep frying, and increases the use of vegetables and seafood instead of meat.

In particular, the restaurateur at Y restaurant is very proud of the ingredients. Only fresh ingredients are used, and dishes are flavored only with salt or soy sauce, never with MSG.[22] This method best brings out the flavors of ingredients. According to the owner, Y restaurant does not use industrially produced sauces, unlike most Chinese restaurants, even high-end ones. He buys black bean sauce fermented in a traditional method in Beijing. Furthermore, he asserts that special ingredients, such as black moss, bamboo fungus, and fresh yam, all good for health, are used in Y's dishes.

An increasing number of Chinese restaurants are trying to keep up with the prevailing trend toward well-being in Korean society. They make efforts to lessen the use of MSG, to replace lard with vegetable oil and to change cooking oils often so that the dishes are light and not greasy tasting, to use vegetables or seafood instead of meat,[23] and to use fruit instead of sugar and vinegar to make sauces sweet and sour. Such restaurants are also attempting to wipe out customers' fears of unsanitary cooking environments. For example, they clean the kitchen frequently and open the kitchen to public view by partitioning the kitchen away from the dining area with glass or by installing a closed circuit TV.

In spite of all this, their efforts do not quite result in the hoped-for outcomes. According to interviews with restaurant managers and owners, their customers do not often know or care about the healthiness of the dishes. The majority of customers do care about flavor, however. The restaurants where I conducted my interviews all emphasize their light flavors achieved through minimal use of MSG, which appeals to the customers. The results of customer interviews also indicate that they do not seriously consider the healthiness of dishes when eating Chinese food. Therefore, it can be said that people who are focused on well-being tend to not choose to dine at Chinese restaurants, primarily due to the strong perception that Chinese food is not aligned with the well-being trend.

If this is the case, why do people go to Chinese restaurants and eat Chinese food? The first reason is simply that they like Chinese food. Interviewee L said, "I like Chinese food, especially Chinese Cold Noodles (*jungguk naengmyeon*), Noodle Soup with Seafood (*jjamppong*), and Braised Sea Cucumber, Shrimp, and Beef (*ryusanseul*). I stayed in Beijing for six months and I liked the food there, which was quite different from Chinese food in Korea. And back in Korea,

I often go to Chinese restaurants with friends." Interviewee J[24] stated, "I go to Chinese restaurant from time to time. It's not because I particularly like Chinese food, but because my roommate likes it. We like to eat Deep Fried Chicken with Soy Sauce (*yuringi*) and Stir Fried Seafood over Crispy Rice (*haemul nurungji-tang*)." Both respondents think that Chinese food is not exactly healthy, but they choose to eat it rather than become unhappy by not eating it.

People choose Chinese food when they want to have a cheap and simple meal, with Chinese-style noodles being a very typical choice. Even though many different varieties of food can be delivered nowadays, for years Chinese food was the only kind of food that could be delivered. When people want to have a quick and simple meal, they often order Chinese noodle dishes for delivery at their homes, schools, offices, or wherever they happened to be.

Another reason is that children ask adults to buy Chinese food. When begged by kids to buy Chinese food, especially *jajangmyeon* and *tangsuyuk,* representative favorite treats for kids, adults sometimes meet these demands. Interviewee S said, "Sometimes my kids pester me to buy *jajangmyeon*. I try not to buy my kids Chinese food because it's not good for one's health. But when they bother me so much, I can't help buying *jajangmyeon* from time to time."

People also go to Chinese restaurants for meetings. The high-end Chinese restaurants are perceived as good locations for meetings because they are quiet, clean, and relatively cheap. When a venue is chosen for a banquet or meeting, the menu is not seriously considered. The place itself is the most important deciding factor. Interviewee K stated, "When I dine with friends, alumni, and co-workers, or have a meeting with colleagues, I sometimes go to Chinese restaurants. Year-end parties especially are mostly held at Chinese restaurants."

There are also various reasons why people chose not to eat Chinese food or dine at Chinese restaurants. Interviewees in their forties told me they frequently ate Chinese food when they were young. In the 1970s and 1980s, Chinese food was one of their favorite meals. However, some said that they seldom ate Chinese food nowadays because they thought it was unhealthy, and rarely went to Chinese restaurants because they were unclean. They confessed that they had been influenced by the negative representation of Chinese food and Chinese restaurants in mass media.

Some people do not regularly go to Chinese restaurants because their dining companions might not want to. Interviewee S said, "Our family seldom goes to Chinese restaurants because my husband doesn't want to go there. He frequently eats Chinese food outside the home, so we avoid going to Chinese restaurants when eating out as a family." Interviewee M[25] said, "We, our family, don't go to Chinese restaurants often because my elderly parents-in-law don't like Chinese food. They say that Chinese food is too greasy and hard to digest."

All in all, people usually tend to choose Chinese restaurants as places to eat out because they or their companions like Chinese food. They also select Chinese restaurants for banquets or meetings. When well-being is their primary consideration, they rarely appear to choose Chinese restaurants. If health or environment is to be considered when selecting Chinese food, they choose a well-being Chinese restaurant or a well-being menu item.

Conclusion

Well-being is a comprehensive and complex term. It includes the positive state of one's body, mind, and finances. Well-being discourse in Korean society began abruptly and spread rapidly thanks to the active intervention of mass media and the business sector. Though well-being is linked to social movements that offer alternatives to the lifestyle of industrialized societies, it has lost some of this meaning in Korean society. Well-being discourse in Korea often focuses on aspects of health and body, and it is extensively commercialized. As far as diet is concerned, well-being tends to emphasize low calories, low cholesterol, reduced MSG, and environmentally friendly food.

This trend has had a negative impact on Chinese food and restaurants. While Chinese food has been successfully localized and is much loved, the preference for Chinese food and restaurants began to decrease beginning in the 1980s and has accelerated through the spread of well-being discourse for being regarded as being incompatible with well-being. Some Chinese restaurants are making efforts to overcome this negative image and trying to take advantage of the well-being trend. They reduce their use of MSG, use vegetable oil instead of lard, replace pork or beef with vegetables or seafood in certain dishes, change the frying oil frequently, and clean the kitchen often in order to combat prevailing perceptions.

The strength of the well-being trend and the negative image of Chinese food and restaurants seem to have exerted an influence upon the consumption pattern of Chinese food in Korean society. Those who consider well-being first tend to not eat Chinese food. However, many still eat Chinese food because they enjoy it. For decades, Korean people have enjoyed and loved Chinese food and continue to eat it despite concerns about well-being. Some also think that if they enjoy Chinese food, eating it, rather than stressing about not eating it, is the correct way to practice well-being. However, such Korean consumers appreciate the efforts of Chinese restaurants to adapt to the well-being trend.

Notes

An earlier version of the present essay was published in 2010 in *Korea Journal* 50(1): 85–109.
1. Previous research on the sociocultural aspects of food and diet is very extensive. Well-known and influential studies include Lévi-Strauss (1970), Douglas (1971), Mintz (1985), Goody (1986), and Appadurai (1988).

2. Studies on well-being began to be published in Korean in 2003. When I searched for studies on well-being in October 2009 through the Research Information Service System provided by the Korea Education and Research Information Service, I found 611 domestic journal articles, 652 doctorate and master theses, and 1,544 books, all of which were published since 2003.

3. The data for this research were gathered in the Seoul area.

4. Vegetarian ideas and lifestyles have a long history, but vegetarianism here is directly related to the vegetarian movement that started in earnest by the formation of the Vegetarian Society in Britain in 1847.

5. For lower-body bathing, one soaks the lower body (under the navel) in warm water for around twenty minutes. It is said to promote the circulation of the blood and help excrete waste from the body.

6. Korean government certifies environmentally friendly agricultural products based on inspections by special certification institutions that include the National Agricultural Products Quality Management Service (NAQS) and some fifty private institutions designated by NAQS.

7. The environmentally friendly product certification system began to apply to livestock products in 2005.

8. This interviewee was a female in her early forties with upper-middle-class background.

9. This interviewee was also a female in her early forties with upper-middle-class background.

10. This interviewee was in her late thirties with lower middle class background.

11. In the 1910s, there were several high-end Chinese restaurants in Seoul and Incheon.

12. In the late 1950s, the population of Chinese in Korea was around 20,000 and there were about 1,700 Chinese restaurants. The population increased to around 30,000 in the early 1970s, with around 2,500 Chinese restaurants.

13. In the 1990s, in response to expanding imports of foreign food items, especially agricultural products from China, the discourse of "body and soil are one" (*sinto buri*) became widespread in Korean society, with an undertone of nationalism, asserting that agricultural products from Korea are better for Koreans than foreign products. I assumed that this trend negatively influenced the popularity of Chinese food and positively influenced that of Korean food.

14. Refer to Jeon (2005).

15. Among seventeen interviewees who were mostly female between their mid-twenties and early forties, thirteen interviewees mentioned greasiness as the representative characteristics of Chinese food. The merits of Chinese food that they mentioned are that it can be cooked quickly, it has diverse flavors and ingredients; nutritional loss is minimal because it is mostly cooked quickly in high heat; and it stimulates the appetite with unique flavors.

16. This interviewee was a female in her mid-forties with middle-class background.

17. This restaurant was located in Cheongdam-dong, which was one of the wealthiest neighborhoods in Seoul with luxury houses and apartments as well as luxury shops. The prices for the dishes were quite high. Because of the prices and the location, the customers were said to be mainly middle class and above.

18. This restaurant is located in Jamsil-dong, which is the residential area for the middle and upper middle class and the commercial area, and they employed both a Korean chef and a Chinese chef from Shanghai. So they tried to develop new dishes by combining Korean- and Chinese-style cooking. The majority of customers were families headed by people in

their middle ages because the restaurant was in the residential area and the light flavors of the dishes appealed to middle-aged and older people.

19. This restaurant is located in Dogok-dong, which is also one of the wealthiest neighborhoods in Seoul. The restaurant here was the first chain store of several chain stores later opened. The customers largely consisted of couples with young children.

20. This restaurant is also located in Cheongdam-dong. The owner had worked as a manager for nineteen years at several restaurants in five-star hotels. He majored in Korean cuisine at a college, thus his specialty was Korean cuisine. He created the menu by combining his specialty of Korean cuisin, the cooking technique of the chef who worked at a Chinese restaurant in a five-star hotel and the knowledge about Chinese cuisine he acquired from his work experience and a lot of food tours in China. The prices of dishes were high, thus the customers seemed to be middle class and above, but not to be limited to a certain age range.

21. The owner informed me that he was planning to add more steamed dishes and to gather them together in a new category on the menu.

22. The restaurateur said that they kept the ingredients in refrigerator for no more than three days.

23. For example, some restaurants sell sweet and sour snapper, puffer fish, or shiitake mushrooms cooked in the same preparation as sweet and sour pork or beef (*tangsuyuk*), one of the most popular Chinese dishes in Korea.

24. This informant was a female in her early thirties with middle-class background. She worked out regularly and watched out for unhealthy food.

25. This interviewee was a female in her early forties with upper-middle-class background.

References

Ahn, Hyun-Young, and Kwang-Ick Cho. 2006. "IPA-reul iyonghan paeseuteu pudeu-ui welbing menyu-ui pyeongga" (Evaluation of Well-being Menu of Fast Food Restaurants Using IPA). *Gwangwang yeongu* (Tourism Research) 21(3): 237–254.

Anderson, Eugene N. 1988. *The Food of China.* New Haven, CT: Yale University Press.

Appadurai, Arjun. 1988. "How to Make a National Cuisine: Cookbooks in Contemporary India." *Comparative Studies in Society and History* 30(1): 3–24.

Bak, Su-jeong. 1993. "Yeongyang bochungje mit geongang sikpum-ui seopchwi siltae-wa siksaenghwal mit geongang-gwaui gwangye" (Study on the Relations among the Intake of Nutrient Supplements and Health Foods, Dietary Behavior and Health). MA thesis, Dongguk University.

Bourgois, Philippe. 1995. *In Search of Respect: Selling Crack in El Barrio.* Cambridge: Cambridge University Press.

Chang, K. C., ed. 1977. *Food in Chinese Culture: Anthropological and Historical Perspectives.* New Haven, CT: Yale University Press.

Cheng, Sea-ling. 2002. "Eating Hong Kong's Way Out." In *Asian Food: The Global and the Local,* edited by Katarzyna J. Cwiertka and Boudewijn Walraven, 16–33. Richmond, Surrey: Curzon.

Cheung, Sidney C. H. 2001. "Hakka Restaurants: A Study of the Consumption of Food in Post-war Hong Kong Society." In *Changing Chinese Foodways in Asia,* edited by David Wu and Tan Chee-Beng, 81–95. Hong Kong: The Chinese University Press.

———. 2002. "The Invention of Delicacy: Cantonese Food in Yokohama Chinatown." In *The Globalization of Chinese Food,* edited by David Wu and Sidney Cheung, 170–182. Honolulu: University of Hawaii Press.

Chua, Beng Huat, and Ananda Rajah. 2001. "Hybridity, Ethnicity and Food in Singapore." In *Changing Chinese Foodways in Asia,* edited by David Wu and Tan Chee-Beng, 161–197. Hong Kong: The Chinese University Press.

Clark, Scott. 2009. "Pleasure Experienced: Well-Being and the Japanese Bath." In *Pursuits of Happiness: Well-Being in Anthropological Perspective,* edited by Gordon Mathews and Carolina Izquierdo, 189–210. New York: Berghahn Books.

Colby, Benjamin Nick. 2009. "Is a Measure of Cultural Well-Being Possible or Desirable?" In *Pursuits of Happiness: Well-Being in Anthropological Perspective,* edited by Gordon Mathews and Carolina Izquierdo, 45–64. New York: Berghahn Books.

Derné, Steve. 2009. "Well-Being: Lessons from India." In *Pursuits of Happiness: Well-Being in Anthropological Perspective,* edited by Gordon Mathews and Carolina Izquierdo, 127–146. New York: Berghahn Books.

Douglas, Mary. 1971. "Deciphering a Meal." *Daedalus* 101: 61–82.

Fernandez, Doreen G. 2002. "Chinese Food in the Philippines: Indigenization and Transformation." In *The Globalization of Chinese Food,* edited by David Wu and Sidney Cheung, 183–190. Honolulu: University of Hawaii Press.

Goody, Jack. 1986. *Cooking, Cuisine and Class: A Study in Comparative Sociology.* Cambridge: Cambridge University Press.

Heil, Daniela. 2009. "Embodied Selves and Social Selves: Aboriginal Well-Being in Rural New South Wales, Australia." In *Pursuits of Happiness: Well-Being in Anthropological Perspective,* edited by Gordon Mathews and Carolina Izquierdo, 88–108. New York: Berghahn Books.

Izquierdo, Carolina. 2009. "Well-Being among the Matsigenka of the Peruvian Amazon: Health, Missions, Oil, and 'Progress.'" In *Pursuits of Happiness: Well-Being in Anthropological Perspective,* edited by Gordon Mathews and Carolina Izquierdo, 67–87. New York: Berghahn Books.

Jankowiak, William. 2009. "Well-Being, Cultural Pathology, and Personal Rejuvenation in a Chinese City, 1981-2005." In *Pursuits of Happiness: Well-Being in Anthropological Perspective,* edited by Gordon Mathews and Carolina Izquierdo, 147–166. New York: Berghahn Books.

Jeon, Jeong-won. 2005. "Welbing ihu oesik sobijadeul-ui saenghwal seonghyang byeonhwa-e daehan yeongu: hansikdang-eul jungsim-euro" (A Study on the Changed Lives of Customers Visiting Korean Restaurants after the Spread of the Well-Being Fad). *Hanguk jori hakhoeji* (The Korean Journal of Culinary Research) 11(1): 87–104.

Ju, Yeong-ha. 2000. *Jungguk, juggugin, jungguk eumsik* (China, Chinese People, Chinese Food). Seoul: Chaeksesang.

Kang, Soo Min. 2007. "Oesik sobija-ui welbing-e daehan insik-gwa silcheon jeongdo-ga welbing eumsikjeom seontaek sokseong-e michineun yeonghyang" (The Effect of the Restaurant Customers' Perception and Practice Regarding Well-Being on Restaurant Attributes). MA thesis, Sejong University.

Kim, Gi-yeong, Jin-cheol Yeom, and Wu-je Jo. 2003. *Oesik saneop gwalliron* (Management of Food Service Industry). Seoul: Hyeonhaksa.

Kim, Ji Yun. 2008. "Welbing raipeu stail-i wain seontaek sokseong-e michineun yeonghyang" (Study on the Effect of Well-Being Lifestyle toward Wine Selection Attributes). *Gwangwang yeongu* (Tourism Research) 26: 19–34.

Kim, Kwang Ok. 1998. "Sangsang-i gyeongjaenghaneun gonggan: hangukeseoui jungguk eumsik" (The Space Where Imaginations Contest: Chinese Food in Korea). In *Hanguk illyuhak-ui seonggwa-wa jeonmang* (The Outcomes and Prospects of Korean Anthropology), edited by Anthropology Study Group, Seoul National University, 201–217. Seoul: Jipmoondang.

———. 2001. "Contested Terrain of Imagination: Chinese Food in Korea." In *Changing Chinese Foodways in Asia,* edited by David Wu and Tan Chee-Beng, 201–218. Hong Kong: The Chinese University Press.

Kim, Min-jeong, and Byeong-sook Kim. 2005. *Sobi munhwa kodeu-ro bon welbing* (Well-Being as a Code for Consumer Culture). Daegu: Taeilsa.

Kim, Tae-hui. 2002. "Paemilli reseutorang gogaek-ui yeongyang-gwa geongang menyu-e daehan taedo" (Family Restaurant Customers' Attitudes toward Nutrition and Healthy Menus). *Hanguk siksaenghwal munhwa hakhoeji* (Journal of the Korean Society of Dietary Culture) 17(5): 629–637.

Ko, Jae-Youn. 2007. "Gungnae wain sobija-ui welbing insik-gwa wain gumae seontaek sokseong-gan-ui gwangye" (Relationship between Well-Being Perception and Wine Purchase Choice Attributes). *Wain someullie yeongu* (Journal of Wine Sommeliers) 16(1): 155–172.

Lévi-Strauss, Claude. 1970. *The Raw and the Cooked,* translated by John and Doreen Weightman. London: J. Cape.

Lewis, Oscar. 1959. *Five Families: Mexican Case Studies in the Culture of Poverty.* New York: Basic Books.

———. 1961. *The Children of Sanchez.* New York: Random House.

———. 1966. *La Vida: A Puerto Rican Family in the Culture of Poverty—San Juan and New York.* New York: Random House.

Mathews, Gordon, and Carolina Izquierdo, eds. 2009. *Pursuits of Happiness: Well-Being in Anthropological Perspective.* New York: Berghahn Books.

Min, Seong-hui, and Oh Hye-suk. 2002. "Gangwon jiyeok sikpum jeongong haksaengdeul-ui oesik haengdong-gwa jungguk eumsik-e daehan insik josa" (A Survey on the Eating Out Behaviors and the Perception about Chinese Foods of Food-Related Major College Students in Gangwon-do Areas). *Hanguk siksaenghwal munhwa hakhoeji* (Journal of the Korean Society of Dietary Culture) 17(3): 309–314.

Mintz, Sidney W. 1985. *Sweetness and Power: The Place of Sugar in Modern History.* New York: Viking.

Naroll, Raoul. 1983. *The Moral Order: An Introduction.* Beverly Hills: Sage.

Park, Eun Kyung. 1994. "Jungguk eumsik-ui yeoksajeok uimi" (Historical Significance of Chinese Food). *Hanguk munhwa illyuhak* (Korean Cultural Anthropology) 26: 95–116.

Plath, David W. 1980. *Long Engagements: Maturity in Modern Japan.* Stanford: Stanford University Press.

Seo, Dong-jin. 2005. "Welbing sidae-ui sobi munhwa bipan-eul wihayeo" (For Criticizing Consumer Culture in the Age of Well-Being). *Munhwa gwahak* (Cultural Science) 41: 72–85.

Su, Jianling. 2001. "The Changing Foodways of a Village in the Pearl River Delta Area." In *Changing Chinese Foodways in Asia,* edited by David Wu and Tan Chee-Beng, 35–45. Hong Kong: The Chinese University Press.

Tam, Siumi Maria. 1997. "Eating Metropolitaneity: Hong Kong Identity in *Yumcha.*" *Australian Journal of Anthropology* 8(3): 291–306.

Tamotsu, Aoki. 2001. "The Domestification of Chinese Foodways in Contemporary Japan: Ramen and Peking Duck." In *Changing Chinese Foodways in Asia*, edited by David Wu and Tan Chee-Beng, 219–233. Hong Kong: The Chinese University Press.

Tan, Chee-Beng. 2001. "Food and Ethnicity with Reference to the Chinese in Malaysia." In *Changing Chinese Foodways in Asia*, edited by David Wu and Tan Chee-Beng, 125–160. Hong Kong: The Chinese University Press.

———. 2007. "Nyonya Cuisine: Chinese, Non-Chinese and the Making of a Famous Cuisine in Southeast Asia." In *Food and Foodways in Asia: Resource, Tradition and Cooking*, edited by Sidney Cheung and Tan Chee-Beng, 171–182. London and New York: Routledge.

Tan, Mely G. 2002. "Chinese Dietary Culture in Indonesian Urban Society." In *The Globalization of Chinese Food*, edited by David Wu and Sidney Cheung, 152–169. Honolulu: University of Hawaii Press.

Thin, Neil. 2009. "Why Anthropology Can Ill Afford to Ignore Well-Being." In *Pursuits of Happiness: Well-Being in Anthropological Perspective*, edited by Gordon Mathews and Carolina Izquierdo, 23–44. New York: Berghahn Books.

Weisner, Thomas S. 2009. "Well-Being and Sustainability of Daily Routines: Families with Children with Disabilities in the United States." In *Pursuits of Happiness: Well-Being in Anthropological Perspective*, edited by Gordon Mathews and Carolina Izquierdo, 228–247. New York: Berghahn Books.

Wu, David Y. H. 2001. "Chinese Café in Hong Kong." In *Changing Chinese Foodways in Asia*, edited by David Wu and Tan Chee-Beng, 71–80. Hong Kong: The Chinese University Press.

———. 2002a. "Improvising Chinese Cuisine Overseas." In *The Globalization of Chinese Food*, edited by David Wu and Sidney Cheung, 56–66. Honolulu: University of Hawaii Press.

———. 2002b. "Cantonese Cuisine (*Yue-cai*) in Taiwan and Taiwanese Cuisine (*Tai-cai*) in Hong Kong." In *The Globalization of Chinese Food*, edited by David Wu and Sidney Cheung, 86–99. Honolulu: University of Hawaii Press.

Wu, David, and Sidney Cheung, eds. 2002. *The Globalization of Chinese Food*. Honolulu: University of Hawaii Press.

Yang, Young-Kyun. 2005. "*Jajangmyeon* and *Junggukjip:* The Changing Position and Meaning of Chinese Food and Chinese Restaurants in Korean Society." *Korea Journal* 45(2): 60–88.

Yu, Hyeon-jeong. 2006. "Welbing teurendeu-e daehan sobija uisik mit welbing haengdong" (Consumer Consciouness toward Well-Being Trend and Well-Being Behaviors). *Hanguk saenghwal gwahakhoeji* (Korean Journal of Life Science) 15(2): 261–274.

Zhuang, Kongshao. 2002. "The Development of Ethnic Cuisine in Beijing: On the Xinjiang Road." In *The Globalization of Chinese Food*, edited by David Wu and Sidney Cheung, 69–85. Honolulu: University of Hawaii Press.

CHAPTER 12

The Social Life of American Crayfish in Asia

Sidney C. H. Cheung

Recent studies on foodways have brought attention to changes in the local dynamics of production, representation, identity construction, postmodern consumerism, and several other social and political changes. For an understanding of the traditional side and its relevant changes in the mode of production of food and foodways, therefore, a holistic understanding of the agricultural innovation that took place in some important farming grounds of human societies should not be overlooked. The globalization of local foodways, as well as the localization of foreign foodways, remind us that foodways are simultaneously local and global in terms of production, manufacturing, and marketing. Meanwhile, much scholarly attention has been given to the social and cultural construction of foodways, yet a truly comprehensive view of food cannot neglect the politics of food production (Nestle 2002). Nor should we overlook the global movement of ingredients (Phillips 2006). The travels of these ingredients not only reminds us of how objects and materials travel, but also of how (our) concepts of food are changing, especially in terms of eating and cooking styles among various human groups (see Kurlansky 1999, 2002).

The historical movement of sugar helps to illustrate this point. The fact that the consumption of sugar has been actually a complicated social development in the modern history of cultural interaction (Mintz 1985) has inspired detailed studies on such items as tea, tobacco, coffee, etc., all which have brought significant contributions to the understanding of our modern economy and politics. And Theodore Bestor (2004) has also demonstrated to us how a local fish market, Tsukiji (in Tokyo), has been affecting the social economy of the global food network. By focusing on food to better understand the sociocultural practices of globalization, we have also seen recent studies on soy products, improvising Chinese cuisine, American fast food, etc., among Asian countries (also see Cwiertka and

Walraven 2000; Cheung and Tan 2007; Du Bois, Tan and Mintz 2008; Watson 1997; Wu and Cheung 2002).

Asian Response to the American Crayfish

In this chapter, I examine the influences brought about by the movement of the red swamp crayfish (*Procambarus clarkii* and *Pacifastacus leniusculus*) from North America to Asia, especially after their rapid growth in Lake Akan, Hokkaido in Japan, and Xuyi, Jiangsu, in Mainland China, and investigate individual and community responses toward adaptation, consumption, and conservation since the introduction of crayfish in 1930. Crayfish, commonly called crawfish or crayfish in English (words derived from the old French word *écrevisse*), are freshwater crustaceans resembling marine lobster but smaller in size. Different from those previous studies on cuisines or processed products, the introduction of crayfish to areas that originally did not exist helps us to investigate the impact brought by the American crayfish in Asia. They appeared as exotic animals in the early and middle of the last century, but were promoted as local food in order to support regional economy as well as agricultural development. Therefore, the social economic impacts brought to both Asian societies cannot be neglected.

In the following section, I would like to focus on crayfish farming history in Louisiana before describing how the introduction and cultivation of a foreign species has contributed to changes in the agricultural system of these regions as well as the trade network in mainland China and environmental conservation in Japan. In Louisiana, crayfish culture existed probably since the eighteenth century; however, systematic and massive crayfish farming did not exist until the 1960s, and crayfish were continuously caught in the wild swampy areas among local people until today (McClain and Romaire 2004), given the fact that the farmed crayfish and wild caught crayfish become available in the market during different periods of the year. But nowadays, besides the local crayfish, some inexpensive packed frozen meat are imported from various countries where Louisiana crayfish was originally introduced as foreign and exotic species for different reasons many decades ago. Of course, crayfish is not an exception among many exotic species settled in a local environment; we have seen how many invasive (exotic or alien) freshwater fish have had enormous negative impacts on their new environments. A few examples are the Nile perch in Australia and Tanzania, the black bass in Japan, janitor fish in the Philippines, the bullfrog in South Korea, and grass carp and snakehead in North America. However, there are some species that have brought new foodways to their new habitat, such as the popular tilapia (an African food fish) in Asia, rainbow trout in Japan, and the red swamp crayfish (*Procambarus clarkii*) in China. Tracking down the spread of the red swamp crayfish both in Japan and China provides a wonderful case study, as it has spread globally and impacted two different countries in many ways. By focusing on the two Asian journeys of the red swamp crayfish, a native Louisiana freshwater crustacean, this chapter seeks to examine how it was widely accepted as a delicacy and a new crop, as well as an agricultural product, in mainland China while it conversely became a destructive, invasive creature "excluded" from agricultural production in Hokkaido's freshwater lakes after its introduction more than seven decades ago.

Crayfish live in freshwater while lobsters live in the sea; crayfish resemble the appearance of marine lobsters and have been marketed as "little lobsters," particularly in mainland China because of the upscale image of lobster there. There are more than five hundred varieties of crayfish in the world and in some countries they are a popular food item; the most well-known culinary style would be spicy Cajun cuisine, which originated in Louisiana and is widely considered a working-class food in the southern part of the United States. Apart from the Cajun cuisine, many Americans still consider crayfish too "dirty and muddy" for eating. However, crayfish is a popular ingredient in both Sweden and Australia. For example, I was told that Swedish people hold crayfish (eating) parties at the end of summer, while *yabby* and *marron* are commonly eaten in Australia. The marron, for that matter, is considered an expensive ingredient for upscale restaurants. In my own experience, I found some Australian yabby and marron kept alive and sold in a Hong Kong upscale supermarket that were considered expensive ingredients in other Asian countries as well.

Louisiana Crayfish (*Procambarus clarkii*) in New Orleans

Historically speaking, New Orleans plays an important role in the cultural roots of the United States. On the one hand, many Americans consider New Orleans to be the "hometown" of the United States given the origination of jazz music there, its early role as the gateway for immigrants, its rural scenery, and the emergence of new values since the end of slavery as well as the end of the American Civil War; on the other hand, most Americans are indeed not familiar with the history and culture of Louisiana. For example, when I talked to Americans living on the East Coast, many of them would give me a strange look when I asked them if they had ever tried any crayfish dishes, and they would tell me that they are not interested in those "mudbugs," as they were usually called outside Louisiana, especially in the northern part of the United States. On top of this, we should remember the historical development of New Orleans since the Louisiana Purchase in 1803, since the changing lifestyles of the French descendants should not be overlooked. For example, I met one man in his early sixties who told me that his family had been living in Louisiana for seven generations; however, he is the first generation to speak English instead of French.

In order to gain a better understanding of how crayfish farming developed, I conducted some basic field study in the United States. In the summer of 2011, I started in New Orleans as it is the most connected transportation hub in the state of Louisiana, and it seemed appropriate to start there before visiting any other relevant areas. However, in New Orleans, when I told people that I was there for the study of crayfish farming, most people gave me the same response: not only had I came to the wrong place, but I had come at the wrong time. Most rice farmers were busy with the rice harvesting; the cultivation period had not started yet. Also, it was the end of the season for wild catching and fishers shifted to catching shrimp, oysters, and fish in the wild. With a friend's help, I was able to see some sacks of crayfish in a local seafood market, together with some local and Chinese-processed and packed frozen crayfish tail. Apart from my concern specifically with crayfish, I not only visited the public seafood market that was formed after the damage of Hurricane Katrina in 2005 (as local fishermen got together in order to retail the seafood they caught directly to customers, after troubles with wholesalers), but also the French Market right outside the French Quarter, which was changed into a touristic shopping spot in the 1960s as locals started purchasing goods from supermarkets and stopped visiting local wet markets. All these experiences broadened my understanding of the changes in the seafood trade network in New Orleans over time.

During my first visit to Louisiana, I was told that I should instead go to Lafayette, which is a three- to four-hour drive from New Orleans. Lafayette is famous for agriculture including rice, soy, sugar cane, and crayfish, so I expected to meet some farmers and to collect some personal histories regarding why and how they got involved in the rotation systems among different crops. With the introduction of the curator of a local museum on southern food and beverage in New Orleans, I was put in touch with the very knowledgeable people in the town of Erath. There I met some rice farmers in order to understand the importance of crayfish from a local perspective. On the way back, I stopped in Crowley, which is known as the rice capital of Lafayette. There, I had a chance to try different crayfish dishes in a meal set called Crawfish Festival, including a crawfish bisque, gumbo, and deep-fried crawfish, among others. For my tastes, it was a rich and "heavy" whole meal, but very enjoyable. The trip was short but fruitful, and I was able to meet and talk with one farmer and some people who are very familiar with the rotation between rice and crayfish farming. After I met two rice farmers in Crowley, I began to realize how and why farmers would choose to farm crayfish instead of working on the second rice crop; weather, labor costs, and taxation were all significant factors. When the price of rice is low and the milling cost is high, and the second crop has low yield compared to the first crop, farmers reflood their fields to encourage the growth of crayfish, and also prevent overgrowth of grass in the field. Compared to rice, which is more like a structured cash crop, crayfish is a bonus, a "real" (untaxed) cash crop, so the farmer makes the decision to rotate based on his/her experience.

Besides conducting interviews with people and visiting markets in New Orleans, I also studied some basic information about crayfish farming available on the internet and from bulletins issued by Louisiana Wildlife and Fisheries Commission, and realized that the massive cultivation of crayfish only began in late 1960s, and that before then all crayfish was wild, caught from bayous and drainage (LaCaze 1966, 1970). Initially I had assumed that this might be related to the decline of the farming population in the 1960s, but nobody I spoke with thought that was even a contributing factors. I then looked at tourism development in the 1960s, the enactment of the Wilderness Act since 1964, the decline of the price of rice in the 1970s, and so on. When I asked locals about the origin of crayfish dishes and how and why they became so popular in Louisiana, I was often told that the consumption of crayfish has a long history and that, for the most part, they had become so popular because they were delicious. Certainly, I could understand the emotional attachment of local people to crayfish, which symbolizes an identity as well as a sense of belonging; but more importantly, as an anthropologist, I aim to uncover how the changing individual taste is related to the social and political environment. Thus, I am still trying to seek the connections between the popularization of crayfish and socioecological changes that have taken place during the last several decades.

To understand why crayfish went from being subsistence crop to a cash crop, we first of all need to know the natural cycle of crayfish reproduction. In the summer, female crayfish create burrows that look like chimneys and hide themselves about 3 meters below ground level where it is wet and humid. Inside the burrow, the female crayfish lay around five to eight hundred eggs and wait for the cooler and wet environment so that the baby crayfish will be brought out from the burrow to grow in the rice field. The small crayfish forage on foliage and the stems of the rice plants. In order to understand the cycle of crayfish reproduction in the wild, we should pay attention to the characters of the lower basin of the Mississippi river. With the formation of high water flow from the melting ice of the upper basin, the depth of water in the lower basin becomes a nurturing ground for crayfish during the spring season. The summer, when the water level goes down, becomes the best harvest time for the wild crayfish. This cycle of wild-caught crayfish fills the gap in rice-field harvest of the farmed crayfish. As the other half of the crayfish supply in Louisiana, we can see the significance of wild-caught crayfish from bayous and rivers. With this in mind, I would like to now draw your attention to the survival of crayfish and their relevant agricultural development in Japan and China.

American Crayfish into Japan in the Early Twentieth Century

Historically speaking, the introduction of food in the form of agricultural product to certain developing countries was mostly for nutritional reasons, and Japan was not exceptional in the early twentieth century. Beginning in the Meiji period, the Japanese government had plans for changing Japanese diets in order to improve nutrition and health, and milk and bread were introduced as part of the change. Also, the nutritional policy that was taking place within the armed forces in the 1920s was considered the turning point of Japanese dietary change (Cwiertka 1999). On the other hand, the ecological changes brought through the Food Increase Project should not be overlooked; rainbow trout, bullfrogs, and the *Uchida* crayfish (*Pacifastacus leniusculus*) were just a few foreign water species that were introduced to Japan from North America in the prewar period, together with the red swamp crayfish to feed the bullfrogs.

However, the bullfrog for the most part died out in the 1960s as a result of the excessive use of agricultural pesticides. Meanwhile, both kinds of crayfish remained and grew rapidly all over Japan, especially in Hokkaido. One might ask why Hokkaido has more American crayfish compared to other regions. First, we need to understand that Hokkaido was renamed from *Ezo-chi* after the Meiji Restoration in 1868, and was designated as the largest piece of land by the Meiji government for experimentation with imported Western agricultural technologies (Morris-Suzuki 1994). At that time, Western technologies included the production of dairy products, salmon aquaculture, and canned product processing. These imported modern technologies enabled the steady supply of food to mainland Japan, thus justifying the idea of colonizing Hokkaido during the early Meiji period (1868–1912). It was within this context that American crayfish were introduced into several self-contained lakes in Hokkaido.

Japan has its own native crayfish (*Cambaroides japonicus*), which is relatively small compared to those from North America. However, Japanese did not eat crayfish except in some parts of Hokkaido until two decades ago. The imported species—red swamp crayfish (*Procambarus clarkii,* which was introduced to Japan in 1930 as feed for the American bullfrog) and *Uchida* crayfish (*Pacifastacus leniusculus,* which was introduced to Hokkaido in 1926 as food for human consumption and also as feed for rainbow trout) competed with the Japanese native crayfish (*Cambaroides japonicus*) and managed to win the battle for survival (Nisikawa, Motohara, and Nakano 2001). Yet recent data shows that the overgrowth of the exotic *Uchida* crayfish in Lake Akan was related to a serious decrease in the amount of rainbow trout in the area (see figure 12.1). More importantly, *marimo* (a kind of spherical algae found at the bottom of Lake Akan and a government-recognized natural heritage in Japan) was also damaged by crayfish (Cheung 2005).

Lake Akan is geographically located so that anyone traveling from Sapporo (the major city in the southern part of Hokkaido) has to go to Kushiro or Kitami and take the local bus to reach the area. It is located in the eastern part of Hokkaido, with Kushiro marshland on its south. In Ainu (indigenous ethnic group currently living in Hokkaido and Honshu) language, *akan* means stable as well

Figure 12.1. *Uchida* crayfish found in Lake Akan.

as not moving, which enhances its stability given that there are active volcanoes and areas with hot springs around Lake Akan. Together with the lake (with an area of 13 square kilometers and 38 meters in depth), "male" mountain Akan (1,317 meters in height), "female" mountain Akan (1,503 meters in height), and a developed area along the coast of the lake with residential and business activities form the basic components of its physical landscape. Together with the natural scenery, hot springs, and the government-recognized natural heritage (a kind of spherical algae called *marimo* found at the bottom of the lake) in 1921, Lake Akan has been a well-known tourist destination since the 1920s. In addition, with the establishment of Akan National Park in 1934, Lake Akan has been recognized as an important tourist attraction in Hokkaido.

Most Japanese think crayfish carry some muddy taste and are considered dirty as a freshwater creature. Yet practically speaking, some Japanese do eat the crayfish in a simple way of cooking. I only had a chance to eat boiled crayfish in a small restaurant in Lake Akan, which is run by some local fishermen (see figure 12.2). Lake Akan and Lake Toro in Kushiro area are the only two locations where fishery cooperatives gained rights to collect and catch *Uchida* crayfish for commercial usage, starting from fifteen to sixteen years ago. *Uchida* crayfish is caught for food consumption, and sold for both canned soup processing and seafood for some local restaurants (see figure 12.3). After 2004, *Uchida* crayfish was labeled

Figure 12.2. Boiled crayfish served in Lake Akan.

Figure 12.3. Cooking *Uchida* crayfish in Lake Akan.

an "invasive" species, and the demand has clearly dropped since then. Before that, local fishermen caught five to six tons of *Uchida* crayfish in Lake Akan each year, but in the last few years that amount is down to three to four tons annually. A representative of the Lake Akan Fisheries Cooperatives stated in an interview that there were two major reasons for the decline in crayfish demand in Hokkaido. First, the image of invasiveness was a generally negative one for locals. However, that might not be the major factor. Once *Uchida* crayfish were labeled as an invasive species, they could not be transported alive and had to be cooked or frozen before transport. Therefore, some hotels and restaurants that used to order live crayfish for cooking stopped buying from the suppliers and fisheries cooperatives.

Besides being served as a boiled dish, crayfish has been processed into canned "lobster soup" for domestic consumption. As I was told, about one ton of *Uchida* crayfish is needed for ten thousand cans of "lobster soup," which is sold at 500–600 yen per can in retail stores in the Lake Akan area (see figure 12.4). This soup is often sold as a gift set for visitors to Akan. Aside from the situation at Lake Akan and Lake Toro, Lake Toya offers a different case for how *Uchida* crayfish were treated as invasive. According to my informant, at Lake Toya crayfish cannot be sold because there is no permit. Therefore, the only way to get rid of them (to maintain the ecological balance) is to continue catching them and simply throw them away.

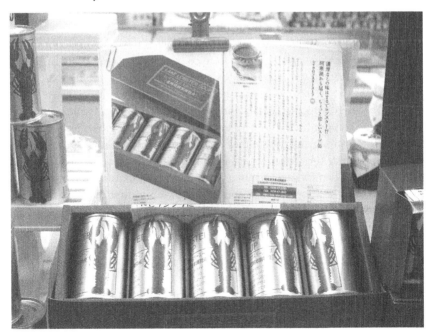

Figure 12.4. Five cans of "lobster" soup in a gift set.

Making Crayfish into Lobster in Mainland China

Procambarus clarkii was brought to Jiangsu area by the Japanese in 1930, although the reason they did so is still unclear. According to my informants, local Jiangsu people tended to believe that there was a Japanese conspiracy to use the crayfish to destroy their rice paddies; crayfish like to eat the roots of crops and, more importantly, they dig holes that drain water away from the rice paddies. Therefore, the local people did not welcome the crayfish at all. Given that crayfish brought no benefits to the people, and that they could still survive in dirty water, they were not considered edible by most. Even now, Chinese people in Jiangsu are frequently surprised to learn that crayfish has become a popular dish in the mainland. Again, for those in Jiangsu who do enjoy crayfish, they told me that they would only ever buy the live green-shelled crayfish at the market for cooking at home as opposed to eating them in restaurants; once cooked it is difficult to single out the "dirty" ones. Yet local villagers in Xuyi told me that in the past they caught crayfish in the river as a kind of leisure-time activity and ate them in a simple cooking style—mainly by boiling them. Commercially speaking, for a long time no one paid any attention to them. Then came the emergence of a dish called Nanjing little lobster (*longxia*), which appeared in the early 1990s, and its rapid growth in popularity was not limited to Nanjing but extended to large cities such as Shanghai, Wuhan, Beijing, and so on during the last decade. Starting from 1992, the redclaw crayfish (*Cherax quadricarinatus*) from North Australia was also introduced to China (Chen and Edgerton 2001). It is important here to explore how the demand for crayfish has expanded and what the impact has been on red swamp crayfish farming in the local context. In Louisiana, crayfish aquaculture is dominated by *P. clarkii* (red swamp crayfish) and *P. zonangulus* (white river crayfish), while the species that became popular in the Jiangsu area is the red swamp variety, which is cooked with ample heat and spices (Huner 1992).

My first encounter (in 2006) with red swamp crayfish in China was at a local restaurant in Nanjing city, where the "little lobster" was cooked in the Sichuan style (hot and spicy). At that time, it was sold at relatively low price (about 1 yaun [RMB] each). When I visited Nanjing again in 2008, however, I was brought to an upscale restaurant for this dish and was surprised to find that the price was RMB 128 for a dish in which there were about twenty to thirty cooked crayfish prepared in a hot, spicy style. Many people in Xuyi told me that eating crayfish in restaurants was becoming too luxurious and they could no longer afford it. Interestingly, I noticed at the above Nanjing restaurant a small leaflet on our table that stated, "Today I am a little lobster, but one day I will be an Australian lobster." While freshwater crayfish obviously will not grow into a marine lobster. Apart from the growing demand and rising prices in the last decade, I also speculated that spicy crayfish has become a welcome and signature dish offered by local hosts for their guests visiting Nanjing.

What had happened in Nanjing demonstrates not only the rising price of crayfish marketed as "little lobster," but also the upscale move of crayfish from a peasant's food of unknown origin to a luxurious gourmet food that represents new Nanjing foodways. With this surprising upward mobility, I consider this a timely example for the investigation of land use and agricultural changes brought by China's emerging rural enterprises. Regarding the nationwide catching of "little lobster" for food consumption, it is mentioned that only 6,700 tons were harvested in the early 1990s; subsequently it was recorded that 6.55 million tons were harvested in 1995 and increased to around 10 million tons in 1999 (Xia 2007, 3). If we only consider the production in the Jiangsu area, the amount of "little lobster" harvested in 1995 was 3 million tons, while it increased to 6 million tons in 1999 (Xia 2007, 3). In order to understand the local production of crayfish from the farmers' perspectives, I made two visits to Xuyi and interviewed several farmers regarding their experiences in crayfish farming and discussed with them their thoughts on the future of their businesses.

Xuyi is located about two hours from Nanjing. Its history can be traced back 2,200 years, together with the mystical underwater Sizhou City, Tieshan Temple in the National Forest Park, and the mausoleum of the grandfather and great grandfather of the founding Ming Emperor Zhu Yuanzhang. Naturally speaking, Xuyi is located in the lower basin of the Hao River and the southern side of Hongze Lake. It has a population of more than 0.7 million within a total of 2,500 square kilometers. Xuyi's environment is famous for its hilly terrain, and is very suitable for agriculture. Xuyi is in Jiangsu province, but the local foodways shares influences from both Anhui and Zhejiang, and are therefore a bit more spicy compared to other Jiangsu areas. During the last two decades, because of the farming of crayfish and the organization of an international festival, tremendous changes have taken place in agriculture and tourism. Local people's living standards have improved significantly, and the income of local farmers has gone up from the 1970s, when Xuyi was one of the poorest counties.

Crayfish farming in Xuyi takes up more than 100,000 mows (1 mow is equivalent to 7,274 square feet), and related practitioners take up another 100,000, and the annual output of up to several billion RMB, coupled with the opportunities for cooperation abroad leads locals to believe that this is a bright industry for the future. Chinese agriculture, however, is suffering from the abandonment of fertile ground as farmers choose to leave their homes for work as migrant factory workers in the Yangtze River Delta and Pearl River Delta regions. I wanted to explore, therefore, whether crayfish farming might provide a positive solution for solving the agricultural problems in some rural areas in today's mainland China. In order to understand the farmers' perspectives, I started my fieldwork in Xuyi by interviewing various local farmers.

The first farmer I met in Xuyi used to be a crab farmer, who explained, "crab easily gets diseased and the feed for crab is much more expensive compared to the feed for crayfish." I realized how cheap the feed for crayfish could be upon visiting the second farmer, who used to be a lotus root farmer. He said that, apart from some corn powder, typically leftover parts from butchering chicken and duck were purchased to feed the crayfish (see figures 12.5 and 12.6). The reason that he started cultivating crayfish was his discovery of the crayfish's habits of hiding beneath the lotus leaves in order to seek shelter from the heat (see figure 12.7).

However, when I interviewed another crayfish farmer (a former necktie trader from Zhejiang, who moved to Xuyi to invest in crayfish cultivation), I was told that crayfish farming was not the easy job that most local farmers thought it was, with the belief that crayfish can grow anywhere. In fact, the Zhejiang trader was not the only one to say so. Another investor from a nearby county said that the reason they needed to have a large-scale operation for high-quality crayfish was that the harvest rate they could expect was far less than the estimation of many local farmers. Therefore, they made a total investment of RMB 50 million for the 2,000-mows farming area in Xuyi in 2007, and planned to develop tourism together with food production as a kind of ecologically friendly resort project. Another crayfish farm I visited with a similar idea for development was a joint venture between a local company and an Australian company that occupied far more space. Their business was obviously much larger than any fishpond I had

Figure 12.5. Crayfish fed by corn powder in Xuyi.

Figure 12.6. Farming crayfish in a lotus pond.

ever seen in Xuyi. The total farming capacity is estimated to be 50,000 mows, with 10,000 mows run by the company and 40,000 designated as supporting areas cultivated by other farmers for the same brand. I wondered how much of the rice paddy was turned into a crayfish pond, and how will the production of a stable food be affected in the long run. I do not have the answers at this time, but I am confident that this will be an important issue for the Jiangsu area in the coming decade.

Together with the establishment of the Xuyi Lobster Museum in 2005 and the outdoor stadium with an audience capacity of 80,000, which is only used for the International Lobster Festival (which started in 2001 as a local festival and was developed into an international one by inviting delegation from other countries to participate), we can begin to see the positive support that the government provided in building up Xuyi as the City of Lobster. However, as I was told by some local people, there was a serious shortage of crayfish in terms of supply, and many of the crayfish consumed during the festival were actually transported from other areas. Therefore, if Xuyi is going to be developed as the trade center for crayfish, it will have to consider how to maintain a stable supply, along with the issues of fair pricing and food safety issues. As far as I have heard from different farmers in Xuyi, there is no standardization of feed, or official technical support, or quality control in crayfish cultivation. Of course, there is not even any control over cray-

Figure 12.7. Crayfish cultivated in Xuyi.

fish that come from outside of Xuyi, even though these imports are branded as "Xuyi Longxia." Another farmer I interviewed in Xuyi acknowledged that critical stories about the cleanliness of the crayfish could negatively affect his business. Ultimately, though, most farmers felt that nothing could be done to stop the spread of negative information.

In fact, this prediction came true in late 2010 when twenty-three persons got sick after eating crayfish in restaurants located in Nanking. Initially there were different opinions over why this happened, but it was finally confirmed that it was because of Haff disease (which is the development of rhabdomyolysis, swelling and breakdown of skeletal muscle, with a risk of acute kidney failure), developed within twenty-four hours of ingesting seafood. Staring from late 2010, it was not difficult to find many crayfish eateries that had either closed down or were performing very poorly in Shanghai and Nanjing, and the fears over Haff disease was a major cause of this. In an attempt to attract customers, the Xuyi prefectural government claimed that if anyone were to fall ill after eating Xuyi longxia in the registered eateries, a compensation of RMB 500,000–1,000,000 would be paid out. However, when I visited Xuyi in 2012 for the 12th International Lobster Festival, there seemed to be little to no concern over the previous cases of Haff disease. At the "Lobster Banquet for Ten Thousand People," an event held the day after the opening of the festival, I witnessed the consumption of twenty to thirty tons (my estimation) of cooked crayfish in one evening. Further, during my stay in Xuyi in June 2012, Xuyi people kept telling me that the Haff disease incident was just an exceptional case.

Technically speaking, biologists remained concerned about excessive production based on a small genetic pool, and this is a worry for those involved with mass production of *Procambarus clarkii* in the Jiangsu area. In 2004, biologists discovered a common bacteria existing in both crayfish and Shanghai mitten crab (Wang et al. 2005). Therefore, the information I found online about bacteria carried by crayfish and the fact that crayfish can survive in contaminated water not suitable for human consumption should not be overlooked. In the future, I would like to investigate how crayfish farming will be affected by these circumstances as farmers try to maintain economic returns from mitten crab farming while, more importantly, dealing with the safety issue of crayfish consumption in China. Finally, in addition to the local consumption of crayfish in China, large amounts of frozen crayfish tails are exported "back" to the United States, causing political responses by Louisiana crayfish producers that could affect international trade policy. The exportation of frozen crayfish back to the United States and such European countries as Sweden has led to important debate in relation to foreign trade policy, protectionism, and the intervention of the state government. Through this issue we can see the meanings of foodways from a political perspectives (Thies and Porche 2007).

Conclusion

We have looked at two stories of crayfish farming and harvesting in Japan and China and it is clear how the impact on local communities is very different. The problem in Hokkaido is obviously an environmental one, which will be a challenge for the government, the fishery cooperative, restaurants, and the local fishing community. Therefore, it is important for us to keep an eye on its development and investigate how various interests (farmers, investors, consumers, and the government) can work together for natural conservation and safety. For mainland China, I would like to focus on the negative image people have about the cleanliness of crayfish while acknowledging that many also have their own methods for choosing and consuming quality ones. With the socioeconomic changes taking place in mainland China through its Open Door policy since 1978, it is important to understand how the concept of food production has changed, especially from the basic daily necessities to luxurious gourmet eating among local people, and from domestic consumption to international exports. Regarding the changing foodways in Asian societies, James Watson and Melissa Caldwell (2005) remind us that the major concerns over food security are no longer about whether there is enough food to eat, but whether our food is up to safety standards, and whether the supply is sustainable and the quality can be maintained. By combining my field research on the development of American crayfish farming with an ethnographic study of a new agricultural economy resulting from state policies on rural reform, a further understanding of mainland China's changing lifestyles both in the urban and rural areas will be expected.

Notes

The research for this chapter was made possible by the GRF Grant provided by the Hong Kong SAR Research Grants Council on the project entitled, "The Social Life of American Crayfish in Three Cultures." An earlier version of this chapter was published in 2010 in *Globalization, Food and Social Identities in the Asia Pacific Region*, edited by James Farrer (Tokyo: Sophia University), which can be found at http://www.fla.sophia.ac.jp/icc/publication/cheung.htm.

References

Bestor, Theodore C. 2004. *Tsukiji: The Fish Market at the Center of the World*. Berkeley: University of California Press.

Chen, Xiaoxuan, and Brett F. Edgerton. 2001. "Freshwater Crayfish Culture in China." *Aquaculture Magazine*, November–December: 41–44.

Cheung, Sidney C. H. 2005. "Rethinking Ainu Heritage: A Case Study of an Ainu Settlement in Hokkaido, Japan." *International Journal of Heritage Studies* 11(3): 197–210.

Cheung, Sidney C. H., and Tan Chee Beng, eds. 2007. *Food and Foodways in Asia: Resource, Tradition and Cooking*. London and New York: Routledge.

Cwiertka, Katarzyna J. 1999. *The Making of Modern Culinary Tradition in Japan*. Unpublished doctoral dissertation, Lieden University.

Cwiertka, Katarzyna, and Boudewijn Walraven. 2000. *Asian Food: The Global and The Local*. Surrey: Curzon.

Du Bois, Christine M., Tan Chee-Beng, and Sidney Mintz. 2008. *The World of Soy*. Chicago: University of Illinois Press.

Huner, Jay V. 1992. "Chinese Crawfish and the Louisiana Crawfish Industry." *Aquaculture Magazine*, March–April: 6–13.

Kurlansky, Mark. 1999. *Cod: A Biography of the Fish that Changed the World*. London: Vintage.

———. 2002. *Salt: A World History*. New York: Penguin Books.

LaCaze, Cecil. 1966. *More about Crawfish*. Wildlife Education Bulletin No. 96. Baton Rouge: Louisiana Wildlife and Fisheries Commission.

———. 1970. *Crawfish Farming*. Fisheries Bulletin No. 7. Baton Rouge: Louisiana Wildlife and Fisheries Commission.

McClain, W. Ray, and Robert P. Romaire. 2004. "Crawfish Culture: A Louisiana Aquaculture Success Story." *World Aquaculture* 35(4): 31–35, 60–61.

Mintz, Sidney W. 1985. *Sweetness and Power: The Place of Sugar in Modern History*. New York: Viking Penguin.

Morris-Suzuki, Tessa. 1994. *The Technological Transformation of Japan: From the Seventeenth to the Twenty-first Century*. Cambridge and New York: Cambridge University Press.

Nestle, Marion. 2002. *Food Politics: How the Food Industry Influences Nutrition and Health.* Berkeley: University of California Press.

Nisikawa, Usio, Motohara Konishi, and Shigeru Nakano. 2001. "Species Displacement Between an Introduced and a 'Vulnerable' Crayfish: The Role of Aggressive Interactions and Shelter Competition." *Biological Invasions* 3: 179–185.

Phillips, Lynne. 2006. "Food and Globalization." *Annual Review of Anthropology* 35: 37–57.

Thies, Cameron G., and Schuyler Porche. 2007. "Crawfish Tails: A Curious Tale of Foreign Trade Policy Making." *Foreign Policy Analysis* 3: 171–187.

Wang, Wen, et al. 2005. "A Novel Spiroplasma Pathogen Causing Systemic Infection in the Crayfish *Procambarus Clarkii* (Crustacea: Decapod), in China." *FEMS Microbiology Letters* 249: 131–137.

Watson, James L. ed. 1997. *Golden Arches East: McDonald's in East Asia.* Stanford: Stanford University Press.

Watson, James L., and Melissa L. Caldwell, eds. 2005. *The Cultural Politics of Food and Eating: A Reader.* Malden, MA: Blackwell.

Wu, David Y. H., and Sidney C. H. Cheung, eds. 2002. *The Globalization of Chinese Food.* Surrey: Routledge Curzon.

Xia, Aijun. 2007. *Little Lobster Cultivation Technique* (in Chinese). Beijing: China Agriculture University Press.

CHAPTER 13

Eating Green
Ecological Food Consumption in Urban China
Jakob A. Klein

The most recent decades of dietary globalization have involved not only the intensification of international food trade and the growing presence of transnational retail and restaurant chains, but also the spread of "organics," fair trade, Slow Food and other movements that are critical of dominant social and ecological relations of food production, distribution and consumption, along with the growth of markets in "alternative" or "ethical" foods (Wilk 2006; Nützenadel and Trentmann 2008). In cities in the People's Republic of China, the rise since the early 1990s of globalized fast foods, packaged foods and drinks, and supermarkets (Watson 2006; Yan 2000; Zhang et al. 2008) has been followed by the emergence of markets for "organics" and other ecologically certified foods, and by the growing involvement of environmental NGOs and entrepreneurs in the promotion of such foods (Sanders 2006; Klein 2009).[1]

Movements, such as Slow Food and "organics," are often criticized for simply contributing to the construction of niche markets for affluent consumers rather than providing equitable, sustainable alternatives to the "global food system" (e.g., Pilcher 2006; Laudan 2004). According to this critique, "alternative" or "ethical" food consumption is beyond the means of most shoppers and has little if any positive impact on farming communities and ecosystems, not only because of the relatively low levels of consumption compared with "conventional" foods but also because the "alternative" markets often come to be appropriated and production "conventionalized" by highly capitalized, profit-driven corporations (Guthman 2004; Shapin 2006). In China, food activists and relatively small-scale, ideologically motivated "organic" food producers have arrived on an ecological food scene already dominated by a combination of agribusiness and state interests (Sanders 2006; Thiers 2002, 2005; Klein 2009). Thus, it makes little sense to talk about the "mainstreaming" or "conventionalization" of Chinese organic and other ecological foods. Nevertheless, the powerful interests involved in these industries may undoubtedly compromise the more radical transformative potential of ecological foods as envisioned by some Chinese activists and activist-entrepreneurs (Klein 2009), although this is not an issue explored here (for a critique of Chinese ecological food production and certification, see Thiers 2002, 2005).

This chapter is instead concerned with the meanings of ecological foods within the culture of consumption in urban China. In this context, the critique of "organic" food consumption as an elite practice needs to be considered. Chinese consumers of "organic" and other ecologically certified foods are often described by observers as members of the "new rich" or emerging "middle class," an affluent and educated minority who can afford to purchase these foods and who have developed a "health consciousness" and an "awareness" of food safety issues in the wake of the country's recurring food safety scandals (e.g., Chen 2006; Sanders 2006; Wang et al. 2008). Arguably, the consumption of ecologically certified foods in China is shaped by both economic ability and considerations of social status, although how these foods figure within China's emerging class configurations has not been adequately researched. One of the objectives of this essay is thus to begin to explore the "class" dimensions of ecological food consumption in urban China.

At the same time, however, to dismiss Chinese ecological food consumption as relevant to only a small minority of affluent consumers is somewhat misleading. Instead, I argue here that the depiction of Chinese consumers of ecological foods as a "health-conscious" or "quality-seeking" elite, while not entirely wrong, nonetheless obscures other important dimensions of Chinese ecological food consumption. These include, in particular, the extent to which ecological food consumption resonates with popular cultural understandings of food and health and is embedded within widespread experiences of, and reactions to, rapid urban development, including the industrialization of the food supply.

The chapter draws on four months of ethnographic research carried out between 2006 and 2009 in Kunming, the capital of Yunnan province in Southwest China.[2] The following section outlines the recent emergence in Kunming of a "scene" in ecologically certified foods. I will then consider the ways in which Kunmingers articulated these foods with social hierarchies, before juxtaposing the food-centered narratives of committed consumers of "organics" to those of other people of various social backgrounds living and working in the city, in order to demonstrate how the consumption of "organics" and other ecologically certified foods is shaped by experiences of rapid changes to the urban food supply and is embedded in a wider, popular food culture. I will then develop this argument further by considering the consumption of ecologically certified foods as one of many tactics Kunmingers pursued to cope with the changing food supply. The concluding section considers the extent to which ecological food consumption in Kunming can be understood as an ambivalent and sometimes overtly critical commentary on rapid urban development.

Ecologically Certified Foods in Kunming

Although a relatively poor, landlocked province still heavily dependent on its tobacco industry, since the 1990s Yunnan's economy has grown rapidly and diversified into areas including tourism and specialized agricultural production, not least of fresh vegetables and flowers, which are now sold to cities along China's Eastern seaboard, to Southeast Asia and further afield. Kunming, according to some accounts a "sleepy, backward" town in the early 1990s (Blum 2002: 150), has emerged as a major hub linking southern China with Southeast Asia, and the newly built city center boasts broad avenues, high-rise buildings, and shopping centers replete with international brands, multinational supermarkets, and fast-food chains (Zhang 2006; Blum 2002; Horton 2007). Often perceived by both locals and outsiders as a "late developer," "lagging behind" cities like Beijing and Shanghai (Zhang 2006), Kunming now boasts a new middle class, albeit alongside a growing underclass of rural labor migrants and laid-off workers (Zhang 2006: 465; Zhang 2008). The city had an official, registered urban population of 1.5 million in 2000, but it has continued to expand during the last decade and many locals I spoke with estimated the population in the urban areas at three million or more.

Many Kunmingers associated the arrival of ecologically certified foodstuffs with the rise in the city since the turn of the millennium of multinational supermarkets like Carrefour and Wal-Mart. During the time of my research these supermarkets remained the city's main retail venues for ecologically certified foods, in particular for fresh vegetables. All of the large supermarket chains had special sub-sections for such products in their fresh vegetable sections, and some also had special sections for ecologically certified meats. Other ecologically certified goods found in Kunming supermarkets, such as fresh fruit, packaged snacks, oils, rice, eggs, teas, dairy products and wines and spirits, could be found in amongst their "conventional" counterparts. Many of the city's ecologically certified foods, including most of the fresh vegetables, fruit, and meat, were produced in the province, mostly by companies that were also producing for export to other provinces or abroad.

As in other Chinese cities, Kunming's ecologically certified foods belonged to three different legally recognized categories with quite different production requirements (see also Sanders 2006; Thiers 2002, 2005). Most "organic foods" (*youji shipin*) available in the city were certified by China's internationally recognized Organic Food Development Center (OFDC), a body initially set up in 1994 by the then State Environmental Protection Agency. These foods were allegedly produced according to rigorous "organic" standards, which included the avoidance of all chemical fertilizers and pesticides and GMOs, and strict controls of pollution levels at the production site. Fresh vegetables were the most common "organic" products in the city. The "green food" (*lüse shipin*) and "no public harm" (*wugonghai*, sometimes translated as "hazard free" or "pollution free") schemes were set up and administered by the Ministry of Agriculture. With the exception of those "green- food" products labeled "AA," which I have not seen sold in Kunming, the "green- food" scheme permits the restricted use of a limited number of agrichemicals and does not meet international "organic" standards. "Green- food" products and the "green food" logo were highly visible through advertising, and packaged "green foods" such as yoghurts and teas were sold not only in supermarkets but also in smaller shops and kiosks throughout Kunming. "No public harm" foods were guaranteed to be carefully checked for residues of potentially harmful levels of pesticides or other chemical residues, and production sites were allegedly checked for industrial pollution, but "no public harm" foods were not otherwise required to differ in their production methods from other "conventional" foods. Kunming supermarkets sold "no public harm" fresh vegetables, and the Yunnan-based Gao Shang Gao and Shen Nong companies sold their "no pubic harm" pork not only in the supermarkets but also from their own shops located in some of the covered markets and in popular shopping areas.

Certification requirements for "organic," "green," and "no public harm" foods differed as much as those between "organic" and "conventional" produce in some other countries, but in Kunming these foods were often lumped together. Most of my acquaintances could not or did not distinguish between them, and some referred to the different categories collectively using terms like "ecological foods" (*shengtai shipin*), "health foods" (*jiankang shipin*), "green foods," or "no public harm foods." By contrast, "organic foods" was not much used beyond a small number of producers, activists, and informed consumers. Indeed, the Chinese term carries none of the positive connotations of its English-language equivalent. Several people complained that the term sounded "foreign," and an official at the Kunming office of the OFDC argued that Kunmingers often associated the term with organic chemistry and thought that these foods contained more chemicals than other foods.

The lumping together of the different foods in everyday speech reflected the extent to which the categories were blurred in the marketplace. In the supermarkets' special vegetable sections, for example, "organic," "green food," and "no public harm" vegetables were often not clearly differentiated from one another. Instead, vegetables here were carefully packed in plastic in what one producer described to me as "family size" portions. Although prices on certified "organics" were sometimes significantly higher than other packaged vegetables, many supermarkets charged the same prices for "organics" as for other certified vegetables— in 2008 and 2009 typically about three times the price of the "conventional" equivalents they sold.[3] The packaged vegetables only occasionally sported stickers from the certifying body, but usually had labels with the producer's name. The foods were packaged in such a way as to emphasize the two contradictory dimensions of "purity" in foods outlined by Sidney Mintz (1996). On the one hand, images of sun-drenched fields and texts describing the foods as being "natural" (*ziran*) and "healthy" (*jiankang*) suggested that these foods were healthful because they were unadulterated by humans. On the other hand, the carefully washed vegetables and neat plastic packaging brought home the message of "hygiene," that these foods were "safe" because they were cleansed and protected from bacteria through human intervention involving the use of "scientific" technology. At one supermarket I visited in 2008, the special vegetable section had huge posters from Kunming's major supplier of fresh "green food" and "no public harm" vegetables, the locally based Chen Nong. The posters articulated the company's products with notions of "hygiene," "modernity," and "cosmopolitanism," and included photographs of its state-of-the-art packaging facility with staff in white lab clothes and face masks, and a map with arrows emanating from Kunming indicating all the places in China and around the world to which Chen Nong claimed to sell its products, places including Beijing, Shanghai, Hong Kong, Japan and Australia. In short, producers and supermarkets charged premiums for ecologically certified foods on the grounds that such foods were supposedly safer and healthier than conventional equivalents, and attempted to gain consumers' trust by presenting these foods as "natural," "uncontaminated," and "modern." That they were sold in international supermarkets and were claimed to be consumed by foreigners arguably underscored the modernity of these foods and, in the wake of China's recurring food-safety scandals, their trustworthiness.

In contrast to the supermarkets, members of Kunming's emerging network of ecological food activists and activist-producers were more likely to emphasize distinctions between the different categories of foods. Local producers and purveyors of "organic foods" were keen to inform consumers that their foods were produced to the "highest" ecological standards, and developed various strategies for educating potential consumers about the differences between the categories and what they saw as the benefits of "organics" (see Klein 2009). By 2008, Kunming had two such producers of certified "organic" vegetables. One was Haobaoqing, whose production site outside the city was certified by the OFDC in 2005 and which for three years was the main local supplier of "organic" vegetables to the supermarkets. However, in 2009 Haobaoqing pulled out of the supermarkets following disputes, which according to the producer included disagreements over prices and Haobaoqing's dissatisfaction with the supermarkets' failure to distinguish their "organics" from other categories of ecologically certified vegetables. Haobaoqing now supplied Kunmingers primarily through a home-delivery box scheme, which it was hoping to rapidly expand beyond the one hundred or so regular customers it had in March 2009.

The other local producer was Sino-Agriculture (*Zhong-Nong*), a mainland Chinese offshoot of the Taiwanese Buddhist organic food company, Li-Ren. Sino-Agriculture's production site to the north of Kunming was certified by the OFDC in 2008. The farm supplied vegetables to the company's organic vegetarian center in downtown Kunming, which also opened in 2008. The center had a restaurant and a shop, which mostly sold products imported from elsewhere in mainland China and from Taiwan. In August 2008 the center had about three hundred members, but the following year Sino-Agriculture expanded its facilities, publicized itself more widely, and opened up its shop to nonmembers.

Both Sino-Agriculture and Haobaoqing were profit-oriented (if not actually profit-making) corporations. Similar to agribusinesses such as Chen Nong, production was organized through contracts with farmers or paid wage labor. Nevertheless, both were committed to ecological agriculture on environmentalist and other ethical grounds. For Sino-Agriculture, "organics" was part of a wider agenda to improve social morality and increase compassion for all living creatures, and the center ran regular classes for its members on food, health, and environmental protection, and also organized classes for children and parents in the Confucian classics—although many staff described themselves as Buddhists, Sino-Agriculture insisted that they did not proselytize in mainland China, where such activities were illegal, and drew instead more explicitly on Confucian teachings in order not to jeopardize their operations there.

In addition to these "activist-entrepreneurs," some environmental activists in the city were also promoting the consumption of "organic" and similar foods. Several activist groups enjoyed good relations with Haobaoqing, and in June 2009 the producer invited some of them to a meeting, in the hope that they would help find new customers for their expanding box scheme. One of the groups, the Pesticide Eco-Alternative Center (PEAC), an NGO committed to reducing the use of chemical pesticides in the Yunnan countryside, organized campaigns to educate urban Kunmingers in the benefits of ecologically certified foods, in particular of "organics" (Klein 2009). In 2009, the web-based, English-language Green Kunming was established to supply products from Haobaoqing and other ecological producers in the province, primarily to the city's resident foreigners.

To summarize, during the first decade of the twenty-first century there emerged a small yet visible scene in ecologically certified foods in Kunming. Actors included international supermarkets, export-oriented agribusinesses, ethically motivated entrepreneurs, government certifying bodies, environmental activists, and, of course, consumers. At one end of the scene, the international supermarkets downplayed differences between the various categories of certified foods and instead promoted all such foods as "hygienic" and "natural" alternatives to consumers willing to pay a premium for food safety and health. At the other end, locally based "organic" producers and activist groups singled out "organic" foods as particularly worthy of promotion and articulated these foods not only with messages of food safety and consumer health but also with agendas such as environmental protection, rural livelihoods, and social morality. However, there was a great degree of overlap between the two ends of the scene. For example, until recently the supermarkets were the main retail outlet for Haobaoqing, and in their consumer campaigns environmental activists have often downplayed farmers' issues and have promoted the supermarkets' ecological foods (see Klein 2009). Instead, like the supermarkets, activists' and activist-entrepreneurs' messages centered on "health" and "food safety," and they too often tried to associate ecologically certified foods with a "modernity," whose locus was identified with places far from Kunming—Beijing, Shanghai, Taiwan, Japan, or "the West." In 2009, a large poster at Sino-Agriculture's vegetarian organic center read:

> Sino-Agriculture Health Center
> Safe, Natural, Green, Healthy
> Our promise:
> • No chemical additives
> • Healthy, vegetarian ingredients
> • Balanced nutritional composition
> • Advanced, foreign equipment

Notions of ecologically certified foods as "healthy," "safe," "modern," and "foreign" were all significant when we consider the place of these foods within Kunming's emerging class hierarchies.

Ecological Foods and Social Differentiation

There are some good grounds for the description of consumers of ecologically certified foods as an "elite minority." China's domestic consumption of such foods relative to its consumption of "conventional" foods is small in comparison with North America, Western Europe, and Japan, and has largely been limited to urban areas (Milbrodt 2004; Chen 2006: 10). This is particularly the case with certified "organics," which are hard to find outside of the major cities (Sanders 2006), and which can cost up to ten times more than "conventional" produce.[4] Within Chinese cities, food consumption in the post-Mao era has become highly segmented and stratified (Veeck and Veeck 2000). For example, according to one report, young and well-educated Beijing consumers are now willing to pay price premiums for food safety (Wang et al. 2008). A recent study published by the United States Department of Agriculture (Gale and Huang 2007) argues that among China's urban poor, estimated in the study at about 50 percent of the urban population, the demand for increased quantities of what are described by the authors as "basic" foods such as eggs, poultry, and pork continues to rise with growing incomes. By contrast, the wealthiest 20 percent are no longer purchasing greater quantities of most foods, but are instead turning to "high-quality items like japonica rice from northeastern China, imported jasmine rice, refined soybean oil, 'green food,' or organic food products" (Gale and Huang 2007: 19).

My own, primarily qualitative, data suggest that food consumption patterns in Kunming were similarly stratified. For example, managers at both Haobaoqing and Sino-Agriculture described their regular customers and members as being mostly well to do and well educated. Sino-Agriculture initially recruited its members from amongst the regular customers of the expensive jewelry shop that the company had been running in Kunming since the mid-1990s. Regular consumers of ecologically certified foods I interviewed were indeed greatly concerned with dietary health and food safety, as I describe in more detail in the next section. Most of these informants could be described as members or aspiring members of the city's emerging middle class. In a recent article, the anthropologist Li Zhang describes membership in Kunming's new "middle class" (*zhongchan jieceng*) not simply as a fixed position based on wealth but rather as a cultivated and performed identity (2008). Key to this identity, she argues, is the ownership of a home in one of the city's newly built-up market communities (*xiaoqu*), along with one's ability to consume in a way considered to be compatible with home ownership in such a community. Car ownership, children's schooling, manners, food, and dress are all important, but Zhang highlights that exactly what kinds of goods and behaviors are considered respectable and suitable to middle-class membership are under constant negotiation, resulting in a great deal of anxiety among Kunming's aspiring middle class.

Ecologically certified foods, and perhaps "organics" in particular, appear to have emerged as a class of goods through which middle-class identities in Kunming could be performed, particularly when the consumption of these foods was combined with other practices of self-cultivation. According to the head teacher of a yoga club, the consumption of "organic" foods was part of a "health-conscious lifestyle" pursued by his often quite wealthy and mostly female students. For a while he even sold Haobaoqing's vegetables from his club. Several of my informants were educated women in their twenties and thirties who bought organic vegetables, had a keen interest in nutrition and dietary health, and studied (or taught) the art of tea drinking.

At Sino-Agriculture, I was able to speak to a few of the mothers who took their children to weekend classes in the Confucian classics. Ms. Shen, for example, had her son take classes at Sino-Agriculture because she felt that it was particularly important for boys to learn to be well mannered and to have the ability to interact with the outside world. Her friend, Ms. Wang, ran a private nursery and was married to a successful restaurateur. She hoped that classes at Sino-Agriculture would help her five-year-old daughter become less naughty. Both Shen and Wang were concerned with the dietary health of themselves and their families and approved strongly of Sino-Agriculture's foods. Wang, who lived in a villa in a gated community to the south of the city center, regularly consulted a private dietician. Shen, who ran a real estate business with her husband, was largely vegetarian—except when the family had guests—and often bought certified "organic" vegetables from Metro supermarket. Sino-Agriculture provided the kinds of foods, environment, and education where people like Shen and Wang could cultivate their family's health and middle-class sensibilities.

The emergence of ecologically certified foods as middle-class goods is arguably linked not only to their alleged health benefits and safety but also with their association with places deemed to be more "advanced" or "modern" than Kunming. This association was, as we have seen, highlighted in in-store advertising. Several people, including ecological activists, food producers, and certifiers, told me that Kunmingers, in contrast to Shanghainese, Beijingers, and "foreigners," lacked "awareness" and "understanding" of ecological foods. That this was taken by some a sign of Kunming's perceived "underdevelopment" (Zhang 2006) was put to me most bluntly by a mid-level manager at a "no public harm" pork company, who complained that Kunming consumers were simply too "backward" (*luohou*) to appreciate their company's products. In consuming such foods, aspiring members of the city's middle class might identify themselves with more "advanced" places. This was perhaps particularly the case with "organics," a foreign-sounding term with which few people were familiar.

The association between ecologically certified foods and elite status was also made by many non-middle-class Kunmingers. Several non-elite informants described ecologically certified foods as "aristocrats' foods" (*guizu shipin*), beyond the means of "ordinary people" (*pingmin baixing*). Even non-middle-class informants who were positively inclined to these foods claimed they could not afford to buy them very often, particularly following the rapid rises in food prices in 2007 and 2008. In so far as these foods were consumed for their alleged safety and health benefits, their high prices can be seen as a dimension of China's increasingly unequal access to health, health products, and safe foods (Chen 2001, 2008). Moreover, in addition to describing ecologically certified foods as expensive, some of my less-well-off informants, such as Master Chen, a roadside tailor from Sichuan province, argued that "the rich" cared more about their health than ordinary people. Several others of comparable economic means suggested that a concern for personal health, reflected in a preference for lightly flavored (*qingdan*) foods and for moderation in the consumption of meat and alcohol, was a sign that a person had "quality" (*suzhi*) and education and was "advanced" (*xianjin*).

Ecologically certified foods were thus implicated in the growing social differentiation in urban China. In Kunming, the consumption of these foods, along with the health consciousness and civility that it signified, had become part of wider strategies people could deploy to present themselves as "middle class."

But social differentiation, while important, is only one dimension of ecological food consumption in Kunming. In other ways, this consumption resonated with a broader popular food culture and shared experiences of rapid urban development. In the following section I consider more closely how consumers of "organics" portrayed their own interest in these foods, and go on to juxtapose these portrayals to broader stories of change to Kunming's food supply and food culture.

Ecological Food Consumption, the Food Supply, and Urban Development

As I have already suggested, food safety and health were the concerns most frequently highlighted by interviewees when talking about their interests in "organic" foods. Ms. Zhao, a teashop owner in her forties who had been ordering a weekly vegetable box from Haobaoqing for about a year when I interviewed her in June 2009, expressed dismay at the increase over the last thirty years in the use of pesticides and other agrichemicals. She was convinced that people's health in her native Kunming had deteriorated since the 1990s, and that changes in food production were largely to blame:

Klein: Were you aware [of the increase in agrichemicals] already [in the 1990s]?

Zhao: I was, but there was nothing to be done about it. And it is all these people becoming ill. There is so much illness now, things like cancers, all kinds of terrible diseases, cancers at every turn. Really it is the food now that is the main cause, otherwise there would not be so much illness.

Some described their consumption of "organic" foods as a part of personal health strategies. Mr. Zhang, a man in his thirties who ran a small travel bureau together with his wife and brother, was convinced that his frequent spells of dizziness, lapses of memory, and exhaustion were caused by what he called the "pollution" (*wuran*) in the foods he ate. In 2008 he arranged a tour for a group of Taiwanese visitors associated with Sino-Agriculture, and learned about the company through them. He became a member, regularly attended Sino-Agriculture's classes, and occasionally bought some of their foods, although when I first met him in 2008 he could not afford to do so regularly.

Similarly, during her time at university and shortly thereafter Ms. Pu had been fond of Western-style fast foods, hot spices, barbecues, hotpots, and meat. Increasingly, however, she had put on weight and suffered from spots and constipation. Pu, in her late twenties at the time of the interview in 2008, worked for an environmental NGO, and came to learn about organic farming there. She came to believe that many of the foods she was eating were unhealthy and had been the cause of her symptoms. She started to eat "organic" vegetables as often as she could, but also changed her diet to include more vegetables and less meat, and to avoid barbecues, fast foods, and hotpots (although she was too fond of chillies to stop eating spicy foods).

These cases were not at all different from the practices, reported in Chinese communities around the world (e.g., Anderson and Anderson 1975; Farquhar 2002: 47–77), of changing one's diet in response to illness. Indeed, both Zhang and Pu reported that on changing their diets they had also begun to prepare dietary therapies with traditional Chinese medicines. A few people I interviewed in fact spoke about "organic" foods as "medicines," and as I mentioned earlier ecologically certified foods were sometimes referred to as "health foods." Ms. Wu, a recently retired accountant in her fifties, first visited Haobaoqing in 2008 and immediately began to order regular deliveries. She claimed that her husband, who suffered from back pain and sleeping problems, felt much better once they started eating "organic" vegetables. Wu argued that buying these vegetables is like "buying health" and that Haobaoqing "should sell them not as food, but as medicine!"

Along with food safety and health, consumers of "organics" often stressed "taste" as a key factor in their choice of foods. Ms. Zhao argued that the vegetables from Haobaoqing taste "so very sweet, just the way they used to when we were little." Ms. Wu claimed that these days, "People don't behave like human beings [literally, don't have the 'flavor of human feelings'], vegetables don't taste like vegetables, meat doesn't taste like meat" (*ren mei you renqingwei, cai mei you caiwei, rou mei you rouwei*), suggesting that the loss of taste in foodstuffs paralleled a wider decline of social relations in the city, an issue I return to below. Wu said that when she first tried Haobaoqing's products she felt that it was the first time in years that she had enjoyed the true taste of vegetables. And once she started ordering a regular box from the farm, her husband, who used to eat mostly meat, began to eat vegetables with great enthusiasm. (Her husband, who was present at the conversation but said little, smiled and nodded in agreement at these claims.)

Few Kunmingers I spoke with were as enthusiastic about "organic" vegetables as Wu, Zhao, Zhang, and Pu. Moreover, Pu was university-educated and financially independent although not a homeowner, while Wu and Zhao owned homes and private cars. For Zhang, who like Pu came from a farming family, his interest in Sino-Agriculture was arguably linked to middle-class aspirations. As their business improved in 2009, he frequently ate at the restaurant together with his wife and son and the couple was planning to send their son to Sino-Agriculture's Confucian classics classes. Nevertheless, the stories that Wu, Zhao, Zhang, and Pu told me of dietary change, including their descriptions of growing concerns with food safety, dietary health, and a loss of taste, resonated closely with those related to me by Kunming people of a variety of social backgrounds and economic means, including those who had little interest in "organics" or other ecologically certified foods. In the remainder of this section I will expand on some of the recurring themes in stories of changes to the food supply and dietary practices told to me in Kunming.

It should be stressed that these stories were not always nostalgic. Older informants contrasted the abundance of today with the severe hardships and periods of hunger they had experienced when growing up. Even those in their thirties recalled ration tickets, queues, and shortages. Nevertheless, tales of progress were tainted by recurring expressions of culinary rupture and loss, often in the same interview. Similar to the narratives recorded by anthropologists in other contexts, these stories displayed a profound ambivalence about culinary modernization (Holtzman 2009; Counihan 2004). Foods were described as increasingly tasteless, and people blamed this on new production methods. Many were scathing of the intensively produced "feed pigs" (*siliao zhu*), "feed chickens" (*siliao ji*), and "feed eggs" (*siliao dan*), which now dominated the markets. One young woman claimed that pork from pigs raised on industrial feed and growth hormones (*jisu*) has a strong smell (*xingwei*) and a bad taste and poor mouthfeel (*kougan*), and that "feed chickens" "really have no taste whatsoever." Similarly, people claimed that vegetables grown with chemical fertilizers and pesticides (*nongyao huafei*) were "pretty" (*piaoliang*) but lacked taste and wouldn't become properly soft when cooked (*zhubupa*). This last complaint was something I heard from scores of people. It reflected the importance of green vegetables in Kunming cuisine and a popular method of cooking leafy greens, which involved simply boiling them in water without flavorings and serving them in the water and with a side dip of spices. This method was meant to bring out the sweetness (*tianwei*) of the vegetable itself and to achieve a mouth-melting texture, known in the local dialect as *pa*.

Many Kunmingers lamented the fact that foods sold in the markets were being grown further and further away from the city itself. The short food chains of the 1960s and '70s were to a great extent a result of the policies of local self-sufficiency (Skinner 1981). But the "free markets" that appeared all over the city from the late 1970s were for a long time dominated by farmers from nearby, selling their own surplus. However, as Ms. Zhao recalled: "There used to be so many farmers' markets in Kunming. It was all farmers from the peri-urban areas carrying vegetables into the city. Now there are very few farmers carrying vegetables to sell, it is all transported into the city and sold on by vegetable vendors. Really it was very good when we were young and the farmers carried their vegetables into town." Indeed, Kunmingers were often critical of the increasing number of foods that were now available out of season, be they imports from other regions or more locally grown "greenhouse vegetables" (*dapengcai*). Ms. Xiao, in her early thirties, was indignant that eateries now served the local snack, *doumenfan* (rice stewed with broad beans and ham) throughout the year, even though the dish was according to her really only tasty around the Chinese New Year, the proper season for local broad beans. Seasonality was not only an issue of taste, however, at least for elderly Kunmingers of my acquaintance. One retired man, who was visiting Haobaoqing on a day trip with his family, told me:

> Man: There are lots of non-seasonal (*fan jijie*) vegetables available now, from Guangdong or Southern Yunnan. Communications are good now.
>
> Klein: How do they taste?
>
> Man: There is nothing wrong with the taste of these vegetables. Foods used to be more monotonous (*dandiao*). At that time fresh fruit from Xishuang Banna [in Southern Yunnan] was highly prized. But a person should not eat too much of these non-seasonal vegetables. A person from a particular place should eat the foods of that place, should live in harmony with the natural environment (*ziran huanjing*).

In a similar vein, Mr. Jia, a retired mechanic who was born in Dali in northwest Yunnan in 1939 and moved to Kunming at the age of three, argued that it used to be that every season had its proper vegetables, but now everything was muddled (*luantao le*). Jia found nonseasonal vegetables to be tasteless. Moreover, seasonal vegetables helped people to adapt to the changing weather conditions. He gave the example of a common variety of Chinese cabbage, known locally as *da kucai,* which is eaten by Kunmingers in winter. "In the wintertime, it is rather cold. People then are externally cold and internally hot (*wai leng nei re*), and just at that time *da kucai* arrive on the market, and help cool the body (*qingre*)." He later added, "It is as if it were planned by God (*Shangdi anpai de*)."

Such ideas about seasons, locality, and health expressed by Jia and others were not unique to Kunmingers. In his recent book on Shanghai food culture, the historian Mark Swislocki (2009) highlights the significance in late imperial and Republican times of the notion that each locality has its own distinctive *fengtu* ("wind and soil"). According to Swislocki, *fengtu* was embedded in a wider correlative cosmology, and implied that just as certain crops are well suited to the environmental conditions of a particular locale, so too are cooking methods and flavorings adapted to those conditions and so too is the health of the people of that locale dependent on its food products and cooking styles. In contemporary Kunming there was a widespread discomfort with what was experienced as a blurring of the relationship between food and seasons, and some Kunmingers explicitly articulated theories of correlation between food, people, and place, according to which eating seasonally was an aspect of a person's integration in his or her native place, and also vital to maintaining bodily balance and health.

In addition to issues of taste, texture, and seasonality, meats and vegetables sold in the markets were a constant source of anxiety, in particular concerning their effects on eaters' health. Many informants expressed fears about the possible adverse effects of food additives (*tianjiaji*) in general and growth hormones (*jisu*) in "feed chickens" and "feed pigs" in particular. Most prevalent was a fear of being poisoned by residues of chemical pesticides used on vegetables, a fear that undoubtedly was reinforced by frequent media reports of Chinese vegetables being found by domestic or foreign authorities to contain illegal levels of residues.[5] Several interviewees spoke about foods becoming increasingly "polluted" (*wuran*), and used this term to cover not only air, water, and soil pollution, but also all additives used in food production. In Mary Douglas's (1966) terms, for Kunmingers these were all pollution in the sense of being "matter out of place." Such pollution and the use of plastic greenhouses were frequently described as "unnatural" (*bu ziran*). The urban food supply was experienced as being increasingly disconnected from "natural" processes and seasonal cycles.

Kunmingers' articulations of culinary "disconnection" from the past and from natural cycles need to be seen in the context of the massive social and physical transformation the city has gone through since the economy took off in the mid-1990s. The anthropologist Li Zhang notes the city's increasing social polarization, and writes about the profound rupture experienced by Kunmingers, as "90 percent of the old neighborhoods were destroyed and tens of thousands of residents were forced out of the city" during a three-year period alone in the late 1990s (2006: 466).

Recent rural migrants to the city I interviewed complained about the "tastelessness" of Kunming foodstuffs, and such complaints should probably be understood both as idioms through which migrants' expressed their experiences of homesickness and hardship, and as reflections of changes to Kunming's food supply. Similarly, among long-standing residents, articulations of culinary loss could be understood as metaphors for experiences of rapid urban change, but they were also a part of it. For example, for many Kunmingers one of the outstanding features of the city's food culture was the variety of its snack foods, and it was often argued that more and more of these local snack foods were being lost. Ms. Yang, a recently retired librarian who was herself originally from Nanjing, complained that it was now difficult to find real Yunnan snacks like "simmered rice-cake pieces" (*shao erkuai*) in Kunming, and that the food courts in the new shopping malls carried mostly snacks from outside the province. "Everywhere all you get is Yangzhou fried rice!" she exclaimed. Yang put this change down to the growing number of outsiders (*waishengren*) in the city, claiming: "One hardly meets any real Kunmingers anymore."

The role of snack foods in Kunming's culinary identity has not only to do with the foods themselves, but also with the ways in which they have featured in the urban landscape. Kunmingers complained bitterly that the small snack shops, cafes, and food hawkers that lined the streets of the city in the 1980s and early '90s had all but disappeared with the broadening of the avenues and increasing urban regulations. Ms. Xiao, who was mentioned earlier in this section, recalled walking to school as a young girl along Jinbi Road in downtown Kunming, with its French-style buildings, parasol trees (*wutongshu*), and above all the fragrance of newly roasted Yunnanese coffee (*xiaoli kafei*) emanating from the cafés where her father and other men enjoyed their morning snacks. She lamented that these had all now disappeared with the rebuilding of the city. She added that Kunming's snack foods were no longer any good, and claimed that one had to go to the provincial towns (*dizhou*) to get snacks that tasted like they used to.

In addition to the now disappearing local-style snack-food shops and local farmers' markets, the urban environment had itself once been a source of various foods. Some people had grown their own vegetables inside the city. Ms. Su, a retired glass-factory worker, described how she and her neighbors had grown cabbages and other vegetables in the 1970s on unused government land, before a road was built there. Middle-aged and elderly men and women described picking medicinal herbs inside the city into the 1980s. The parks in the hills just outside the city had once been full of mushrooms and wild vegetables, I was told. The city's waters, too, had been a source of abundance. A taxi driver in his forties recalled childhood joys of fishing in the Panlong River, which runs through the city. Other informants described collecting "seaweed flowers" (*haicai hua*) from Cuihu, the large lake in the heart of the city. These were used to make pickles (*haicai zha*). Even after the disastrous land-reclamation campaign of the early 1970s (Shapiro 2001), fish from nearby Lake Dian remained abundant and popular into the early 1990, but now no one dared eat the fish. The city itself had once provided a sense of security. Its lakes and rivers, parks, and yet-to-be-built-up areas could be used to supplement the monotonous and often inadequate diets of the socialist redistributive economy. Increasingly, though, the city was a threat, a site of distance from the "natural" cycles into which it had once been integrated. Dietary change reflected and was implicated in profound changes in Kunmingers' "senses of place" (Feld and Basso 1996).

Coping with the Changing Food Supply

Seen against the backdrop of these stories of rapid urban change and the industrialization of the food supply, the consumption of "organics" and other ecologically certified food can be understood not only as practices of social differentiation and lifestyle consumption, but also as a pragmatic tactic to access foods that were deemed to be safe, healthful, and tasty. Moreover, by arriving at the "correct" time of the year and tasting "the way they should," such foods might help to "reconnect" people with their surroundings and their pasts, healing ruptures caused by rapid urban development and migration (see also Sutton 2001).

Still, most Kunmingers I met rarely purchased ecologically certified foods, and fewer still bought "organics." Informants cited several reasons for this. Cost was an important factor for many, as suggested earlier, as was a lack of familiarity, especially with "organics." Indeed, the well-known "no public harm" fresh pork from Gao Shang Gao and, especially, Shen Nong commanded much lower premiums than ecologically certified vegetables, and a number of informants with modest incomes reported purchasing these products at least occasionally.[6] There was also a widespread distrust in labels and certificates, which were thought to be easily faked, and several people I spoke with were convinced that enterprises were simply packaging conventionally produced foods and selling them as "ecological." Establishing trust was indeed regarded as a core issue for food enterprises, and Haobaoqing and some other ecological producers encouraged people to visit the farms to see for themselves how the food was grown.[7] Furthermore, many of my interviewees did not buy ecologically certified vegetables because these did not fit into their shopping practices or meet their aesthetic standards. Such vegetables, as we have seen, were typically sold in supermarkets. While practically all of the households I studied, including native working-class and rural migrant households, did shop at supermarkets, most did so no more than a couple of times a month, and only a few bought vegetables there. Most purchased vegetables several times a week or even daily, and insisted on "freshness" (*xinxian*). Interviewees often considered all supermarket vegetables, including ecologically certified ones, to be not fresh, and avoided them on these grounds.

However, purchasing ecologically certified foods was only one of many tactics my Kunming informants deployed, be it within or outside the market sphere, to acquire foods they regarded as relatively safe, healthful, tasty, affordable, and embedded in local seasonal cycles. These tactics included specific shopping practices at urban food markets, visits to rural farmers' markets, purchasing directly from farmers, collecting wild foods, and utilizing interpersonal networks.

I begin with a discussion of food markets and people's shopping practices. Most food shopping was done at outdoor or covered "vegetable markets" (*cai shichang*), which in fact sold a wide range of fresh, dried, and prepared foods, and at supermarkets (*chaoshi*). The "standard" (*zhenggui*) covered vegetable markets were dominated by specialized retailers selling from hired stalls. Informal vendors, some of them farmers selling their own vegetables or fruit, operated on the peripheries of the covered markets, often selling at cheaper prices than inside the market. These informal vendors also congregated in alleys and residential neighborhoods, and in the several large informal markets that had emerged in the city, often in low-income areas. The informal stands and markets were crucial resources for the urban poor, and the low-income households in my study did much of their shopping there. By contrast, some of my better-off informants avoided them, claiming that they were unhygienic and that mostly laid-off workers, poor pensioners, and migrant workers shopped there.

In the vegetable markets, many shoppers would seek out vegetables that looked slightly tattered and chewed up by insects, the logic being that if insects could eat them, then they could not contain too many chemicals. Ms. Tao was a migrant worker from Sichuan who in 2008 did her daily shopping at an informal outdoor market on Lingguang Street near central Kunming. She often bought marrows and other gourds (*gua*) in the summertime because, she told me, coming from a farm she knew that they did not require large amounts of pesticides. Instead, she bought leafy vegetables in the wintertime, when there were fewer pests and therefore less need to use pesticides. Similarly, some shoppers avoided certain vegetables, such as celery, which they thought were grown with particularly large amounts of pesticides, or unusually large vegetables, which might contain growth hormones. Several people also reported soaking their vegetables at home for half an hour or longer in an attempt to wash away any chemical residues.

Some shoppers regularly asked the origins of vegetables before buying them, and some cultivated relations of trust with vendors who sold products from particular localities. Some would only buy from farmers selling their own goods. Localities perceived to be mountainous and poor were often regarded as having the least pollution and lowest use of agrichemicals and therefore the "purest" foods, and Kunmingers often specifically sought out foodstuffs from these areas. One couple, Mr. Xu and Ms. Jiang, had recently retired from the city's Environmental Protection Bureau. They used their detailed knowledge of the water sources around Kunming to only purchase vegetables from areas with the least-polluted water. Some hawkers were aware of these kinds of geographies, such as the woman in an informal market outside the now closed-down Kunming Textile Mill who loudly announced the origins of her cabbages and peppers to passers-by, "They are from Tuanjie county, no pesticides!"[8] Auntie Liu, a retired textile worker who bought her vegetables from farmers selling outside her former work unit, explained:

> There are two types of vegetable hawkers [at the Kunming Textile Mill market], middlemen (*erdaoshang*) and those who sell what they have grown themselves. [The latter] arrive very early to sell and leave after an hour or two. They are from Tuanjie County, and there are also those farmers from around Baisha He, all local farmers who grow their own. They are a bit more expensive but not much, just an extra five *mao* per kilo or so. The middlemen are a bit cheaper, but they sell greenhouse vegetables [*dapeng cai*] and those are not good to eat.

When it came to meat, some informants reported reducing their consumption of pork, opting instead for beef or lamb, which they regarded as being less likely to be raised with the use of feed and growth hormones. Indeed, some argued that Hui Muslim butchers sold more hygienic meat than Han (cf. Blum 2001: 138), and some Hui butchers were now claiming that their chicken, beef, and lamb were both *qingzhen* (a Chinese Islamic term that encompassed "halal") and "ecological" (*shengtai*).[9]

Still others sourced foods directly from the countryside. Picking wild mushrooms and wild vegetables was a popular pastime, one that tied people into local seasonal cycles. Indeed, there was something of a mushroom frenzy in Kunming during the wet summer months. Fishing was also popular, and for a fee one could fish at certain ponds and reservoirs outside the city. Perhaps even more popular was "farmhouse fun" (*nongjiale*). Since the late 1990s farmers throughout the Kunming area had been setting up facilities such as dining spaces, guest rooms, fishing ponds, mahjong tables, and karaoke machines in the hope of attracting tourists from the city. Many also had orchards or vegetable gardens where visitors could pick their own foods. Often advertised as sites of "ecotourism" (*shengtai lüyou*), Kunmingers described the food at these places as simple and coarse, but more flavorsome and "natural" than foods in the city.

Some people also purchased meat, poultry, eggs, or vegetables directly from farmers. Together with friends, Xu and Jiang had on several occasions commissioned a farmer to raise a pig for them without using industrial feed or additives, which they then slaughtered themselves and divided up amongst friends and family. Several of my acquaintances shopped at periodic rural markets. One couple, Mr. Yang and Ms. Li, began shopping regularly at rural markets when they retired in the late 1990s. They had an intricate knowledge of the markets in the Kunming area. In the summer of 2009 my research assistant, Ms. Miao, and I went on a shopping trip with them and their son-in-law, Mr. Hu, who was driving. We drove for two hours to Dong Cun, a small market town to the north of the city. In that area, Yang and Li told us, the food was more "ecological" (*shengtai*) than elsewhere, because there was little industrial pollution and because it was a mountainous area with lots of minority peoples, where farmers used little fertilizer or pesticides because they basically grew food for their own consumption and only sold what they themselves could not eat. As we were leaving Kunming, Yang and Li claimed that they visited rural markets mostly for fun and just bought a bit of food while they were at it. On the return journey, having filled the car with several kilos of pork, four chickens, eggs, wild mushrooms, potatoes, aubergines, spring onions, Chinese chives, green beans, chillies, watermelons, pears, and twenty liters of distilled maize liquor, they conceded that they in fact hardly ever bought food in the city.

Picking wild foods, visiting farmhouses and buying from farms and rural markets were combined by some during weekend outings with family or friends, and were obviously easier for better-off households with their own cars. Nevertheless, some rural villages and many markets were accessible by public transport, and at weekends hoards of Kunmingers went by bus, train, or bicycle to visit the massive periodic farmers' markets held in peri-urban areas, most famously at Ma Gai (or "Ma Jie" in standard Mandarin).

Foods collected or purchased in rural areas were sometimes distributed to family and friends, as suggested above. Foods were also acquired outside the market through networks that people maintained with relatives and friends living in the countryside. This was not least true for recent migrants in the city. Tao's relatives, for instance, always brought homemade preserved pork (*yanrou*) and pressed tofu (*doufugan*) from their Sichuan village when visiting Tao and her family in Kunming. Some registered urban residents maintained similar networks. My research assistant lived with her parents, her elder sister and the latter's husband, Mr. Ao. Ao hailed from a peri-urban Kunming village and regularly received vegetables grown by his mother. These vegetables were considered much tastier by the family than those bought in the market, and their faith in the relationship with the grower meant that they could eat her cucumbers raw—something they would never do with vegetables from the market. Xu and Jiang, whom I interviewed in 2008, received all of their rice from relatives in Xu's home village in southern Yunnan, a village he had left some fifty years earlier.

None of the various strategies described here were mutually exclusive, of course, and for example an enthusiastic consumer of "organic" vegetables like Mr. Zhang also maintained close ties with his relatives in his home village in northwest Yunnan, from whom he received foods like fruit, meat, and buckwheat. Zhang argued these foods were less polluted than foods sold in Kunming markets, and referred to both foods from back home and organics as "environmental protection foods" (*huanbao shipin*).

Not only was the consumption of ecologically certified foods perfectly compatible with other strategies, arguably the various food acquisition practices were also to some extent informed by the emerging discourses on, and markets in, ecologically certified foods, not to mention wider discourses on the environment, as suggested by Mr. Zhang's talk of "environmental protection foods." Indeed, terms like "green food," "no public harm," and "ecological" foods had become a part of everyday speech in Kunming, and were often used indiscriminately to describe foods that were thought to have been produced without agrichemicals. In the markets in 2008 and 2009 (though not in 2006) I heard hawkers claim that their foods were "green foods, no chemical fertilizer or pesticides," while restaurant menus used the term "ecological cucumbers" (*shengtai huanggua*) to indicate raw cucumbers served with a dipping sauce. A retired factory worker I spoke to at a crowded bus station on the way to the market at Ma Gai told me when I asked why so many people wanted to go there: "To buy farmers' products, products that farmers themselves bring to market." "Why do they want to buy farmers' own products?" I asked. "Because they are 'no public harm,'" he replied. "What does that mean?" "Green products! Green foods!" he exclaimed.

Conclusion

Ecological foods, including ecologically certified foods and noncertified "green" or "ecological" foods, carried several, often overlapping social meanings in Kunming. In the supermarkets, these foods were sold as "hygienic," "natural," "healthy," and "safe," yet expensive, alternatives to conventional foods. To activists, activist-entrepreneurs, and to some of their consumer members, the consumption of such foods was also seen as a means to achieving wider social agendas, such as protecting the nonhuman environment, increasing compassion for all living things, or improving the health and livelihoods of China's farmers. As "globalized," "modern" commodities some of these foods, and the practices of moral and bodily self-cultivation with which they were sometimes linked, were bound up with aspirations to cosmopolitanism and performances of middle-class identities.

Seen against the backdrop of a widespread distrust of the rapidly industrializing food supply, however, the purchase of ecological foods could be seen as one of many practical tactics Kunmingers of all social "classes" deployed in order to access foods they perceived to be healthy, safe, and tasty. Further, while Kunming consumers of certified and uncertified "ecological" foods I spoke to rarely claimed to be motivated by a concern with producers' welfare or by a desire to "protect nature," there were nonetheless important critical dimensions to this consumption, which should not be overlooked. The histories people told of dietary change were often critical of the rise of intensive and chemically dependent methods of food production, the lengthening of food chains, and what was seen as the loss of local food culture and seasonality. These often nostalgic narratives tied into what Li Zhang (2006: 469–472) describes as "alternative views" of Kunming's recent, state-led urban transformation, views which, Zhang explains, were expressed both in personal memories of a loss of the city's once bustling street life, as well as in the popular publications and exhibitions centering around images of "old Kunming." Similarly, the shopping practices described above can be seen not only as practical responses to changes in the officially promoted mechanisms of urban food supply and distribution, but also as nostalgic attempts to "reconnect" with memories of lost times and places, and as expressions of ambivalence or critique toward ongoing urban modernization projects.

Indeed, Li Zhang discusses the attempts since the late 1990s by officials to promote "standard" covered markets, while cracking down on mobile hawkers and spontaneous markets, as these "run against the official effort to establish a regulated and formalized spatial order" (2006: 473). These crackdowns were carried out enthusiastically between 2006 and 2009. In the run up to the 2008 Beijing Olympics, most of the hawkers that convened around the covered markets in central Kunming were chased off. In the summer of 2009 the authorities abruptly closed down not only the small informal Lingguang Street market but even the huge periodic market at Ma Gai. The latter closure, which received a great deal of attention in the local press, was publically justified on the grounds that the market posed a threat to public order, sanitation, food safety, and the flow of road traffic, although shoppers and vendors I spoke to on Ma Gai's final market day expressed skepticism toward the official claims, some citing the new building projects that were planned for the site. The fate of the market at the Kunming Textile Mill was thought by local residents to be in the hands of the development company that now controlled that land.[10]

But in spite of these attempts to "cleanse" urban space in the name of modernization (Herzfeld 2006), farmers continued to seek out spaces in the city where they could sell their goods, and urban residents sought out rural markets elsewhere, or developed other tactics, within the constraints of their specific economic abilities, to acquire tasty, healthful, "green" foods. In conclusion, while the consumption of ecologically certified foods highlights divisions and inequalities in Chinese cities, it also resonates with and informs broader food cultures and widely shared experiences of, and critical responses to, rapid changes to the urban food supply and to other aspects of urban "development."

Notes

1. The indigenous and state-led origins of Chinese ecological agriculture and certification in the 1980s and 90s should not be overlooked, and the bulk of ecologically certified foods consumed in China are also produced there (Sanders 2000; Milbrodt 2004). Nevertheless, the recent development of ecological food production and domestic consumption needs also to be understood within contexts of globalization. Transnational supermarket chains play a leading role in the retail of ecologically certified foods in Chinese cities (Milbrodt 2004; Chen 2006). Furthermore, international debates articulating food with environmental and social issues have had a certain impact in China, including through networks linking Chinese environmental NGOs with international activists and other bodies outside the country (Klein 2009; see also Yang 2005). Significantly, moreover, China is now one of the world's leading exporters of "organic" foods (Paull 2007). The Chinese state promotes the export of ecologically certified foods in the name of "sustainable rural development"; in order to meet food safety requirements imposed by importing countries and international trade regimes; and in the hope that these foods will find their way onto the Chinese market and have a positive effect on domestic food safety standards (Thiers 2005; Sanders 2006; Paull 2007).

2. Research included numerous conversations and observations in food markets and shops in and around Kunming, in restaurants and at ecological farms, and interviews at the offices of environmental NGOs, government agencies, and businesses. Much of the material used in this piece comes from interviews on food shopping, cooking, and eating conducted in 2008 and 2009 with members of twenty-five Kunming households. Usually, the main shopper of the household was interviewed, and in many cases more than one person from the household took part. Interviews took place in people's homes, at workplaces, cafes or restaurants, and lasted between fifty minutes and two hours. All but two of the interviews were recorded and transcribed. Follow-up meetings were arranged wherever possible, and in some cases interviewees were met with several times.

   Households were met through contacts and snowballing. No attempt was made to interview a statistically representative sample of the Kunming population. Roughly half of the interviewees might be described as "middle class," and worked at, or had retired from or were married to a person who worked at, jobs such as journalists, university professors, entrepreneurs, and government bureaucrats. Many of these people resided in some of the city's new upmarket residential neighborhoods (see Zhang 2008). The other interviewees included migrant workers, poor pensioners, laid-off workers, and housewives married to manual workers. Household size and composition ranged from single-person households to one household where four generations lived together under one roof. Eight of the households included frequent consumers of "organics" or other ecologically certified foods, while many others occasionally purchased such products.

Fieldwork in Kunming was funded by small research grants from the British Academy (SG-43053 and SG-50545), with additional and also greatly appreciated support from the Universities' China Committee in London (UCCL) and from the SOAS Internal Research Grants scheme. The work of my research assistant, Miao Yun, in helping to locate, contact, and interview informants, gather miscellaneous information, and transcribe interviews has been invaluable. The present chapter is indebted by insightful support from Professor Kwang Ok Kim and Professor Okpyo Moon. I am also grateful to Dr. Yuson Jung and Professor Melissa Caldwell for their helpful comments.

3. Local producers of "organic" foods told me that premiums were much higher in Beijing and Shanghai and that distinctions between the different ecological categories were more rigidly maintained there than in Kunming, and this was also suggested by the data collected in Beijing by my research assistant (see note 4). During a visit to Kunming in 2012, part of a separate research project, I observed that in two major supermarkets the products sold in their sections for "top-quality vegetables" (*jingpin shucai*) were no longer labeled "organic," "green," or "no public harm" at all.

4. In a Beijing supermarket in February 2009 my research assistant, Miao Yun, recorded a price of RMB 18.50/kilo of "organic" carrots, compared to RMB 1.80/kilo for "conventional" carrots in the same shop, while "organic" tomatoes cost RMB 19.80/kilo and "conventional" ones RMB 5.50/kilo. Other categories of ecologically certified foods sold there were cheaper, but still generally two to three times the price of "conventional" equivalents.

5. One case that was mentioned by several acquaintances in Kunming in the summer of 2009 had occurred in May of that year in Luoping County in Qujing City, Yunnan. Sixty-five people, including over ten schoolchildren, had been hospitalized after eating cabbage with illegal levels of pesticide residues (Jiang 2009). Interestingly, the melamine milk scandal, which erupted just as I was leaving Kunming in the summer of 2008, did not figure as much in my informants' conversations the following summer as I had expected it to. Nineteen of the twenty-five household studies were conducted in the summer of 2008, prior to the scandal, and only one of the six households studied in 2009 had a child. It is not unlikely that melamine-tainted milk would have figured more prominently had the bulk of my household studies been carried out in 2009.

6. In 2012 some supermarkets were advertising "organic pork" (*youji zhurou*).

7. Many of those who did regularly consume organic foods felt strong ties to particular producers, and in some cases it was clear that such ties were more significant than a belief in some generic notion of "organics." Ms. Wu, for example, became strongly committed to Haobaoqing and after she had been a member for half a year she started helping them out with their accounting. By the summer of 2009, Mr. Zhang had been on several trips to Sino-Agriculture's farm to help out with the harvest. Visiting producers could be detrimental to trust, however. Following a recent visit to a self-styled "ecological farm," the retired librarian Ms. Song (interviewed in 2008 together with her friend and colleague,

Ms. Yang) was very unhappy about the plastic greenhouses that were used there, exclaiming that "these were not entirely ecological ... [the crops] should be planted in nature and grow naturally." Ms. Zhao was a frequent visitor at Haobaoqing, and sometimes had lunch there with her friend Ms. Wu. While she was very positive about the vegetables, she thought that their chicken, while good, did not taste like it used to when she was a child. Having seen that they did not grow grain at the farm, she concluded that an important reason for this was that there was no chaff for the chickens to eat.

8. Tuanjie County is populated largely by ethnic Yi and Bai peoples, and the hawker was wearing the kind of headscarf and shoes often worn by local Yi women. Ethnicity may have played a part in people's shopping geographies, as ethnic minority groups often signified simplicity and backwardness to urban Kunmingers (Blum 2001).

9. One Kunming-based Islamic ecological food company, Huaxi, sold variously certified Green Food, hazard-free and organic meats and eggs at shops all over Kunming. Their products included Ecocert-certified organics eggs, which were sold locally and exported to the European Union. The manager of one Huaxi shop insisted that over half of their customers were non-Muslims, and mostly elderly.

10. In 2012 I learned from local residents that this market had in fact been closed down the previous year.

References

Anderson, E. N., and Marja L. Anderson. 1975. "Folk dietetics in two Chinese communities, and its implications for the study of Chinese medicine." In *Medicine in Chinese Cultures,* edited by Arthur Kleinman et al., 143–175. Washington, DC: US Government Printing Office.

Blum, Susan D. 2001. *Portraits of "Primitives": Ordering Human Kinds in the Chinese Nation.* Lanham: Rowman and Littlefield.

———. 2002. "Ethnic and linguistic diversity in Kunming." In *China Off Center: Mapping the Margins of the Middle Kingdom,* edited by Susan D. Blum and Lionel M. Jensen, 148–166. Honolulu: University of Hawai'i Press.

Chen, Nancy N. 2001. "Health, wealth, and the good life." In *China Urban: Ethnographies of Contemporary Culture,* edited by Nancy N. Chen et al., 165–182. Durham, NC: Duke University Press.

———. 2008. "Consuming medicine and biotechnology in China." In *Privatizing China: Socialism from Afar,* edited by Li Zhang and Aihwa Ong. pp. 123-132. Ithaca and London: Cornell University Press.

Chen, Ursula. 2006. "China, People's Republic of; organic products; South China organic food market brief 2006." USDA Foreign Agricultural Service, *GAIN Report,* CH6608.

Counihan, Carole. 2004. *Around the Tuscan Table: Food, Family, and Gender in Twentieth Century Florence.* London: Routledge.

Douglas, Mary. 1966. *Purity and Danger: An Analysis of the Concepts of Pollution and Taboo.* London: Routledge.

Farquhar, Judith. 2002. *Appetites: Food and Sex in Postsocialist China.* Durham, NC: Duke University Press.

Feld, Steven, and Keith H. Basso, eds. 1996. *Senses of Place.* Santa Fe, NM: School of American Research Press.

Gale, Fred, and Kuo Huang. 2007. "Demand for food quantity and quality in China." Economic Research Service, United States Department of Agriculture, *Economic Research Report* 32. http://www.ers.usda.gov/publications/err32/.

Guthman, Julie. 2004. *Agrarian Dreams: The Paradox of Organic Farming in California.* Berkeley: University of California Press.

Herzfeld, Michael. 2006. "Spatial cleansing: Monumental vacuity and the idea of the West." *Journal of Material Culture* 11(1–2): 127–149.

Holtzman, Jon. 2009. *Uncertain Tastes: Memory, Ambivalence, and the Politics of Eating in Samburu, Northern Kenya.* Berkeley: University of California Press.

Horton, Chris. 2007. "The rise of the Kunming consumer." *Emerging China,* 13 July. www.emerging-china.com/articles/163239.html.

Jiang Qiongbo. 2009. "Luoping 65 ren chi baicai zhongdu (65 people in Luoping poisoned from eating cabbage)." *Chuncheng Wanbao* (Chuncheng Evening News), 10 May, A06.

Klein, Jakob A. 2009. "Creating ethical food consumers? Promoting organic foods in urban Southwest China." *Social Anthropology* 17(1): 74–89.

Laudan, Rachel. 2004. "Slow Food, the French terroir strategy, and culinary modernism." *Food, Culture and Society* 7(2): 133–144.

Milbrodt, Carola. 2004. *Organic Food Industry in China: Current State and Future Prospects.* Unpublished MA thesis, Berlin.

Mintz, Sidney W. 1996. "Color, taste, and purity." In *Tasting Food, Tasting Freedom: Excursions into Eating, Culture, and the Past,* 84–91. Boston: Beacon Press.

Nützenadel, Alexander, and Frank Trentmann, eds. 2008. *Food and Globalization: Consumption, Markets and Politics in the Modern World.* Oxford and New York: Berg.

Paull, John. 2007. "China's organic revolution." *Journal of Organic Systems* 2(1): 1–11. http://www.orgprints.org/10949.

Pilcher, Jeffrey M. 2006. "Taco Bell, Maseca and Slow Food: A postmodern apocalypse for Mexico's peasant cuisine?" In *Fast Food/Slow Food: The Cultural Economy of the Global Food System,* edited by Richad Wilk, 69–81. Lanham, MD: Altamira Press.

Pratt, Jeff. 2007. "Food values: The local and the authentic." *Critique of Anthropology* 27(3): 285–300.

Sanders, Richard. 2000. *Prospects for Sustainable Development in the Chinese Countryside: The Political Economy of Chinese Ecological Agriculture.* Aldershot, Hants: Ashgate.

———. 2006. "A market road to sustainable agriculture? Ecological agriculture, green food and organic agriculture in China." *Development and Change* 37: 201–226.

Shapin, Steven. 2006. "Paradise sold: What are you buying when you buy organic?" *The New Yorker,* 15 May.

Shapiro, Judith. 2001. *Mao's War Against Nature: Politics and the Environment in Revolutionary China.* Cambridge: Cambridge University Press.

Skinner, G. William. 1981. "Vegetable supply and marketing in Chinese cities." In *Vegetable Farming Systems in China,* edited by Donald L. Plucknett and Halsey L. Beemer, Jr., 215–280. London: Frances Pinter; Boulder, CO: Westview Press.

Sutton, David E. 2001. *Remembrance of Repasts: An Anthropology of Food and Memory.* Oxford and New York: Berg.

Swislocki, Mark. 2009. *Culinary Nostalgia: Regional Food Culture and the Urban Experience in Shanghai.* Stanford: Stanford University Press.

Thiers, Paul. 2002. "From grassroots movement to state-coordinated market strategy: The transformation of organic agriculture in China." *Environment and Planning C: Government and Policy* 20: 357–373.

Thiers, Paul. 2005. "Using global organic markets to pay for ecologically based agricultural development in China." *Agriculture and Human Values* 22: 3–15.

Veeck, Ann, and Gregory Veeck. 2000. "Consumer segmentation and changing food purchase patterns in Nanjing, PRC." *World Development* 28(3): 457–471.

Wang, Zhigang, Yanna Mao, and Fred Gale. 2008. "Chinese consumer demand for food safety attributes in milk products." *Food Policy* 33: 27–36.

Watson, James L., ed. 2006 [1997]. *Golden Arches East: McDonald's in East Asia,* 2nd ed. Stanford: Stanford University Press.

Wilk, Richard, ed. 2006. *Fast Food/Slow Food: The Cultural Economy of the Global Food System.* Lanham, MD: Altamira Press.

Yan, Yunxiang. 2000. "Of hamburgers and social space: McDonald's in Beijing." In *The Consumer Revolution in Urban China*, edited by Deborah S. Davis, 201–225. Berkeley: University of California Press.

Yang, Guobin. 2005. "Environmental NGOs and Institutional Dynamics in China." *The China Quarterly* 181: 46–66.

Zhang, Li. 2006. "Contesting spatial modernity in late-socialist China." *Current Anthropology* 47(3): 461–484.

———. 2008. "Private homes, distinct lifestyles: Performing a new middle class." In *Privatizing China: Socialism from Afar,* edited by Li Zhang and Aihwa Ong, 23–40. Ithaca and London: Cornell University Press.

Zhang, X., et al. 2008. "Consumption and corpulence in China: A consumer segmentation study based on the food perspective." *Food Policy* 33: 37–47.

CHAPTER 14

From Food Poisoning to Poisonous Food

The Spectrum of Food-Safety Problems in Contemporary China

Yunxiang Yan

The safety of the foods that we eat every day, once an ordinary issue too mundane to warrant scrutiny from society or the state, has become a focal point in public opinion, scholarly research, professional management, and government regulations throughout the contemporary world. In Europe, although food-safety standards have been raised and the actual number of people who die or are sickened by food poisoning is small, the fear of food-safety problems remains strong and features centrally in the political agendas of governments (Jensen and Sandoe 2002; Pawsey 2000). The rising importance of food-safety concerns is widely attributed to the fundamental changes in food production, circulation, and consumption (Pawsey 2000), the profit-seeking politics in the corporate world of the food industry (Nestle 2010), and the anxieties associated with the growing abundance of food choices in a globalizing market (Rozin 1989).

In a very literal way, the food-safety issue confirms, once again, Ulrich Beck's insightful observation that being scared is a new psychological state among those who live in post-industrialization societies (Beck 1992). In his much-celebrated theory of risk society, Beck argues that at the stage of modern society, hazards mainly resulted from industrialization and thus were relatively calculable, but at the stage of risk society, the potential impact of some incalculable and uninsurable risks—such as climate change—threatens the existence of everyone, rich and poor alike. These risks, ironically, are the reflexive consequences of modernity and thus challenge almost all existing social theories. Because the risk of food safety indeed bears some features of risk society, it is by no means accidental that Beck's theory has been widely adopted since the 1990s to study food-safety problems in different societies (Enticott 2003; Smith 2009; Thiers 2003; Zhang 2007).

Perhaps nowhere else is more impacted by food-safety scares than China, where incidents of food contamination and poisoning have been exposed in succession, the use of chemical fertilizers and pesticides ranks number one in the world, exported foods are often rejected by foreign countries due to chemical contamination (Calvin et al. 2006), and the public consistently considers food safety a top concern in official surveys (Chinese Ministry of Commerce 2004–2008). In the West, organic food, local food, and small-scale farming movements are regarded as solutions to the looming food-safety crisis, but in China the responses have been quite different. As Ann Veeck, Hongyan Yu, and Alvin Burns observe, Chinese consumers often blame small local food producers and the government for the worsening food-safety situation and embrace, rather than reject, the market economy and modern and large-scale enterprises as possible solutions. The relevance of risk society theory, they argue, is discounted in the Chinese case (2008). Why? The following example may offer some helpful insights.

Along with its astonishing economic growth since the 1980s, Chinese dietary patterns have changed rapidly, especially meat and egg consumption. For example, China's meat output reached 78 million tons in 2005, representing 29 percent of the world's total output; in the same year per capita meat consumption was 63 kilograms (Li 2009). To meet the high market demands, Western technologies of battery farming have become the most popular in the livestock sector, resulting in a number of food-safety concerns, including the proper disposal of diseased animals. According to Li, three out of the eight layer farms that his research team studied sold dead chickens to employees who in turn resold them to food dealers or restaurants, and five out of the seven pig farms disposed of dead pigs by selling them to vendors who collected the diseased animals for small street-food stalls. This practice can be traced back to the 1990s and has been repeatedly exposed by the Chinese media and food-safety professionals, yet the problem persists (Li 2009: 235–236).

Although diseased chicken ending up in restaurants or roast-chicken shops is hardly news in recent years, the Chinese public was shocked when the Chinese scientist Jiang Gaoming and his research team in 2007 released the results of a multiyear research project on the poultry industry. They found that most of the 4.7 billion chickens consumed in China per year are raised in battery farms where various forms of animal cruelty are regarded as normal and necessary. To make sure broiler chickens can grow to maturity in less than fifty days and egg layers can produce nearly three hundred eggs per year, farmers add a large quantity of additives, antibiotics, and hormones to the chicken feed and restrain the movement of birds to narrow and crowded cages. These "normal" conditions of battery farming alone have caused so many food-safety threats that even the chicken farmers, who do not want to consume the chickens they raise, told the researchers: "We just sell them to the cities" (Jiang 2007). But this is only part of the food-safety problem; a much darker side involves the dead chickens.

The average rate of unnatural deaths on Chinese chicken farms is 5 percent, which amounts to more than 200 million birds every year. How have these diseased chickens been disposed of? Jiang and a group of investigative reporters found that nearly 80 percent of the diseased chickens ended up in the human food chain in a number of ways. First, farmers regularly sold fresh carcasses, along with obviously sick chickens, to producers of roast chicken who could make bigger profits due to the much lower price for the dead chickens. The next channels were the sausage factories that accepted even carcasses that have started to decay and thus were even cheaper to buy. The factories then processed the meat with colorants, flavor additives, and preservatives. The worst and most problematic way of distributing dead chickens found by Jiang's research team was in the least likely place—the avian hospitals. In one animal hospital, for example, everyday 25–50 kilograms of diseased chicken carcasses were sold for US $0.10 per kilogram to pig farmers who then blended the chicken meat into pig feed. Although the central government imposes strict regulations regarding the disposal of carcasses and compensates farmers with cash to incinerate the diseased chickens on the farm (especially during the outbreak of bird flu), local government agencies are reluctant to implement these regulations as it may affect their own cash flows. Frustrated by the various obstacles created by local government agencies and attracted by the instant profits from the market, most farmers choose to sell the diseased chickens to illegal vendors instead of burning them (Jiang 2007; see also Zhou et al. 2007).

Clearly the supposedly modern yet unnatural conditions on the battery farms produce unsafe or potentially unsafe chicken and eggs, a typical food safety problem that exists to varying degrees in almost all modern societies from Europe to America. Because of its huge population, Chinese demand for chicken meat and eggs is huge, thus increasing the impact of unsafe chicken and eggs. However, the illegal trade of diseased chicken among farmers and vendors constitutes a different kind of food-safety problem in China because it is intentional and calculated, revealing not only the loopholes in market regulation but also the existence of a serious ethical problem. The selling of chicken carcasses by avian hospitals is indicative of the corruption of the professionals who are supposed to be the guardians of food safety. The negative role of local government agencies in regulating the disposal of diseased animals reveals another level in the Chinese food-safety problem, that is, the regulatory failure of the state. The key to better understanding the food-safety challenge in contemporary China is to first identify the characteristics of the food-safety problems in the context of the Chinese political economy.

In the following, I will first review the development of food-safety problems in China from the 1950s to the present, noting that the emergence of poisonous food is indicative of a shift from a food-hygiene problem to a food-safety problem. Next I take a closer look at the four types of food poisoning that continue to cause national food scares. In the final section, I offer a sketch of the food-safety problems, grouping them into food hygiene, unsafe food, and poisonous food. My central argument in this chapter is that food safety is not a singular issue in contemporary Chinese society; rather, it manifests itself as a set of problems in both temporal and social terms. Recognizing and unpacking this complexity is critical to further understanding and solving the food-safety problems in contemporary China.

From Food Hygiene to Food Safety

The notion of food safety (*shiping anquan*) is relatively new in Chinese discourse, emerging in the 1990s in the Chinese media and becoming a household term by the turn of the century. In the early decades of the People's Republic, foods were regarded unsafe to consume only when they were severely contaminated by bacteria or badly spoiled. Yet, pressed by economic shortages, many people risked consuming these foods and thus were often sickened by food poisoning. Outbreaks of food poisoning, which tended to peak in summer and early autumn, were regarded strictly as a health problem or food-hygiene problem, because they mainly resulted from the lack of hygiene in food preparation, the consumption of spoiled foods, microorganisms in foods that were not well sanitized, and other unhealthy habits. Except for health professionals, few people paid attention to the issue unless they became a victim. The official media rarely reported food-poisoning cases unless they were politically significant.[1] This marks a sharp contrast to the late 1990s when public concerns about unsafe foods in everyday life increased steadily, the media were filled with reports of food-safety incidents, and earlier health hazards evolved into clear and present dangers in everyday life.

To have a basic understanding of the evolution of food-safety problems, I conducted a noninclusive survey of the published public-health literature from 1950 to 2002 and classified a total of 356 cases of food poisoning into eight types in accordance with the major causes of each outbreak. The Chinese government promulgated the first food-safety law (provisional) in November 1982, indicating official recognition of the prevalence and seriousness of food-safety problems, and formally enacted a final version of the law in 1995 (still called the Food Hygiene Law). Accordingly, in table 14.1 I divide the five decades into two periods, comparing the conditions before and after the 1982 Provisional Food-Hygiene Law (trial version).

It should be noted that the cases in table 14.1 have little statistical significance as my survey is noninclusive and the public-health journals surveyed were not scientifically selected. Moreover, these cases have been reported and studied primarily by public-health professionals whose primary interest was in the medical and public-health aspects of the unsafe food problem. Cases that have more

Table 14.1. A comparison of food-poisoning cases (that involved one hundred victims or more) during two periods

Type	Major causes of food poisoning	Number of cases in 1950–1982	Number of cases in 1983–2002
A	Meat of diseased animals	26	18
B	Spoiled foods	27	18
C	Pesticides or other chemicals	23	15
D	Problematic canteens	49	55
E	Toxic plants	4	1
F	Improper food preparation	6	
G	Unsafe foods from restaurants or markets	4	87
H	Foods with toxic additives from restaurants or markets		23
		139	217

social meanings might have escaped the attention of these health professionals and might have been neglected by the ideologically charged official media under Maoism. Furthermore, the 1983–2002 literature is limited to larger cases involving at least one hundred people or one death, a threshold standard for registering a case with the Ministry of Health; cases of food poisoning occurring in private homes during the second period therefore generally are not included.

Nevertheless, a survey of this literature on food poisoning still reveals some important information about the various problems related to unsafe foods. First, during the period prior to the provisional food hygiene law, 49 out of 139 cases of food poisoning were caused by public canteen problems (type D in table 14.1), which include poor sanitation, unsafe storage of leftovers, lack of hygiene regulations, improper cooking methods, and the use of spoiled foods (Wang 1975). The concentration of food-poisoning cases in public canteens is related to the fact that in the pre-reform era most urban employees ate at least one meal per week in their work-unit canteens, and rural collectives offered lunch to peasants during busy seasons. Public canteens therefore were a major venue of food consumption, second only to private homes; but as the economic reforms and privatization proceeded after the mid-1990s, public canteens began to lose their importance.

Second, the causes of food poisoning in public canteens, however, are not much different from those occurring in private homes, such as spoiled foods (type B in table 14.1) or poor sanitary conditions. The consumption of diseased animals (type A) causing food poisoning in both public canteens and private homes during this period, such as workers in a Shanxi factory who ate diseased pork in a 1960 case (Zhang 1961), Jiangxi peasants who ate diseased cattle in a 1961 case (Ouyang 1961), and villagers who ate diseased donkey meat in a 1972 case in Henan province (Zhao 1974). This is why most authors in the public-health literature attribute these cases to problems of backwardness, namely, the lack of modern scientific knowledge and regulations, and they identify education and hygiene regulations as the main solutions (see, e.g., Sun 1980; Wang 1975; and Zhou 1958). During the second period, the number of type A and B food-poisoning cases declined, whereas new types of cases emerged and took the lead.

Third, when food poisoning was caused by contaminated or spoiled foods during the first period, chances are that, for economic reasons, the victims knowingly consumed the inferior foods. Until the early 1980s, the market played a minimum role in the food supply; citizens and work-unit canteens all purchased food from state-run stores or rural cooperatives. Under the planned economy, staff members in these stores merely performed their duties at assigned jobs, without any profit-making incentive. The meat of diseased animals and low-quality or spoiled foods were all openly sold at lower prices. At the time, the Chinese term for such substandard goods was *chulipin,* meaning defected goods. Many people were attracted to the defected goods because of their low price, which was a major coping strategy to survive the poor living standards in Maoist China. During the collective period (1956–1983), there were still independent vendors selling homemade food at rural marketplaces; but due to the low mobility these vendors had a fixed circle of customers from the nearby villagers. As a result, when they sold substandard food products, such as meat from diseased animals or spoiled foods, they made no effort to cheat the customers and merely used the lower prices to attract buyers. Thus, in most cases customers and public canteens willingly and knowingly purchased substandard, contaminated, or even spoiled foods to save money.[2] But the situation changed dramatically when the market economy was introduced to China in the 1980s. Health concerns increased among the Chinese due to both the spread of scientific knowledge as the health professionals had hoped and the improvements in living standards since the 1980s. Under the new circumstances, profit-driven food suppliers, regardless if they were state owned or private, no longer sold substandard or problematic foodstuffs as *chulipin*; instead they began to use various ways to disguise the substandard food and to sell it as normal produce on the market.

Fourth, food poisoning caused by pesticides or other harmful chemicals (type C) began to occur in the 1970s; the number of recorded cases increased during the early 1980s and then declined in the 1990s. A close reading of the reports, however, shows that in most cases pesticides had caused the food poisoning because it was mistakenly directly consumed. The most common occurrence was the use of pesticide containers to store food (Lu 1981); in several cases, public canteen staff accidently put pesticides or other chemicals into the foods (Hu 1982). Most cases of the users of pesticides becoming food-poisoning victims occurred in rural China. Interestingly, none of the type C food poisoning cases were attributed to pesticide residuals; this might be due to the fact that growers used only a limited amount of pesticides during the 1960s and 70s and did not apply pesticides repeatedly. When peasants became more familiar with pesticides and their use during the 1983–2002 period, the number of type C food-poisoning cases among farmers declined.

The final yet probably most important clue revealed in table 14.1 is the emergence of two new types of food-poisoning cases, namely, those caused by consuming foods purchased at markets and/or in restaurants (type G and H). These two types of cases actually are both due to the profit-driven market that reemerged in the early 1980s. But they differ from one another because of the clear identification of toxic additives or chemicals in the latter, which has been reported in the literature since the late 1990s. Consumers purchased unsafe foods in the markets without knowing the dangers because these foods had already been processed, packaged, and disguised as normal and healthy foods. For example, children in a Zhejiang kindergarten were sickened after drinking milk powder contaminated by magnesium oxide (Zeng and Xiang 1994), more than 130 customers at a restaurant became sick by eating foods tainted with nitrite (Yi 1994), and primary-school students were poisoned by spoiled soybean milk purchased at the school canteen (Tang 1998). In these cases, the contaminated foods were traced to restaurant owners or producers and retailers of processed food, all of whom were private entrepreneurs, a new group of business people that quickly ascended to prominence and wealth during China's market reforms.

Since the late 1990s, certain toxins, such as nitrite, have frequently been the primary cause of food poisoning because they were regularly used to lower the costs of processed foods. Food poisoning has also been caused by harmful chemicals contained in animal feed. In other words, the new types of food-poisoning cases are due to the intentional addition of toxic chemicals to foods. These developments motivated Chinese health professionals and food experts to think beyond the conventional boundaries of food hygiene. In 2001 nearly five hundred people in Guangdong province were poisoned by eating tainted pork containing clenbuterol that had been used in pig feed to promote lean meat; the case raised new concerns because the use of clenbuterol in pig feed was forbidden by the Chinese government (Wang 2002). By the turn of the century a new Chinese phrase was coined to describe the contaminated foods that caused types G and H food poisoning: *youdu shipin,* which literally means "poisonous food."

The New Challenge of Poisonous Food

The defining feature of the phenomenon of poisonous food is the deliberate contamination of food. During the 1950–1982 period, food poisoning was caused mainly by poor sanitation conditions, sloppy operations in public canteens, poverty-driven consumption of substandard foods, and the accidental mixing of pesticides with foods, none of which were deliberate acts. But when producers intentionally add toxins to foods, processing factories adulterate foods with chemicals, and sellers sell unsafe foods through deception and falsification and the government regulatory agencies turn a blind eye to these illegal practices (as revealed in the case of the dead chickens that I present at the beginning of this chapter), food poisoning is no longer caused by human error. Those responsible for poisonous foods are fully aware of the harmful impact on consumers when they add the toxins to foodstuffs and they do this intentionally, calculating profit motives over people's health. This change transformed the food-hygiene problem into a food-safety problem, a radical shift that is also marked by a completely new stage in government regulation of the food industry and the rise of public fears of a new threat—poisonous food.

The establishment of the State Food and Drug Administration (SFDA) in 2003 reflected both the increase in regulatory efforts to enforce food safety by the Chinese government and the worsening of unsafe-food problems. Under the previous Food Hygiene Law, the Ministry of Health played a major role in regulating circulation and preparation links in the food industry; production and processing were largely left to other agencies to monitor, such as the Ministry of Agriculture, the State Administration for Industry and Commerce (SAIC), and the General Administration of Quality Supervision, Inspection, and Quarantine (GAQSIQ). Directly under the State Council, the role of the newly established SFDA was to coordinate and oversee all other health, food, and drug agencies. It is particularly noteworthy that there are two departments in the SFDA that are dedicated to the urgent work of food regulation, namely, the Food Safety Coordination Department and the Food Safety Supervision Department (Liu 2010; Tam and Yang 2005). A cat-and-mouse game has been played between the regulatory state and the unruly and defiant players in the food industry as more regulations are issued by the government and then more violations and legal loopholes are identified. This battle climaxed in 2009 when a new Food-Safety Law was enacted to replace the outdated 1995 Food-Hygiene Law (Ramzy 2009).

At the same time, concerns about food safety became a regular in feature discussions in media reports and public opinion. Starting from 2004, the Ministry of Commerce has carried out an annual investigation on food-safety conditions and has issued a yearly report. Year after year, the investigation shows that Chinese consumers are highly concerned about food-safety problems. Among urban consumers, the rate of concern increased from 79 percent in 2005 to 96 percent in 2008 and among rural residents it increased from 58 percent in 2006 to 94 percent in 2008. The 2008 report admits, quite diplomatically, that the increase in public concern about food safety may be an indicator of the decline of consumer confidence in the government's ability to regulate food safety (Ministry of Commerce 2008). In 2006 the SFDA admitted that more than 60 percent of surveyed consumers viewed food-safety conditions in China as bad or very bad. In 2007 an online survey conducted the official Xinhua Net revealed that 95 percent of the respondents agreed that there are too many problems with the food-safety situation in China (cited in Mou 2007).

In this new wave of food-safety scares, the most frequently used term is *youdu shipin,* or poisonous food. For Chinese consumers, the first decade of the twenty-first century has been filled with cases of various kinds of poisonous foods. It started in 2001 with poisonous rice in Guangdong province and the scandal of a famous moon-cake maker using spoiled cake filling from the last year. In 2003 public fears rose when people learned that several producers of the famous Jinhua hams in Zhejiang province had soaked the meat in dichlorvos, a strong insecticide used for fumigation, to prevent spoilage and insect infestation during the warm weather. The severity of food-safety problems finally attracted the attention of the top leaders in 2004 when fake milk powder that was widely sold in Anhui province caused the deaths of more than seventy babies due to malnutrition and other illnesses (Zhou 2004). The scandal led Premier Wen Jiabao to order that the SFDA send a team of experts from Beijing to investigate the case. In 2006, acting on a tip from district inspection agency in Beijing, more than two thousand tons of stale rice containing *Aspergillus flavus,* a carcinogenic toxin that may cause cancer in humans, was discovered on the market. To hide the food-poisoning case from the central government, Beijing government agencies issued false statements denying the fact (Wang and Yang 2006). The strengthened regulatory efforts by the central government did not seem to have much effect, as fears of poisonous foods became global in 2007 when China-made pet foods, contaminated with melamine, caused the death of dogs and cats in the United States and fake drugs made in China caused deaths in Panama (Cha 2007). For Chinese people, however, baby formula contaminated with melamine in 2008 was the most shocking and frightening because of the large number of babies affected by the toxic milk power, the reputation of the milk powder company as one of China's most trustworthy enterprises, and the involvement of local government agencies in the scandal (more on this below). Although the Chinese government tightened regulation of the food industry and enacted the new Food-Safety Law in 2009, large-scale poisonous-food scandals continued to occur, such as the case of adulterated cooking oil recycled out of sewage and restaurant waste that was exposed in 2010. Professor He Dongping, who led a research team to investigate the case, asserts that the tainted cooking oil was widely found in eateries and food-processing factories as well as private homes, probably used to prepare one out of every ten meals in China (Barboza 2010).

The poisonous foods can be grouped into the following four major types. The first and perhaps most common is adulterated food. Seeking higher profit returns, food processors and/or producers resort to cheaper, inferior, or less desirable materials in the production of processed or cooked foods. On its own, this is not that dangerous. In most cases, however, inferior foods must be polished with chemicals, such as coloring unripe strawberries or cherries with carmine dye so that they appear to be of good quality and thus be sold at higher prices. Using toxic chemicals to preserve processed foods is also common; for example, formaldehyde (甲醛) or sodium formaldehyde sulfoxylate (吊白块) are widely used to whiten seafood and grains (see Zhou 2007: 87–123).

The Chinese media frequently expose scandals of food adulteration, especially the use of toxic agents in the process of adulteration. For example, in 2004 several companies producing Longkou cellophane noodles in Yantai, Shandong province, were found to make the noodles from cornstarch instead of green beans. To make the cornstarch noodles as transparent and chewy as those made of green beans, the companies added sodium formaldehyde sulfoxylate, a toxic industrial bleach, and lead-based whiteners to their products. The scandal became headline news because Longkou is a long-established and famous brand name in China, and this brand of cellophane noodles is the number-one choice among consumers both in China and overseas. In the same year, Chinese media revealed that Sichuan pickled-vegetable factories, another well-known regional food specialty, had been using industrial-grade salt to pickle the vegetables and spraying pesticides on the pickled vegetables before shipment. The most disgusting yet perhaps the most widely consumed adulterated food, however, is the cooking oil that is extracted from the oil in sewage pipes or leftover foods collected from restaurants.

Food additives constitute the second most frequent channel by which a variety of toxins enter the food chain. Antibiotics, colorants, and hormones are widely used as additives to animal feeds and processed foods. Well-known examples include using Sudan dye IV (苏丹红4号) to feed chicken or ducks to produce eggs with red yolks, or using ciprofloxacin (环丙沙星), enfloxacin (恩诺沙星), flavomycin (黄霉素), or simply contraceptive pills to feed farm fishes, or adding melamine to a number of foods including baby milk powder, as in the case of the 2008 baby formula scandal (more on this below). In 2006, Hong Kong banned the import of turbot from China because it was found that a high amount of illegal antibiotics had been deposited in the fisheries. Other cities, such as Shanghai, Beijing, and Hangzhou, quickly followed suit. More often than not, farmers openly use illegal food additives, such as clenbuterol, that have long been banned by government regulation. Clenbuterol is a drug originally developed to help patients with breathing disorders. It causes central nervous system stimulation and increases in aerobic capacity the metabolism rate. Therefore, it is also used by bodybuilders to reduce their body fat. Once used in excessively large amounts in pig feed, clenbuterol can also reduce the amount of fat in pigs and thus was experimented with as a pig-feed additive in the United States during the 1980s. But the practice was soon banned in the United States and other Western countries due to its harmful effects on humans. In the 1990s clenbuterol was introduced to

China as a pig-feed additive to increase the production of lean meat, reportedly by Chinese scientists returning from a visit to the United States, and was sold in the market under the Chinese name *shouroujing* (瘦肉精), meaning "lean meat powder." The first case of food poisoning from clenbuterol-contaminated pork was reported in Guangzhou in 1998, followed by a string of similar cases. In 2001 alone, more than 1,100 people in Beijing, Guangzhou, and Hangzhou were victims of tainted pork, leading the Chinese government to take clenbuterol off the list of accepted food additives and to ban its use in animal feed. However, pork contaminated by clenbuterol has continued to be found in the market since 2001, with the most recent case reported in late 2009 (CNN 2009).

The third type of poisonous food results from the direct application of pesticides, especially in the course of food processing. For a number of food producers, pesticides serve as a cheap yet strong preservative, as in the above-mentioned cases of pickled vegetables in Sichuan province and Jinhua ham in Zhejiang province. In Xianghe county, Hebei province, farmers used a strong pesticide called 3911 to soak the roots of chives so that the vegetable would grow extremely large and strong. From 1999 to 2004, the pesticide was used on thousands of acres of chive fields. This was an open collective action; when the pesticide was applied there was a very strong acrid odor in the entire area. Yet, until an investigation team from a journal sponsored by the GAQSIQ exposed this illegal operation, no local government agency bothered to question this harmful practice (Wang 2004).

Modern farming relies heavily on the use of chemical fertilizer and pesticides, making pesticide residuals the most common threat to food safety throughout the world. The problem of pesticide residuals widely exists in China and has worsened as farmers are using an ever-increasing amount of pesticides and shortening the nonspray time before the harvest to avoid infestations of insects from neighboring farms, thus creating a vicious cycle of pesticide residuals. The abuse of pesticides by food-processing companies differs from pesticide residuals because in the former case food producers and processors intentionally violate the laws and regulations to directly add toxins to foods and resort to chemicals and other techniques to make sure that the consumers are not aware of the toxins. This is why Chinese consumers carefully distinguish the pesticide residuals and the abuse of pesticides, calling the former *nongyao canliu* (pesticide residuals) and the latter *youdu shipin* (toxic foods).

The last type of poisonous food is a challenge to the imagination—it is simply fake or counterfeit food, such as the above-mentioned Anhui province case of fake milk powder made out of starch in 2004. The earliest and perhaps also the most common practice is the production of fake medicine. As early as June 1985, an investigative report was published in the party's mouthpiece, the *People's Daily*, exposing a large business scam that involved more than one thousand participants and various local government agencies in Jinjiang county, Fujian province.

Local food-processing factories had begun to produce fake medicines made of starch, sugar, and other common foodstuffs as early as 1980. Peasant producers managed to sell the fake medicine to state-owned hospitals and pharmacies by giving cash kickbacks to those in charge, thus reaping huge profits from the extremely low-cost fake products. By 1985 a total of fifty-seven factories in the county were specializing in the making of more than one hundred kinds of fake medicine, making them strong competitors to the state-owned pharmaceutical companies. With more details revealed in other reports, provincial party boss Xiang Nan, an important figure in promoting economic reform in south China, resigned, the highest-level political casualty of the food-safety problem in the history of the PRC. However, the fake medicine did not disappear along with the fall of Xiang Nan; rather, counterfeiting drugs still constitute a large share of the Chinese market and are also exported to foreign countries, with serious medical consequences. Shaoguang Wang (2003: 40), describing this as a sign of the weakness of the Chinese state, cites some horrifying figures: "In 2001, 192,000 people died after using bogus or poor-quality medications. Despite government efforts that led to the shutting down of 1,300 pharmaceutical factories, or half of the entire industry that year, the first half of 2002 brought an additional 70,000 deaths from fraudulent drugs." Fake liquor made out of industrial alcohol is also common on the Chinese market. An early incident occurred in early 1998 when small liquor producers in Shanxi province made a strong liquor by mixing water with methyl alcohol that was more than nine hundred times the officially permitted alcohol content. The fake liquor caused twenty-seven deaths and more than two hundred hospitalizations (Hooper 1998). The severity of this case attracted the attention of the central government, and Jiang Zemin, the top party boss at the time, condemned the makers of the fake liquor in a public speech. Although a number of villagers were punished, the practice never ceased and fake liquor continued to show up in Chinese markets in subsequent years.

The making of fake foods often involves heavy doses of toxic chemicals and the use of cheaper and inferior substitute materials. For example, fake soy sauce made out of human hair and chemicals was found in 2004 because human hair can be collected as recyclable waste at an extremely low price; fake chicken eggs made out of water and chemicals appeared in different regions between 2005 and 2007; and fake pig-blood pudding made out of water and chemicals caused a new food scare in 2009. Many consumers commented that even thinking of the poisonous and unclean contents of these fake foods would cause a person to fall sick.

Mapping the Range of Food-Safety Problems

At this point it becomes clear that food safety in China is not a single-dimensional issue, nor is it merely a social risk associated with the arrival of modernity.

Instead, it exists on at least three levels, with complicated and extended implications. I refer to the three levels or dimensions as food hygiene, unsafe food, and poisonous food respectively.

First, the conventional food hygiene problem continues to exist but with a shift of the primary site from the family kitchen or public canteen to food factories and various types of eateries. During the past three decades, Chinese consumers have increasingly relied on *fangbian shipin,* or convenient food, that is, processed, precooked, or semi-cooked foodstuffs. Many urban employees including migrant workers rely on lunch boxes, another type of convenient food, offered by street vendors or available at small eateries. Invariably, these convenient foods are either canned or packaged and most are ready to eat. The increasing demand for convenient foodstuffs may be expected in cities, but it also exists in the countryside. In the village where I worked since the 1980s, the most popular items in the village stores are sausages, instant noodles, and roasted chicken or pork (in order of their sales volume). Food processing has thus become a booming business in the food industry and has created a growing demand for food-safety regulation. People have little knowledge about the origins, ingredients, and the actual making of their foods, which by and large are left to the various food factories. This disconnection and sense of alienation associated with foods have long been regarded as a major cause of public fears of food safety as well as of actual incidents of food safety (Pawsey 2000; Smith 2007).

Yet, as many have pointed out, small-scale family workshops, with more than a 70 percent market share, dominate the food-processing business in China. The highly fragmented and primarily household-based food-processing sector presents a challenge to regulatory agencies for public health, quality control, food processing, and transportation, and the corruption in these regulatory agencies creates an additional problem of enforcement (Li 2009; and Tam and Yang 2005). Many of the family workshops operate under poor sanitary conditions with little modern technology. For example, an investigative report in 2003 revealed that newly 70 percent of the food-processing enterprises in Guangzhou had to be closed down because of failure to meet official quality-control standards. Among them, many cooking-oil processing plans actually operated in apartment units where families lived. In Hunan it was reported that 80 percent of the food-processing workshops actually did not have production permits and/ or business license (cited in Tam and Yang 2005: 26). Packaging and labeling procedures are also poorly regulated and official corruption and counterfeiting are often prevalent. As an informant explained to me, "What you need is just to buy the good-looking packaging materials, wrap your products, and seal the package. Better yet, you can buy packaging materials with famous brand names or super-quality labels. This really helps."[3] In 2005 two men were found guilty of making fake brandy under the brand names of Hennessey and Remy Martin. The bottles of their fake liquor all had laser-burned lot numbers and special anti-counterfeiting labels, making the fake product appear to be authentic (Lin 2009: 56–57).

"Never ask what is inside a sausage" is a truism in most societies. The increased reliance on processed convenient foods, however, makes this an even more relevant issue in the everyday lives of contemporary consumers. According to the Chinese Ministry of Health, the number of victims of food poisoning by microbial contamination exceeds the number of those poisoned by farm chemicals (Calvin et al. 2006). This is also why Wu Yongning, a senior scientist at China's Center for Disease Control, argues that media coverage of food scares in China in 2007 misinformed the public. Citing statistical results from a national survey on diet and health status, Wu asserts that, despite the striking news stories about chemical contamination, the main food-safety threat remains microorganisms (see Ellis and Turner 2007).

At the second level, unsafe foods result mainly from the heavy use of chemical fertilizers, pesticides, hormones, steroids, preservatives, flavor enhancers, colorants, and pollution and environmental degradation in the larger context. Non-seasonal growing and intensive battery livestock farming also contribute to the production of unsafe foods. Among other problems, pesticides stand out as the number-one cause of food-safety problems in China. As a Chinese promoter of organic food has noted, in Shanghai the excessive use of pesticides is profit driven and regarded as a survival strategy by vegetable farmers, who apply four times the recommended amount of pesticides to boost yields (Moore 2010). According to research by Paul Thiers, about one-third of the pesticides sold in China are unregistered and untested. Safety information rarely reaches down to the level of farmers and consequently ten thousand or more Chinese farmers die of pesticide poisoning every year (Thiers 1997). It has been estimated that by 2005 only about 6 percent of the volume of Chinese agricultural production was pollution-free and only 1 percent was green (Calvin et al. 2006: 20).

The unsafe food problem associated with chemical contamination and other modern agricultural techniques is a global phenomenon, and China has only followed the Western path and in a number of ways copied the Western model. For example, in the past most people in China enjoyed meat only during the holidays. However, due to the changing modes of meat production and circulation, meat has now become a daily staple. Because many problems of unsafe food actually derive from modern farming technologies and food processing as well as from modern consumerist ideology, the food-safety problem is also an inherent and reflexive part of modernity. Moreover, as science and modern technology have proved not to be omnipotent forces and as the global scale of food production and circulation has made it almost impossible to predict and control some of the most serious problems of unsafe food, the food-safety problem remains a daunting risk of Beck's second modernity (1992). Therefore, organic and local food and small-scale farming movements have been on the rise in Western societies, where the active participation and leadership of ordinary citizens is crucial.

In this connection, the Chinese case differs from its counterpart in the developed world as the Chinese state, most of the elite and the general public firmly uphold modernization as China's primary goal of development and consequently have yet to see the problem of unsafe foods as a consequence of modernization. Science and technology are regarded as a solution, instead of a liability, to food-safety problems. This may explain why movements of local food and small-scale production do not have much attraction to Chinese consumers, many of whom rely on the market, big corporations, and modern technology (see Veeck et al. 2008).

At the third level, the poisonous food phenomenon stands out as a new and devastating development in Chinese food-safety problems. Unlike the food-hygiene problems or the unsafe foods caused by modern modes of production and processing, poisonous food does not enter the food chain on an everyday basis, nor is it produced on a regular and national scale. Thus, statistically, the actual number of people sickened or dying from consuming poisonous foodstuffs is less than the number of those who suffer from food-hygiene problems or unsafe foods. However, almost every incident of poisonous food, after being exposed by the media or on the Internet, has caused large-scale panic and nationwide food scares. During my interviews, most people cited incidents of poisonous foods as justification for their worries about food safety, and almost without variation, my informants wondered why on earth someone would put toxins in foods for the sake of profit making. This widely expressed disbelief was regularly followed by a strong expression of distrust because, as many informants told me, "nowadays you never know what is inside a package of food; anything is possible."[4] Outraged and morally disturbed, many informants lamented that they no longer knew what was safe to eat and who could be trusted.

What do the above-mentioned four types of poisonous foods have in common? The first is the deliberate contamination of foods. The food producers or processors use an array of legally banned toxic chemicals that are added to food or animal feeds. Second, by doing so the producers, processors, and circulators of poisonous food not only intentionally violate government laws and regulations but also intentionally put business profits above the health of consumers. The making of poisonous food is accompanied by moral abasement. Third, fully aware of the illegality of their actions, the harm to consumers, and the punishment if they are caught, the retailers of toxic foods need to hide the true nature of the toxic foodstuffs and sell it as normal and healthy products. The latter distinguishes poisonous food from the other counterfeit products that flood the Chinese market, especially fraudulent luxury goods such as fake cosmetics, watches, bags, and famous-brand clothing, because the fact they are sold is an open secret of a defiant lifestyle (for a systematic study of counterfeiting culture in China, see Lin 2009).

In other words, what makes these poisonous foods so harmful is not only the toxic chemicals but also the social toxins inherent in the making of the foods, namely, the disregard or even dismissal of other people's health and safety, the intention to harm others for the sake of self profit making, the secrecy and deception necessary for the production and circulation of toxic foods, and the indifference and failure of the regulatory agencies that are closely associated with the flows of poisonous food. Toxic chemicals cause physical and thus visible harm to the well-being of consumers; social toxins threaten the existence of both people and society in a number of invisible yet equally substantial ways.

The most morally disturbing fact is the well-organized and large-scale production and distribution of poisonous food, which often involves various government institutions. Many people, most of whom are ordinary workers on the frontlines of production and processing, actively participate in the deliberate contamination of food. Others are the economic or political elite at various levels, such as entrepreneurs, managers, professionals in quality-control agencies, and government officials. Poisonous food beyond the household workshop level causes serious damage to public health and social ethos, easily causing national panics, such as during the 2008 case of the tainted baby formula by the Sanlu Group, a well-known joint-venture giant in the Chinese dairy business.

To artificially increase the amount of protein in inferior milk that was either diluted with water or spoiled, melamine, a chemical used to make plastic and tan leather, was added, and the contaminated milk was used to produce baby formula, ice cream bars, and other products. By 15 September 2008, only products by Sanlu had been found with melamine, and the company recalled seven hundred tons of its baby formula. But on the following day a nationwide test conducted by the General Administration of Quality Supervision, Inspection, and Quarantine (AQSIQ) revealed that the milk products of 22 out of 109 inspected firms were also contaminated with melamine, including products at Yili and Mengniu, two top firms. Although most contaminated products were being sold on the domestic market, some were also being exported to Hong Kong. Sanlu Group milk products enjoyed the privilege of a quality inspection waiver by the AQSIQ, and the reports on the Sanlu problematic baby formula were not disclosed by the local government and its agencies for several months until the New Zealand partner company contacted the authorities in Beijing. Obviously, the production and distribution of hundreds of tons of contaminated milk powder would not have been possible without negligence and dereliction of duty by a number of government agencies in charge of the safety and quality of dairy products, including the AQSIQ, the Bureau of Food and Drug Supervision, the Ministry of Health, and the Bureau of Industry and Commerce. The Sanlu tainted milk powder stands out as one of the worst cases of poisonous food, causing 6 deaths, 51,900 hospitalizations of children with serious kidney problems, and 24,900 cases of children suffering from other problems. Seeking justice for the families of the victims remains is ongoing and it remains an open wound even after harsh legal punishments were meted out to a few individuals who played a major role in the scandal (Barboza 2009; Yoo 2010).

The tripartite classification of China's food-safety problems is obviously for analytic purpose; in reality the boundaries between the lack of food hygiene, unsafe food, and poisonous food are often blurred, especially most cases of food adulteration. The recycling of cooking oil from sewages and restaurant waste is a good example. Yet, the social causes of these three types of food-safety problems differ from one another, even though in some cases they may overlap. As most food-hygiene problems are caused mainly by lack of health knowledge, sloppy personal hygiene habits, and negligence of sanitation in the work environment, they can be addressed through the application of scientific knowledge and modern technology. Ironically, the unsafe foods are mainly a by-product of science and technology advancements in modern farming and agribusiness and the impact of global consumerism, in accord with the pursuit of modernization as a top priority on the national agenda. The poisonous-food problem, however, is caused by a number of social and moral changes in Chinese society, chief among which is the widespread resentment among those who have fallen behind in the national trend of wealth accumulation and feel social discrimination. Let me cite a few examples to illustrate this last point.

In the case of the diseased chicken presented at the outset of this chapter, chicken farmers told the researcher that they do not eat the chicken they raise because of the food-safety problems associated with battery chicken farming—they only sell the chicken to urbanities. In her study of villagers' experiences and coping strategies with cancer in Sichuan, southwest China, Ann Lora-Wainwright finds that her rural informants are fully aware of the current food-safety problems and many attribute the widespread cancer to the consumption of foods contaminated with harmful chemicals. This knowledge, however, does not affect the use of chemicals in farming as the villagers feel compelled to apply large volumes of pesticides and other chemicals to increase crop yield; they do, however, carefully grow organic foods for themselves and proudly offer the safe foods to people whom they know, including the visiting anthropologist. While regarding this strategy as the exercise of agency by villagers to fight against the threat of unsafe foods, Lora-Wainwright also notes: "To the extent that farmers produce food for the market with profit rather than the wellbeing of the consumers in mind, their engagement with the market economy is disembedded from social relations" (2009: 68). Although these two cases belong to the category of unsafe food, the above-cited case of soaking of chive roots in pesticide reveals the same psychology, that is, the toxic products will be sold to strangers, first and foremost to urban people (Wang 2004).

In 2008 I had a rare opportunity to interview a migrant worker in Shanghai who admitted he used to make fake blood pudding but had stopped doing so by the time of our meeting. When asked whether he was aware that his product would cause harm to consumers' health, he replied without any hesitation: "I knew but I did not care. Why should I? I don't know them at all." Two more clues emerged as our conversation proceeded. At first, he told me that it was acceptable to sell fake food to people in cities because urbanities had medical insurance. "If they get sick, they can afford to see a doctor." Then he recalled his painful experiences working in two cities during the last twelve years and how on several occasion he was seriously beaten by the "*chengguan dui,*" a self-supporting patrol force in charge of maintaining order in urban food markets. "I actually felt good when some of them ate my blood pudding and I hoped that they would become seriously ill," he admitted triumphantly.[5]

Is the making of poisonous food this man's way of making money or taking revenge or both? More importantly, how much have we learned about the motivations and moral justifications among violators of food-safety regulations at all three levels, especially those at the poisonous-food level? These are some of the daunting questions that beg for answers. Distrust and disregard of strangers is deeply rooted in traditional Chinese ethics that emphasizes the centrality of particularistic ties, especially those based on kinship and community, in one's moral universe. As I explore elsewhere, some Chinese individuals seem to hold different moral principles when dealing with people from different social circles and thus a good Samaritan can become the victim of extortion by the very person whom the good Samaritan has just helped (Yan 2009). In a similar vein, the problem of poisonous food reveals a dark side of the particularistic ethics.

Obviously, due to space limits it is impossible in this chapter to examine the complex causes of food-safety problems at all three levels as well as the moral universe of producers, processors, and retailers of problematic foodstuffs. The point I want to make here is that to address the food-safety issue in contemporary Chinese society we must first identify the specific real-life problems, understand their patterns and causes, and, more importantly, fully consider why people knowingly do things to harm the health of others.

Conclusion

To conclude, food safety constitutes a new, urgent, and multifaceted challenge to Chinese people, society, and state, involving a number of social, political, and ethical problems beyond food safety itself. The complexity of the food-safety challenge, however, has yet to be fully recognized, evidenced by the lack of a detailed account of the typology, major features, and wider implications of food-safety problems. To address this issue, I have reviewed the development of food-safety problems, identifying the shift from the public hazard of food poisoning to the social fear of poisonous food as a key to understanding the changing patterns of food-safety problems during the last six decades. I classify the food-safety problems in contemporary China into three types, namely, problems of food hygiene, unsafe food, and poisonous food. Although the traditional problem of food hygiene persists and calls for continuing attention from health professionals, unsafe food caused by modern modes of farming and food processing has quickly become a dominant and increasingly large-scale cause of the food-safety problems affecting the health and lives of Chinese people. Socially and ethically, however, it is the type of poisonous food that presents the most serious challenge to public trust, regulatory governance, and the general well-being of Chinese individuals, not to mention the physical and psychological damage that each poisonous food scandal produces at the society level.

The tripartite problems also cut through temporal space and thus reflect a time-compressed feature of modernization in China. Although the unsafe food problem certainly presents a social risk of second modernity or postindustrial and late modern, it occurs in the Chinese context of a much-fragmented market of food production and processing, where most problems exist at household farms and workshops where food-hygiene problems persist. The disregard and distrust of strangers, reflected in the making and circulation of poisonous food, however, is indicative of the breakdown of the traditional ethical system during China's transition from a kinship-based society of acquaintances to a highly mobile society where interactions with strangers are increasingly common. This premodern-to-modern problem, however, has a contemporary twist of increased social inequality and injustice caused by the Chinese model of growth and development that in turn allows many to justify their immoral behavior when making and selling poisonous food.

In this regard, the food-safety problems present a clear and present danger to social solidarity and political stability of first modernity on top of the social risk of Beck's second modernity. It is common in China for science, technology, and modernization generally to be regarded as the solution to food-safety problems and as the proper way to control food risks. For example, Veeck, Yu, and Burns discovered that most Chinese consumers do not attribute food-safety problems to the unknowable consequences of scientific advancement, and many consumers turn to the famous brands of large companies and other market mechanisms to minimize their food risks. Such behavior seems to contradict risk society theory (Veeck, Yu, and Burns 2008). In a similar way, the majority of my informants, both urban and rural, placed the blame for the outbreak of food-safety problems on individual farmers, manufacturers, and retailers of toxic foods for being too greedy and for lacking morality, while others criticized the government agencies for regulatory failures or traced the origins of all food scandals to corrupt officials. After all, humans are the source of all chemical toxins. Moreover, because of the dominance of household workshops in China's food-processing sector, chemicals are used in low-tech and labor-intensive processes, without the input of scientific knowledge. As one elderly villager put it succinctly: "No poison can be poisonous without the touch of human hands."[6] These folk explanations and attributions are precisely the same as the explanations offered by Chinese journalists and scholars in media reports and academic research, albeit in a much more systematic and sophisticated fashion in the latter.

In other words, the epistemological role of science and technology and modernity in the formation of contemporary food-safety problems remains a blind spot in Chinese public opinion and professional discourse. But does the existence of this blind spot cancel out the actual link between modernity and contemporary food-safety problems? Does not knowing of this link eliminate the felt risk of poisonous foods among Chinese consumers? Do the counter-facts make the theory of risk society irrelevant in Chinese reality, as suggested by Veeck and her colleagues? In my mind, the answer to these questions is clearly "no." What it does show us is perhaps the unquestionable centrality of modernity and the much stronger influence of its control-logic among Chinese people across all walks of life, which is missing from risk society theory because it aims to explain postindustrial or second modernity in Western Europe.

The significance of modernization in developing countries tends to be underestimated by Western scholars because modernity has never been a most sought-after objective in Western history: it gradually arrived even before people found a name to call it. In contrast, modernization was the Holy Grail when China was fighting for national survival and nation building and it remains so to this day as the country is trying to redefine its position on the global stage. It is impossible to review China's spiral path in pursuit of modernity here, but what I want to point out is that in the post-Mao era, this Holy Grail has been interpreted and understood almost exclusively in materialistic terms. Such an understanding was first made possible through the state-sponsored national debate in 1978 that concluded that practice is the sole criterion for testing truth. It was then specified in material terms in Deng Xiaoping's well-known definition of Chinese modernization.[7] Ever since the early 1980s the promotion of science and technology and the maintenance of political stability have been sacredly guarded by the Chinese state as the secret recipe to realize the dream of modernization, and since the early 1990s this way of thinking has been widely accepted and practiced by the majority of both the elite and ordinary people. It is not surprising, therefore, that few in China—scholars and ordinary people alike—could (or would want to) attribute the food-safety problems and food risks to the unintended consequences of science-technology advances and modernity's control-logic.

Therefore, the Chinese case of food safety, as I argue in studies on individualization and moral change (see Yan 2009 and 2010), must be understood in light of China's own path and history of modernization and explored in the context of a combination of theories that fully consider the complexity and particularities of the Chinese case.

Notes

1. A noteworthy exception is a 1960 case in Shanxi province when sixty-one peasants were poisoned by a fellow worker who had placed arsenic in the food cooked in the public canteen to vent anger over what he felt was unfair treatment. The victims were saved due to air delivery of an effective medicine from Beijing. During the subsequent four months, the Chinese media focused on the party-state's power and effort to save the victims' lives and published thousands of reports and commentaries, with a special report entitled "For the sake of our 61 working class brothers" in the *China Youth Daily* taking the lead. But details about the food poisoning and the culprit, who was soon executed, were not covered in the media and remained unclear to the public until the late 1990s.

2. When I lived and worked in rural collectives in the 1970s, I consumed meat from horses that had died of unknown diseases on two occasions. At the time, many villagers jokingly commented that we might end up sick or even dead if we ate the horse meat, but it was still worth it because "we will be happy ghosts with meat in our stomachs." During the 1970s, rural people only had the opportunity to eat meat during the Chinese New Year or when the collectives held banquets. Therefore, when a draft animal died of disease or old age, many villagers were happy because of the unexpected opportunity to consume meat.

3. Personal interview conducted in Shanghai, June 2007.

4. My informants most frequently mentioned the cases of fake chicken eggs, fake soy sauce, diseased roast chicken, and cooking oil from sewages. These foods may not be the most toxic but they all contain ingredients that challenge a basic principle of food ethics and thus cause panic and fear (see Jensen and Sandoe 2002; Smith 2007; and Zwart 2000).

5. Personal interview conducted in Shanghai, July 2009.

6. Personal interview conducted in rural Heilongjiang, August 2008.

7. When he met a British delegation on 21 March 1979, Deng Xiaoping brought up the notion of a "Chinese way of modernization," specifying that this was the realization of the modernization of agriculture, industry, national defense, and science and technology. On another occasion, when meeting provincial leaders on 28 July 1979, Deng further defined the specific standards for Chinese modernization: "It would be quite good if we could reach the level of GNP U.S. $1,000 per capita (by the year 2000). [Chinese people] would be able to eat well, dress well, and use good appliances." In 1984 Deng lowered this expectation to US $800 per capita. It should be noted that in the late 1970s per capita GNP in China was about $300.

References

Barboza, David. 2009. "Death Sentences Given in Chinese Milk Scandal." *New York Times,* 2 February. http://www.nytimes.com/2009/01/22/world/asia/22iht-milk.3.19601372.html (accessed 10 September 2010).

———. 2010. "Recycled Cooking Oil Found to Be Latest Hazard in China." *New York Times,* 31 March. http://www.nytimes.com/2010/04/01/world/asia/01shanghai.html

?scp=1&sq=recycled%20cooking%20oil%20found%20to%20be%20latesthazard%20 in%20china&st=cse (accessed 28 October 2010).

Beck, Ulrich. 1992. *Risk Society: Towards a New Modernity,* translated by Mark Ritter. London: Sage Publications Ltd.

Calvin, Linda, et al. 2006. "Food Safety Improvements Underway in China." *Amber Waves* 4(5): 16–21.

Cha, Ariana Eunjung. 2007. "China Food Fears Go From Pets to People." *Washington Post,* 25 April. http://www.washingtonpost.com/wp-dyn/content/article/2007/04/24/AR200704 2402539.html (accessed 28 October 2010).

CNN. 2009. "China: 70 Ill From Tainted Pig Organs." http://www.cnn.com/2009/WORLD/ asiapcf/02/22/china.poisonings/index.html (accessed 22 September 2010).

Ellis, Linden, and Jennifer Turner. 2007. "Food Safety: Where We Stand in China," 18 December. http://www.wilsoncenter.org/index.cfm?topic_id=1421&categoryid=EE4F5 78C-D321-2150-ABD87895FEF607D8&fuseaction=topics.events_item_topics&event _id=329237 (accessed 29 August 2010).

Enticott, Gareth. 2003. "Risking the Rural: Nature, Morality and the Consumption of Unpasteurized Milk." *Journal of Rural Studies* 19: 411–424.

Hooper, Beverley. 1998. "From Mao to Market: Empowering the Chinese Consumer." *Harvard Asian Pacific Review* 2(2): 29–34.

Hu, Bing. 1982. "Chi zhimagao yinqi de yichang fengbo" (An Incident Caused by the Consumption of Sesame Cake). *Zhongguo shipin* (Chinese Food) 5: 21.

Jansen, Karsten Klint, and Peter Sandoe. 2002. "Food Safety and Ethics: The Interplay between Science and Values." *Journal of Agricultural and Environmental Ethics* 15: 245–253.

Jiang, Gaoming. 2007. "The Truth about Dead Chickens." *China* Dialogue, 14 June. http:// www.chinadialogue.net/article/show/single/en/1096-The-truth-about-dead- chickens (accessed 12 August 2010).

Li, Peter J. 2009. "Exponential Growth, Animal Welfare, Environmental and Food Safety Impact: The Case of China's Livestock Production." *Journal of Agricultural and Environmental Ethics* 22: 217–240.

Lin, Yi-Chieh Jessica. 2009. "Knockoff: A Cultural Biography of Transnational Counterfeit Goods." PhD dissertation, Department of Anthropology, Harvard University.

Liu, Peng. 2010. "Tracing and Periodizing China's Food Safety Regulation: A Study of China's Food Safety Regime Change." *Regulation & Governance* 4(2): 244–260.

Lora-Wainwright, Anna. 2009. "Of Farming Chemicals and Cancer Deaths: The Politics of Health in Contemporary Rural China." *Social Anthropology* 17(1): 56–73.

Lu, Jianhua. 1982. "Youjilin nongyao wuran dami yinqi shiwu zhongdu de diaocha" (An Investigation of Food Poisoning Caused by Pesticide Contamination). *Anhui Yixue* (Anhui Medicine) 2: 54–55.

Ministry of Commerce. 2008. "The 2008 Report on Food Safety in the Circulation Domain."

Moore, Malcolm. 2010. "China Goes Organic after Scandal of Cooking Oil from Sewers." *The Telegraph,* 30 August. http://www.telegraph.co.uk/news/worldnews/asia/china/7971983/ China-goes-organic-after-scandal-of-cooking-oil-from-sewers.html (accessed 28 October 2010).

Mou, Xiurui. 2007. "Shiping anquan zhi you" (Worries about Food Safety). *Zhongguo shiping anquan wang* (China Food Safety Net), 14 March. http://www.ce.cn/cysc/sp/info/ 200703/14/t20070314_10686083.shtml (accessed 27 August 2010).

Nestle, Marion. 2010. *Safe Food: The Politics of Food Safety*, 2nd ed. Berkeley: University of California Press.

Ouyang, Jian. 1961. "Shamenshijun ganran diaocha baogao—Yin shi bingsi niurou suozhi shiwu zhongdu 122 bingli fenxi" (Investigative Report on Salmonella Infection: An Analysis of 122 Cases of Food Poisoning Caused by the Consumption of Diseased Cattle). *Jiangxi Medicine Journal* 7: 27–28.

Pawsey, Rosa K. 2000. "Food and its Safety." *Medicine, Conflict and Survival* 16(2): 192–200.

Ramzy, Austin. 2009. "Will China's New Food-Safety Laws Work?" *Time*, 3 March. http://www.time.com/time/world/article/0,8599,1882711,00.html (accessed 2 September 2010).

Rozin, Paul. 1989. "Disorders of Food Selection: The Compromise of Pleasure." *Annals of the New York Academy of Sciences* 575(1): 376–386.

Smith, David. 2007. "Food Panics in History: Corned Beef, Typhoid and 'Risk Society.'" *Journal of Epidemiol Community Health* 61: 566–570.

Sun, Ruixing. 1980. "Ershinian shiwu zhongdu de qingkuang fenxi" (An Analysis of the Causes of Food Poisoning in the Past Twenty Years). *Jiangsu Medicine* 7: 4–5.

Tam, Waikeung, and Dali Yang. 2005. "Food Safety and the Development of Regulatory Institutions in China." *Asian Perspective* 29(4): 5–36.

Tang, Chen. 1998. "Yin shiyong bianzhi dounai yinqi xiaoxuesheng jidi shiwu zhongdu de diaocha" (An Investigation of Food Poisoning Caused by Spoiled Soybean Milk among Primary School Students). *Shanghai Preventative Medicine* 7: 311–322.

Thiers, Paul. 1997. "Pesticides in China: Policy and Practice." *Pesticide Outlook* 8(1): 6–10.

———. 2003. "Risk Society Comes to China: SARS, Transparency and Public Accountability." *Asian Perspective* 27(2): 241–251.

Veeck, Ann, Hongyan Yu, and Alvin C. Burns. 2008. "Food Safety, Consumer Choice, and the Changing Marketplace in Urban China." In *Papers of the 33rd Annual Macromarketing Conference*, 39–44. Clemson, SC: The Macromarketing Society, Inc.

Wang, Jianmin, and Yang Zhongqing. 2006. "Beijing dumi an qipian zhongyang." (Cheating the Central Government in the Case of Poisonous Rice in Beijing). *Yazhou zhoukan* (Asia Weekly) 6.

Wang, Jinfu. 1975. "Ziboshi shisinian shiwu zhongdu fenxi" (An Analysis of Food Poisoning During the Past Fourteen Years in Zibo City). *Shandong Medicine* 4: 15–18.

Wang, Liming. 2004. "Qinli Xianghe dujiucai jinjing" (Experiencing the Arrival of Poisonous Chives from Xianghe). *Zhongguo zhiliang wanglixing zazhi* (Journal of Quality Supervision in China) 4.

Wang, Shaoguang. 2003. "The Problem of State Weakness." *Journal of Democracy* 14(1): 36–42.

Yan, Yunxiang. 2009. "The Good Samaritan's New Trouble: A Study of the Changing Moral Landscape in Contemporary China." *Social Anthropology* 17(1): 9–24.

———. 2010. "The Chinese Path to Individualization," *British Journal of Sociology* 61(3): 489–512.

Yi, Xiang. 1994. "Xi'an you fasheng yiqi yanzhong shiwu zhongdu shijian" (Another Serious Incident of Food Poisoning in Xi'an City). *Shipin yu jiankang* (Food and Health) 1: 46.

Yoo, Yungsuk Karen. 2010. "Tainted Milk: What Kind of Justice for Victims' Families in China?" *Hastings International and Comparative Law Review* 33(2): 555–575.

Zeng, Bo and Xiang Rongsong. 1994. "Yiqi youer xuesheng yanghuamei shewu zhongdu de diaocha baogao" (A Report on Food Poisoning Caused by Magnesium Oxide Contamination among Kindergarten Students). *Gongye weisheng yu zhiyebing* (Industrial Hygiene and Occupational Disease) 6: 363.

Zhang, Guining. 1961. "Zhuhuoluan shamenshijun shiwu zhongdu ganran de liuxingbingxue baogao" (An Epidemic Report on Food Poisoning Caused by Salmonella Cholerae). *Shandong Medicine* 5: 12–15.

Zhan, Xiaofang. 2007. "Shipin anquan yu hexie shehui" (Food Safety and Harmonious Society). MA thesis, School of Philosophy and Sociology, Shanxi University.

Zhao, Jiabao. 1974. "Shiyong silurou wuran shushanghan shamenshijun yinqi 111 li shiwu zhongdu de diaocha baogao" (Report on 111 Cases of Food Poisoning Caused by Consumption of Diseased Donkey Contaminated with Salmonella Typhimurium). *Weisheng yanjiu* (Hygiene Studies) 2: 186–188.

Zhou, Qing. 2007. *Min yi heshi weitian: Zhongguo shipin anquan xianzhuang diaocha* (What Kind of God: A Survey of the Current Safety of China's Food). Beijing: Zhongguo gongren chubanshe.

Zhou, Renjie. 2004. "Fuyang liezhi naifen shijian shouxi pilu siyingshu" (The Total Number of Infant Deaths Caused by Adulterated Baby Formula is Released). *Jingji banxiaoshi* (Half an Hour of the Economy), CCTV, 22 April.

Zhou, Shunan. 1958. "Nongcunzhong fasheng shiwu zhongdu de yuanyin yu yufang" (Causes of Food Poisoning and Prevention in Rural China). *Zhongguo yikan* (Chinese Medicine Journal) 1: 25–27.

Zhou, Siyu, et al. 2007. "Siji zheyang zouxiang canzhuo" (The Way Diseased Chicken Ends Up at the Dinner Table). *Nanfang zhoumo* (Southern Weekend), 19 July.

Zwart, Hub. 2000. "A Short History of Food Ethics." *Journal of Agricultural and Environmental Ethics* 12(2): 113–126.

Contributors

Sangmee Bak is a professor of cultural anthropology at Hankuk University of Foreign Studies in Seoul, Korea. Graduated from Seoul National University and Harvard University (PhD), she taught at Dartmouth College and Queens College of the City University of New York. She has been working on anthropology of food and identity, cultural heritage, and globalization in Korea and East Asia. Dr. Bak is a member of the Cultural Heritage Committee (World Heritage and Folklore Sections). Her publications include "The Flow of Kimchi: Food Exchange Networks and Changing Gender/Family Identities in Korean Society" (2006) and "Intangible Cultural Heritage and Cultural Tourism in Korea" (2011).

Melissa L. Caldwell is professor of anthropology at the University of California, Santa Cruz. She is also the co-director of the University of California Multi-Campus Research Program on Studies of Food and the Body and the editor-in-chief of *Gastronomica: The Journal of Critical Food Studies.* Her research focuses on changing political and economic systems in Russia, with particular attention to food. She has written on such topics as fast food and globalization, food nationalism, gardens and natural foods, food insecurity, and food relief programs. She is the author of *Not by Bread Alone: Social Support in the New Russia* and *Dacha Idylls: Living Organically in Russia's Countryside,* and editor, with Yuson Jung and Jakob Klein, of *Ethical Eating in the Socialist and Postsocialist World.* Her current research examines the shifting terrain of art, science, creativity, and play through a study of molecular gastronomy and do-it-yourself food science.

Sidney C. H. Cheung is professor of the Department of Anthropology, associate dean of the Faculty of Arts, and associate director of the Institute of Future Cities at the Chinese University of Hong Kong. His research interests include visual anthropology, anthropology of tourism, heritage studies, food and identity, fragrance and ethnicity; his coedited and edited books include *Tourism, Anthropology and China* (White Lotus, 2001), *The Globalization of Chinese Food* (RoutledgeCurzon,

2002), *Food and Foodways in Asia: Resource, Tradition and Cooking* (Routledge, 2007) and *Rethinking Asian Food Heritage* (forthcoming, 2015). He also serves as a partner of the UNESCO Chair project of Tours University, France on "Safeguarding and promotion of Cultural Food Heritage," and member of the Scientific Committee of Greenline Heritage conference series in Portugal since 2008.

Jean DeBernardi is professor of anthropology at the University of Alberta. She received her training as a cultural anthropologist at Stanford University, Oxford University, and the University of Chicago and has been teaching in Canada since 1991. She has conducted ethnographic research on Chinese popular religion in Malaysia and Singapore, and recently completed a study focusing on religious and cultural pilgrimage to the Daoist temple complex at Wudang Mountain, China. She has recently launched a new project exploring contemporary tea culture in China and its introduction to Canada.

Kyung-Koo Han is a cultural anthropologist trained at Seoul National University and Harvard University (PhD). He is currently dean of the College of Liberal Studies, Seoul National University. He was editor of *Korean Cultural Anthropology* and of *Korean Social Science Journal*. He also served as president of the Korean International Migration Association, and the Association for the Studies of Koreans Abroad. His numerous articles on Japan and Korea include "The 'Kimchi Wars' in Globalizing East Asia: Consuming Class, Gender, Health, and National Identity" (2011) and "Some Foods are Good to Think: Kimchi and the Epitomization of National Character" (2000).

Michael Herzfeld is Ernest E. Monrad Professor of the Social Sciences in the Department of Anthropology at Harvard University, where has taught since 1991, and also serves as IIAS Visiting Professor of Critical Heritage Studies at Leiden University and Professorial Fellow in the Faculty of Arts, University of Melbourne. Editor of *American Ethnologist* in 1995–99, he has authored eleven books—including *Cultural Intimacy* (1997), *The Body Impolitic* (2004), *Evicted from Eternity* (2009), and *Siege of the Spirits* (forthcoming, 2016)—and numerous articles and reviews, and has produced two ethnographic films (*Monti Moments* [2007] and *Roman Restaurant Rhythms* [2011]). A recipient of both the J.I. Staley Prize and the Rivers Memorial Medal in 1994, he has also received honorary doctorates from the Université Libre de Bruxelles (2005), the University of Macedonia, Thessaloniki (2011), and the University of Crete (2013). His field research to date has focused on Greece, Italy, and Thailand.

Hsin-Huang Michael Hsiao is distinguished research fellow and director of the Institute of Sociology at the Academia Sinica and professor of Sociology at National Taiwan University. He had previously served as a national policy advisor to the president of Taiwan between 1996 and 2006. His areas of specialization include civil society and new democracies, the middle class in the Asia local sustainable development, and NGO studies. His most recent publications include *Ethnic Economy of Vietnamese Spouses in Taiwan* (coeditor, 2012), *Changing Faces of Hakka in Southeast Asia: Singapore and Malaysia* (editor, 2011), *Cross-Border Marriage with Asian Characteristics* (coeditor, 2010), and *Rise of China: Beijing's Strategies and Implications for the Asia-Pacific* (coeditor, 2009).

Yuson Jung, trained in social anthropology at Harvard University (PhD), is assistant professor in the Department of Anthropology at Wayne State University, Detroit. She has been conducting ethnographic research in Bulgaria on issues of consumption, globalization, food, and postsocialism since 1998. She has coedited (with Jakob Klein and Melissa L. Caldwell) *Ethical Eating in the Postsocialist and Socialist World* (2014) and is completing a manuscript entitled "Balkan Blues: Everyday Consumption and the Poverty of the State." Her publications have appeared in many journals, including *Food, Culture and Society*. Since 2008 she has been working on the *Cultural Politics of Wine: The Transformation of the Bulgarian Wine Industry* based on ethnographic fieldwork in Bulgaria.

Kwang Ok Kim (DPhil Oxon.) is professor of Anthropology at Seoul National University, Yongje Chair Professor at Yonsei University, Korea, and also Distinguished Professor at Shandong University, PRC. He is also on the Presidential Committee for Culture in the government of Korea. He served as president of Korean Society for Cultural Anthropology. He has conducted extensive fieldwork in Korea, mainland China, and Taiwan with interests in politics of culture, religion, ritual, history, lineage, and material culture including food. His numerous publications include *Chinese Peasant in the Middle of Revolution and Reform* (2000), *Yangban: The Life-world of Korean Scholar-gentry* (2004), *Ethnicity Beyond the Myth* (2006), *Politics of Culture and Power Structure of a Korean Local Society* (2012), *China in Everyday Practice* (forthcoming).

Jakob A. Klein is lecturer in Social Anthropology at SOAS, University of London. Focusing on China, his research interests include food consumption, local specialty foods, and ethical food movements. Publications include *Consuming China: Approaches to Cultural Change in Contemporary China,* coedited with K. Latham and S. Thompson (2006); "'For Eating, it's Guangzhou': Regional Culinary Traditions and Chinese Socialism," in H. G. West and P. Raman, eds., *Enduring Socialism: Explorations of Revolution and Transformation, Restoration and Continuation* (2009); "Everyday approaches to food safety in Kunming," *The China Quarterly* 214 (2013); and, coauthored with H. G. West and J. Pottier, "New Directions in the Anthropology of Food," in R. Fardon et al., eds., *The SAGE Handbook of Social Anthropology* (2012).

Khay Thiong Lim is associate professor in the Graduate Institute of Southeast Asian Studies, National Chi Nan University, Taiwan. His research interest lies in the study of Southeast Asian Chinese culture and Chinese and Vietnamese culinary cultures. He has published articles on Southeast Asian Hakka Chinese, Vietnamese eateries in Taiwan, and Malaysian Chinese culinary culture. He is currently working on an edited volume on Hakka Chinese in Southeast Asia.

Okpyo Moon (DPhil Oxon.) is professor of Anthropology at the Academy of Korean Studies and currently the president of the Korean Society for Cultural Anthropology. She has been visiting professor at the Edwin O. Reischauer Institute, Harvard University, and at the National Museum of Ethnology, Osaka, Japan. Her research interests include family and gender, urban and rural community making, ethnic minorities, tourism, consumption, material culture, and heritage policies in Japan and Korea. She has recently edited and coauthored *Foreign Cultures in Us: Culinary and Touristic Consumption of Otherness in Contemporary Korea* (2006); *Japanese Tourism and Travel Culture* (2009); and *Consuming Korean Tradition in Early and Late Modernity: Commodification, Tourism, and Performance* (2011).

David Yen-Ho Wu, Senior Fellow and professor, the East-West Center, Honolulu, and Anthropology Faculty of the University of Hawaii, did fieldwork in the South Pacific, Southeast Asia, China, Japan, and Taiwan on issues of minority cultural identity and globalization of cuisines. His many publications include *The Chinese in Papua New Guinea* (1982), *Where is Home* (2011), *Overseas March: How the Chinese Cuisine Spread?* (coedited, 2011), *Globalization of Chinese Food* (2002), and *Changing Chinese Foodways in Asia* (2001).

Yunxiang Yan is professor of anthropology and director of the Center for Chinese Studies, University of California, Los Angeles. He earned his BA in Chinese Literature from Peking University in 1982 and PhD in Social Anthropology from Harvard University in 1993. He is the author of *The Flow of Gifts: Reciprocity and Social Networks in a Chinese Village* (Stanford University Press, 1996), *Private Life under Socialism: Love, Intimacy, and Family Change in a Chinese Village, 1949-1999* (Stanford University Press, 2003), and *The Individualization of Chinese Society* (Berg, 2009). His research interests include family and kinship, social change, the individual and individualization, and the impact of cultural globalization. Among other projects, he is currently writing a book on individualization and moral changes in post-Mao China.

Young-Kyun Yang is a professor of anthropology at the Academy of Korean Studies. He received a BA and MA from Seoul National University and a PhD from the University of Pittsburgh. His recent works include "Jajangmyeon and

Junggukjip: The Changing Position and Meaning of Chinese Food and Chinese Restaurants in Korean Society," "Education and Family in Korean Society," "Nationalism, Transnationalism, and Sport: A Case Study on Michelle Wie," and coauthored books such as *Foreign Cultures in Us: Culinary and Touristic Consumption of Otherness in Contemporary Korea* (2006), *Ethnic Relations of Overseas Koreans* (2006), *Ethnic Relations of Korean American in Los Angeles* (2008).

Index

.

Lightning Source UK Ltd.
Milton Keynes UK
UKOW07n2101240215

246819UK00006B/61/P